The Discipler's Manual

Books by F. E. Marsh

Devotional Bible Studies
Emblems of the Holy Spirit
500 Bible Study Outlines
Illustrated Bible Study Outlines
Major Bible Truths
1000 Bible Study Outlines
Practical Truths from First Thessalonians
The Discipler's Manual
Why Did Christ Die?

The Discipler's Manual

F. E. Marsh

KREGEL PUBLICATIONS
Grand Rapids, Michigan 49501

The Authorized King James Version is used in the text unless otherwise indicated. Those marked NIV are from The Holy Bible, New International Version, © 1978 by International Bible Society, used by permission. Those marked RSV are taken from the Revised Standard Version, © 1946, 1971 by Division of Christian Education of the National Council of Churches of Christ in the United States of America. Used by permission.

Cover & Book Design: Al Hartman

Library of Congress Cataloging-in-Publication Data

Marsh, F. E. (Frederick Edward) 1858-1919.
[Fully Furnished]
The Discipler's Manual / F. E. Marsh.
p. cm.
Reprint of the 1969 ed. published under the title: Fully Furnished.
Includes indexes.
1. Christian Life. I. Title.
BV4501.M34646 1991 248'.4 79-2550
CIP

ISBN 0-8254-3238-3 (pbk.)

1 2 3 4 5 Printing/Year 95 94 93 92 91

Printed in the United States of America

Contents

Foreword

The thoughtful Christian is faced with an awesome enigma, a thing hard to understand and explain: an unreached world with more than half its four billion inhabitants yet to hear about God's offer of salvation in Christ Jesus. Millions each year pass into eternity with no chance to receive God's provision for their sin. What a terrifying, overwhelming state of affairs!

The child of God has a mandate from his risen Lord to love and confront this world with the issues of the Gospel, but he isn't doing it. The individual Christian is not impacting the world, because he is not equipped to perform the task his Lord has committed to him. In our day, sad to say, the roles of personal evangelism and discipling have been replaced by the electronic church, mass evangelism, and other modern outreach methods.

There is no substitute for the New Testament concept of spiritual reproduction (2 Timothy 2:2). Thousands who have been converted to Christ remain in spiritual babyhood for want of leadership into the abundant life promised by the Savior (John 10:10). Hosts of Christians are bored and disenchanted because they have allowed themselves to settle for far less than God's best. They are failing to go on to spiritual maturity (Hebrews 6:1-3). They have accepted Christ, believe in God, consent in general to the truths of the Scriptures, but something is missing that makes the difference between an elemental, superficial believism and a vital, life-changing fulfilling reality. They remain converts: they need to become disciples.

Dr. F. E. Marsh has recognized the need to spell out the elements in the discipling process. In these thirty-four studies he has set forth in a comprehensive manner all that a well-equipped servant of Christ needs to know of God's purpose and method of reaching and building men and women for God. Dr. Marsh is possessed by an uncompromising confidence in the integrity and authority of the Bible and in the perfect sufficiency of the Holy Spirit to teach, equip, lead and empower the Christian witness. In this single volume we are presented with a complete manual for discipling.

I have owned and used a copy of this work, formerly published as *Fully*

Furnished, for more than forty years. Many of my best sermons had their seeds in these studies. What a treasure of precious gems is found in this Spirit-prompted production! What a blessing it is that this work should be republished now to meet the need for discipling!

Every preacher and teacher of the Word of God is obligated to lead the congregation of God into the green pastures of spiritual maturity. Developing an awareness of the ingredients of "the abundant life" will be all the Holy Spirit needs to produce effective, fruitful disciples for "the work of the ministry" and the evangelization of the world.

W. Herbert Scott

World Vision International, 1979

Introduction

Carey's words, "Attempt great things for God, and expect great things from Him," have stimulated many a heart, and urged many a tired worker to lift up the hands which were hanging down. Yet there seems to be something requisite in addition to the noble man's words, for he looks at things mainly from the human standpoint and if I might, without casting any reflection upon him, I would say, "Accept great things from in God, and then He will attain great things through you," for the secret of all attainment in the spiritual life, is the obtainment of the Holy Spirit in His fulness; hence, the measure of the latter always gauges the advance of the former. This thought runs through the whole of the Epistles. The Spirit, in the fullness of His power, is always the Adjustment for every fault, and the Advancement in every grace.

Let us briefly see how this thought runs through the seven epistles which Paul addressed to the churches.

The Holy Spirit is the "Spirit of Life," to overcome the self-life. There are no less than forty-one personal pronouns in Romans 7. The chapter is full of "I's," "Me's," and "My's." What is the antidote? "The law of the Spirit of Life in Christ Jesus" (Romans 7:2), this emancipates from the law of sin and death. As the law of gravitation causes the piece of lead to fall to the ground, when it is released from the hand which holds it, so the tendency of self is naturally to selfishness and earthly things. But when that piece of lead is attached to a balloon, then it rises with the object to which it is united. The same is true of the believer. When he is in vital union with Christ, and energized by the Spirit's uplifting presence, then he is freed from the downward tendency of things.

The Holy Spirit is "the Spirit of God" in contrast to the impotence and incompetency of man. The epistles to the Corinthians deal with a body of believers who were man centered; hence, they were "carnal." The apostle reminds them that they cannot of themselves understand the Word of God, nor fathom the deep things of God, nor apply the truths of God; for the Spirit is the Unfolder of the Word, the Enlightener of the mind, and the Communicator of the gospel. This is all brought out in 1 Corinthians 2, where the Spirit is said to be "the Spirit of God" (verses 11, 12, 14), in connection with the four things which are "of God" in verses 1, 5, 7, 10). As long as the woman with the issue of blood was occupied in seeking good from others by her own resources, she was not improved, but as soon as she came in contact with Christ, by touching the hem of His garment, then the power in Him flowed into her, and she was healed of her malady. The same is true in the Spirit's realm. In order to have His competency we must be under His control.

The Holy Spirit is "the Spirit" in contrast to the flesh. The grievous error into which the saints at Galatia had fallen was the substitution of fleshly energy for the Spirit's working, which led to the ignoring of the grace of God, and brought them into bondage. The Holy Spirit, right through the epistle, is referred to as "the Spirit" (Galatians 3:2, 3, 5, 14; 4:6, 29; 5:5, 17, 18, 22, 25; 6:8) and as such the sovereignty of His claim is brought before us. No one nor anything must be substituted for Himself. This is made known in the words—"If we live by the Spirit, by the Spirit let us also walk" (Galatians 5:25 RSV) Man in his self-energy and fleshly endeavor can never climb the heights of God's holiness, nor comprehend the riches of His grace, but the Spirit is the One who can lift us into both, and make us cease from the flesh, even as the whirlwind carried Elijah into the realms of glory; and being transformed, the mantle dropped from him, for being an earthly garment, it could not remain upon a spiritual body.

The Holy Spirit is the Atmosphere in which the child of God is to live. The command "to be filled in (margin) the Spirit" (R.V., Ephesians 5:18), is given in the epistle to the Ephesians. There are two things, among others, which the atmosphere is—it is a purifler and an eradiator. The foul air is dissipated by the atmosphere, and absorbed by the vegetable kingdom, and it is also by means of the atmosphere that the sun's rays are eradiated. The same may be said of the Holy Spirit. He is the Cleanser to remove every defiling thing from the life, and the Eradiator to cause the sun of the holiness of God to shine into and out of our lives. There are seven things which we are told not to do in Ephesians 4:25-31. We are (1) not to lie, (2) to be angry and sin not, (3) not to give place to the devil, (4) not to steal, (5) not to allow our tongue to be a medium of "corrupt communication," (6) not to grieve the Holy Spirit, (7) and not to allow bitterness and its attendant evils to be associated with us. These things cannot be done in our own power. The Spirit of God must be the Putter-away. Following the command to "be filled with the Spirit," there are seven things believers are to do in relation to each other in the different relationships in which they are found. Generally, believers are to submit to each other: wives are to be subject to their husbands: husbands are to love their wives: children are to obey their parents in the Lord: parents are to be considerate for their children: servants are to serve the Lord in their earthly service: and masters are to regard their servants with kindly interest. The practicality of the Spirit's infilling can easily be gathered from these things. He is the One who fulfils these responsibilities in our lives, as we prayerfully trust Him,

The Holy Spirit is the Medium through which we have fellowship with the Lord and each other. It is in the epistle to the Philippians that we read of "the fellowship of the Spirit" (Philippians 2:1) and it is in that epistle we find the apostle urging the sisters who had quarrelled to "be of the same mind" (4:2) and again and again we have the exhortation to be "of one accord," to have "one spirit," to be of "one mind" (1:27; 2:2). As the sap is the uniting power which unites every part of the tree, so the Spirit is the uniting power which enables believers to be of one accord with each other. The concord of mutual interest is found in being in accord with the Holy Spirit, even as the tire of the wheel keeps the spokes of the wheel in union with the hub.

The Holy Spirit is the In-letter to the fulness of the glorified Christ. The epistle to the Colossians brings before us the fulness of Christ as the Head of creation from whom are all things, and in whom all things are held together (1:15-17) and also the Head of the Church (1:18, 19), to whom believers are united (see the "with Hims" in chapters 2 and 3), and in whom they are made full (Colossians 2:10 RSV). Now the Holy Spirit is only mentioned once in the epistle (1:8) by name, but while this is the fact, He is made known again and again. Take seven things in chapter one, namely, spiritual understanding (verse 10), spiritual walk, spiritual fruit (verse 20), spiritual power, spiritual endurance (verse 11), spiritual affinity (verse 24), and spiritual ministry (verse 29). Like the unseen bar which ran through the boards of the tabernacle and kept them steady on the foundation (Exodus 24:28), so the Holy Spirit is the Secret Worker who leads us into the fulness of the living Christ, and makes true in our experience what is true for us in Him.

The Holy Spirit is the Safe-Guarder of the Christian worker's life and labor. He makes the message of the gospel effective through the believer's lips (1 Thessalonians 1:5). He gives joy amid suffering, and makes the affliction a means of gladness (1 Thessalonians 1:6). He guards us by His presence, even as the fence protects the garden, lest we should presume upon His love (1 Thessalonians 4:8). He reminds us we are not to "quench" any flame which He has kindled in another (1 Thessalonians 5:19), and frequently admonishes us lest we should forget the purpose the Lord had in saving, namely, the setting apart of our being for His hallowed occupation (2 Thessalonians 2:13).

1

The Discipler's Assurance

"His testimony lacks authenticity and conviction. Because of that, it is likely to do more harm than good," said an experienced believer in Christ, after hearing one whose words came in a hesitating way. The same may be said of many professed Christians. For that reason it will be wise, in the opening chapter of *The Discipler's Manual*, to look at the true meaning of the believer's judgment, for his sin and sins, in Christ's death. Unless we Christians are sure about this, we are not likely to bring assurance to others.

As flowers may have many hues, and as a number of different colored flowers in a bouquet enhance the beauty of each other by their contrast, so in the cross of Christ, the attributes of God are brought out in wondrous contrast, yet with consistent harmony. Indeed, in the cross we see His name was glorified, His love manifested, His majesty upheld, His justice satisfied, His truth vindicated, His law magnified, and His righteousness displayed, in the putting away of sin.

Is it not a logical as well as a Scriptural statement, that since Christ has been judged on the cross for the sin and sins of the believer, therefore the latter will *not* be judged for his sin and sins, at the judgment of the Great White Throne? For all that God would have had to judge in us as sinners, at the Great White Throne, He has judged in Christ on the cross. There, He became answerable for us, and made up for our failures and shortcomings. Therefore, as someone has aptly said, *"If anyone is to be kept out of heaven for my sins, it is Christ."* Because of His sacrifice, it is the privilege of each believer to know, and say,

> "He bore on the tree the sentence for me,
> And now both the Surety and sinner are free."

Let us now turn to God's Word, and see what He says about this subject. In so doing, there are three propositions which I want to make. *First,* the fires of God's judgment are set ablaze by man's sin. *Second,* Christ bore the judgment of God against sin, for those who receive Him as their Substitute; therefore in Him, they have died for their sin. *Third,* the Word of God assures us, there is no condemnation for the believer in Christ.

First, the fires of God's judgment are set ablaze by man's sin.

There are two words that are rendered "judgment" in God's Word. One has to do with the act of judging, in order to get the facts of the case; the other, which is generally rendered "condemnation," signifies the carrying out of the sentence of judgment already passed. As to the first, God's conclusion in relation to man universally is that all are guilty before Him (Romans. 3:19); and as to the second, God is waiting in grace to see if men will accept His Son as their Savior, in order that they may be delivered "from the coming wrath" (1 Thessalonians 1:10). If they will not, then there is nothing left but "a fearful expectation of judgment and of raging fire that will consume the enemies of God" (Hebrews 10:27 NIV).

There are three reasons for the judgment of God against man's sin.

1. *The judgment of God comes upon man because of what man is*. ". . . just as the result of one trespass was condemnation for all men . . . through the disobedience of the one man the many were sinners . . ." (Romans 5:18, 19 NIV). Adam, by his act of disobedience, made himself a sinner, and all his posterity too. As one drop of deadly poison in a glass of water will make the whole poisonous, so Adam's transgression has poisoned the whole race of man. As a consequence of the fall, man's nature is evil; hence, the natural man is evil, and does evil. Samuel Coleridge said it well: "It is a fundamental article of Christianity, that I am a fallen creature . . . that an evil ground existed in my will, previously to any given act, or assignable moment of time in my consciousness; I am born a child of wrath. This fearful mystery I pretend not to understand. I cannot even conceive the possibility of it; but I know that it is so . . . and what is real, must be possible."

This natural bent for evil within calls for the judgment of God upon it, as it did in the days of Noah. Of this evil we read, "The Lord saw how great man's wickedness had been, and that every inclination of the thoughts of his heart was only evil all the time . . . So the Lord said, I will wipe man, whom I have created, from the face of the earth . . ." (Genesis 6:5-7 NIV). The sinfulness of man means guiltiness, and guilt brings punishment, as the late H.C.G. Moule remarked in speaking of the Christian's knowledge of indwelling evil: "He was sinful before he sinned. He also knows that this antecedent sinfulness, cannot be rightly conceived as mere misfortune; it was implicit rebellion, real guilt. It was the free attitude of his real personality; when it came to expression, that expression was not due to a mastering fate, wrong while the victim—self—was right, though weak. It was due to himself."

2. *The judgment of God comes upon man because of what he has done*. When the judgment of the dead takes place, we read that they are "judged according to their works" (Revelation 20:12). What they have been determines what they shall be; thus, those who have been filthy and unjust, will be the same, yea, more so (R.V. margin, "Yet more," Revelation 22:11). What men have done will determine the measure of their punishment. One thing which impresses itself upon the mind, as the conversation goes on between Abraham and Lazarus, is that the latter makes no complaint as to the justness of his punishment (Luke 16:19-31). From this we may gather, the unsaved will see, and own, the

righteousness of the sentence which will be passed upon them, and will confess with the thief on the cross, "We are getting what our deeds deserve" (Luke 23:40, 41 NIV).

3. *The judgment of God comes upon man because of what he has not done.* Some of God's most terrible judgments have come, and will come, because of things not done. This is plainly brought out in the following scriptures from the NIV where omissions to duty are censured and condemned:

"Did not come" (Judges 5:23).
"Does not" (Matthew 7:26).
"Does not love" (1 Corinthians 16:22).
"Do not know" (2 Thessalonians 1:8).
"Do not obey" (2 Thessalonians 1:8).
"Do not believe" (John 16:9).

The consequent judgment mentioned in each of the above scriptures came because of something which was not done. Meroz was cursed because help was not given; the storm of wrath overthrew the house of the man because he did not build on the rock; the "anathema" will be passed upon those who have no affection for Christ; everlasting destruction and separation from the glory of God's presence will come, because He was not known and obeyed and the sin of all sins is that men will not believe on the Lord Jesus Christ.

Christ further illustrates, in the parable of the wicked servant, the evil consequence of not fulfilling His will, for He makes the Judge say, "I will judge you by your words, you wicked servant! You knew, did you, that I am a hard man, taking out what I did not put in, and reaping what I did not sow? Why then, didn't you put my money on deposit so that when I came back I could have collected it with interest? Then he said to those standing by, 'Take his mina away from him, and give it to the one that has ten minas.' 'Sir,' they said, 'he already has ten!' He replied, 'I tell you that to everyone who has, more will be given, but as for the one who has nothing, even what he has will be taken away'" (Luke 19:22-26 NIV). A similar pronouncement is given to the servant who did not use his talent, with the addition, "And throw that worthless servant outside, into the darkness, where there will be weeping and gnashing of teeth" (Matthew 25:30).

Do we not gather from these statements how different man's conception of sin is from what God thinks of it? Man thinks if he keeps away from wrongdoing, he does not sin; God's thought about sin is *failure to do the right,* and this, whether man knows it or not—for the meaning of the word sin is to miss the mark, that is, to fall short of what God demands—is how he should see it.

Second, Christ bore the judgment of God against sin for those who receive Him as their Substitute; therefore, in Him, they have died for their sin.

The three causes of God's judgment upon men as sinners have their counterpart in Christ's death for sin, for He was judged for what the believer *was*, as a sinner; for what he *did*; and for what he *failed to do*.

1. *Christ died for what we were.*

We are in ourselves sinners, with a sinful nature, and as such, we must be judged. In the NIV we read, "God did by sending his own Son in the likeness of sinful man to be a sin offering. And so he condemned sin in sinful men" (Romans 8:3). Moule rendered the latter part of the above verse, and commented upon it as follows: "'*And as sin-offering,*' expiatory and reconciling, '*sentenced sin in the flesh*'; not pardoned it, observe, but sentenced it. He orders it to execution; He kills its claim and its power for all who are in Christ."

We know from the Scriptures that while our actual sins are forgiven for the sake of Christ (Ephesians 1:7; 1 John 2:12), our sinful nature is not forgiven, but is judged in His death. This is wondrously and minutely typified in the sin-offering.

Let us ponder the following four questions in relation to this aspect of the subject. What was the sin-offering called? Where was the sin-offering taken? What was done with the sin-offering? Who killed the sin-offering?

What was the sin-offering called?

It was called a sin-offering (see Leviticus 4), and it was offered to God for the sin of ignorance. The sin of ignorance was a sin committed through indwelling evil, but the committer was none-the-less guilty, even though he did it unwittingly (Leviticus 5:17). In the Hebrew, the words sin and sin-offering are identical; thus, when we read, "*It is a sin-offering,*" we might as literally read, "*It is sin.*" Thus the sin-offering is treated as sin, and judged as sin. This is also true with reference to Christ as the Sin-Offering. He was treated on the cross, by God in righteousness, as the personification of sin. As Martin Luther said, "He was my sin," or better, as the Holy Spirit says, "God made him who had no sin, to be sin for us, so that in him we might become the righteousness of God" (2 Corinthians 5:21 NIV).

Where was the sin-offering taken?

The Bible says, ". . . the rest of the bull—he must take outside the camp" (Leviticus 4:12). Outside the camp was the place of judgment. It was the place to which the leper was separated (Leviticus 12:46). Thus, Miriam was shut out of the camp for seven days, when she was smitten with leprosy, because of her sin against her brother (Numbers 12:15). The Sabbath-breaker was stoned to death, outside the camp, when he came under the judgment of God, because of his willful transgression of God's commandment (Numbers 15:35, 36). Christ the great Anti-type, when He was judged for our sin, "suffered outside the city gate" (Hebrews 13:12). Christ, the Spotless One, went to the place of uncleanness, the place of death, the place of judgment, that He might be treated as the transgressor, as the unclean one, and as the sinner. This is clearly stated in God's Word. In 2 Corinthians 5:21, He is said to be "made . . . sin," and in Galatians 3:13, He is said to have become "a curse." The reference in the last passage of Scripture is to the judgment of the prodigal and rebellious son, mentioned in Deuteronomy 21:18-23, who, after he had been stoned to death outside the camp, was hanged, and of whom it was written, ". . . anyone who is hung on a tree is under God's curse." Such words being associated with Him who died for us, tell us on the one hand what we deserve, and on the other hand the terrible death He underwent. A doctor gives medicine to heal the sick, but Christ took our disease that He might heal us. A man pays a ransom to free a slave, but Christ paid the ransom by *becoming* a slave, that He might free us.

In the history of Israel there is one scene which is painful in its sinful blackness. I refer to the whoredom of Israel at Baal-Peor. Why do I refer to this? Because the being hanged on a tree is incidentally mentioned. We read, "So Israel joined in worshiping the Baal of Peor. And the Lord's anger burned against Israel. The Lord said to Moses, 'Take all the leaders of these people, kill them and expose them in broad daylight before the Lord, so that the Lord's fierce anger may turn away from Israel'" (Numbers 25:3, 4). Then we have described to us the faithful action of Phinehas, who executed one of the princes for his sin. In so doing, Phinehas was acting on divine authority, as may be gathered from Deuteronomy 13:6-9. I refer to this incident to show that as Christ is said to be accursed in His being hanged on a tree, it therefore identifies Him with the worst of sins, and tells how thoroughly He was identified with us, in being treated as we should have been treated. The prince, Zimri, suffered for his own sin at the hand of Phinehas, and thus the anger of the Lord was turned away (Numbers 25:10-15). Christ suffered for our sin, at the hands of God, as foretold by the prophet Zechariah (13:7). In this, God's anger is turned away from us (Isaiah 12:1).

St. Vincent de Paul was, for some time, almoner-general to the prison ships in the chief harbors of France. During the reign of Louis XIII, while visiting those ships at Marseilles, he was so struck by the broken-down looks, and exceeding sorrowful countenance of one of the convicts, that, on discovering his own sorrow was less, he absolutely changed places with the convict. The prisoner went free, and St. Vincent took the convict's chain, did a convict's work, lived on convict fare, and, worst of all, had only convict society. When He took our place and died our death, Christ did something very similar, that we might go free.

What was done with the sin-offering?

"But the hide of the bull and all its flesh, as well as its head and with the legs . . . all the rest of the bull—he must take outside the camp to a place ceremonially clean where the ashes are thrown, and burn it in a wood fire on the ash pile" (Leviticus 4:11, 12). These words plainly tell us that the sin offering was to be utterly consumed, except the fat (Leviticus 4:8.10).

In the Book of Leviticus, there are two words used in speaking of burning. Each has a very different meaning. The word which occurs in Leviticus 1:9, 13, 15, 17; 2:2, 9, 12, 16; 3:5, 11, 16; and 4:10 means to turn into fragrance by fire; to burn as incense. This fragrance went up to God as a sweet-smelling savor. This is typical of Christ in the God-glorifying aspect of His death, as the One in whom the believer is accepted (Eph. 5:2). But the word used to describe the burning of the sin-offering outside the camp, means "to consume utterly." It is expressive of God's judgment against sin, as when we read that the one, who was discovered with the sacred things of Jericho which were devoted to the Lord, should "be destroyed by fire, along with all that belongs to him. He has violated the covenant of the Lord and has done a disgraceful thing in Israel" (Joshua 2:15).

This word of judgment being associated with the sin-offering points out that Christ has borne the fiery judgment of God against our sinful nature. Speaking of this fact B.W. Newton wrote: "God sending His own Son in the likeness of sinful flesh, and 'concerning sin, damned sin in the flesh,' that is, *our indwelling sin*. Thus the wrath due to both our sin, and to our sins (I speak of believers) was borne by the Holy One, who Himself had neither sin, nor sins. There it expended itself; there it burned until nought but ashes remained; there faith sees both the sin and the sins of all believers, ended forever, as regards the judicial estimate of God. We may stand, as it were, by the side of that burning pile. We see the flame fiercely raging in the full intensity of its devouring power; at length, we behold it lessen; at last, flicker and decay, till it smoulders among the embers. We may watch the last expiring spark that glimmers there, and when that ends—when nothing but the cold ashes remain—we see an emblem of the relation which the fire of holy wrath bears to all the believing people of God. Its power is expended; it has burned itself out; ashes only remain."

Who killed the sin-offering?

The offerer killed the sin-offering. If Leviticus 4 is read, it will be found that four different cases are supposed. But whether it were a priest (verses 3, 4), the whole congregation (verses 13-15), one of the rulers (verses 22-24), or one of the common people (verses 27-29), there were three things that had to be done in each case: 1) the offering had to be brought to the door of the tent of the congregation; 2) the offerer had to lay his hands on the head of the offering as identifying himself with it; and 3) he had to kill it himself. All this speaks of a personal need, a personal reliance upon the sacrifice for remittance of sin's penalty. It required a personal act of faith, in taking the knife and plunging it into the animal, which was offered up in the offerer's stead. In its typical application, we are reminded, by the offerer killing the antmal for sacrifice, that it was our personal sin which put the Lord Jesus Christ to death. There is a sense in which the words of Peter may be applied to each of us: "You killed the author of life" (Acts 3:15). It was *our* sins which nailed Him to the accursed tree.

2. *Christ died for what man had done.*

In the *Arabian Nights*, in the story of Alladin, we are told that Alladin could only get the desire of his heart by rubbing the lamp which the genie had given him. In like manner, it is only as we rub the lamp of divine truth by prayerful and submissive meditation, that we get the soul-satisfying blessings of the gospel. The Holy Spirit has been pleased to couple with the blackness man's sins, and the golden girdle of Christ's all-sufficient sacrifice, certain expressions. These demonstrate and illustrate how completely the healing balm of His atonement covers the terrible wound of man's transgressions. Let us briefly see how this is brought out in the following nine passages of Scripture (the NIV text), where "sins" are specially mentioned:

"... take away our *sins*" (1 John 3:5).
"... offered for all time one sacrifice for *sins*" (Hebrews 10:12).

"... gave himself for our *sins*" (Galatians 1:4).
"... the atoning sacrifice for our *sins*" (1 John 2:2).
"... sacrificed ... died for *sins*, the righteous for the unrighteous" (1 Peter 3:18).
"once to take away the *sins* of many" (Hebrews 9:28).
"... bore our *sins* in his body on the tree" (2 Peter 2:24).
"Blood ... poured out ... for the forgiveness of *sins*" (Matthew 26:28).
"... died for our *sins*" (2 Corinthians 15:3).

In each of the above scriptures, there are two great truths presented—1) the sins of the sinners, and 2) the sacrifice of the Savior. While we keep these two truths before us. I want to emphasize one point in each of these verses as found in connection with the fact of Christ's atoning death. These nine statements might be called, "Nine rays which radiate from the sun of Christ's atoning sacrifice."

First Ray—Manifestation. "He was *manifested* to take away our sins" (1 John 3:5 KJV). The meaning of the word "manifested" is, for one to reveal himself, who had been hidden behind a curtain. The Greek word *phaneroŏ* is rendered "*shewed*" in John 21:1, 14, where our attention is directed to the fact of Christ appearing after His resurrection. In the verse before us, we have it distinctly stated that Christ appeared in human form for one specific purpose (1 Timothy 3:16; 1 John 1:2), namely, to take away our sins. As the scapegoat, on the day of atonement, was separated to take away the sins of Israel (Leviticus 16:21), so Christ was manifested to take away our sins by His death—to take away the penalty which they merited, and to destroy the power which they had gained over us.

Second Ray—Perfection. "Offered for all time *one* sacrifice for sins" (Hebrews 10:12). In this verse, the emphasis is on the word "*one*," calling attention to the fact that Christ's one offering, once offered, is sufficient to meet the necessity of the case. The Holy Spirit repeats again, and again, the words "*once*" and "*one*" (see Hebrews 9:12, 26, 28; 10:2, 10, 12). The contrast is between the many offerings, offered at many times, which proclaimed their imperfection; and the one Offering, offered once, which tells out its perfection. Christ the Perfect One offered Himself as the Perfect Offering, which perfectly deals with our sins, and gives to the believer a perfect conscience, in consequence.

Third Ray—Consecration. "*Gave* himself for our sins" (Galatians 1:4). We read in Acts 19:31, that some of Paul's friends urged him not to "*venture* into the theatre" at Ephesus, lest he should come to harm; and in 2 Corinthians 8:5, we read of those to whom the apostle wrote, that "they *gave* themselves first to the Lord." Let us take these scriptures and apply them to Christ. He did "venture" (the words "*adventure*" and "*gave*," are the same as rendered "*gave*" in Galatians 1:4) His life on our behalf, for He gave Himself to the task of taking the punishment of our sins. This He did in consecration to God's will, for He was acting at His bidding.

Fourth Ray—Atonement. "The atoning sacrifice for our sins" (1 John 2:2). Christ is the propitiatory sacrifice, who answers to God's justice on behalf of our sins. The Greek word *Hilasmos*, rendered propitiatory, answers to the Hebrew word *caphar*, which means to effect a reconciliation with God, by atonement. Christ has given to God, by His death, all He asked from us. Because of this, we are covered in the all-sufficiency of what Christ gave to God, when He died in our stead.

Fifth Ray—Substitution. "Died for sins, the righteous for the unrighteous, to bring you to God" (1 Peter 3:18). The preposition *huper* rendered *for* in the sentence "Righteous *for* the unrighteous," means on behalf of, as when one person bends over another, in order to protect him. So Christ was acting on our behalf, in receiving the blow which was aimed at us, and thus suffered in our place. He, the Righteous One, received the punishment due to the unrighteous one on account of his sins. On the 10th of June, 1770, the town of Port-au-Prince, in Haiti, was utterly overthrown by a terrible earthquake. From one of the fallen houses the inmates had fled, except a black woman, the nurse of her master's infant child. She would not desert her charge, though the walls were even then giving way. Rushing to its bedside, she stretched forth her arms to enfold it. The building rocked to its foundation; the roof fell in. Did it crush the hapless pair? The heavy fragments fell indeed upon the woman, but the infant escaped unharmed; for its noble protector extended her bended form across the body, and, at the sacrifice of her own life, preserved her charge from destruction. This old account of a courageous rescue is a small illustration of how Christ died for us, in bearing in His body, the just due of our sins.

Sixth Ray—Imputation. "Once to take away the sins of many" (Hebrews 9:28). The meaning of the word *"take away"* is to bring, carry, or lead up, as when Christ *"led them up"* (His disciples) into a high mountain (Mark 9:2). Another picture . . . of this sacrifice is seen when an offerer brought an animal to the altar. This animal was then offered up on behalf of the offerer, and bore his sins upon itself. Christ led our sins up to the altar of the cross. He then bore the due weight of their punishment, in that He was treated as though He had committed the sins. Bengel remarks, "Our sins were laid on Him; when, therefore, He was lifted up on the cross, He bare up our sins along with Him."

Seventh Ray—Identification. "Bore *our sins* in his body on the tree" (1 Peter 2:24). On one occasion, the customs authorities asked Peter why his Master did not pay tribute. Christ, knowing what had taken place, directed Peter to go and catch fish, and in the mouth of the first one he would find a piece of money, which he was to give to the authorities, as Christ says, "For my tax and yours" (Matthew 17:24). The preposition "Anti" translated "for," which Christ uses in speaking of the money *"for* my tax and yours," is one which signifies something which is set over against something else; it may be in opposition to something else, as when the man of sin is called the *"Anti-*Christ," or it may be that which is an equivalent to a claim made, and thus meeting it. Christ uses this preposition when He speaks of giving ". . . his life a ransom *for* many" (Matthew 20:28; Mark 10:45).

The one thing I want to emphasize is this: Christ in His death, not only died in our stead, as the Substitute acting *apart* from us, but as the tribute money was for Christ and Peter, so Christ *identified* Himself with us. Thus His death is our death for our sins. In Hebrews 1:3 we read that Christ Himself "provided purification *for* sins," or as Rotherham translates the sentence, "made for Himself a purification for our sins."

Personally, Christ did not need to purify Himself, for He was "without sin"; but *representatively* He did, for He was acting as our Head. Christ Himself illustrated this when He allowed John the Baptist to plunge Him beneath the waters of Jordan *as a sinner* (compare Matthew 3:6 with Matthew 3:13-15). As we remember our oneness with Him in His death, it gives a new meaning to the possessive pronoun in Isaiah 53:4, 5, where we read,

He bore "*our* infirmities."
He "carried *our* sorrows."
He was "pierced for *our* transgressions."
He was "crushed for *our* iniquities."
The "punishment that brought *us* peace was upon him."
". . . by his wounds *we* are healed."

Coupling these scriptures with the words, "Christ bore *our* sins," there flashes from the cross the wondrous rays of His grace and love for *us*. As Dr. Denney says, "It was *His* death, certainly, for He had *come* to die; but it was *not* His, for He knew no sin; it was *for* us, and *not for Himself*, that He made death His own."

Eighth Ray—Remission. "This is my blood of the covenant, which is poured out for many, for the forgiveness of sins" (Matthew 26:28). The meaning of the word "remission" (KJV) is, according to Liddle and Scott, "A letting go, a setting free, as of a slave or captive. Or more fully and completely from a biblical standpoint, "dismission, discharge, a setting free. In the Septuagint, and New Testament, setting free, remission of debt or punishment; hence, the forgiveness of sins on the part of God, and with reference to the future judgment; total remission and forgiveness, excluding all idea of punishment."

As in the year of jubilee, which began on the Day of Atonement, the debtor was freed from all liabilities; so Christ frees us from the bondage and guilt of sin, by shedding His blood for us.

Ninth Ray—Revelation. "Christ died for our sins according to the Scriptures" (1 Corinthians 15:3). In his *Studies in Theology* Dr. Denney relates an incident which illustrates the effectiveness of Christ's substitutionary work. He says, "A fishing-tackle maker, and an enthusiastic fisherman, once told me of losing his bait in a mysterious way without catching anything. The explanation was, that by some accident or other, the barb had been broken from the hook. It was my friend himself who made the application of this, when he said that this was exactly what happened when people preached the love of God to men, but left out of their Gospel, the essential truth, that it is Christ on the cross, the Substitute for sinners, in whom that love is revealed. In other words, the condemnation of our sins in Christ upon His Cross is the barb on the hook."

The barb of the gospel is unmistakably the Atonement of Christ. Without it, there is no catching of men out of the Great Sea of sin; but on the other hand, the hook upon which the barb is welded, is the Word of God. It is in it, we are told, He died according to its revelation. Take the Scripture away and the Christ is removed, and we exclaim with Mary, "They have taken my Lord away, and I don't know where they have put him" (John 20:13). But in the gold of Holy Writ we discover the jewels of Christ's death, even as the precious stones were secured in the breastplate of Israel's High Priest by the settings of gold.

Well may we sing with Frances Ridley Havergal, as we think of what Christ has done for us, and say to Him:

> What hast Thou done for me, O Mighty Friend,
> Who lovest to the end!
> Reveal Thyself, that I may now behold
> Thy love unknown, untold,
> Bearing the curse, and made a curse for me,
> That blessed and made a blessing I might be.
>
> Oh, Thou wast crowned with thorns, that I might wear
> A crown of glory fair;
> "Exceeding sorrowful," that I might be
> Exceeding glad in Thee;
> "Rejected and despised," that I might stand
> Accepted and complete on Thy right hand.
>
> Wounded for my transgressions, stricken sore,
> That I might "sin no more";
> Weak, that I might be always strong in Thee;
> Bound, that I might be free;
> Acquaint with grief, that I might only know
> Fulness of joy in everlasting flow.
>
> Thine was the chastisement, with no release,
> That mine might be the peace;
> The bruising and the cruel strips were Thine,
> That healing might be mine;
> Thine was the sentence and the condemnation,
> Mine the acquittal and the full salvation.
>
> For Thee revilings, and a mocking throng,
> For me the angel-song;
> For Thee the frown, the hiding of God's face,
> For me His smile of grace;
> Sorrows of hell and bitterest death for Thee,
> And heaven and everlasting life for me.
>
> Thy cross and passion, and Thy precious death,
> While I have mortal breath.
> Shall be my spring of love, and work of praise,
> The life of all my days;
> Till all this mystery of love supreme
> Be solved in glory—glory's endless theme.

3 . *Christ died for what man did not do.*

There are many things which man should have done, that he has not done. Man should have fulfilled God's law in every iota and particular; and he should have glorified God in an absolute and perfect consecration to His will. Since he has done neither, he has come short of God's glory (Romans 3:23), and he has been guilty of enmity against God (Romans 8:7). Christ, in striking contrast, has been obedient to the will of God, and glorified Him. There are two "I have's" in the Gospel according to John, which bring out these facts. In speaking of

Himself as the Good Shepherd, who gives His life for the sheep, and His authority for so doing, Jesus says, "This command I received from my Father" (John 10:18) and in looking over His life's work, in the light of the Atonement He was about to make, He said, in speaking to His Father, "I have brought glory on earth by completing the work you gave me to do" (John 17:4). In every particular, He was the Perfect One. There was no blemish in His character. It always sounded forth, "Glory to God in the highest." There was no flaw in the devotion of His life. It stands unique and alone in its marvelous beauty. There was no fault in the consecration of His service, it was Perfect with the holiness of God. There was no stain in the texture of His nature, it was pure in every part. There was no alloy in the gold of His holiness, it was uncorrupted by self. There was no spot in the sun of His testimony, it was truly noble, and nobly true. There was no flaw in His obedience, for it was perfect in its delight to do God's will, and to finish His work. And there was no defect in the work He undertook when He died to meet God's claims, and to bring glory to His name. His death on behalf of His own went up to God as a sweet smelling savor (Ephesians 5:2), which not only satisfied the claims of His Throne, but brought joy to His heart.

Because of this believers find themselves perfect in His comeliness (Ezekiel 16:14); beautiful in His beauty (1 John 4:17); holy in His holiness (1 Corinthians 1:30); righteous in His righteousness (2 Corinthians 5:21); precious in His preciousness (1 Peter 2:7); living in His life (1 Peter 2:5); accepted in His acceptableness (Ephesians 1:6); enriched in His riches (Philippians 4:19); blessed in His blessedness (Ephesians 1:3); seated in His exaltation (Philippians 2:6); sufficient in His meekness (Colossians 1:12); strong in His grace (2 Timothy 2:1); gladdened in His joy (John 15:11); and loved in His love (John 15:12). All these blessings have stamped upon them the hallmark of Christ's perfect Atonement.

The Word of God's grace assures us that there is no condemnation for the believer in Christ.

We can conceive nothing better than Bengel's rule for searching the Word of God with profit—"Apply yourself wholly to the text; apply the subject wholly to yourself." Where this double application exists, there is sure to be a double blessing—the mind will be enlightened by the soul's knowledge, and the heart will be assured of the soul's warmth. But the two must go together. The beam of truth in relation to the soul must be balanced, on the one hand, by the scale of reverent study of the Scriptures guided by the Holy Spirit. On the other hand, it requires the scale of obedience to the truth known, and whole-hearted response to it.

In thinking over the specific statements of the Bible (NIV), which assure believers of their interest in Christ, the following seven points have been suggested:

1. *An Undeniable Difference*. The outlook for believers and unbelievers is unmistakably different. This is very clearly seen, if we note two appointments and two reservings. Of the unsaved it is said, ". . . man is destined to die once and after that to face judgment" (Hebrews 9:27); and ". . . the Lord knows how

to . . . hold the unrighteous for the day of judgment, while continuing their punishment" (2 Peter 2:9). The outlook for unbelievers is black with the clouds of coming judgment and wrath, which loom before them. The outlook for believers stands out in vivid contrast. It is lit up with the brightness of life and immortality, for we are told, "For God did not appoint us to suffer wrath, but to receive salvation through our Lord Jesus Christ" (1 Thessalonians 5:9); and that He has "reserved" "an inheritance that can never perish, spoil or fade" (1 Peter 1:4). There is as much difference between these two appointings and two reservings, as there is between light and darkness, holiness and sin, Christ and the devil, blessing and curse, salvation and wrath, joy and misery, heaven and hell.

2. *An Unambiguous Distinction*. "Not be condemned with the world" (1 Corinthians 11:32). The context tells us that the reason why God chastens His people is that they should not be condemned with the world. The words suggest two alternatives, the condemnation of the world, and the not being condemned with the world. The latter applies to the children of God. Beneath the surface of the words, we may draw an inference, namely, that when God condemns the world, the children of God will be where condemnation cannot reach them. His word to His own is, "Go, my people, enter your rooms and shut the doors behind you: hide yourself for a little while, until his wrath has passed by" (Isaiah 26:20). There is a threefold direction in this command. *First*, God's people are to enter into *their innermost* (for so the word means) rooms; *second*, they are to shut their doors behind them; and *third*, they are to hide themselves. Likewise those who are hidden in the Atonement of Christ are shut in, in the perfection of His finished work, and abiding in the innermost chamber of His love, are where the indignation of judgment cannot reach them.

3. *An Unapproachable Sphere*. "Therefore, there is now no condemnation for those who are in Christ Jesus" (Romans 8:1). Condemnation can never reach Christ, therefore it can never reach those who are in Him. The position in which the believer is found, is "in Christ." What does it mean to be in the circle of these gracious words—"in Him"?

In Him, as Noah and his family were in the ark, and thus saved from the avenging flood of God's wrath against sin, for He is the Ark upon whom the flood of righteous indignation against sin has surged and fallen. In Him we are safe, for He has borne the brunt for us; yea, we have borne it, in Him.

In Him, as the children of Israel were in the blood-sprinkled houses on the night of the passover, and thus delivered from the darkness and eternal death of sin; for He is the Lamb whose blood was shed for us, which blood, being sprinkled on the door-posts and lintel of our conscience, speaks peace to us.

In Him, as the unintentional man-slayer who fled to the city of refuge was saved from the avenger, and was safe till the death of the high priest, if he abode in the refuge (Numbers 35:25-28). Our great High Priest will never die, for He lives in the power of an endless life; thus He saves to the uttermost, that is "evermore" (Hebrews 7:25, margin), for He is the "Author of eternal salvation unto all them that obey Him" (Hebrews 5:9). The avenger of the broken law can never touch us, for we are in Him.

In Him, as Rahab was in the house with its scarlet symbol of assured protection from the judgment about to fall on Jericho. The scarlet thread of Christ's precious blood gives assurance, that since He died, the question of our sin will never be opened again.

In Him, we have passed the judgment due to our sin, and are now seated with Him in heavenly places even as the stones taken from Gilgal and placed in Jordan, and the stones taken from Jordan and erected in Gilgal (Joshua 4:3-9, 20), indicated the reproach of Egypt rolled from Israel (Joshua 5:9).

We may well call this an unapproachable sphere, for who can reach us, since we are in Him? We often see at the entrance gates of large office buildings, "No admittance except on business." Likewise there are some who have no admittance into the realm of these words, "In Him." Who are they? Sin with its condemning power, law with its terrible curse, justice with its righteous demand, Satan with his accusing voice, hell with its burning flame, death with its biting sting, and the world with its deceptive lusts.

4. *An Unqualified Assurance*. "He that believeth on Him is not condemned" (John 3:18). How positive are the words, "Is not condemned." The words really mean, "is not judged." The one that believes is not sentenced; hence, he can never have condemnation, through having the experience of bearing the execution of the sentence.

The light of heaven flashes upon the diamond words, *"is not."* There is no uncertainty about them. When Christ uses an *"is not,"* there is no mistake as to the meaning of these emphatic words; there is the positive statement of God. Let us take three *"is nots"* by way of confirmation and illustration. He says of the fire which is to feed upon the wicked, "the fire *is not* quenched" (Mark 9:44, 46, 48). He says of him who gives to any thing or any one, the place He should occupy, that he *"is not* worthy of Me" (Matthew 10:37, 38); and Christ also said, in rebuking His disciples because of a sectarian spirit which they displayed, "He that *is not* against us is on our part" (Mark 9:40). We understand these to be positive statements, against which there is no court of appeal. Therefore, we take the *"is not"* of John 3:18, as the positive assurance of the Lord Jesus Christ to those who believe on Him, that there is no judgment upon, nor for them.

5. *An Unmistakable Promise*. "Shall not come into condemnation" (John 5:24). I remember once asking a believer, "Which side of the judgment are you?"

"Oh," she replied, "we must all appear before the judgment-seat of Christ."

I pointed out to her she was confusing things which differ, for only believers will be at the judgment-seat, and that they are there, not to be judged, but that their *works* may be tested, so that their place in Christ's coming kingdom may be determined.

She then reminded me of the scene described in Revelation 20; but I pointed out to her, that only one class of people are judged there, namely, "the dead." Then I gave her the promise of Christ in John 5:24: "Shall not come into judgment" (RSV).

When the Holy Spirit says, "Sin *shall not* have dominion over you" (Romans 6:14), it means that sin shall not exercise its lordship. When we read, "I *shall not* want" (Psalm 23:1), because the Lord is my Shepherd, it means that every need shall be supplied. When Jehovah said to Israel, "The plague *shall not* be upon you for a destruction" (Exodus 12:13, margin), it was God's promise that Israel should be safe from judgment. In the same way, when the Savior assures those who believe in Him, that they "*shall not* come into condemnation," we may rest content that He will keep His word. Someone may object, and say, does it not say, "It is appointed unto all men once to die, and after this the judgment" (Hebrews 9:27)? No, it does not. It says, "It is appointed unto men," not "*all* men." Besides this, the gist and point of the Scripture quoted is lost sight of if we don't read the "as" and "so" of the passage. The words are: "And *as* it is appointed unto men once to die, but after this the judgment: *so* Christ was once offered to bear the sins of many; and unto them that look for Him shall He appear the second time without sin unto salvation" (Hebrews 9:27, 28). The meaning of the passage is, death and judgment are the common lot of humanity, because all have sinned; but the believer in Christ is looking for neither death nor judgment, but for the coming Christ, for Christ has died the death, and borne the judgment. Thus believers can say with the captain, who, when the passenger said to him, as he pointed to some clouds, "There is a storm coming, captain," replied, "No, we are on the weather side of the storm."

6. *An Unspeakable Privilege*. "Herein is love with us (margin) made perfect, that we may have boldness in the day of judgment because as He is, so are we in this world" (1 John 4:17). The day of judgment does not fill us with dread as it does other men, and the reason for this is, "As He is, so are we." Canon Fausset says of this: "The ground of our 'confidence' is, 'because even as He (Christ) is, we also are in this world' (He will not, in that day, condemn those *like Himself*); we are *righteous* as He is righteous, especially in that which is the sum of righteousness, *love* (chapter 3:14). Christ is righteousness and *love* itself in heaven; so are we, His members, still 'in this world.' Our oneness with Him even now in His exaltation (Ephesians 2:6), so that all that belongs to Him of righteousness, etc., belongs to us by perfect imputation and progressive impartation, is the ground of our *love* being *perfected, so that* we can have confidence in the day of judgment."

7. *An Unrivaled Question*. "Who is he that condemns?" (Romans 8:34). Who can condemn us? Can God? No, for He has justified us. Can Christ? No, for He died for us. Can the Holy Spirit? No, for He is One with the Father in our salvation. Can sin condemn us? No, for it has been answered for in Christ's death. Can Satan condemn us? No, for Christ has rendered him powerless by His victory over him. Can the law condemn us? No, for Christ is the end of the law for righteousness to everyone who believes. Can death condemn us? No, for Christ has taken away its sting. Can justice condemn us? No, for it is satisfied.

Why is it there is no condemnation? Let it be repeated once again. It is because Christ died.

> Buried in the grave of Jesus, I believe what God has said;
> Faith, His judgment acquiescing, reckons now that I am dead.

Death and judgment are behind me, grace and glory are before;
All the billows rolled o'er Jesus, there exhausted all their power.

First-fruits of the resurrection, He is risen from the tomb;
Now I stand in new creation, free—because beyond my doom.

Jesus died, and I died with Him, buried in His grave I lie;
One with Him in resurrection, seated now in Him on high.

I await the full redemption, when the Risen One shall come;
And my mortal body changed, shall be fashioned like His own.

Precious and once-bleeding Surety, nothing would I know but Thee:
Nothing would my heart desire, but, my Lord, Thy face to see.

Here I share in Thy rejection, Thy reproach and cross I love;
Here I stand in Thine acceptance in the Father's sight above.

Help me here to walk obedient to Thy holy will and word,
Counting all my joy to please Thee, owning Thee, alone, my Lord.

2

The Discipler's Acceptance

"He hath made us accepted in the Beloved" (Ephesians 1:6).

One of the most essential things for the Christian worker is this: he should be perfectly clear as to his personal acceptance in Christ, for if he is in doubt about this, and sees men "as trees walking," he is not likely to be helpful in his ministry to others, for his testimony will be weak and wavering.

A well-known and much loved servant of Christ, in giving a Bible reading, said: "There are four rules I lay down for Bible study. *First*, I consider the text; *second*, I notice words and phrases; *third*, I refer to the context and *fourth*, I give a practical exposition of the subject." In looking at this subject, let us follow, in some measure, the same rule:

The Text

We shall look at the whole of Ephesians 1:6, although we only call special attention to that part of it which speaks of the believer's acceptance in the Beloved. The Authorized Version is: "To the praise of the glory of his grace, wherein he hath made us accepted in the Beloved." Green, in his twofold Testament, renders it: "In order" (speaking of God's good pleasure) "to a glorious praise of His grace, wherein He dealt graciously with us in the Beloved." Rotherham translates it: "Unto the praise of the glory of His favor, wherewith He favored us in the Beloved One." Dean Alford gives it: "To the praise of the glory of His grace, which He freely bestowed upon us in the Beloved One." The Revised Version is: "To the praise of the glory of His grace, which He freely bestowed on us in the Beloved." The New International Version has it: ". . . to the praise of his glorious grace, which he has freely given us in the One he loves."

Notice the Word "Accepted"

The Greek word *"karitoo,"* means to be endued with special honor. It only occurs in one other place in the New Testament—Luke 1:28—and is rendered *"highly favored"*; it is in connection with Mary as the mother of Jesus when the angel said to her: "Hail! thou that art *highly favored* (or, as the margin has it, '*graciously accepted*, or *much graced*'), the Lord is with thee!" The margin of the Revised Version has it, "endued with grace."

Look at the Context

The apostle, in the third verse of Ephesians 1, praises the Lord because He has blessed us in Christ with all spiritual blessings; and then he goes on to enumerate them:

Chosen according to His own mind for one purpose, *i.e.*, that we should be holy and without blame before Him in love.

Making us His own children, according to His own pleasure, that He Himself might be glorified by what He has done for us, on the ground of His own delight in us, and by virtue of His Son's atoning death.

Now it is His own pleasure and delight to deal with us, and bless us according to the riches of His grace.

Exposition

We will take the different readings as bringing out, in some measure, the meaning and fulness of the Scripture.

I. "He hath made us accepted in the beloved" (A.V.)

A *wondrous manufacture—"Made."* By our sins we had made God hide His face from us (Isaiah 49:2, margin); and before He could bless us, Christ had to be made sin for us, that we might be made the righteousness of God in Him (2 Corinthians 5:21). Now God has made Christ unto us, Wisdom, Righteousness, Sanctification, and Redemption, and also made us accepted in the Beloved.

A *gracious Provider to praise—"He."* Not our prayers, not our repentance, not our faith, not our attendance upon the means of grace, not our efforts, not our holiness, not what we are or can promise to do, not our good works, not anything that is of us or man, but He, Himself, because He would, and because Christ died, has provided for us.

A *blessed certainty—"hath."* It is not may, or has, or will, but blessed Divine certainty—"hath." A present, blessed, and eternal "hath." As true as God lives, as certain as Christ died and rose again, as stable as God's steadfast throne, as sure as His ever abiding Word.

Unworthy receivers—"us." We, who were once dead in trespasses and sins, hath He quickened. We, who were once rebels, hath He reconciled; we, who were once under the curse, hath He blessed; we, who were once under condemnation, hath He justified; we, who were once in the world, hath he taken out, and put in the children's place.

A *glorious truth—"Accepted."* I call your attention to three illustrations of this truth, in the Old Testament. *First,* Genesis 4:7 "If you do what is right, will you not be accepted? But if you do not do what is right, sin is crouching at your door" (NIV). The Newberry Bible has it, "A sin-offering croucheth at the entrance." It seems as if God said to Cain: "Abel has been accepted because he came as a sinner, and by bringing the burnt-offering, has confessed his need of atonement, and by faith has laid hold of, and is resting in the work of My Son, which in the fulness of time He shall accomplish. But you have come and brought Me a cursed offering, by bringing the fruit of the earth, which is cursed on account of sin. Why not come in My own way? There is even now a lamb crouching at the door, and if you come in My way you shall be accepted as much as Abel." This brings before us four points—(1) There must be the confession of the need of atonement on the part of the sinner; (2) there must be atonement made by another; (3) there must be faith in the atonement made; (4) and the result is, the one who rests in Christ is accepted by God.

Again, look at Leviticus 1:4: "He is to lay his hand on the head of the burnt offering, and it will be accepted on his behalf to make atonement for him." The burnt offering brings before us Christ, as the One wholly devoted to do His Father's will, the One in whom the Father delighted, the One in whom He was well pleased, and who perfectly glorified Him. The Israelite who brought the offering, and laid his hand upon it was thus identified with it, and accepted. In a far higher sense are we today accepted, namely, in all the worthiness of what Christ is to God.

Again, consider Exodus 28:36-38 (NIV): "Make a plate of pure gold and engrave on it as a seal, Holy to the Lord. . . . It will be on Aaron's forehead continually, so that they will be acceptable to the Lord." The pure gold brings before us Christ, as the Son of God. The engraving, like the engraving of a signet, and the words "Holy to the Lord," tell us of what Christ is as Man—the Holy One to God. Aaron wore the golden plate on the mitre for a definite purpose, namely, that the children of Israel (who were identified and represented by him) might always be accepted before the Lord. Our Divine High Priest, in all the glory of His person, the completeness and worth of His work, the spotlessness of His humanity, and the purity of His holy character, represents every believer, and in Him every child of God is accepted. Because He is accepted, so are we; because He is holy, so are we; because He is righteous, so are we; because He is the Object of God's delight, so are we; because He lives, so shall we; because He abides forever, so shall we.

A *secure position, and a wondrous fact—"in the Beloved."* As Goodwin says: "The sun, you know, shines upon all the world; but if you take a burning glass and hold it in the point of union or concentration, between the shining sun and something that you would have inflamed, hereby the sunbeams are contracted, and fall upon that object with a more intense heat and fervor, even to an inflammation of it; and this, by reason, that the beams were first contracted in the center of the glass and then diffused, and with more vehemency darted upon the object under it. Thus God loves all His creatures; His love is over all His works—so the Scripture expresses it—but He loves them not in His Beloved; He accepts them not in Him. But now for the sons of men, that Son of God who is His Beloved, contracts all the beams of God's love in Himself, and they fall upon Him first; and then they, through Him, shine and diffuse themselves upon us all, with a ray infinitely more strong and vigorous than they would have done, if we had been considered in ourselves alone. And this is the advantage of being accepted in the Beloved. God loves us with the same love wherewith He loves His Son."

So dear, so very dear to God,
  More dear I cannot be;
The love wherewith He loves the Son,
  Such is His love to me.

"Praise of His Grace, wherein He dealt graciously with us in the Beloved" (T. S. Green, M.A.).

Dealt with us, not as we deserve, but as Christ deserves. Dealt with us, not according to law, but according to the riches of His grace. Dealt with us, not according to justice, but according to His own loving purpose. Dealt with us, not as a rich man doling out charity, but as His equals. Dealt with us, not merely in pity, but plenteously; not grudgingly, but graciously; not as man, but as God. Ugly stones we were, in the quarry of sin, but He has made us precious and beautiful in His building; beggars we were, on the dunghill of the world, but He has set us among princes; slaves to Satan we were, but sons of God we are; brands we were, fit only for burning, but branches we are of the Living Vine; and poor as Lazarus we were, but rich as Christ we are.

"His favor, wherewith He favored us in the Beloved One" (Rotherham).

We are favored, because we are in Christ. God has set His love upon us, even as Ahasuerus loved Esther more than all other women, and she obtained grace and favor in his sight (Esther 2:17). God has favored us in His Favorite One, even as Pharaoh favored Hadad the favorite, and gave him the queen's sister to be his wife (1 Kings 11:19). He has brought us into favor, even as He did Daniel with the prince of the eunuchs (Daniel 1:9); only in our case, it is with Himself. By His love He has granted us life and favor, even as Job confessed (Job 10:12). In His favor there is life (Psalm 30:7). He satisfies us with favor, even as Naphtali was satisfied (Deut. 33:23). And, verily, His favor is as dew upon the grass (Prov. 19:12), refreshing, stimulating, and satisfying.

"To the praise of the Glory of His Grace, which He freely bestowed upon us in the Beloved One" (Dean Alford).

There are two precious "B's"—"Bestowed," "Beloved" in this verse. Christ as our Head, is our Beloved, and therefore we are enriched by the bestowment of His blessings, but it is in the Beloved. As Dyer says: "Why was the Bread of Life hungry, but that He might feed the hungry with the Bread of Life? Why was the Rest Himself weary, but to give the weary rest? Why was the Prince of Peace in trouble, but that the troubled might have peace? None but the Image of God could restore us to God's image; none but the Beloved of God could make us dear to God; none but the natural Son could make us sons! None but the Wisdom of God could make us wise; none but the Prince of Peace could bring the God of peace and the peace of God to poor sinners."

"He hath freely made us well thought of in the Beloved" (Trapp).

Three times in the Song of Solomon, do we find the Bride referring to the fact that she has the Beloved, and the Beloved has her; but we also find progress in the apprehension of the fact. First she says; "My Beloved is mine, and I am His"; second: "I am my Beloved's, and my Beloved is mine"; and third: "I am my Beloved's, and His desire is toward me" (Song of Solomon 2:16; 6:3; 7:10). At first she is taken up with the fact that she has the Beloved; second, she recognizes that the Beloved has her; and third, she finds that the Beloved delights in her, and His desire is toward her. God thinks a good deal of His people. They are (NIV)—

1) His portion—"The Lord's portion is his people" (Deuteronomy 32:9).
2) His treasure—"My treasured possession" (Exodus 19:5).
3) His joy—"I will rejoice over Jerusalem" (Isaiah 65:19).
4) His crown—"You will be a crown of splendor" (Isaiah 62:3).
5) His inheritance—"His glorious inheritance in the saints" (Ephesians 1:18).
6) His dwelling—"Dwelling in which God lives by his Spirit" (Ephesians 2:22).
7) His rest—"This is my resting place for ever" (Psalm 132:14).

"He hath highly favored us in the Beloved" (Luke 1:28).

In Luke 1:28, the word *"accepted,"* is rendered *"highly favored"* (NIV). Reading these words into Ephesians 1:6, they make it read, "He has highly favored us in the Beloved." Why did God single out Mary to be the mother of Jesus? Was she better than other women? No. But He did so because He would. Why did the Lord Jesus select 153 great fishes at the Sea of Tiberias, and leave the small ones? Because He chose to do so. Why did God choose Israel as a nation, and not reckon them among the nations? Because it was His pleasure. Why were the twelve disciples chosen? Naaman the leper cleansed before all other lepers? The widow of Sarepta fed before all other widows? Saul of Tarsus chosen to be Paul the Apostle before all other persecutors? Because it pleased the Lord. Why has He so highly favored us who are His? Because we are better than others? No. He has taken us out of the world, to be a people for Himself, to be His love gift to Christ, and to be the body and bride of Christ, because it is His purpose.

Chosen not for good in me;
Wakened up from wrath to flee;
Hidden in the Savior's side;
By the Spirit sanctified:
Teach me, Lord, on earth to show,
By my love, how much I owe.

"His grace, which he has freely given us in the One he loves" (NIV)

We shall take along with this the marginal reading of the R.V. in Luke 1:28, which is "endued with grace." We will briefly refer to two points, i.e., the *freeness* of the blessings bestowed, and the *fullness* of the grace given.

The freeness of the blessings bestowed. If we go back to the beginning, we find God dealing thus with our first parents. He told them they might eat freely of every tree except the tree of the knowledge of good and evil (Genesis 2:16), but they abused His goodness. Now, Christ having died and risen again, God will give every thirsty soul the Fountain of Life freely (Revelation 21:6). The invitation is free and full: "Whosoever will, let him take the water of life freely." Having done so, we are justified freely by His grace through the redemption that is in Christ Jesus (Romans 3:24). And the measure of His dealings with us now is according to His own loving purpose and the worthiness of His Son and since this is the case, may we not ask the question, with the apostle Paul, "He who did not spare his own Son, but gave Him up for us all—how will he not also along with Him, graciously give us all things?" (Romans 8:32). And the Spirit of God has been given to us, that we may know the things that are freely given to us of Him (1 Corinthians 2:12). Oh, how free are His blessings! They are as free as the air we breathe, as the water we drink—freer—for there are no rates to pay; free as the sun that shines alike on mud hut and mansion; free as the food that Christ gave the five thousand; and free as the year of jubilee was to the Israelite of old.

The fulness of the grace given. It is grace upon grace, and yet it is grace the same. Grace to suit and meet our varied need, and yet always the grace of God. Think of what that means. It means that He has given us all things, yea, even His fulness.

There is fulness of acceptance for us in Him, therefore we do not doubt Him; there is fulness of peace, therefore we trust Him; there is fulness of life, therefore we abide in Him; there is fulness of blessing, therefore we delight in Him; there is fulness of power, therefore we wait upon Him; there is fulness of grace, therefore we receive from Him; there is fulness of love, therefore we must return His love; there is fulness of teaching, therefore learn of Him; there is fulness of joy, therefore rejoice in Him; there is fulness of fulness in Him, therefore be full in Him; there is fulness of riches, therefore we count upon Him; there is fulness of strength, therefore we lean upon Him; there is fulness of light, therefore we walk with Him; and there is fulness of energy, therefore we must be subject to Him.

3

The Discipler's Attraction

Satan's motto is, "Anything but Jesus." Religion, philanthropy, or pet pursuits, may engross us. But if by these the mind be diverted from "Jesus only," the one Soul-Satisfier, how poor we are! The voice of the Father, the teaching of the Spirit, and the utterance of the Word are one on this point. "Jesus only." God's fulness is centered in Christ: His thoughts are of Christ, who communicates God's thoughts to us. If we would know God, then we must know Christ.

All approach to God is through Him, so that if we would draw near to God, we must come in His name. All God's gifts are in Christ. If we would possess them, we must have Christ by being *in Him*. God's strength is Christ: He is the "Power of God": to have strength, we must have Christ. The love of God is manifested in Christ: If we would experience the glow of that love, it must be as we are in touch with Him. All that God is, is revealed in Christ: "He who has seen me has seen the Father." The glory of God is seen in the face of Jesus Christ. Let us therefore abide in His presence, so that we may reflect His glory. What better attraction could we have than *Jesus Himself*? Jesus Himself having us, and we having Him—let this theme engage our thoughts.

The work Jesus completed on the Cross is our salvation and our stay

In his second prayer in the epistle to the Ephesians, the apostle Paul asks that the saints at Ephesus "may be able to comprehend with all saints, what is the breadth, and length, and depth, and height" (Ephesians 3:18). Of what? The love of Christ is the usual answer. We think this is incorrect. He expresses his desire that the saints may know that, in verse 19. I believe the breadth, length, depth, and height, refer to Christ Himself: the breadth of His power: the length of His love: the height of His glory: the depth of His sufferings. We would now direct attention to the last, especially in connection with the benefits that flow to us, as the outcome of His death.

Many passages of the Bible tell us, in touching and telling words, that Christ died for us; but the one word which makes them so touching and telling, is—"Himself": "Who gave *Himself* for our sins" (Galatians 1:4); "Gave *Himself* for me" (Galatians 2:20); "Christ also loved the Church, and gave *Himself* for it"

(Ephesians 5:25); "Who gave *Himself* for us" (Titus 2:14); "When He had by *Himself* purged our sins" (Hebrews 1:3); "He appeared to put away sin by the sacrifice of Himself" (Hebrews 9:26); "Who gave *Himself* a ransom for all" (1 Timothy 2:6).

We believe that *the finished work of Christ* is the hub around which all the spokes of our blessings meet, and the tire by which they are held together, and in which they are all secured. The work of Christ for us in His atonement on the Cross is central to our faith, the hinge on the door to eternity.

An old novel tells the story of a New England woman, whose fame was bright among the poor and lawless, whom she perseveringly befriended. She was not a believer, never "went to meeting," and smilingly put aside the arguments of a boyish young minister who tried to reason her into faith. But one whom she had befriended became a murderer, and she had, with infinite reluctance, to surrender him to justice. The next Sunday she went to church for the first time in twenty-five years.

"'I ain't got much to say about it,' said she, 'but I'm goin' to say this much—it ain't no more'n right I should, though I don't believe in a lot of palaver about things like this. I've made up my mind that I'm going to believe in Jesus Christ. I ain't never, but I'm going to *now*, for'—her voice turned shrill with passion—'*I don't see any other way out of it for John Gleason.*'"

She felt that the case of the murderer was so desperate that no one but the Lord Jesus Christ, in the sufficiency of His atonement, could meet it. This is true in the case of everyone who really knows himself. The seeds of every evil thing lurk in our nature, and only need circumstances to bring them out. Hence, every one needs Christ, whether he or she feels that need or not. But we who have received Christ, know Him as our Stay and Support. We glory in the sufficiency of His death, in its Godward and manward aspects, for just as each of the boards of the Tabernacle rested in, and on, two sockets of silver, so we rest on, and are identified with Him who died to meet the righteous requirements of a holy and righteous God, who must by the very necessity of His nature punish sin. And Christ by that same death meets our need as sinners. Those who thus know Christ, can sing—

> Thy death, not mine, O Christ,
> Has paid the ransom due;
> Ten thousand deaths like mine
> Would have been all too few.
> To whom, save Thee,
> Who can alone
> For sin atone,
> Lord, shall I flee?

Christ, at the Right Hand of God in His position and person, is the measure of our acceptance and standing

"Christ . . . gave *himself* up for us, an offering and a sacrifice to God for an odor of a sweet smell" (Ephesians 5:2, RSV). As the burnt offering went up a sweet-smelling savor to God (Leviticus 1:9), typical of the delight the Father has in Christ (Matthew 3:17), so we are in Christ a sweet-smelling offering to Him.

To be saved *by* Jesus is *good*, even as the first-born of the children of Israel were saved from death by the sprinkled blood of the paschal lamb, in Egypt. To be saved *in* Christ is *better*, as Noah and his family were saved in the ark, and passed through the waters of judgment. But to be safe *as* Christ is *best*, for this means that we are as secure as He is.

A friend once said to the late George Silwood, of Keswick, "How blessed it is to be 'safe in the arms of Jesus!'"

"Yes," he replied; "but I am safer than that."

"Safer than that!" replied the friend in astonishment. "How much safer can you be?"

George Silwood replied, *"I am safe as an arm of Jesus."* And so it is.

An old writer, in speaking of the believer's completeness in Christ, says: "There is life in Christ, and glory in Christ: Christ our Life and His glory, our glory, which agrees with the words of the Savior, 'Because I live, ye shall live also'; and 'where I am, you shall be.' As if the Lord had said, 'My beloved saints, you are as safe as I am; your lives and your glory are bound up in Mine. I laid down My life to take up yours, and now I have laid up your life as sure as My own, both in My Father and your Father's bosom. I in the Father, and you in Me: My love, My fair one, My undefiled, you are where I am.'"

Well might Luther exclaim, on realizing his position in Christ before God, "Oh, the blessedness of knowing, that as Christ is before God, so am I!" Well might the apostle ask, "Who will bring any charge against those whom God has chosen? It is God who justifies. Who is he that condemns? Christ Jesus, who died—more than that, who was raised to life—is at the right hand of God and is also interceding for us." God, who in His righteous grace has pronounced us righteous, will never bring an accusation against us, and Christ who died and rose, and is seated at God's right hand pleading in our behalf, will never condemn us. Since those who have the right to charge us and to condemn us, will not do so, we need fear none. This being so, the conclusion of the whole matter is—

In Christ we are as His worthiness, in His acceptance (Ephesians 1:6).
In Christ we are as His likeness, in His completeness (Ezekiel 16:14).
In Christ we are as His perfection, in His spotlessness (2 Corinthians 5:21).
In Christ we are as His sanctity, in His holiness (Hebrews 10:10).
In Christ we are as His fulness, in His plenitude (Colossians 2:9, 10; Ephesians 1:22).
In Christ we are as His beauty, in His loveliness (Song of Solomon 4:7).
In Christ we are as Himself, in His glory (1 John 4:17).

Christ's possessions is the amount of our blessings and property

". . . what was said in all the Scriptures concerning *Himself*" (Luke 24:27). Such are the weighty words that describe, and sum up the conversation, the Lord Jesus had with the two disciples, as He journeyed with them to Emmaus. There were two main things of which He spoke, i.e., His sufferings and His glory. But how significant are these things! And they are so, because they are about Himself, and He Himself is the One who has done all. His sufferings are the foundation of the house of His grace, and His glory is its peak. But what a store of things there is in Himself, who is the House of God's provision!

We can never be poor with Christ, because we can never have a poor Christ. We should have no riches at all if it were not for Christ: therefore, Christ is our riches. Just as the image of the cherubim were worked into the beautiful curtain called "The Tabernacle" (Exodus 36:8), so Christ's gifts are all in Himself, and He Himself is in all His gifts.

When John the beloved disciple was banished to the Isle of Patmos, being in the Spirit, he heard a voice behind him. It told him wondrous things. But they were no more marvelous than what we hear, when we listen to Christ as He speaks to us in His Word.

In musing upon Christ in His gifts, the writer was waiting upon Christ to reveal Himself upon this line of thought, when a voice seemed to say, "Call to mind, and look up in My Word, what I say in connection with the word 'My,' as illustrating what you have, in possessing *Myself*, and thus see what you have, and what I expect in consequence."

As I began to meditate, it seemed as if Christ said, "My *body* (Matthew 26:26) I gave to be bruised for you, in suffering in your stead. My *blood* (Luke 22:20) I gave for you, to atone for your sins. My *life* (John 10:15) I gave up for you, that you might have eternal life. My *flesh* (John 6:51-56) I gave, that you might be sustained and satisfied. My *hands and* My *feet* (Luke 24:39) I gave for your inspection, that you might ponder and see the completeness of My work. My *Word* (John 5:24) I gave, that you might be assured of your interest in Myself. My *Church* (Matthew 16:18) I give you, to be a member of it, that you may be one with Me. My *Father* (John 20:17) I give to be your Father: He is your Father because He is Mine, and you are Mine. My *yoke* (Matthew 11:29) I give you, to take upon you, that you may know and delight in My will. My *rest* (Hebrews 4:1-5) I give you to enter, as you are obedient to My directions. My *Spirit* (Acts 2:17) I give you, to carry on My work in making you like Myself during My absence. My *laws* (Hebrews 8:10) I give and write in your hearts, that you may do them out of love to Me. My *commandments* (John 14:21) I give you, that you may show Me you love Me by obeying them. My *voice* (John 10:27) I give you to hear, as you heed Me in following My steps. My *joy* (John 15:11) I give you, to enjoy as you abide in Me. My *name* (Matthew 18:20; John 14:13; 15:16; 16:23-26) I give you, as the center of gathering, and as your passport and plea in prayer. My *grace* (2 Corinthians 12:9) I give you, as your sufficiency, to delight in trial and suffering. My *power* (2 Corinthians 12:9, RSV) I give you, to strengthen you in your weakness. My *love* (John 15:9) I give you, that you may give Me your obedience. My *peace* (John 14:27) I give you, that you may be calm amidst life's storms. My *hand* (John 10:28) I give you, that you may be assured of your security. My *barn* (Matthew 13:30) I will give you, to be garnered in, when the great harvest comes. And My *glory* (John 17:24) I give will you to share, that you may be eternally blessed."

These are but a few of the golden beads that Christ gives us, in the necklace of His grace. We may well examine them and discover, as we gaze, fresh beauties of our adorable Lord in whom we have all our possessions, for without Him we would be poor indeed.

Since this is so, let us prize Him above all. He is the Prize that makes all prizes, prizes. He is the Gift that makes the gifts, gifts; for there would no gifts were it not for *the* Gift, for He is all our gifts. He is the Blessing that makes all our blessings, blessings; for there were no blessings in our blessings, were it not for Him, who is the blessing of our blessings.

Christ as our High Priest, and our Advocate with the Father, is an evidence of our dearness to Him

"We do have such a *high priest* "(Hebrews 8:1). "We have an *advocate* with the Father" (1 John 2:1 KJV).

We must not look upon the offices of Christ as our High Priest and Advocate, as one and the same: they are distinct and different. The distinction has been thus defined:

"Priesthood is between *God and His people*; Advocacy is between the *Father and the children*. The one is for us as worshipers; the other is connected with our fellowship with the Father and His Son. The one is preventive; the other, restorative."

These distinctions are seen in the history of Peter. As the High Priest, Christ prays for Peter, that his faith may not fail but as the Advocate, He restores Peter after his failure (Luke 22:31, 32 comp. John 21:15-19). As our High Priest, *He* is able to help us (Hebrews. 2:17, 18), sympathizing with us in our difficulties, even as He did with Paul, when he was in danger of being shipwrecked, by assuring him of safety (Acts 27:23-25). He is able to sustain us in the time of temptation; for as the priest of old, ever looked after the lamps in the lampstand, and kept them burning by supplying them with oil, so our High Priest ever supplies us with all the grace we need (Leviticus 24:3, 4; Hebrews 4:15, 16). He is able to support us in being with us in our trials, even as He was with the young men in the fiery furnace (Daniel 3:25-27). He is able to uplift us in our weaknesses, by enabling us through His strength to glory in them, so that His power may rest upon us, even as it did upon Paul, in connection with his "thorn in the flesh" (2 Corinthians 12:7-9) and this He is able to do, because He has trodden the path before us.

Now, in the position of Advocate, He serves us in removing our defilement, when we confess our sins. God has made no provision for us to sin, but, if through carelessness we do sin, there is provision made, as the following indicates: "I write this to you so that you will not sin. But if anybody sin, we have one who speaks to the Father in our defense, Jesus Christ, the Righteous One" (1 John 2:1 NIV). This present ministry of Christ is illustrated in John 13, when Christ is seen washing His disciples' feet. As we travel this sin-stained world, we become defiled and contaminated. The breath of the world dims the brightness of our confession of Christ, and it needs His master-hand to burnish us. The prince of the power of the air causes the germs of disease to enter and mar our spiritual health. We need the touch of the Divine Physician to heal us. The mud of sin is apt to be splashed upon us by the vehicles of Satan, and the cleansing blood of Christ alone can remove the stain. The root of bitterness is ready to grow in our nature, and this needs to be removed by the Heavenly Gardener. Thus Christ ever lives to succor, save, strengthen, sympathize, and sanctify, as our High Priest and Advocate. This loving and continual service of His proclaims our dearness to Him.

Christ in us is the cause of our Christlikeness and progress in the Christian life

Two expressions are used again and again by the apostle Paul—"In Christ," and "Christ in us" (2 Corinthians 5:7; Galatians 2:20). One is the counterpart of the other, and dependent upon the other, just as the cog-wheels move each other by meshing together. In Christ we have life, hence we live unto God; and Christ as our Life, lives in us, hence we live for Him before men.

Some time ago I saw in a vinery what a gardener calls *inarching*. When from some cause, a vine is not doing very well, the gardener determines to get a healthy young vine, and "inarch" it to the older one. This means that he gets the young vine, and removing a piece of bark from the sides of both vines, ties them tightly together. Thus they grow together and become one. When they are thus bound to each other, the gardener cuts the young one about half through, an inch or so below where they are fastened together. Then when the two are thoroughly united, and the wood of the young vine is ripe, he severs the latter completely from its root, so that all its nourishment is derived from the older vine. After a time the older vine is cut just above where the two are joined; thus all the sap and nourishment from the older goes to the younger tree. In this way the younger partakes of the fruitfulness and fatness of the older.

Even so is it with Christ and us. The bark of our nature was cut when the Holy Spirit convinced us of sin: and the bark of His nature was cut when He gave Himself up to die for us. We are severed from our natural root and standing in Adam and Christ was "cut off out of the land of the living," that the sap of His divine nature might be infused into us, in resurrection power by the Holy Spirit. Thus do we partake of the *fulness* of His life, the *fatness* of His grace, and the *fruitfulness* of His love.

As Christ in His love lives in us we are able to live in love to Him. As Christ in His holiness lives in us we are well-pleasing to Him. As Christ in His gentleness lives in us, we are gentle toward others. As Christ in the sufficiency of His grace dwells in us we have sufficiency of grace to overcome temptation, and to delight in whatever may come to us. The tree can stand the storms that shake it, by virtue of the life that is in it, and roots itself firmly in the ground. As Christ lives in us the fruitfulness in the ninefold cluster of "the fruit of the Spirit" (Galatians 5:22, 23) is manifest in our lives even as the grapes show the fatness of the vine. For Christ-likeness, we must have Christ. For the imitation of Christ, we must have the Christ *within* us, so that we may imitate the Christ to those around us.

What Christ was in His life, is the Object of our desire, and we are to imitate Him

"Christ pleased not *Himself*" (Romans 15:3). When we consider the character of Christ as revealed in the Gospels, we are attracted to Him like an oasis in a desert.

What kind of life was His?

Godward, it was a life of prayer, telling out His dependence upon His Father. It was a life of perseverance in His Father's will: a life of purity from which there radiated a holiness that was pleasing to God. It was a life which, from beginning to end, went up as a sweet-smelling aroma in which the Father delighted.

Manward, the life of Christ was one of incessant "doing good." His *compassion* for the lost, His *concern* for the welfare of the people, His *care* to faithfully represent the Father, and His *completed work* upon the Cross, all bear testimony to His intense love to, and for, mankind. "It has been said by a great poet, that great characters and great souls are like mountains—they always attract storms; upon their heads break the thunders, and round their bare tops flash the lightnings, and the seeming wrath of God. Nevertheless, they form a shelter for the plains beneath them."

So with Christ. He was always a Shelter for the fallen and downtrodden—a willing Listener to the penitent cry of anguish. He was ever ready to respond to the touch of the child, as in clinging confidence it nestled to His side. It is true, He brought down on Himself the lightning of man's hate, but He sheltered those who confided in Him. What He was, we should seek to be, and we can only be like Him, as He Himself lives within us; *for the indwelling Christ can alone imitate the Christ*. He alone must use our fingers to copy the perfect lesson that He puts before us, otherwise the down-strokes will be crooked, and the up-strokes clumsy—not to speak of the number of blots in the copy-book of our lives, and the omissions in copying.

We are all agreed that we could not have a better Copy; but we are also assured that He who is the Copy must Himself be the Copyist, if there is to be a reproduction of His life, and the representation in our lives of His lovely character.

What Jesus says is the ground of our authority, and the reason for our action

"Jesus Himself . . . said" (Luke 24:36). We are always under orders. The Lord in His grace does not leave us to our whims and fancies; but He bids us act according to His will and command. He is our Lord and we are His bondservants, and since this is the case, we look for no will in the matter, for the way of His will is our only desire. His commands are our comforts, for there is no comfort except in obeying His commands. His Word is our guarantee, and we want no license but His Word. His directions are our delight, and there is no delight but in carrying out His directions. "Thus saith the Lord" is our plea in prayer, and our power with men and we have no plea in prayer, nor power with men, but as we have "Thus saith the Lord" for our direction. His precepts are our foundation, and we have no stay but in His sayings. His behests are our blessings, and there is no blessing but in carrying them out.

"Whatsoever He saith unto you, do it," was the wise utterance of Mary. And as the servants got the waterpots which had been filled with water, filled with wine, so are we filled with joy by doing whatsoever He tells us. We love to do what He commands, for love makes the work worth doing. An old writer puts it well: "A musician is not recommended for playing long, but for playing well: it is obeying God willingly that is accepted. The Lord hates that which is forced. It is rather paying a tax than making an offering. Good duties must not be pressed or shaken out of us, as the waters came out of the rock when Moses smote it with a rod, but must freely drop from us as myrrh from the tree, or honey from the comb. If a willing mind is wanting, there is wanting that flower which perfumes our obedience, and makes it a sweet-smelling savor to God."

What Christ will yet do, is the hope of our expectation: and what He is, will be the measure of our likeness

"Christ loved the church, and gave *himself* up for her to make her holy, cleansing her by the washing with water through the word, and to present her to *himself* a radiant church, without stain, or wrinkle or any other blemish, but holy and blameless" (Ephesians 5:25-27 NIV). These are the graciously glorious words used by the Holy Spirit to describe what Christ has done, and is doing, and will yet do, for His Bride, the Church.

Like the steps of Solomon's throne, these verses lead us to the place of blessing:

1) There is *affection*—"Christ loved the church."
2) There is *substitution*—He "gave himself."
3) There is *absolution*—He has cleansed.
4) There is *sanctification*—He has separated us to God.
5) There is *regeneration*—He reminds us by His Word and Spirit, of what He has done for us, and as we listen and heed, we are renewed.
6) There is *presentation*—He is going to present us to Himself.
7) There is *classification*—We are told what we shall be by His grace.

It is to the *presentation* mentioned above I direct that our thoughts:

"The thought," says H. C. G. Moule, "is of the Heavenly Bridegroom welcoming the glorified Bride at the marriage feast hereafter. True, she is now His Spouse and His Body: but the manifestation then will be such as to be, in a sense, the marriage as the sequel to the betrothal. The words 'present to Himself,' suggest that the Bride is not only to be welcomed then by her Lord, but welcomed as owing all her glory to His work, and as being absolutely His own."

The words "present to Himself" bring to our mind the promise of our now absent Lord, in John 14:3: "I will come back, and take you to be with *me* that you also may be where I am." Having prepared a place for His Bride, and His Bride for the place, He comes to receive her to Himself, that she may be with Him forever.

As Eliezer presented Rebecca to Isaac, who received her to himself to be his henceforth, so the Holy Spirit will conduct us to our Lordly Bridegroom, when, by His power, we shall rise to meet Christ in the air. The Lord shall then receive us to Himself, we shall be like Him, and be forever with Him.

"What would Jesus do?" is the guide of our life, and our inspiration in service

He "made *himself* nothing, taking the very nature of a servant . . . he humbled *himself* and became obedient to death" (Philippians 2:7, 8)—"Entrusted *himself*" (1 Peter 2:23). In the above Scriptures Christ is seen in *service*, in *sanctification*, and in *suffering*. Running through all that He did—as the golden thread in the ephod of the High Priest—was the consuming desire: "What would My Father wish Me to do?" So must it be with us: our wishes should sink under the thought: "What would Jesus do?"

What would Jesus do in the *home?* He would brighten it by His presence, as the light gladdens the weary watcher. He would cheer all by His loving manner, as the mother comforts her child; He would lighten all by His gentle help, as one who takes the burden from the shoulders of the weary traveler; He would sweeten the home by His tender words, as the scent perfumes the garments; He would purify it by His holy influence, as the disinfectant kills the germs of disease; He would hush every disturbing voice, as with His "Peace, be still," on Galilee's troubled waters; and He would deny Himself for the good of others, even as He did when He died for us on the cross.

What would Jesus do in the *Church?* He would love all its members, as a mother loves her children; He would be interested in all its work, even as the father takes note of the rough model that his boy has been making; He would be present at the gatherings for worship and prayer, as the High Priest, at the appointed time, was present to trim the lamps; He would be sure to visit those of its members who were sick, and would cheer them as friend cheers friend; He would feed and encourage those who were young in grace, as the shepherd specially tends the lambs of his flock; He would seek to restore those who had backslidden, even as the shepherd searches for the stray sheep; He would admonish those who were unruly, as the father corrects his child; and He would be an Example to all, even to the washing of the disciples' feet (John 13).

What would Jesus do in the *world?* He would reflect the holy character of His Father, as the mirror reflects the face; He would tell out the Word of God in His testimony, as the wax reveals the impression of the seal; He would lend a helping hand to the downcast and fallen, as He often did when He was here on earth; and He would contemplate the godless multitude with a compassion which could alone reveal the love of God, as the moon reflects the sun's light.

What would Jesus do in *temptation?* He would trust in God to deliver Him; in the strength of God, He would overcome; and by the Word of God, He would frustrate every evil suggestion of the enemy.

What would Jesus do under *persecution?* He would neither plead His own cause, nor stand up for His rights, but commit Himself to the righteous vindication of His Father.

Finally, what would Jesus do *always?* In a word, He would consult His Father by prayer, and thus obtain His guidance and grace. This consideration of what Jesus would do is a safe means of guidance for the disciple who follows in His steps.

What Christ is in Himself, is the delight of our hearts, and the joy of our song

"*Jesus himself* stood among them" (Luke 24:36). These words describe the manifestation of Christ to His sorrowing disciples, gathered in the upper room at Jerusalem. It was no optical delusion, but the illustrious Person of their divine Lord who addressed the astonished disciples. The One they had on the cross in shame and agony but a short time ago now stood before them in glory and grace. The One whom they saw but lately, distressed on account of contact with sin's penalty, now confronts them with "Peace be unto you." To assure them, He further adds: "It is *I Myself!*" No wonder that their joy was great. In those days He revealed Himself in person: but not the less really, does He manifest Himself to the obedient heart of today (John 14:21).

"Which would you rather have—happy feelings without Christ, or Christ and no happy feelings?" asked the writer of a young Christian who was seeking joy in her feelings, rather than in the possession of the Lord Himself. She did not take long to decide that she would rather possess Christ, and let the happy feelings go. As do many of greater experience, she had been seeking her joy in something outside of *Himself*.

Now the way to miss joy, is to be taken up with the possession of *it,* while the secret of possessing the joy, is to have the *Lord* of the joy. If we have the Giver, we are sure of the gifts; if we have the Treasury, we possess the treasure. If we are united to the Promiser, we are certain of the fulfillment of the promises. If the Lord is our Delight, our delight will be the Lord, and so the Lord shall answer to every blessing, and to every need. There is no greater need than to be without Christ; but possessing Christ, we have *no need to want*. The Christian who seeks for highest joy apart from Christ, will, like the prodigal, discover himself to be in want. He who has the Lord, on the other hand, shall never want. The Christian who is taken up with some happy experience is like Peter, whose soul did not rise above the happy surroundings of "being here" (Matthew 17:1-8); the Transfiguration scene was felt by him to be "good"; but having Christ amid circumstances ever so adverse, we can say: "Lord, it is good to be with You." We shall be above circumstances when we can truthfully say this. Let us learn to spell our own blessings, gifts, doctrines, and graces with one word of five letters—

"J-E-S-U-S"

Once it was the blessing; now it is the Lord;
Once it was the feeling; now it is His Word.
Once His gifts I wanted; now Himself alone;
Once I sought for healing: now the Healer own;
Once 'twas painful trying: now 'tis perfect trust;
Once a half salvation; now the uttermost.
Once 'twas what I wanted; now what Jesus says;
Once 'twas constant asking; now 'tis ceaseless praise;
Once it was my working; His it hence shall be;
Once I tried to use Him; now He uses me.
Once the power I wanted; now the Mighty One;
Once I worked for glory; now His will alone.

4

The Discipler's Confession

One of the most important things to observe in our Christian life and service is the condition attached to any blessing that we may need. "Make this valley full of ditches" (2 Kings 3:16) was the word of the Lord, through the prophet Elisha, to the king of Israel; and after they had made the ditches, then the Lord caused the water to come and fill them. In like manner, when we fulfill the Divine condition, there follows abundant blessing and continuous victory. True confession of sin is making, as it were, the ditches: then follows, as a consequence, the filling. For clarity, we are using the NIV in this chapter.

It is also most important to observe the order of Divine blessing. Confession of sin leads to cleansing from sin, and consecration to God follows. Power with God and man comes as a result of purity of heart, and persistency in prayer. Separation to God is a consequence of salvation from the power and love of self. Following this comes availability for the Master's use. This is illustrated in the case of Isaiah (Isaiah 6). As he viewed the holiness of God, and saw himself in the light of His presence, the vision caused him to cry out, "Woe to me! I am ruined" (or, as *The Newberry Bible* has it, "I am dumb"; this may mean, "I have no words to utter on my own behalf"; or, "I have been guilty of silence"), because I am a man of unclean lips," etc. Then came the cleansing. The seraph took the coal from the altar (the emblem of the accepted sacrifice), and placing it on the prophet's lips (the application of the sacrifice), said: "See, this has touched your lips; your guilt is taken away and your sin purged," or atoned for. Then Isaiah willingly responded to the voice which was saying, "Who will go for us?" "Here am I. Send me!" and he was immediately commissioned. Thus we see that there is—first, *confession* of sin; then *cleansing* from sin; and then *consecration* to the Lord for service.

We are not now considering the confession of national sins, though we should do that also, even as Nehemiah did, when he confessed, "I confess the sins we Israelites, including myself and my father's house, have committed against you. We have acted very wickedly toward you. We have not obeyed the commands, decrees and laws you gave your servant Moses" (Nehemiah 1:6, 7). Think, too, of Daniel, who, when he made his confession, said, "We have sinned and done wrong. We have been wicked and have rebelled; we have turned away from your commands and laws" (Daniel 9:5). There is ample reason why we as a country should confess our national sins. And when we also remember the infidelity, intemperance, and impurity, which as a three-headed monster goes stalking through our land, there is sufficient reason to fast with Nineveh, to lament with Jeremiah, to be sad at heart with Nehemiah, and to humble ourselves with Daniel.

In considering the believer's personal confession to God, we are not called upon to consider the failures and faults of our fellow-believers, though with Paul we have had cause to lament that many who did run well, have turned out to be stony-ground bearers; and we have had people like Alexander to slander us (2 Timothy 4:14), and Demas to forsake us (2 Timothy 4:10). Again, there is great cause for confession when we think of the envy, hatred, malice, worldliness, unbelief, lack of love to souls, leaning toward error, neglect of prayer, and want of conformity to Christ, which we see in so many of those who profess His name.

But we are considering, as servants of the Lord, the need to humble ourselves under His mighty hand, to confess to Him our individual sins, our own peculiar failures. Like, Isaiah we need to be cleansed, and go forth, in renewed power and energy, with the Lord in His service.

There are two things which lead to confession: 1) The examination of ourselves and our service under the microscope of God's Word, which will help us to see the flaws and failures. 2) The measuring of ourselves in the light and presence of Him, who is "a Consuming Fire." This will give us a deeper understanding of His character and claims, and our experience will be intensified. Every new manifestation of Christ will mean a fresh impetus to our service, and a fresh experience in our souls. Before every such revelation a deep humbling, and a specific confession of sin and unworthiness on our part is experienced. We will refer to several illustrations in Scripture to bear out this statement, and we will point out the special sin or hindrance that led to the manifestation. May the Holy Spirit bring the truth home to us!

Abraham (or walking before others)

"When Abram was ninety-nine years old, the Lord appeared to him, and said, 'I am God Almighty; walk before me and be blameless'" (Genesis 17:1). The Lord seems to say, "Be upright. No more listening to and walking before Sarah in unbelief. Walk before Me. I am the Almighty God; I am quite able to keep to My word and fulfil My promise. It is true you are old, and Sarah is as well; but although your bodies are dead, I will do as I have pledged Myself to do." We see Abram's mistake but do we not often fall into the same snare? Do we put on an act before others, seeking to please men, instead of pleasing God and doing everything as under His eye, according to His truth, by His power, and for His glory? What scheming there is to carry on the Lord's work! What efforts we make to be big before others! One of the evils of today is that many are adopting worldly means to carry on the Lord's work (so-called). The Saturday evening concert takes the place of the prayer meeting. The Lord's people, instead of praying to Him, and using their privilege and responsibility to give heartily to Him for His work, set up a bazaar or bake sale, thus asking the world to patronize the Church. The political lecture takes the place of, or is added to, the exposition of the Word. And in the process the line of separation between the world and the Church is rubbed out. Believers and unbelievers seem to be going hand in hand.

At one time, the danger was that the Church would go down to the world, as Abram went down to Egypt; but now the evil is, that the Church is not only going down to the world, but is inviting the world into the Church, and is seeking to entertain it, instead of preaching the Gospel. How true the words of Dr. Bonar; "I look for the Church, and I find it in the world; and I look for the world, and find it in the Church!"

Christians, are we not to blame for this? Have we been faithful to our Lord in speaking out upon these things? Or, at least, do we realize the mischief these things have caused? Have we forgotten that One is our Master, even Christ, and that we are responsible to Him to abide by the directions He has given us in His Word? Do we fail to remember that the path of separation is the place of power and blessing? Thank God if He has kept us from the spirit of this age! To Him be the glory! Let us not in any way judge others in a self-righteous spirit, but, remembering that there are those who have erred, and recognizing our oneness in Christ as members of His body, let us confess their failures and our own faults as well, for they are many.

Jacob (or self-aim)

Jacob was always looking out for himself. He didn't care who suffered, so long as he succeeded. His natural character shows itself in his parting with his mess of pottage, on condition that he receive the birthright; in preparing a delicious meal for his father as a fit opportunity to obtain the coveted blessing; in serving Laban so long as it meant profit to himself; and in sending a present to Esau, that he might, if possible, appease the anger his conscience told him to expect. But the Lord meets with him, wrestles with him, and asks his name. Look at what Esau said of him, "Isn't he rightly named Jacob? He has deceived me these two times; he took away my birthright, and, behold, now he hath taken away my blessing" (Genesis 27:36). Jacob himself confirms, and confesses that he is Jacob—the deceiver and supplanter. Men of less cunning might afford to miss the chance of coming face to face with God. Jacob must come into close quarters with Him. Can we wonder at Jacob's astonishment as his whole past life of self-interest comes up in review at Peniel? "I have seen God face to face, and my life is preserved." Did he not feel that he deserved to die?

Jacob, however, discovered that his name suited him well, and that discovery paved the way for blessing. Let us welcome the Divine scrutiny which robs us of our "Jacob" nature for the spirit that actuated this man is in us all. Oh, this horrid self! It asserts itself in our holiest moments: stalking into the pulpit, suggesting recourse to some flight of eloquence, some poetical utterance which begs for applause from men. Nor is it wanting when we draw near to the Lord in prayer. There is such a strong tendency to *pray before* men, rather than to *plead for* them. Look at how we seek for power, too, so that it may be seen how powerful *we* are, and that others, seeing the feather in *our* cap, may acknowledge the same to our glory! How dishonoring this is to the Lord! How it must grieve the Holy Spirit! What Berridge says of pride, we say of self: "It is the first thing on in the morning, and the last thing off at night."

Moses (or looking to self instead of to God)

When the Lord appeared to Moses in the burning bush, He commanded him to go down to Israel in Egypt, and told him that He would use him to accomplish His purpose. Then Moses began making a whole host of excuses. He referred to himself, and said, "Who am I, that I should go unto Pharaoh, and that I should bring forth the children of Israel out of Egypt?" Who, indeed, if *only* Moses? But the Lord met that by saying, "Certainly I will be with you." That should have been quite sufficient for him. Then Moses borrowed misery by supposing what Israel would say: "Behold, when I come unto the children of Israel, and shall say unto them," etc; but the Lord met that by telling him, He was the I AM, who was sufficient for all. Moses now raised another difficulty, saying that the children of Israel would not believe him, nor hearken to him; then the Lord showed him His power by turning his rod into a serpent, and by causing his hand to be covered with leprosy, and cleansing him from it. He also promised to perform like miracles through him. Moses next pleaded that he was not eloquent, that he was slow of speech and could not speak; but the Lord overcame that by giving him his brother Aaron as a spokesman (Exodus 3 and 4).

In all this, we see Moses looking to himself, instead of to the authority of God. And how often have we done the same! Is there not one of two extremes into which we are apt to run? Either we look to our own strength, or to our own weakness. The former causes us to be puffed up with pride, and the latter casts us down in discouragement. When we are inflated with pride, we rob God of His glory; and when we allow our weakness to prostrate us, as Elijah did when he ran away from Jezebel and lay down under the juniper tree, we limit the Holy One of Israel by our unbelief. Let us remember, as Hudson Taylor once said, "It is a sin to be discouraged." Oh, how often the Lord cannot use us because we look to our own resources! "God's commands are His enablings," says Ralph Erskine; that is, when the Lord bids us do anything, He gives us the power to accomplish it. There is cause for confession when we bear in mind our proneness to be influenced by our surroundings, depressed by our circumstances, and discouraged by our weakness.

Joshua (or self-authority)

When Israel was before Jericho, Joshua saw a Man with a drawn sword, and exclaimed, "Are you for us or for our enemies?" And He replied, "Neither, but as commander of the army of the Lord have I now come" (Joshua 5:13-15). The Lord wanted Joshua to know that he was *not* commander of the Lord's army, but that the Lord Himself was. Joshua must take a second place—the servant's place. It seemed almost as if Joshua, before this, had assumed a position he had no right to take; so the Lord, by manifesting Himself as commander of the Lord's army, made him understand that the authority was His, and that the government was to be upon His shoulder.

Have *we* taken the right position as servants of the Lord? Has there been a lording it over God's heritage, as though it were ours? Have we followed in the steps of Him who came "not to be ministered unto, but to minister, and to give His life a ransom for many"? Remember, He took the slave's position, washed the disciples' feet, and did the bondservant's work! Have we fully comprehended that we are the *servants* of the Lord Jesus, for His Church and the world? Have we carried out the maxim of the Lord: "He that is chief, let him be the servant of all"? Have we not assumed, rather, an air of superiority? How unlike Him who was meek and lowly in heart, gentle in manner, tender in expression, humble in life, and loving in ministry!

Gideon (or unbelief)

With what a shower of "Oh's" and "If's" Gideon met the Lord when He appeared as the Mighty One of valor!—Reading Judges 6:12, 13: "The Lord is with you, even the Lord mighty in valor," is the correct one, and not that which makes Gideon appear the mighty one of valor. But note how Gideon met Him with his vocabulary of unbelief. There was the *exclamation of unbelief*—"But Lord"; the *uncertainty of unbelief*—"*If* the Lord be with us"; the *language of unbelief*—"*Why* has all this happened to us?"; the *consternation of unbelief*—"*Where* are all his wonders that our fathers told us about, when they said, Did not the Lord bring us out of Egypt?"; the *wail of unbelief*—"*But* now the Lord has abandoned us and put us into the hand of Midian." The Lord turned to him and said, "Go in the strength you have, and save Israel out of Midian's hand: Am I not sending you?" Then Gideon showed the *strength of unbelief*—"But Lord, how can *I* save Israel?" and, lastly, the *resources of unbelief*—"My clan is the weakest in Manasseh, and *I* am the least in my family."

How often have we been like Gideon, looking around at our circumstances, and influenced by our surroundings, instead of looking up and trusting in the Lord!

> Faith, mighty faith, the promise sees,
> And looks to God alone.

We see the importance of being strong in—and full of—faith, from four instances we have recorded of the Lord blessing others for the sake of those who came to Him on their behalf (Mark 2:5; Matthew 8:10; 15:28; John 4:50). The palsied man was healed, the centurion's servant raised up, the Syrophoenician woman's daughter was liberated, and the nobleman's son restored, because of—and for—the faith's sake of those who brought them to Christ. Unbelief hinders the hand of God, and keeps Him, as it did Jesus of old, from doing many mighty works through us. Unbelief is like a brake upon the gospel, which hinders its progress, and is a libel upon the character of God.

Isaiah (or sins of the lip)

"Woe is me! for I am undone"—or, as otherwise rendered, "for I have been silent"—"because I am a man of unclean lips." This is a twofold confession. First, "I have been silent." He seems to say, "I have not told the people their sins, I have not declared Your will to them, and I have not preached Your Word." Second, "I am a man of unclean lips." "I have sinned myself, so how can I speak of sin? And I am unclean, so how can I speak to others?"

Christians, have we been silent on any subject? Have we kept back part of the price? Have we declared the whole gospel? Have we preached the Lordship of Christ, as well as Jesus the Savior? Have we held up the Person of Christ as the Holy Spirit does in 1 John, when He says we are to be holy as Christ is holy, righteous as He is righteous, pure as He is pure, to walk as He walked, and to walk in the light as He is in the light? Have we insisted on full surrender to Christ, so that His life may be manifested in our mortal bodies?

Can we say, as the apostle Paul could, in addressing the elders at Ephesus, "I have not neglected to declare unto you all the counsel of God"? Could we say, if today were to be the end of our earthly course, "I have *fought* a good fight, I have *finished* my course, I have *kept* the faith?" Have we reproved the unruly, warned the selfish, and told out with no uncertain sound the result of decision for Christ? Have we told the sinner of his doom, as well as the saint of his destination? Have we declared that God is Light as well as Love, Majesty as well as Mercy, a Consuming Fire as well as Compassion, and the Righteous One as well as the Redeemer?

Have we told out the twofold nature of sin to the unsaved—that man is a sinner because of what he is, and because of what he has done? Have we spoken of the death of Christ as the expression of God's righteousness, as well as of His love? Have we declared how the grace of God affects the whole person—not only his position and welfare hereafter, but *here*, the body of the believer being the temple of the Holy Spirit?

Why have we been silent? Has it been because the fear of man? Or has it been because we have not experienced a full comprehension of Christ ourselves? The secret of all failure in this respect, is the neglect of the *prayerful* study of the Word, and not applying to ourselves what we preach to others. Oh! for the spirit of the saintly M'Cheyne! It is common to find him speaking thus in his diary : "*July 31st*—Sabbath afternoon: On Judas betraying Christ. Much more tenderness than I ever felt before. Oh! that I might abide in the bosom of Him who washed Judas's feet, and dipped His hand into the same dish with him, and warned him, and grieved over him, that I might catch the infection of His love, of His tenderness, so wonderful, so unfathomable!"

Let us remember that the truth of God—as a matter of experience—is only the truth of God to us, as we prove it to be so.

Peter (or partial obedience)

We are all acquainted with the failure and disappointment of the disciples when they had been fishing all night and had taken nothing (Luke 5:4-7). As they were washing their nets, the Lord Himself came to them, and said to Peter, "Put out into the deep water, and let down the *nets* for a catch." Peter answered, "'Master, we've worked hard all night, and haven't caught anything. But because you say so, I will let down the net.' When they had done so, they caught such a great multitude of fish that their *nets* began to break." Now the Lord had told Peter to let down the *nets*, but he did so reluctantly and with little faith; the consequence was the nets broke. On another occasion, when the Lord told them to let down a *net*, we read, they "drew the net to land full of large fish, a hundred and fifty-three; and although there were so many, the net was not torn"

(John 21:6, 11). We must beware of partial obedience. It means damage when we quibble and question the Lord's word. We may be sure that we will smart for it. When we hesitate over His command, instead of heartily obeying it, we will suffer.

It is only partial obedience when we follow Christ as Peter did—afar off—instead of being like Caleb, who followed the Lord fully; or, like the psalmist, when he said, "My soul clings to you" (Psalm 63:8). (Or "is joined to You"; for it is the same word that is translated "joined" in connection with the scales of leviathan, of which we read, "They are *joined* fast to one another; they cling together, and cannot be parted" Job 41:17.)

There is only partial obedience when we are occupied with the work of the Master, as Martha was, and do not sit at the feet of the Master, as Mary did, in contemplation of Him. What we want, the late Mr. Bewley of Dublin well expressed to those surrounding his death-bed; "See that you have the characteristics of the three in the home at Bethany—Lazarus, the risen man; Mary, the listener to the word of Jesus; and Martha, active for Christ."

There is only partial obedience when we are taken up with the blessings of the Lord—not with the Lord Himself. Thomas Lye says, "Outward enjoyments are indeed sweet but my God, the Author of them, is infinitely more sweet. They have all, even the most delicate of them, a tang and smack of the cask and channel through which they come. A single God is infinitely more sweet than the enjoyment of all created good things that come from Him. Though, indeed, I can smile when my corn and wine and oil increase, and bear a part with my valleys when they stand so thick with corn that they even laugh and sing—alas! this without the enjoyment of a God is but a mere leaping of the head after the soul is gone. True, indeed, these are some of God's love-tokens; but what are these to His person and presence? These, indeed, are rich cabinets; but, oh! the light of His countenance—that, that is the jewel! In having these, I can say with Esau, 'I have much'; but, give me *Him*, I can exult, and, triumphing, say with Jacob, 'I have all.' These are some of His left-hand favors, some of His bottles of milk, and gifts, a fit portion for Ishmael . . . but it is an Isaac's inheritance, waters of the upper fountains, which my soul thirsts for; those right-hand blessings, His presence, His soul-ravishing presence, in which there is 'fulness of joy, and pleasures for evermore.' These may serve for my comfortable passage, but nothing but Himself can content and satisfy. He alone can fill up all the gaping chinks and chasms of my soul. He is my Sun and Shield, my Root and Branch, my Foundation and Corner Stone. He only can answer all my desires, all my necessities. My God and my All!"

There is only partial obedience when we preach the *comforts* of the gospel, and not the *claims* of the gospel. Is there not abundant room for confession to the Lord, when we think of our lack of conformity to Christ; our lack of love to Him who loved us unto the death; our half-heartedness in the service of Christ; our need of humility and likeness to Him, who is meek and lowly in heart; the opportunities that we have let slip for doing good; our ease and selfishness; our coldness toward other Christians; our jealousy toward others who have been used of God; and our failure to rejoice in the success of others? Verily, as we bow ourselves before the Lord, we have to confess with one, who has long since gone into the Master's presence, "I am nothing, I do nothing. I compare myself to Lazarus, with this difference, his sores were all outside, but mine are all inside."

Christians, let to Psalmist's twofold prayer be ours, "Search me, O God, and know my heart: try me, and know my anxious thoughts. See if there is any offensive way in me, and lead me in the way everlasting" (Psalm 139:23, 24). *Search*, then *lead*. Search us with eyes of fire, then lead us to see the value and virtue of that precious blood which cleanses from all sin.

Search us! Look at us as You looked at Peter (Luke 22:61), and bring home to our hearts the selfishness that has characterized our life and service—the self-aims, the self-sufficiency, the self-love, the self-seeking, and the self-glorying; then lead us to Yourself—to Your heart of love, that beats in sympathy for us; to Your hand of power, able and willing to uphold us; and cause us to abide in You, so that You may manifest Your own life through us, that with your servant Paul we may say—because of the work of Your grace—"We live, we labor, we speak, and yet not we, but Christ."

Search us, to show us our weakness, our inability to do, or to be anything apart from You, and our entire dependence upon You, and also to know in the truest, fullest sense, that without You we can do nothing; then lead us to rest in You, and to know that Your strength is made perfect in our weakness, as Your love has been made perfect in our unworthiness and also to prove each moment, that strengthened *by*, and in You, we can do all things (Philippians 4:13).

Search us, by putting us in Your sieve, so that all the chaff of worldliness may be winnowed away; then lead us to delight in You alone, for as You are the Object of our hearts, the pride of life must give way to humility of soul; the lust of the flesh must give place to love to You; and the lust of the eyes must give place to entire satisfaction in gazing upon You.

Search us! Put us in the crucible, to remove the dross of sin and self which gathers on our spirits, and hides the reflection of Your own lovely face, so that our lack of conformity is seen, instead of Your beauty; then lead us, that Your own character may appear, and Your own loveliness be manifested.

Search us! Bring the knife of Your Word, and remove from us all the fruitless and unprofitable things in our lives, all the questionable things that are like so many suckers, draining away the strength that should go to help that which is fruitful and useful; then cause us to bring forth fruit—the fruit of the Spirit in His manifold perfection, the *more* fruit of abundant grace, the *much* fruit of more abundant labor, and the fruit that shall *remain*—of souls blest, who will be our crown and rejoicing in the day of Your appearing.

Search us! Chasten us with the rod, if necessary, but let us not despise Your dealing, nor faint under it; only let the desired effect be produced, namely, the peaceable fruits of righteousness; then lead us to learn the lesson You would teach, so we shall bless the hand that strikes, and know it is but an expression of Your Fatherly love and tender care, for whom You love You chasten.

Search us! Search our hearts, and see if there be any wrong motive, or impure desire; search our thoughts, see if they are wandering from You; search our ways, see if there are any wrong actions, any doubtful things in the life which are hindering us, any stumbling-blocks over which weaker Christians are falling; then lead us, that our affections may be set only on You, and every thought be in subjection to You—so shall our ways please You.

Searcher of Hearts!—from mine erase
  All thoughts that should not be,
And in its deep recesses trace
  My gratitude to Thee!

Hearer of Prayer!—oh, guide aright
  Each word and deed of mine;
Life's battle teach me how to fight,
  And be the victory Thine.

Giver of All!—for every good
  In the Redeemer came—
For raiment, shelter and for food,
  I thank Thee in His Name.

Father and Son and Holy Ghost!
  Thou glorious Three in One!
Thou knowest best what I need most,
  And let Thy will de done.

—George Pope Morris

5

The Discipler's Authority

The Christian worker's authority, for all he says and does, is the Word of God. That is why he should have no doubt as to the inspiration of the Scriptures, for, as we are told in 2 Timothy 3:16, 17: "All Scripture is God-breathed, and is useful for teaching, rebuking, correcting, and training in righteousness, so that the man of God may be thoroughly equipped for every good work" (NIV here and throughout the chapter). If there is any doubt that the Scriptures are God's Word, there can be no authority in testimony, for to be "thoroughly equipped for every good work," we must be thoroughly convinced as to the truth of God's good Word.

I need not point out that the subject of the inspiration of the Scripture is one of great and pressing importance. It is the very core of Christianity. It is the keystone to the arch of truth. It is the foundation of our faith. It is the pillar of our profession.

The inspiration of the Scriptures is the *core of Christianity*. Take this away, and the whole building will topple over, and those in it will be swallowed up in doubt and agnosticism. The inspiration of the Scriptures is the *keystone to the arch of truth*. As the keystone is connected with the other stones, making the arch secure, and without it the arch is incomplete, so the truth that the Scripture is the Word of God is absolutely necessary to give strength and security to all the truths of the Sacred Writings. If this is taken away, the whole is weakened and easily overthrown.

The inspiration of the Scriptures is the very *foundation of our faith*. As the house must be well founded, if it is to stand the strain of the tempest, so, unless there is the belief—the firm conviction—that the Scripture is the Word of God, our faith will soon be shaken to its downfall by Satan; it will be overthrown by doubt, and carried away by the drift and current of rationalism. As one has well said, "It is not strange that upon the Word of God all the forces of the foes of Christianity should be massed. If confidence in that Word can be undermined; if, by subtlety and sophistry, its infallible inspiration may be made to appear like an old wife's fable, or groundless tradition; if in any way, men may feel at liberty to slash on the sacred roll, and cut out of it whatever is offensive to the proud reason or the wayward will of the natural man—the devil will have achieved his greatest triumph."

The inspiration of the Scriptures is the *pillar of our profession*. The two pillars which gave strength and solidity to the Temple, were suggestively named "Jachin" (meaning "He will establish") and "Boaz" ("In Him is strength"): so the two facts that give us strength and security, and uphold our profession, are the complete and the verbal inspiration of the scriptures. Thank God, no modern Samson can bring these pillars down. Men have been trying long enough to do it; but it has been to their own injury and confusion.

God has spoken to us in three ways.

He has spoken to us in the works of creation

"By faith we understand that the universe was formed at God's command, so that what is seen was not made out of what was visible" (Hebrews 11:3).

"By the word of the Lord were the heavens made, their starry host by the breath of his mouth. He gathers the waters of the sea as into a heap; he lays out the deep into storehouses. Let all the earth fear the Lord; let all the people of the world revere him. For he spoke, and it came to be; he commanded, and it stood firm" (Psalm 33:6-9).

"The heavens declare the glory of God and the skies proclaim the work of his hands. Day after day they pour forth speech; night after night they display knowledge. There is no speech nor language where their voice is not heard. Their voice goes out into all the earth, their words to the end of the world" (Psalm 19:1-4). The sun in his splendor, the moon with her silvery rays, the planets in their order, the "milky way" with its mystery, the sea with its roar, the earth with its countless treasures, all speak to us, and declare God's eternal power and Godhead.

God has spoken to us by His Son

"In the past God spoke to our forefathers through the prophets at many times and in various ways, but in these last days he has spoken to us by his Son, whom he appointed heir of all things, and through whom he made the universe" (Hebrews 1:1, 2). "In the beginning was the Word, and the Word was with God, and the Word was God. He was with God in the beginning" (John 1:1, 2). "The Word became flesh and lived for a while among us. We have seen his glory, the glory as of the one and only [Son] who came from the Father, full of grace and truth" (John 1:14).

"No man has ever seen God, at any time, but God the only [Son] who is at the Father's side, has made him known" (John 1:18). In His *words* He told out the mind of God; in His *works*, the power of God; in His *compassion*, the love of God; in His *dealings*, the grace of God; in His *spotless character*, the holiness of God; in His *death*, the righteous love of God; and in His *resurrection*, the energy of God. Christ is the Divine Logos, the living Oracle of God, the Expression of the Godhead, the Doctrine of Jehovah.

God has spoken to us in His written Word

"You have exalted above all things Your name and Your word" (Psalm 138:2). This is as much as to say, You have written Your name on every part of Your works—on the sun, on every star; but in Your Word Your grace and love are seen. As Watts says:—

Great God, with wonder and with praise
  On all Thy works I look;
But still Thy wisdom, power, and grace
  Shine brightest in Thy Book.
Thy stars, that in their courses roll,
  Have much instruction given;
But Thy good Word informs my soul
  How I may climb to heaven.

How has God made known His will? The answer has already been given in some measure. "In the past God spoke to our forefathers through the prophets" (Hebrews 1:1), "For prophecy never had its origin in the will of man, but men spoke from God as they were carried along by the Holy Spirit" (2 Peter 1:21). In these words we have the answer.

I like the King James Version here: *"sundry times"* (or "many portions")—all was not revealed to each prophet: one received one portion, and another another. *"Divers manners"*—by internal suggestion, by audible voice, by Urim and Thummim, and by visions. *Different persons*—"Holy men . . . spake as they were moved by the Holy Ghost." Men of all classes, ages, and positions, were the writers. How is it there was no contradiction and no confusion? Because the Word was written at the dictation of God, and under His superintendence.

Hastings has well said, "The authorship of this Book is wonderful. Here are words written by kings, by emperors, by princes, by poets, by sages, by philosophers, by fishermen, by statesmen; by men learned in the wisdom of Egypt, educated in the schools of Babylon, trained up at the feet of rabbis in Jerusalem. It was written by men in exile, in the desert, in shepherds' tents, in 'green pastures,' and beside 'still waters.' Among its authors we find the tax-gatherer, the herdsman, the gatherer of sycamore fruit; we find poor men, rich men, statesmen, preachers, exiles, captains, legislators, judges; men of every grade and class are represented in this wonderful volume, which is in reality a *library*, filled with history, genealogy, ethnology, law, ethics, prophecy, poetry, eloquence, medicine, sanitary science, political economy, and perfect rules for the conduct of personal and social life.

"It contains all kinds of writing; but what a jumble it would be if sixty-six books were written in this way by ordinary men! Suppose, for instance, that we get sixty-six medical books, written by thirty or forty different doctors of various schools . . . bind them all together, and then undertake to doctor a man according to that book! What man would be fool enough to risk the results of practising such a system of medicine? Or suppose you get thirty-five editors at work, writing treatises on politics, or thirty-five ministers writing books on theology, and then see if you can find any leather strong enough to hold the books together, when they are done."

Inspiration! The word "inspired" only occurs in the Bible in connection with the word translated "Scripture."

"Inspired" means *"God-breathed."* As God breathed into man the breath of life, and he became a living soul, so God breathed into man, and spoke this Word to him; hence it is Divine in its Authorship and authority.

The early Christians firmly believed in the inspiration of the Scriptures, and never considered it anything else. Dr. Brookes says, "In the early Church . . . there was entire unanimity among those who had a right to be called Christians, as to inspiration itself, an inspiration that was supernatural in its source, unerring in its truthfulness, and extending to the very words of Scripture.

"Thus Clement says: 'Look into the Holy Scriptures, which are the true words of the Holy Ghost'; 'Ye know, beloved, ye know full well the Holy Scriptures; and have thoroughly searched into the oracles of God.'

"Barnabas, in the epistle ascribed to him, writes: 'The Lord hath declared unto us by the prophets'; 'Thus saith the Lord by the prophets'; 'Moses in the Spirit spake.'

"Irenæus testifies: 'Well knowing that the Scriptures are perfect, as dictated (or spoken) by the Word of God and His Spirit.' Hippolytus says: 'Be assured they did not speak in their own strength, nor out of their own minds, what they proclaimed; but first by the inspiration of the Word, they were imbued with wisdom.'

"Origen declares: 'The sacred books are not the writings of men, but have been written and delivered to us, from the inspiration of the Holy Spirit by the will of the Father of all things, through Jesus Christ. The sacred Scriptures come from the fulness of the Spirit, so that there is nothing in the prophets, or the law, or the Gospel, or the Epistles, which descends not from the Divine Majesty.'

"Any amount of similar evidence could be adduced, but it is sufficient to say, that up to the Reformation, if even one voice was raised to advance some theory of inspiration, it was too feeble to be heard."

It is only of late years that men have dared to talk of "degrees of inspiration." Well may Dr. Bishop of America, say, with cutting scorn and biting sarcasm:

"Degrees of inspiration! Shades of varying value in the cadences of the Almighty's voice! He whispers, hesitates, speaks low in Esther . . . He stutters, falters in the genealogies; is inaccurate in figures. He evidently weakens, halts; Almighty God breaks down! Degrees of inspiration! The older theologians, thank God, did not know them—nor own them. Why should they? As well discuss degrees in Deity, in Predestination, in Providence, as talk of degrees in that of which Augustine says: 'Whatsoever He willed that we should read, either of His doings or sayings, that He commissioned His agents to write, as if their hands had been His own hands.'

"'God breathed' sweeps the whole ground. God comes down as a blast on the pipes of an organ—in voice like a whirlwind, or in still whispers like Æolian tones, and saying the word, He seizes the hand, and makes that hand, in His own, the pen of a most ready writer."

As the father guides the hand of his boy in writing a letter (and hence it is the father and not the boy who is writing), so the Lord dictated and directed those whom He used to make known His will, as recorded in His Word. We do not contend, nor do we for one moment mean to infer that the translations of the Scriptures are inspired. As one has said, "We affirm the inspiration and authority of the *original* Scriptures, the sacred autographs, but not of the copies or versions."

But we do most distinctly affirm, without any fear of contradiction, that the natural man could not conceive the Word of God; neither can he comprehend its truth and meaning, apart from the Holy Spirit. As an instance of this, look at

Peter's own understanding of the Lord's words in Matthew 26:22. He saw no reason why Jesus should suffer, and hence his answer, "Be it far from thee, Lord; this shall not be unto thee" (KJV). But Peter on the day of Pentecost had the Spirit's teaching on the subject, which not only made the reason of these sufferings clear to him, but enabled him fully to explain their meaning to others (read Acts 2:22-36).

We believe in the Plenary Inspiration of the Scriptures. What is the meaning of the word "plenary"? The Roman Catholics speak of "plenary indulgence," which simply means an entire remission of penalties due to all sins. From this we see that the word denotes completeness, fulness. Dr. Hodge speaks of plenary inspiration as "a Divine influence, full and sufficient to secure its end." "The end in this case secured," he says, "is the perfect infallibility of the Scriptures in every part, as a record of fact and doctrine, both in thought and verbal expression. So that, although they come to us through the instrumentality of the minds, hearts, imaginations, consciences, and wills of men, they are, nevertheless, in the strictest sense, the Word of God."

Sir Walter Scott's dying request to his son-in-law, "Bring me the Book," showed that it was the Book of books to him. "Bring me the Bible," was what he meant. The Bible is the Book. It is *"the Book"* because it is from Him who is *The One*.

Its *altitude* shows its Divine origin. It towers on high like a majestic mountain, and who can scale its heights? The *blessings* which it brings show its Divine bounty. It comes to those who will receive it, like Joseph to his brethren, fills their sacks with corn, and returns their money; and it gives to them untold good.

Its *claims* speak of its Divine authority. It comes to us, like the still small voice came to Elijah in the cave at Horeb, as the voice of Jehovah. Its *diction* declares its Divine Speaker. "Never man spake like this Man," was the testimony borne to Him who was "the Word made flesh"; so we say of the Book, "Never *Book* spake like *this Book*."

Its *elevating* power shows its Divine strength. It tells of One who takes out of the horrible pit of sin, and the mire of sensuality. It speaks of One who takes from the dunghill of pollution, and sets among princes.

Its *freshness* tells out its Divine Author. It is a living spring, ever fresh and refreshing.

"What a wonderful Book it is!" said one to a well-known Christian.

"Yes," was the reply, "but you see it is a *living* Book."

Its *grace* shows the overflow of Divine love to meet all needs. Like the river mentioned in Ezekiel, it is a river to swim in, and brings joy and health to the receiver. Its *harmony* shows its Divine arrangement. The Old Testament is revealed in the New, and the New Testament is hidden in the Old. Genesis must be unlocked by John in his Gospel and Epistles. Exodus and Leviticus are illustrated and explained in Hebrews. The Revelation is the key to Daniel, and

Christ is the Secret,

the Sum and Substance of it all. Its *invitations* are the pleadings of Divine compassion. As Moses said to Jethro, so the Word says to all, "Come with me, and I will do you good." Its *judgments* show the Divine righteousness, as illustrated in the fulfillment of God's word to Pharaoh, through Moses, in the plagues. Its *kindness* of spirit speaks out the Divine mercy. Its *lucidity* manifests its Divine brightness. It is a lamp to our feet and a light to our path. No traveler will lose his way who follows this guide. Its *miracles* tell out the putting forth of Divine power, whether it be in Moses turning water into blood, or Jesus turning water into wine. Its *nature* testifies to the Divine holiness, for like its Author it is holy. Hence, as water cleanses, so the Word, when received, produces holiness.

Its *order* speaks of a Divine plan. Take the Epistle to the Romans, and mark the progressiveness of its revelation in the five "R's,"—Ruin in the Fall—Redemption in Christ—Reception of Christ—Righteousness in Christ—Reflection of Christ. Its *preservation* shows its Divine Keeper. Men have tried to burn it, but they have met with similar treatment to the men who cast the three Hebrews into the fire—they have themselves been destroyed.

The very house where the agnostic, Voltaire, lived is packed with Bibles, a depot for the Geneva Bible Society, and it is said that his old printing press has been used to print the Word of God!

Its *questions* speak of the Divine Convicter. What sinner can stand before such questions as these—"What will you say when He shall punish you?" "What will you do in the swelling of Jordan?" "Who shall be able to stand?"

Its *ring* tells out its Divine genuineness, as the ring of the coin tells it is not a counterfeit. The fruit the Bible produces, testifies to its Divinity. Its spirit speaks of its Divine Inspirer. There is righteousness without rancor, love without looseness, and goodness without guile.

Its *teachings* testify to its unsullied character. They are powerful, for they penetrate to the heart and conscience: and they are peace-giving, for they say to everyone who believes in Christ, what He said to the troubled lake, "Peace be still!"

Its *unfoldings* are the manifestations of the Divine One. As you put your eye to the telescope, other worlds, unseen by the naked eye, come into your view; so when the Word of God is searched in a prayerful spirit, we have to exclaim with the Bride in the Song of Solomon, "He looketh forth at the windows, showing Himself through the lattice."

Its *wisdom* shows the Divine Teacher. What man could ever conceive the plan of salvation? That God in righteousness should save those who believe in Christ!

Its *excellence* speaks out the fact that it is God-given: that it is in very deed all that it claims to be—inspired of God. There is no need for a further revelation, or the aid of higher criticism, or the reasonableness of man's inner consciousness. The light of man's inner consciousness is blacker than Egyptian darkness.

We believe in the Verbal Inspiration of the Scriptures. What do we mean by the verbal inspiration of the Scriptures? Dr. Hodge explains it in the following words:

"It is meant that the Divine influence, of whatever kind it may have been, which accompanied the sacred writers in what they wrote, extends to the expression of their thoughts in language, as well as the thoughts themselves—the effect being, that in the original autograph copies, the language expresses the thought God intended to convey with infallible accuracy, so that the words, as well as the thoughts, are God's revelation to us.

"That this influence did extend to the words, appears from the following considerations:—

"1. The very design of inspiration is, not to secure the infallible correctness of the personal opinions of the inspired men themselves (Paul and Peter differed, and sometimes the prophet knew not what he wrote), but to secure an infallible record of the truth. But a record consists of language.

"2. Men think in words, and the more definitely they think, the more are their thoughts immediately associated with an exactly appropriate verbal expression. Infallibility of thought cannot be secured, or preserved, independent of an infallible verbal rendering.

"3. The Scriptures affirm this fact: 'Which things also we speak, not in the words which man's wisdom teacheth, but which the Holy Ghost teacheth; comparing spiritual things with spiritual' (1 Corinthians 2:13). 'For this cause also thank we God without ceasing, because, when ye received the Word of God which ye heard of us, ye received it not as the word of men, but, as it is in truth, the Word of God, which effectually worketh also in you that believe' (1 Thessalonians 2:13).

"4. The New Testament writers, while quoting from the Old Testament for purposes of argument, often base their argument upon the very words used, thus ascribing authority to the *word* as well as the thought (Matthew 22:32 and Exodus 3:6 Matthew 22:44 and Psalm 110:1; Galatians 3:16 and Genesis 17:7, are examples)."

Dr. Bishop says: "Verbal and direct inspiration is, therefore, the Thermopylæ of Biblical and Scriptural faith. No breath, no syllable; no syllable, no word; no word, no book; no book, no religion."

Good Bishop Jewell bears similar testimony: "There is no sentence, no clause, no word, no syllable, no letter, but it is written for thy instruction. There is not one jot, but it is signed and sealed with the blood of the Lamb."

The popular theory of today is, that God gave the thoughts, and man clothed them in his own language. What does the Scripture itself say about this? Does it say that God gave the thoughts, or that He spoke? The latter, most certainly. Let us note a few of its many testimonies as to this fact.

The giving of the law. "God *spoke* all these *words*, . . ." (Exodus 20:1). Here the words are as positive and plain as they possibly can be. It is distinctly stated that God spoke the words of the law, *saying* what Moses reiterated.

The testimony of Moses. Moses, in referring to what God said to him when He met him at Horeb, and spoke to him out of the burning bush concerning the bringing of Israel into the land of Canaan, declares, "The Lord our God said unto us at Horeb, 'You have stayed long enough at this mountain. Break camp and advance into the hill country . . .'" (Deuteronomy 1:6, 7 comp. Exodus 3, etc.).

The dying testimony of Joshua. "Not one of all the promises the Lord your God gave you has failed" (Joshua 23:14). Such was the witness of the valiant leader of Israel, before he joined the redeemed who had passed into the unseen world.

The words of Samuel to Saul. "The Lord has done what he predicted through me: for the Lord has torn the kingdom out of your hands" (1 Samuel 28:17). So said Samuel to King Saul, after the latter had consulted the witch of Endor. Samuel had come from Hades to remind the fallen king of his former message to him. "The Lord has torn the kingdom of Israel from you" (1 Samuel 15:28).

The last words of David. "The Spirit of the Lord *spoke* through me; his *word* was on my tongue" (2 Samuel 23:2). Here is the explanation of the fact, that the sweet Psalmist of Israel was able to predict the sufferings of Christ and the glory that should follow, because He who indited the word, was the same who afterwards unfolded that same word about Himself to the sad disciples, as they were gathered together in the upper room at Jerusalem (Luke 24:44-47).

God's promise to Solomon. "Then will I perform my *word* with thee, which I *spake* unto David thy father" (1 Kings 6:12 KJV). If we compare these words with 2 Samuel 7:1-17, we find that God's word came to Nathan the prophet, and through him to David.

Solomon's prayer. Solomon, in his prayer at the dedication of the Temple, says to the Lord, in speaking of His faithfulness to His word, "You have kept your promise to your servant David my father; with your *mouth* you have promised . . ." (1 Kings 8:24). And a little farther on he says, as he is still praying, in speaking to the Lord about the throne of Israel, "Now, O God of Israel, let Your *word* be verified . . ." (1 Kings 8:26). And yet again, he bears his indirect testimony to Verbal Inspiration in referring to the nation of Israel, with regard to their separation to God, and His choosing them for His people: "For you singled them out from all the nations of the world to be your own inheritance, just as you declared through your servant Moses when you, O Sovereign Lord, brought our fathers out of Egypt" (1 Kings 8:53; compare with Exodus 19:5, 6 and Deuteronomy 14:2).

The Lord's answer to the prayer of Hezekiah. When Hezekiah was sick unto death, he prayed to the Lord that his life might be spared. The Lord granted his request by adding fifteen years to his life, and gave him a sign that He had heard him, in that he caused the shadow on the sun-dial to go back ten degrees. The incident is related in the following words: "Hezekiah became ill and was at the point of death. He prayed to the Lord, who *answered* him and gave him a sign" (2 Chronicles 32:24).

Nehemiah's prayer. In the great thanksgiving gathering, at the completion of the building of the wall of Jerusalem, among other things that Nehemiah says in prayer, in referring to what God had done for Israel, is the following: "You came down on Mount Sinai; you *spoke* to them from heaven" (Nehemiah 9:13).

The Psalmist's words. The Psalmist, in speaking of the gracious leading of Israel in the wilderness, by Jehovah, and of His instructions to them, says, "He *spoke* to them from the pillar of cloud" (Psalm 99:7).

Jeremiah's message from the Lord to Judah. "This is the word that came to Jeremiah from the Lord: 'While you were doing all these things, declares the Lord, I *spoke* to you again and again, but you did not listen; I *called* you, but you did not answer. . . . I will thrust you from my presence, just as I did all your brothers, the people of Ephraim'" (Jeremiah 7:1, 13-15). Thus God *speaks* in predicting the punishment that would come upon Judah, when they were carried away into captivity by Babylon, because they had not hearkened to His word, through His servants.

Daniel's prayer about the captivity of Judah. "You have fulfilled the *words spoken* against us . . ." (Daniel 9:12). So says Daniel in calling to remembrance the statements of God through Moses in Leviticus 26:14, etc., where God declares that He will punish His people, by letting their enemies overcome them and lead them into captivity. And as Daniel looked on their condition in captivity, he beheld the literal fulfillment of the *words* of God.

The testimony of the Lord Jesus. When the Sadducees came to Christ, and began to question the fact of the resurrection, He asked, "Have you not read in the book of Moses, in the account of the bush, how God said to him, 'I am the God of Abraham, the God of Isaac, and the God of Jacob'? He is not the God of the dead, but of the living" (Mark 12:26, 27).

The song of Mary. "He has helped His servant Israel . . . even as he said to our fathers" (Luke 1:54, 55). So sang Mary, the mother of Jesus, in the gladness of her heart, as she praised God for the honor He had bestowed upon her, in using her to be the fulfiller of Scripture, especially of the promise made to Abraham (Genesis 17:19; Galatians 3:16).

The song of Zacharias. "Praise be to the Lord, the God of Israel, because he has come and redeemed his people. He has raised up a horn of salvation for us . . . (as he *said* through his holy prophets of long ago)" (Luke 1:68-70). Such were the prophetic words of the man when he regained his speech, as he was filled with the Holy Spirit.

The testimony of the Jews to the blind man. "We know that God *spoke* to Moses" (John 9:29). Such were the words of the Jews, in deriding the Lord Jesus and His utterances, and expressing their self-glorification at being the disciples of Moses.

There are many other places where it is distinctly stated that God *spoke,* but the above will suffice. Let us remember the most emphatic utterance of the Holy Spirit, in the following two verses of Scripture already quoted: "In the past *God spoke* to our forefathers through the prophets"; and "For prophecy never had its origin in the will of man, but men spoke from God *as they were carried along* by the Holy Spirit" (Hebrews 1:1; 2 Peter 1:21).

In the face of these statements, will any man dare to say that God has not spoken? If he presume to do so, then let him remember the following trenchant words, and mark the consequence:

"Do not add to what I command you and do not subtract from it" (Deuteronomy 4:2).

"See that you do all I command you; do not add to it or take away from it" (Deuteronomy 12:32).

"Every word of God is flawless . . . Do not add to his words, or he will rebuke you, and prove you a liar" (Prov. 30:5, 6).

"I warn everyone who hears the words of the prophecy of this book: If anyone adds anything to them, God will add to him the plagues described in this book. And if anyone takes words away from this book of prophecy, God will take away from him his share in the tree of life and in the holy city, which are described in this book" (Revelation 22:18, 19).

A German girl began to mark in her Bible those passages which were precious to her, but she found as she went on, that every word was more or less precious, so she had to leave off, or she would have had to mark every word. Every word is precious to the true child of God, and he recognizes that every word is inspired in what is known as Scripture.

In closing this chapter, there are two things we should like to emphasize, and these are, *first*, the discipler's personal attitude towards the Word of God and *second*, the absolute importance, to keep before the unsaved, certain facts revealed in the Scriptures.

First. The discipler's personal attitude towards the Word of God. There are seven things we should do in relation to it.

1. *Receive the Word of God with meekness*. "Receive with meekness the engrafted Word, which is able to save your souls" (James 1:21 KJV): receive it as *servants*, for it is the voice of the Master; receive it as *saints*, to cleanse from all defilement; receive it as *subjects*, for it is the command of the King; receive it as *soldiers* to equip for the warfare with evil; receive it as *sons*, for it is the Father's will; receive it as *saved ones*, as the direction of grace, and receive it as *surrendered ones*, as the rule for the life.

2. *Let the Word of God dwell in you richly*. "Let the Word of Christ dwell in you richly in all wisdom" (Colossians 3:16 KJV). Let it dwell in the heart, as a *preservative* from evil; let it dwell in the soul, as the *propeller* in service; let it dwell in the mind, as the *plan* for direction; and let it dwell in the affection, as the *power* for conflict.

3. *Keep the Word of God tenaciously*. "They have kept thy word" (John 17:6 KJV), Christ could say of His disciples. We should keep it as a *treasure*—securely; as our *teacher* for instruction; as a *tower* for protection; and as our *trust* we should keep it faithfully and well.

4. *Continue in the Word of God untiringly*. "If you continue in my word, you are truly my disciples" (John 8:31 KJV). Continuance in the Word is the *mark* of true discipleship, the *manifest* evidence that we are true followers of Christ.

5. *Live out the Word of God faithfully*. "You show that you are a letter from Christ" (2 Corinthians 3:3 RSV). The Christian is the world's Bible, a living object lesson. If we are not walking *Bibles*, then we are walking *libels*.

6. *Hold forth the Word of God boldly*. "Holding forth the word of Life" (Philippians 2:16 KJV). As the man holds the lighted torch above his head in the dark night, to show himself and others the path in which to tread, so the Christian is to hold up the Word by his life, and its testimony with his lips, that others may be enlightened and benefited.

7. *Meditate on the Word of God prayerfully*. As the well-watered tree by the river's side, grows and is fruitful, so the Christian who muses on, and meditates in the truth of God, is prosperous in life, and profitable to others (Psalm 1:2).

Second, the absolute importance to keep before the unsaved, certain facts revealed in the Scriptures.

In the New Testament we find a constant and repeated appeal to the Old Testament, as to its authority and power. There are five places where we find the words, "*It is written,*" occurring in connection with, and bringing before us, five most important facts. They have to do with *sin, sacrifice, salvation, sanctification*, and *judgment*.

1. *Sin*. "*It is written,* There is none righteous, no, not one" (Romans 3:10 KJV). Sin is a terrible disease, which has infected all mankind. It has permeated the whole of man's being. All are smitten with it. As to what men are, namely, sinners with a sinful nature, there is no difference. Men *do* wrong, because they *are* wrong. The first thing for the sinner to know is, what he is, and finding this out, he will soon cry out, "God be merciful to me the sinner." Remember it is written—it is a fact, whether man feels it, believes it, or not—that God says he is a sinner.

2. *Sacrifice*. "In the volume of the book *it is written* of me" (Hebrews 10:7 KJV). So said Christ in speaking of His sacrificial work upon the cross. Sacrifice was needed to meet the righteous requirements of God on account of sin. Sacrifice has been made by Christ, the Just One, suffering for the unjust, to bring us to God. The sacrifice has been accepted, in that God raised Christ from the dead. The sacrifice is sufficient for all who will trust in Him who made it.

3. *Salvation*. "*It is written,* How beautiful are the feet of them that preach the Gospel of peace" (Romans 10:15 KJV). The messengers of the gospel tell out the glad tidings of salvation, to those who will trust in Christ—salvation from the wrath to come, and peace with God, through faith in the blood of the Lamb.

4. *Sanctification*. "*It is written,* be ye holy; for I am holy" (1 Peter 1:16 KJV). Being saved, we are set apart for God, to listen to His voice, to do His will, to have fellowship with Himself, to be used in His service, and to learn of Himself alone.

5. *Judgment*. "*It is written,* I will destroy the wisdom of the wise, and will bring to nothing the understanding of the prudent" (1 Corinthians 1:19 KJV). Those who cling to their own opinions, in contradiction to God's declarations, who consult their own whims and fancies, and will not hearken to the claims and call of God in the gospel of His grace, must surely suffer for their willfulness, and that eternally. Don't trifle with the Word of the Lord, for remember—

> "Within that awful volume lies
> The mystery of mysteries:
> Oh, happiest they of human race
> To whom our God has granted grace,
> To read, to fear, to hope, to pray,
> To lift the latch, and force the way;
> But better had they ne'er been born.
> Who read to doubt, or read to scorn."

6

The Discipler's Need

The old Highlander was not far off when he said: "There are two things which the Church has forgotten—the personality of the Holy Spirit, and the personality of Satan." We might go even farther and say, in many cases the Holy Spirit is not so much forgotten as *ignored*, and spoken of in these words by Dr. A. T. Pierson: "The most conspicuous preacher in Brooklyn in past years, and now unhappily conspicuous for his defection from the faith, has published these astounding words. They were the first indication to me that he was wandering from the truth his father had preached before him. He says: 'The Holy Spirit of God is a thin and shadowy effluence, proceeding from the Father and the Son, as the breath proceeds from the human body.' Think of that. It seems to me it comes very close to blasphemy. The Holy Spirit is a Person, just as much as the Father is, or as the Son is a Person. If you deny the personality of the Holy Spirit, practically you deny everything that the Bible reveals about the nature of the Most High God."

If we deny the personality of the Holy Spirit, then follows inevitably that we will deny the personality of Satan. What does the denial of the personality of the Holy Spirit, and the personality of Satan involve? By doing so, we throw overboard all that we hold to be essential to salvation and sanctification. We have no hesitation in saying that the cause of all the declension in spiritual life is the departure from the truth, the truth as to the personality of the Holy Spirit and the personality of Satan. There is a triple consequence, a three-headed monstrosity in the denial of either the one truth or the other. Let one deny the personality of Satan, and the account of the temptation by Satan in the garden of Eden is a myth, its insertion in the Bible a mistake, and the disobedience of Adam does not involve the human race. Thus the federal headship of Adam is eliminated, his act not being a representative one: and likewise such Scriptural statements as, "By one man sin entered into the world, and death by sin, and so death passed upon all men, for that all have sinned"; "In Adam all die"; "By one man's disobedience many were made sinners," are cut out by the knife of rationalism. Following this, the natural depravity of man vanishes, and the words of Christ to Nicodemus, "That which is born of the flesh is flesh," and "Except a man be born again, he cannot see the kingdom of God," are delusive and misleading.

When you remove these two old-fashioned truths, you can argue away the sinfulness of sin till it becomes almost holiness, or at the worst a *slight* misfortune. The sacrifice of the Savior becomes unnecessary, and therefore not vicarious. To put it at its highest, it is but a model of devotion, an ideal of suffering martyrdom. The punishment of the sinner for sin is out of the question, for sin is not sin, Satan is not Satan, hell is not hell, justice is not justice, and punishment is not eternal. Rather, these expressions are only figurative and mystical! Thus the denial of the personality of the devil goes more or less (rather, *very much more* instead of less) with the following three things:

1. The identification and incrimination of the sinner in the fall of Adam.
2. The depravity of man, and his consequent departure from God.
3. The necessity and endlessness of future punishment.

As there is a triple consequence involved in denying the personality of Satan, so there is in denying the personality of the Holy Spirit. *First,* the divine inspiration of the Bible as the Word of God is abandoned; for holy men could not be moved by the Holy Spirit in writing, if there were no Holy Spirit to influence and direct them. *Second,* the miraculous conception of Christ as to His manhood could not happen. The words of the angel to Mary, "The Holy Spirit will come upon you, and the power of the Most High will overshadow you, so the holy one to be born will be called the Son of God" (Luke 1:35 NIV), have no meaning; consequently, our Lord's Sonship is destroyed and His Deity is gone. *Third,* Christ's death has no value for others, for He was only a man. His sacrifice was not an atonement for sin; neither was it substitutionary, but only virtuous, in that He suffered as a martyr.

As the triune leaf of the shamrock withers and dies, when it is plucked from the stem through which life and support are derived from the root, so the denial of the personality of the Spirit destroys the three truths already referred to. The Bible as the revelation of God is gone, hence we are in worse than Egyptian darkness; the Deity of Christ was assumed, therefore He was an impostor; and the death of Christ is valueless, for no mere man could atone for the sins of others. Only as the Son of God could He bear the sins of many. Hence we are forever lost.

I wish to deal, however, not so much with the personality of the Spirit, as the enduement of the Spirit.

The Holy Spirit is spoken of in two ways in the New Testament. Reference is made to His *personality* as taking the place of Christ, who promised "another Comforter." In other parts of the New Testament the Spirit's *power* is referred to, meaning the influence He exerts.

In his elaborate treatise on the Greek article, Bishop Middleton says, in referring to the personality and power of the Holy Spirit, that when the article is used, it refers invariably to the Person of the Holy Spirit, or to the Holy Spirit as a Person, and when the Holy Spirit is spoken of without the article, His gifts and influences are meant. Rotherham makes this clearly understood in his translation of Acts 2:4, describing the disciples on the day of Pentecost: "And they were all filled with Holy Spirit, and began to be speaking with other kinds of tongues, just as *the* Spirit was giving unto them to be sounding forth." In the same chapter the distinction is seen—verses 32, 33. "The same Jesus hath God raised up, whereof all we are witnesses! By the right hand of God, therefore, having been exalted, also the promise of *the* Holy Spirit having received from the Father, He hath poured out this which yourselves do see and hear." The expressions, "Filled with Holy Spirit," and "Poured out this," speak of the influence and power of the Spirit; while the expressions, "The promise of *the* Holy Spirit," and "As *the* Spirit was giving," speak of the personality and presence of the Spirit.

Now, it is possible for us to recognize the personality of the Holy Spirit, to be born of the Holy Spirit, and yet not to have received as a definite and continuous experience, the enduement of the Spirit—the power of the Spirit resting upon us in service. It is just as possible for an employee to recognize his employer, and yet not to be fully under his sway, in the sense of having his interest wholly at heart. In the Acts of the Apostles, there are those mentioned who were believers in Christ, and yet had not been empowered with the Holy Spirit. They recognized the Spirit in a sense, for as *sinners* He had worked in them and led them to Christ; because no man can call Jesus Lord but by the Holy Spirit (1 Corinthians 12:3). And as *saints*, He was indwelling them as God's seal upon them, for "If any man have not the Spirit of Christ, he is none of his" (Romans 8:9). But as *servants*, He was not resting upon them. For instance, there is the case of the Samaritans who had been brought to Christ through the preaching of Philip the evangelist, but who did not receive the enduement of the Spirit until the apostles came and laid their hands upon them. Again, we have the case of Apollos, who knew only the baptism of John, but who was instructed by Aquila and Priscilla in the way of God more perfectly (Acts 18:24-28). Immediately he began to testify that Jesus was the Christ, namely, that He was exalted to baptize with the Holy Spirit. And no doubt he would witness, as Peter did, "God hath made that same Jesus both Lord and Christ"—LORD, as Governor *over* the Church, and CHRIST, as the channel of blessing *to* and *in* the Church. Again, when Paul came to Ephesus, he questioned certain disciples there, "Have ye received the Holy Spirit since ye believed?" and they answered, "We have not so much as heard if there be any Holy Spirit" (or, *that the Holy Spirit has been given*, Acts 19:2).

It is sadly true today that a large number—if not the majority—of believers accept the truth that this dispensation is specially the dispensation of the Holy Spirit as a matter of *theory*. As a matter of *experience*, however, they are living under the old dispensation. In the old dispensation, the Spirit came upon men of God at intervals, but He did not indwell them. To this Christ seems to refer when He says of John the Baptist, "He that is least in the kingdom of heaven is greater than he" (Matthew 11:11). Not greater as to *character*, but greater as to *privilege*. We may go farther and say that we have greater privileges than the Lord Jesus Himself, looking at Him as the Man and the Servant of God, and recalling what He Himself says: "Verily, verily, I say unto you, He that believeth on me, the works that I do shall he do also; and *greater works* than these shall he do; because I go unto my Father" (John 14:12).

In speaking regarding a mission that had been held at a seaside resort, an honored servant of Christ said, "This mission, and missions generally, confirm me in an opinion I have long held, and to which I have given frequent expression, that the supreme need of the age is a *new baptism* of the Holy Spirit upon the Church, making the Church a better Church, holier, more Christ-like, a faithful witness to the truth, and a glorious missionary and soul-saving agency. The mission of missions would be a mission to the Church. That is the first thing. Matters will not be very much different until there be such a mission. Out of it, what missions to the world would come! And what an impression a purged, living, zealous, transformed, God-filled Church would make upon the world! The doctors and reformers are many, and the prescriptions and methods are numerous and varied, and there is a great deal of discussing and conferring. The wise and the learned speak through the press and in other ways. But what the Church really wants is GOD; the fulness of spiritual life; the baptism of the Holy Spirit. There will be little success, the pace of progress will be slow, until the Church gets on her knees, acknowledging her sins, and shortcomings, and unfaithfulness, and pleading with God to make her holy, and to fill her full of Himself."

"The supreme need of the age is a new baptism of the Holy Spirit." We are sure that every child of God will say "Amen" to those words.

The need of the baptism or filling of the Spirit is seen in many ways. Let me mention a few:

The need of the Holy Spirit is seen in many cases because the need is not felt.

As the Church at Laodicea was perfectly satisfied with itself, so there are Christians today who are perfectly satisfied with their lives and labors. It is an easy matter to sing, "I need Thee every hour," but if the actions give the lie to the sentiment, where is the evidence of felt need? Is the Lord wanted when His commands are not obeyed—or only partially so? when His orders are neglected? when His direction is not sought in prayer? when His claims are flaunted? when we trust *our* methods, instead of *His* might? when we make our plans, instead of bringing the clean sheet of paper for Him to draw the plan, recognizing that our part is simply to go by it? Is there not too much human effort in the Lord's work, instead of the happy impulse of the Spirit? Is there not a good deal of Jacob action in our life, struggling in our own strength, unmindful—unconscious, it may be—that we are rebelling against the Lord? Are we not ignoring God's Word as we are influenced by the spirit of the age?

When there is an utter abandonment of self and its plans, and a crying unto the Lord—not a complimentary call—in acknowledged want, then there is evidence of felt need.

The need of the Holy Spirit is manifest if we call to mind the fact that many of God's people are being defeated in conflict with sin, with error, and with Satan, again and again.

What was the cause of Israel's defeat at Ai? It was the Achan in the camp. What was the secret of victory over the Midianites? It was because Gideon was clothed with the Spirit—the power of the Spirit was resting upon him: the Lord as the "mighty Man of valor" was with him.

Is there any Achan in the heart, the life, or the labor, that is spoiling us? The Achan of *doubt* will cripple faith, as we see in the case of the disciples who failed to expel the demon from the man brought to them. The Achan of *worldliness* will hinder holiness, as the sucker of the rose tree hinders its growth and flower. The Achan of *selfishness* will cause the pilgrim to stumble, as the obstacle in the path causes the passer-by to do, to his hurt.

The Achan of *fear* will paralyze confidence, as the stroke of paralysis benumbs and renders useless the limb. The Achan of *men-pleasing* will mar communion, by hiding the Savior's face, as the cloud hides the sun from view. The Achan of *self-confidence* will grieve and wound the Holy Spirit, as the thorn in the hand causes pain.

The Achan of *half-heartedness* will produce an up-and-down experience—a zig-zag walk. The Achan of *pride* will surely bring a fall, as Bunyan depicts Christian when he outran Faithful, and then looking round in self-glorification, fell to the ground. The Achan of *jealousy* will bring a snare, as a man who digs a pit for another, and falls into it himself. The Achan of the *flesh* will cause bondage of soul and bitterness of spirit, as David found to his sorrow and regret. The Achan of *covetousness* will eat as a canker; and the Achan of self will work untold mischief.

As a safeguard, we need to be clothed with the Spirit, or, as Paul puts it, to be "in the Spirit," for "if we live in the Spirit," "we shall not fulfill the lust of the flesh." If we truly feel the need of the Spirit's power, the Achan of sin will be judged in the Lord's presence and put to death.

The need of the Holy Spirit is self-evident, as we call to mind the worldly means that are adopted to carry on what is called the Lord's work, and the identification of Christians with such means, when they profess to believe otherwise.

The one thing that is blighting and blistering the life of the Church today is the adopting of worldly means to carry on what is *called* the Lord's work; but the Lord is not in it, nor will He have anything to do with it. Following upon the heels of this is the departure from the truth of God. This is the reason the Church has so little power, and, like Samson in the lap of Delilah, has been robbed of her strength. The worldliness in the Church is the great barrier to the outflow of the blessing of Christ. This is why the Lord Jesus is outside the Church, instead of having His rightful place in it as Lord and Master.

What harmony is there between wordly melodies and spiritual songs? What likeness is there between Church entertainments, and the early Christians on their knees pleading with God? What resemblance is there between shows in churches and the simple preaching of the Word of God? How do we reconcile luxurious clothing and the Holy Spirit's words about modest apparel? These are distinctly opposed; and if men will seek to mix them, it will not be long before that awful word—*Ichabod* (1 Samuel 4:21—*the glory is departed)* will be plainly visible to all.

Perhaps the saddest feature is that Christians, who profess to be out of sympathy with these things, can yet identify themselves with theatrical amusements by going occasionally to oblige a friend, or by allowing their children to attend.

The need of the Holy Spirit is apparent, if we remember how the Word of God is ignored.

How can the Holy Spirit manifest His presence and power, when the Word He has inspired is ignored, its authority questioned? He cannot. It is an impossibility. A friend of mine—the late Dr. J. H. Brookes of St. Louis—has thus described a kind of preaching which is popular:

"It seems to me more and more evident that the truth is not to win the field in our day; it will have a tremendous fight to hold its own against the ever increasing odds with which it has to contend. If the battle were only with the world and the devil, there would be nothing to fear; but, unhappily, the fight must be carried on principally against professed friends. Insurrection rages within the citadel, and a 'man's foes are those of his own household.' The Church itself is traitorous, and the worst enemy we have to dread. Annihilation, restoration, evolution—a mixture of Darwinism and Jesus Christ—such is the stuff certain popular preachers are giving to their hearers, and editors of religious papers throw up their hats, and shout themselves hoarse, over the power and progress of the Church. Alas! nothing is more apparent to me, than that the professing body, with its false doctrines, its intense worldliness, its scarcely concealed iniquities, is on the rapids just above the Falls of Niagara, and the awful abyss is just below."

Did Dr. Brookes' mind alter after writing those words? Are things better? Here is what he said on the subject in writing more recently:

"The conflict between truth and error is waxing hotter on this side of the sea (in America), as it is in the mother country. Higher criticism, a denial of the inspiration of the Scriptures, future probationism, annihilationism, contempt of the Atonement, ridicule of our Lord's second coming, semi-Unitarianism, and semi-Universalism, even in so-called evangelical Churches, are pushing forward with a bolder front every day; and those who are contending earnestly for the faith once for all delivered to the saints are few and disheartened. But why should we be discouraged or surprised? We are plainly told by our Lord, and by the Holy Spirit, in the inspired writings, that in the last days there shall be difficult times, and we ought to know that just what we see around us must be witnessed before the end shall come."

Anyone who knows what is going on, and who has looked beneath the surface of Christendom, will confirm what Dr. Brookes says. And this comes about through man, in his conceit, consulting his own reason, instead of consulting and being influenced by the truth of God.

Now, on the other hand, the Holy Spirit never fails to bless the truth, if it is faithfully and fully preached in prayerful dependence upon Himself. It was while Peter was speaking the Word in the house of Cornelius that the Holy Spirit fell upon them that heard his words. The secret of all the loose living among professing Christians is the lack of the truth being enforced and enjoined upon them, by those who profess to be the servants of God. As a crooked ruler will make a crooked line, so crooked teaching will make crooked lives. "Take heed to thyself"; "Take heed to the doctrine," said Paul, in writing to Timothy; and how better can we take heed to ourselves than by taking heed to the truth of God?

Do we fully believe the truth we preach to others, because we have proved it as truth in our own experience? Could that be said of us which was said by Hume when he was reproached for going to hear an earnest preacher of his day: "I don't believe all he says, but he does. Once a week at least, I like to hear a man who believes what he says. Why, whatever I think, that man preaches as though he felt the Lord Jesus Christ was at his elbow."

Could the Lord say of us, as He did of the disciples in His memorable prayer, "They have kept Thy word"? *To keep His words is to prove our love to Him;* "If ye love me, ye will keep my commandments." *To keep His words is to show we know Him;* "Hereby we do know that we know Him, if we keep his commandments." *To keep His words is to abide in His love;* "If ye keep my commandments ye shall abide in my love, even as I have kept my Father's commandments and abide in his love."

To keep the words of Christ is to prove our faithfulness to Him; "I have kept the faith," Paul could say at the end of his ministry. *To keep His words is to be blessed;* "Blessed is he that keepeth the sayings of this book" (Revelation 22:9) may be applied to all His words.

To keep His words is to have the protection and commendation which Christ bestowed upon the Church at Philadelphia; "Because thou hast kept the word of my patience, I also will keep thee from the hour of temptation" (Revelation 3:8).

Are we keeping the truth? Are we believing it? Is the truth of God so precious to us that we count it our chief joy to hold fast the Word? Or do we resemble the prophets of Jericho, who when they spoke one thing, believed another, and said to Elisha, "Knowest thou not that the Lord will take away thy master?" But when they discovered that Elijah was missing, they offered to go in search of him, proving that they did not expect the prophet's translation, although they had talked about it.

The need of the Holy Spirit is painfully evident, if we note the difference between the early Christians and the majority of professing Christians today.

One has said, in contrasting the early Church with the Christianity of today, "Is it not a solemn thought, that if the evangelist Luke were describing modern instead of primitive Christianity, he would have to vary the phraseology of Acts 4:32-35 somewhat as follows: 'And the multitude of them that professed were of hard heart and stony soul, and everyone said that all the things which he possessed were his own: and they had all things in fashion. And with great power gave they witness to the attractions of this world, and great selfishness was upon them all. And there were many among them who lacked love, for as many as were possessors of lands bought more, and sometimes gave a small part thereof for a public good, so their names were heralded in the newspapers, and distribution of praise was made to everyone according as he desired."

To further illustrate the difference between modern and primitive Christianity, we quote from a writer in the *Homiletic Review:* "The Apostolic Church, as compared with the Church of our day, was poor in appliances. The sanctuaries that sinners had to come into were close and crude, yet they came in and were converted. There was not much money for the diffusion of the Gospel, but somehow the Gospel was diffused. The ministers were inelegant, but somehow they marvelously impressed their congregations; their sermons were void of brilliancy, but one sermon then converted three thousand men and now it takes three thousand sermons to convert one man. You may have a flourishing congregation, a full and even crowded house, a first-class organist and precentor, an artistic choir and exquisite music, an influential and wealthy board of trustees, and a well-filled church treasury, and yet not have one particle of spiritual power. The house may be full of people, but if the people are not full of the Holy Spirit, saints will not grow in grace and sinners will not be converted to God. When the whole Church was filled with the Holy Spirit, sinners were converted not by scores, but by thousands. Now the churches are filled with worldliness, not with the Holy Spirit, and conversions are infrequent; one church filled with the Holy Spirit could shake a city from one end to the other. One member of the church full of the Holy Spirit will be felt as a spiritual power and force to the farthest limit of the congregation."

Such being the facts, we must admit that the Church needs an infilling of the Holy Spirit, for this alone is the cure for all the ills from which she is suffering.

7

The Discipler's Consecration

I recall climbing Snowdon, in North Wales. On looking back, when about a third of the way to the summit, we were impressed with the beauty of the scenery below; and as we look back upon our past life we are "transported with the view," and we are constrained to praise our loving Father for His goodness and mercy, which have followed and waited upon us, like two faithful attendants.

But if we would reach Snowdon's summit, we must press on, and if we would excel in the Christian life, we must go forward and upward. One thought occurs to us again and again, as we are ascending the mountain: we think we are nearing the summit, but no, it is only *a* height, and not *the* height. So with the Christian life, there are heights above heights. In looking at and musing upon the subject of consecration, there are three lofty peaks that rise one above the other. These are illustrated in the three words which are rendered "consecration" in the Old Testament. Let us notice the Scriptures in which these words occur, and also refer to others illustrating the different renderings.

First, "Kadesh." In 2 Chronicles 31:6, we have an illustration of the meaning of the word "Kadesh." It occurs in the account of the reformation effected by Hezekiah, in his separating from Israel everything attaching to heathen worship and practice. Noticing his steadfast purpose to be loyal to Jehovah's claims, we read: "The children of Israel and Judah, that dwelt in the cities of Judah, brought in the tithe of oxen and sheep, and the tithe of holy things which were *consecrated* unto the Lord their God." Note, it is not said that they consecrated them to the Lord. The tithe was the Lord's portion, and was always to be set apart for Him, according to Leviticus 27:30; and if they failed to render that which He claimed, according to Malachi 3:8, God considered it robbery.

The meaning of the word "consecrated" in the above quotation is "set apart." It is applied to the seventh day—"God blessed the seventh day, and *sanctified* it" (Genesis 2:3); it is applied to the first-born of Israel whom God chose for Himself—"All the first-born are mine: for on the day that I smote all the first-born in the land of Egypt, I *hallowed* unto me all the first-born in Israel" (Numbers 3:13). The same expression is used in reference to the consecration of Aaron and his sons—"Thou shalt take of the blood that is upon the altar, and of the anointing oil, and sprinkle it upon Aaron, and upon his garments, and upon his sons, and upon the garments of his sons with him and he shall be hallowed, and his garments, and his sons, and his sons' garments with him" (Exodus 29:21); and in reference to the cities of refuge which were set apart for the man-slayer mentioned in Joshua 20:7: "They *appointed* Kadesh," etc. The term is similarly applied to the action of David in 2 Samuel 8:11, when he *dedicated* the spoils he had taken in battle, and the gifts sent by foreign potentates, to the Lord.

Second, "Mah-lah." This word is used again and again in connection with the consecration of Aaron and his sons (Exodus 29:9). It means *"to fill."* It is frequently rendered "full." The Psalmist uses the word in speaking of God's providential gifts, as "The earth is *full* of the goodness of the Lord" (Psalm 33:5), of the riches of God (Psalm 104:24), and of the mercy of God (Psalm 119:64). The marginal reading in connection with this word, "Fill the hand," is given in Exodus 29:9; 32:29.

Third, "Nazar." Here we are reminded of the consecration of the Nazarite in Numbers 6, where the word occurs again and again. The same word is applied to the *"crown"* (Exodus 39:30), which was upon the mitre of the High Priest, denoting "separation" and "holiness." Now, taking these three words and their meanings in the light of the New Testament, we get a threefold meaning of Consecration, namely; *Separation, Dedication, Appropriation.*

Separation to God

Our natural condition is separation *from* God. The prophet's description of Israel is true of us all—"Your sins have separated you from me, and your iniquities have caused me to hide my face from you." The Lord Jesus was separated for the work of redemption, as in Israel's early history the paschal lamb was separated to be slain. On the Cross, Christ was separated from God, when He cried in the anguish of His spirit, "My God! My God! why hast Thou forsaken Me?" Christ endured this separation from God that we might be united to God. The believer's separation to God presupposes at least three things— 1) Reconciliation; 2) Redemption; 3) Occupation.

Reconciliation. In speaking of the sufferings of Christ and their purpose, the apostle Peter says, "For Christ also hath once suffered for sins, the Just for the unjust, that He might bring us *to God*" (1 Peter 3:18). Observe, he does not say here that Christ died to save us from hell to heaven, but to bring us *to God*. When the prodigal returned, it was to be reconciled to his father—not merely to escape the swine-troughs that he might enjoy the bounties of his father's table, but to receive the father's smile, feel the father's kiss, hear the father's words of welcome, and enjoy the father's company. Even so, the purpose of Christ's death was to remove the barrier which kept God from the sinner, and the sinner from God. It was also to reconcile the sinner *to* God. Rotherham's translation of 1 Peter 3:18, is, "That He might *introduce* us to God." Happy introduction, beginning the eternal friendship between God and the sinner!

Redemption. Redemption is a higher step than reconciliation. The word "redemption" is a compound word, one part meaning to "buy back" and the other to "set at liberty." The prodigal might have been reconciled to his father, and yet not have been free. For instance, if his prayer to be made a "hired servant" had been granted, he would have been reconciled to his father, but would not have enjoyed the same privileges and freedom as before. Now, the Lord, in His grace, has been pleased not only to bring us near to Himself, but to set us at liberty by virtue of the finished work of His beloved Son. Hence, the song which each believer takes up now and which will occupy the Church of Christ in the coming ages is, "Thou hast redeemed us *to God* by thy blood" (Revelation 5:9).

Occupation. Mentioning his service for the Lord, the apostle Paul introduces himself to the Romans as a "servant of Jesus Christ, called to be an apostle, separated unto the Gospel of God" (Romans 1:1). The very first cry of Paul when the Lord met him was, "Lord, what wilt *Thou* have me to do?" And the call from God Paul recognized as a call *to* God, for Him to use His servant for His glory. As one separated unto the gospel of God, he received his instructions from God. Paul had fellowship with God, such as Enoch in his day enjoyed, and he was used by Him to His praise.

We need to emphasize the words "*to God,*" because there have been those who have been separated from men, but have not been separated to God. Men have been separated to monasteries from their fellow-men; but how few have been separated to God in this self-imposed seclusion!

Again and again we find Paul referring to the fact that the believer is brought to God, and that he is to do everything as to God alone. In speaking of the conversion of the Thessalonians, in his letter to them, Paul refers to the fact in the following words:—"You *turned to God* from idols" (1 Thessalonians 1:9); in declaring the purpose of God in sending him with the gospel to the Gentiles, when before Agrippa, Paul said it was "To turn them from darkness to light, and from the power of Satan *unto God*" (Acts 26:18). Because of our association with Christ in His death—for God reckons all that Christ did as done by us, because He did it on our account—we are to reckon ourselves "dead indeed unto sin, but alive *unto God* through Jesus Christ our Lord" (Romans 6:11). Paul also says we are to yield ourselves *unto God*" (Romans 6:13; 12:1); and to "bring forth fruit *unto God*" (Romans 7:4).

We have heard an Eastern parable which illustrates what we mean. One day a sheik met a woman carrying in her one hand a basin of water, while the other held a torch. He eagerly inquired what she meant to do with each.

The woman replied, "I am going to put out the flames of hell with the water and burn up the glories of heaven with the torch."

"Why are you going to do this?" asked the sheik.

Her reply was, "That men may love God for what He is in Himself, and not for what they escape or receive."

That is it. We are separated to God to serve Him, to love Him, to follow Him, and to obey Him. It is sadly true that too many Christians sigh for the blessings of the Lord, and never long for Himself. Like Jacob, they will serve God for what they can get. "Only bless me and I will serve Thee," is their language to God.

What we want is the spirit of Mary—"They have taken away *my Lord.*" Oh! it was her Master she wanted. Hers was the truly blessed life, because she found her all in Him. Let us, realizing our separation to the Lord, leave behind all worldliness, and, like Israel, come clean out of Egypt. Let us walk in hallowed communion with Him as Adam did before he sinned. Separated to do His bidding, as Moses was, when he did all that the Lord commanded him in connection with the Tabernacle, and separated to Him, we shall experience Elijah's courage to confront our Ahabs, while we are, like Elijah, conscious of the Lord's presence. Separated to Him to take Mary's place, we shall be spared the friction of Martha's service. Fret and worry will give place to calmness. Separated to Him, we shall be ready to do His will and work, even as Christ did.

Dedication to the Lord

As David dedicated to the Lord what he possessed (2 Samuel 8:11), so should the believer hold all he has at the disposal of the Lord for His use and glory. It is an easy matter to sing, "My all is on the altar," and quite as easy to speak of consecration; but mere talk will not tell, sentiment is not sufficient, profession will not prevail. There must be the manifestation of the consecration in practical godliness, self-denial, and reflection of the spirit and ways of Christ.

A threefold cord is not easily broken, so true consecration must be *definite*, *continuous*, and *entire*. Let us briefly note these three characteristics of consecration, as illustrating this point of dedication.

Consecration must be definite. When a man took upon himself the vow of the Nazarite, he had to be very definite. He had to abstain from strong drink, to keep away from dead bodies, and to let his hair grow long (Numbers 6:3-8). As the Nazarite abstained from all that had to do with the vine, so there must be with us the separation from all that would tend to excite nature and add fuel to the fire of passion. As the Nazarite was to keep away from dead bodies, so must we keep away from all those who are dead in trespasses and sins; in a word, from the world and all that is in it—the lust of the flesh, the lust of the eyes, and the pride of life. Remember the word of the Lord on this—"Awake, O sleeper, and arise from the dead" (Ephesians 5:14 RSV); and again, "Come out from among them, and be ye separate, and touch not the unclean thing" (2 Corinthians 6:17). The Nazarite was to let his hair grow long as a sign of his being under the authority of God. Paul reminds the Corinthians that long hair is a sign of subjection (1 Corinthians 11:10-15), so are we to be under the control of Him whom we call *Lord*. Let us understand what definite dedication means. The whole being is open to the sunshine of God's presence; the whole nature is under the sway of Christ; and spirit, soul, and body are to be under the control of the Holy Spirit. Let us count the cost, as definite dedication claims from us:

The *mortification* of the old nature (Colossians 3:5; Romans 8:12, 13).
The *expulsion* of all evil habits (Colossians 3:9; Galatians 5:24).
The *denial of self* (Luke 9:23, 24).
The *enthronement* of Christ in the heart (Ephesians 3:17; 1 Peter 3:15, RSV)
Satisfaction in Christ alone (Matthew 11:29; Psalm 73:25).
Delighting to do God's will (1 Thessalonians 5:18; Psalm 40:8).
Aiming always for God's glory (1 Corinthians 10:31).

This brings us to another important consideration, namely, *Consecration, in order to have lasting results, must be continuous*.

A boy was once asked if his father were a Christian, and he replied, "I think he was once; but he has not been working at it lately." The boy's answer may describe too many professors, who live an up-and-down life, because they do not maintain their attitude towards God as His consecrated ones; for bear in mind, consecration is an attitude maintained, as well as an act done once for all. As I remember a good Irish brother aptly put it, "Consecration is an act once for all, and repeated forever afterwards."

Last of all, *consecration must be entire*. There must be no withholding part of the price (Acts 5:3). The Lord will not be satisfied, even though you present the greater part. He will have all or none. How many there are whose lives might be summed up, after the manner of the announcement placed in the window of an ironmonger's shop, "The bulk of our stock is of English manufacture." Yes. The *bulk*, but not all. The Lord wants all. He claims all. Let Him have all: then your life and being shall be to His glory. You will be like a well-tuned instrument, upon which the Lord will play to His praise. As a good Yorkshire Christian often said: "I am an instrument of ten strings; two eyes to look to Him; two ears to listen to His voice; two hands to work for Him; two feet to run on His errands; a tongue to speak His praise; and a heart to love Him alone."

Appropriation of Christ

God, in His grace, has treasured up in Christ all His fulness, that we may appropriate it, or better, that we may find Christ to meet our every need, and answer to all our deep spiritual necessities in life and service. This is what Paul desired, aimed at, and eagerly sought for. In Philippians 3:8-12 His aspirations are expressed thus: "That I may *win* Christ"; "That I may *know* Him"; "That I may *apprehend* that for which also I am apprehended of Christ Jesus." His desire was threefold.

1. *Winning Christ*. The apostle is not here speaking of salvation, or of possessing Christ. His testimony on this point is calm and clear. Listen to what he says in acknowledging Christ's ownership of him: "Whose I am, and whom I serve" (Acts 27:23). But he is here expressing his determination to see what are the riches which are in Christ for him. An everyday occurrence may help to explain the term "winning." It is a common expression for miners, when they commence working a new coal pit, to speak of "winning the coal." They do not mean to win the right to the mine—that belongs to the proprietor; but they mean to get that which already belongs to him. In like manner, "winning Christ" means that we seek to discover the fulness of grace and power that there is in Christ, and how He meets all our need for walk, warfare, and work.

2. *Knowing Christ*. Again, when the apostle aspires to "know Christ," he does not mean that he does not already know Him. "I know whom I have believed" (2 Timothy 1:12). This is the certainty of faith; doubt as to this would have produced no such ringing witness; but he is here aspiring to know Christ in a practical sense, for he believes that to know Christ is to trust Him; as the psalmist says: "They that know thy name will put their trust in thee" (Psalm 9:10). The more we know Christ, the more we will trust Him. To know Christ is not only to trust Him, but to love and to obey Him.

When St. Columbanus ventured to suppress the ardent thirst for knowledge in his aspirant Lucinus, reminding him that undue love of knowledge had shipwrecked some souls, his disciple humbly remonstrated, "My father, if I learn to know God, I shall never offend Him, for they only offend Him who know Him not."

Let us take to heart the Lord's remonstrance with Israel: "The ox knows his master, the donkey his owner's manger, but Israel does not know, my people do not understand" (Isaiah 1:3 NIV). To know Christ as Savior is to be saved by Him from sinning. To know Christ as Sovereign is to be ruled by Him. To know Christ as Sanctifier is to let Him manifest His own life through us. To know Christ as Satisfier is to delight only in Him. To know Christ as the One who died for us is to die to sin with Him. To know Christ in His resurrection power is to live to God by Him. To know Christ as Cross-Bearer is to take up our cross daily and to follow Him. Oh, to know *Him* in the truest and fullest sense of the word!

3. *Apprehending Christ*. Among the things that were put into the hands of Aaron at his consecration were the breast and shoulder of the ram of consecration (Exodus 28). The shoulder in Scripture is associated with strength, and the breast with affection. Connecting these two thoughts and Paul's desire to apprehend (understand or grasp) Christ, may we not say that he longed to apprehend Christ in the fullness of His love, and in the energy of His power? He himself expressed this when writing to the Ephesians, and praying for them for he uses the same word as he does to the Philippians: "May be able to comprehend (apprehend) with all saints, what is the breadth, and length, and depth, and height" (Ephesians 3:18, 19)—of what? "The love of Christ," says one. Yes, more—Christ Himself: the breadth of His purpose, the length of His love, the depth of His sufferings, and the height of His power. Why has Christ in His love apprehended us? That we may apprehend Him in His love. Why has He by His power quickened us together with Himself? That we may lay hold of His power (Ephesians 1:19 to 2:1). Why has He in His gracious purpose laid hold of us as we were posting on to perdition? That we may grasp His purpose and enter into His secret, and be initiated into His plan, so that we may let all go that is not for His glory, and find our delight and pleasure in Himself. This we assuredly shall do as we apprehend *Him*.

8

The Discipler's Power

The Holy Spirit works in us in a threefold way. He works *upon* us as *sinners;* He works *in* us as *saints;* and He works *through* us as *servants.*

He works upon us as sinners. The prophet Ezekiel offers an illustration of our state when dead in trespasses and sins. It is seen in the vision of the valley of dry bones (Ezekiel 37). As the breath of God came *upon* them, and caused the dry bones to live, so the Spirit of God has come upon us, and quickened us from the death of sin, so that we are now alive unto God, by His power, through Jesus Christ.

He works in us as saints. We read of the Spirit controlling and guiding the "living creatures" in the Book of Ezekiel:—"They went every one straight forward: whither the Spirit was to go, they went . . . Whithersoever the spirit was to go, they went, thither was their spirit to go" (Ezekiel 1:12, 20). Whither the Spirit went, they went. When the Spirit went forward, they went forward. And as the Spirit in the living creatures influenced and controlled them, so He is to influence us. We are saintly in life, upright in conduct, pure in heart, meet for use, as we are under the Spirit's leading. For we work out our salvation, as we let Him work in us to will and to do of His good pleasure. And we are complete, that is, we answer to the end for which we were saved, as we are responsive to the Spirit's working. So the apostle Paul says, in speaking of his ministry, and of himself personally: "We preach, warning every man, and teaching every man in all wisdom; that we may present every man perfect in Christ Jesus: whereunto I also labor, striving according to His working, which worketh in me mightily," or "in power" (Colossians 1:28, 29).

The Holy Spirit works through us as servants. Let us refer again to the living creatures mentioned in Ezekiel. In them we have an illustration of God's working through us, as we let Him work in us. We read, "The spirit of the living creatures was in the wheels. When those went, these went, and when those stood, these stood and when those were lifted up from the earth, the wheels were lifted up over against them: for the Spirit of the living creature was in the wheels" (Ezekiel 1:20, 21). As the Spirit influenced and moved the living creatures, so the living creatures in turn operated upon and regulated the wheels. In like manner, as we know in our lives the power and operation of the Spirit of God, He will use us in moving others.

These three stages in the Spirit's working are further illustrated in the Gospel according to John.

In chapter 3, we have the *Begetting of the Spirit, implanting the new life of salvation, through faith in Christ*, expressed in these words—"born of the Spirit." As the Spirit moved upon the face of the waters, and brought order out of disorder, so has the Spirit brooded over us, convicted us of sin, brought us to Christ, and implanted in us a new nature.

In chapters 14 and 16, we have the *Bestowal and Indwelling of the Spirit, impregnating the being in sanctification, by abiding in Christ*. As Moses was not able to enter the Tabernacle because of the glory of the Lord filling it, so self shall not enter our life as we abide in Christ.

In chapters 1 and 7 of the same Gospel, we have these words, "He shall baptize you with the Holy Ghost"; "Out of Him" (Christ) "shall flow rivers of living water. This spake He of the Spirit." There we have the *Baptism of the Spirit influencing, impressing, and inflaming the worker in service, by receiving from Christ*. As the waters that came from the sanctuary, mentioned in Ezekiel 47, brought life and gladness wherever they went, so shall it be with us, as we are receiving from Christ, for the Spirit shall flow through us to others.

Now, as the Holy Spirit was needed to "quicken us together *with* Christ," and as we need the Spirit to operate in us to produce likeness *to* Christ, so we need the fullness of the Spirit to be *used by* Christ.

The truth about the Holy Spirit has been called the "Lost Gospel." Neglect of the subject has entailed upon the Church of God a great loss. Perhaps the answer that a woman in the north of Scotland is said to have given to her minister when he was catechizing her might be given by some today.

"How many Persons are there in the Godhead?" he asked.

To the astonishment of all present she replied, "There are two Persons in the Godhead, the Father and the Son."

Again the minister put the question, and this time with a caution. The woman was known for her love and zeal in Christian work: so when she gave the same answer the second time, the minister turned to his elders, and the others present. In a pompous manner, he said, "You see what comes of high-flown zeal and hypocrisy. This woman seeks to teach others, and is herself more ignorant than a child. What gross ignorance! Woman! don't you know that the correct answer is, 'There are three Persons in the Godhead, the Father, the Son, and the Holy Ghost?'"

"Sir," replied the woman, "I ken verra weel that the Catechism says sae. But whether am I to believe, the Catechism or yersel'? We hear you mention the Father; an' sometimes, but nae often, ye mak' mention o' the Son in yer preachin'; but wha ever heard you speak aboot the Holy Ghost? 'Deed, sir, ye never sae muckle as tauld us whether there be ony Holy Ghost, lat alane oor need o' His grace."

Somehow the notion has gone abroad that because the Holy Spirit does not speak *from* Himself ("*from Himself*" is the correct reading of John 16:13, as brought out in the Jerusalem Bible), therefore He does not speak *of* Himself.

This is most erroneous, for right through the Word He speaks of Himself as the Executor of the Father's plans, and the Unfolder of the Person of Christ. In creation, in providence, and in redemption, He speaks of Himself in the Word which He has inspired, as the Active Agent of the Godhead.

We need the baptism, the filling, the anointing of the Spirit to rest upon us, and to work through us as a definite and continuous experience as the servants of God. Martin Luther, Richard Baxter, Jonathan Edwards, Charles Finney, Robert Haldane, and others like them, sought, received, and were carried on in their life and service by the power of the Holy Spirit.

"The Spirit of the Lord is upon me," said Christ, in speaking of Himself as the Servant of Jehovah. So also in the Acts of the Apostles, the servants of Christ are spoken of as being "full of the Holy Spirit."

It is as *Servants of Christ* that we now invite your attention to a few of the marks of the servant, who is filled with the Holy Spirit. It may lead some who have not yet received this definite baptism, or filling, of the Spirit, to seek it from the Lord, while those who have known something of the filling of the Spirit may be reminded that it is as we remain in the right attitude of soul, as we continue to fulfill the conditions which He has laid down, that His power will continue to rest upon us, and work through us, to the glory of His name.

One who is filled with the Holy Spirit is full of faith to convict the sinner of his sin of unbelief.

Have we not the Lord's own word for it? "When he is come he will reprove the world of sin, of righteousness, and of judgment: of sin, because they believe not on me." Are we to understand this as the work of the Spirit apart from the believer? I think not; but it is rather the Spirit of God working through the believer. Remember that these form part of those precious words of Christ when assuring His disciples that the Spirit would be with them and dwell in them.

In reference to this passage Bowen says, "What is here promised is such an outpouring of the Holy Spirit as shall not only reveal itself in the consciousness of believers, but substantiate itself as an undeniable and wonderful fact to the onlooking world. Is not the great thing wanted, this, that the Spirit of God should be so poured out on Christ's people, that men should be made aware of His presence with them, and of His presence at the right hand of God?"

We read that Stephen and Barnabas were "full of faith." They were full of faith because they were full of the Spirit. They were full of the Spirit because they were full of faith. Unless we have a simple and strong faith in God ourselves, we cannot expect to convince others; but if, on the other hand, we are allowing the Holy Spirit to work through us, we will be full of faith, and thus His influence through us will be felt. As life gives brightness to the eye, spring to the step, and vigor to the whole body, so the Holy Spirit filling us will give us vigor of spirit, earnestness of manner, boldness of utterance, and spiritual perception.

One who is filled with the Spirit will be full of the truth in testimony.

I "am full of words and the spirit within me compels me" (Job 32:18 NIV). So said Elihu to Job. As Elihu was full of words by the Spirit within him, so shall we be if filled with the Spirit, for the Spirit of God is the Spirit of Truth. The Spirit comes to us through the truth. As the cistern is supplied with water from the reservoir, by the pipes connecting the two, so the Spirit comes to fill us through the truth.

Many preachers might be called *spider-preachers*, for, as the spider spins the web out of its own body, so they delight to amuse their audiences with ideas, conceived in their own brains. A popular method just now is to spend Lord's Day evenings in lecturing on social subjects, and on every conceivable subject but THE SUBJECT.

These are not the lines on which the Holy Spirit works. What was the subject-matter of the apostles' preaching? It was the truth. Right through the Acts of the Apostles, there is one word that we find repeated again and again. It runs through the book like the distinguishing piece of cord that runs through the ropes which come out of His Majesty's different dockyards. It is the word "Word." On the day of Pentecost, those who gladly received the *Word* were baptized; when Peter spoke after the lame man had been healed, many who heard the *Word* believed; after the disciples had been threatened by the council, and forbidden to speak in the name of Jesus, they besought the Lord "that with all boldness they might preach the *Word*," and the Lord answered their prayer, for "they spake the *Word* of God with boldness."

The seven deacons were chosen, that the Apostles might give themselves continually to prayer, and "the ministry of the *Word*"; when the great persecution arose, "the disciples went everywhere preaching the *Word*"; when the apostles heard that the Samaritans had "received the *Word* of God," they determined to send Peter and John to them; and of their visit we read, "They testified and preached the *Word* of the Lord."

When Philip found the eunuch reading from the prophecy of Isaiah, "he began at the same *Scripture*, and preached unto him Jesus"; when Peter was preaching in the house of Cornelius, while they heard the *Word*, the Holy Spirit fell upon them; "the apostles and brethren that were in Judæa heard that the Gentiles had also received the *Word* of God."

Of Paul and Barnabas, when at Salamis, we read: "They preached the *Word* of God"; when Paul was preaching at Antioch we find him saying to the Jews, "To you is the *Word* of this salvation sent." The next Sabbath Day, almost the whole city came together to hear the *Word* of God. At Iconium, Paul and Barnabas gave testimony unto the *Word* of His grace; at Perga, they "preached the *Word*."

Peter, in speaking of his mission before the Apostles and elders at Jerusalem, when the matter of circumcision in relation to the Gentiles was under consideration, says: "Men and brethren, ye know how that, a good while ago, God made choice among us, that the Gentiles by my mouth should hear the *Word* of the gospel and believe" (Acts 15:7). In Paul's second great missionary journey, he and Barnabas continued in Antioch, "teaching and preaching the *Word* of the Lord"; and in referring to the places already visited by the apostles, "Paul said unto Barnabas, Let us go again, and visit our brethren in every city where we have preached the *Word* of the Lord." The Holy Spirit forbade them to preach the *Word* in Asia; they spoke the *Word* of the Lord to the jailer and his household; of the Berean Jews we read, "They received the *Word* with all readiness of mind"; Paul remained at Corinth "a year and six months, teaching the *Word* of God among them"; of his ministry in the neighborhood of Ephesus, we are told, "This continued by the space of two years so that all they which dwelt in Asia heard the *Word* of the Lord Jesus"; and Paul's parting commendation to the elders was: "And now, brethren, I commend you to God, and to the *Word* of His grace, which is able to build you up, and to give you an inheritance among them which are sanctified."

Such was the teaching of the apostles—*the Word!* Let us be full of the same subject and the results that followed their labors will follow ours. Let us use the Word of God in its naked simplicity, in its convincing might, in its arousing energy, in its enlightening power, in its rugged strength, in its comforting grace, in its assuring knowledge, in its peaceful joy, in its Christ-honoring theme, in its God-glorifying teaching, and in its Spirit-giving utterance.

This is the weapon we *shall* wield if we are filled with the Spirit, for one mark of being filled with the Spirit is a capacity to understand the truth, and an apprehension of the mind of the Lord, and this with increased longings to learn more. The Bible will be a new book to us, and as we grow daily more willing to be emptied of our own ideas, the Lord will replace them by His own teaching, and unfold to us what we should never have understood with ever so great an intellect.

Of a certain preacher it was said that his preaching had two faults: first, he was *too straight*, and second, he was *too Scriptural*. Would that no greater censure were ever merited by us as Christian workers.

One who is filled with the Holy Spirit is full of life.

Psalm 106:16 says, "The trees of the Lord are full of sap"—full of life. We will be full of life as we are continually in touch with Him who is the Spirit of Life, by abiding in Christ. It is not for us to waste time in vain regrets over the past, or to bemoan our *inability* as we face the future, but it is for us *to respond to God's ability*. I always like to think of responsibility as being man's response to God's ability.

As the life in the oak enables it to spread its branches and strengthens it against the tempest, so, filled with the Spirit, we will be able to weather the tempests of trial and temptation. As the life in the fruit trees causes them to bear refreshing fruit, so, filled with the Spirit of Life, we will bring forth the fruit of the Spirit in its ninefold cluster—refreshing the heart of God and the souls of men.

As the life in the tree causes it, in the springtime, to throw off the remaining dead leaves of autumn, so, as we are filled with the Spirit of Life, evil habits will be thrown off by Him who fills our being. As the life in the flowers causes them to beautify the earth and perfume the air, so will the Spirit of Life manifest the loveliness of Christ and the odor of His presence through us. As the life in the bird enables it to soar on glad wing above the clouds, into the clear sunshine of heaven, and there sing its thrilling song, so, filled with the Spirit, we will mount above the dust and din, the clouds and commotion of earth, into the clear sunshine of the Lord's presence, to have hallowed communion with Him: and there shall we sing with glad heart and thankful spirit to Him who loves us, for it is said, "Be filled with the Spirit; speaking to yourselves in psalms and hymns and spiritual songs, singing and making melody in your heart to the Lord" (Ephesians 5:19).

As we note the boldness of Peter, the love of John, the holiness of Paul, the sufferings of Stephen, the consecration of Barnabas, the joy of the early Christians, and the activity of the women who labored in the gospel, we ask, "Are these qualities natural to them?" and our answer is, "No." These are the actions of another Person who is living within them, by the Spirit, through the truth. It is the *boldness* of Christ that is seen in Peter; it is the *love* of Christ that is seen in John; it is the *holiness* of Christ that is seen in Paul; it is the *suffering* of Christ that is seen in Stephen; it is the *consecration* of Christ that is seen in Barnabas; it is the *joy* of Christ that is seen in the early Christians; and it is the *activity* of Christ that is seen in the ministering women.

One who is filled with the Spirit is full of power.

The Roman centurion said, "I am a man under authority, having soldiers under me and I say to this man, 'Go,' and he goeth, and to another, 'Come,' and he cometh" (Luke 7:8). The reason the centurion had power to command the soldiers under him was that he was under the power of Rome. Thus, he had all its power at his back. If he failed to recognize his position and his responsibility to Rome, those under him would not recognize him. In the same way, as we are under the authority of heaven, we have authority, and we have no power, save as we recognize the power of God. The Lord will never give us power that it may be a feather in our own cap, so that people should say, "What a powerful preacher he is!" And if, when the Lord uses us, people should speak as though we had power, we should silence them by saying, as the apostle did, "Why look ye so earnestly on us, as though by our own power or holiness we have done this? . . . God . . . hath glorified His Son Jesus" (Acts 8:12). It is only as we feel our weakness, and acknowledge it, that the power of Christ will rest upon us, and then we shall bear Micah's testimony, "I am full of power by the Spirit of the Lord." Not *our* power, but *full of power* because *full of the Spirit*. In prayer one day an old German minister thus expressed it this way: "O Lord, since Thou hast *all* power, we will have *no* power." That is it. What we want is not the power of intellect, the power of argument, the power of science, or the power of philosophy, but the power of God. Then, what was said of Stephen when full of the Holy Spirit, shall be said of us, "They were not able to resist the wisdom and the Spirit by which he spake." God wants not our power, but our weakness; and as His love has been perfected in our unworthiness, so is His strength made perfect in our weakness.

Paul's might lay not in enticing words of man's wisdom but in demonstration of the Spirit and of power. Someone has said, "Many pray earnestly for power, in, and with their work, and receive it not, because they do not accept the only position in which the power can work. We want to get possession of the Power, and use it. God wants the Power to get possession of us, and use us. If we give up ourselves to the Power to rule in us, the Power will give itself to us to rule through us."

One who is filled with the Spirit is full of blessing for others.

In writing to the Romans of a visit he hoped to make, Paul says, "And I am sure that, when I come unto you, I shall come in the fulness of the blessing of the gospel of Christ" (Romans 15:29); or, more correctly, "I will come *in the full measure of the blessing of Christ*" (NIV). How is it Paul could speak so confidently? Because he recognized that the channel of blessing was Christ, who was living, dwelling, and working in him mightily by the Holy Spirit; and since he had Christ, and Christ had him, he was sure that He would communicate blessing through him to others. The secret of Paul's ministry was his recognition that he was an instrument to be used, a vessel to be filled, a channel through which blessing could flow from Christ to others.

Some time ago a friend remarked to me, "There are three ways of spelling CHRISTIAN WORKER, by simply transposing the letters:" and, though the transposition is very simple, I give it here, as it illustrates three stages of Christian experience, and leads on to the highest and most effectual way of Christian service.

CHRISTIAN WORKER. That should stand for something good, noble, and Christlike; but it does not always do so. It was a "Christian worker" who cut off the ear of the servant of the high priest, and afterwards denied his Master. It was a "Christian worker" who wanted to call down fire from heaven upon some who did not see as he did. It was a band of "Christian workers" who strove among themselves who should be the greatest, and the same "Christian workers" forsook their Master in the hour of His direst need.

Now let us transpose the letters of the two words thus:—The "a" being taken out of "Christian," and placed in front of "worker," and the "in" in front of "Christ," then we have, "A WORKER IN CHRIST." Surely this is a higher name. It speaks of one who is abiding in Christ and apprehending Him; one who is in touch with Him, and having fellowship with Him.

We next notice the highest position, and this we get by a very simple transposition indeed—"CHRIST IN A WORKER."

We remember giving this in the hearing of a little boy of eight, who seemed to grasp the idea, and on reaching home, he said, "Ma—

Christian worker is good,
A *worker in Christ* is better, but
Christ in a worker is best."

The little boy's rendering may help us to remember the three states of Christian service. It is good to be a Christian worker, but that may mean simply an agent for Christ. It is better to be a worker in Christ, for that means being in partnership with Him. It is better still for Christ to be in the worker, for this means that He has possession of us. He is working in us to will and to do of His good pleasure. If Christ is in the worker, there is no doubt that there will be blessing, and that we will be full of blessing, because full of Christ, by the Holy Spirit.

We have already referred to the fact that the apostle was full of blessing because full of Christ, as may be inferred from the three "Yet not I" expressions of Paul: "Yet not I, but the Lord" (1 Corinthians 7:10) "Yet not I, but the grace of God" (1 Corinthians 15:10) "Yet not I, but Christ liveth in me" (Galatians 2:20).

If Paul's experience is to be ours, self must be hidden out of sight, and only Christ seen. When Moses had accomplished all the will of God respecting the Tabernacle, placing everything according to the divine order, the glory of God came and filled the place. In the same way as we follow the line of God's truth, knowing its power in our own experience, and witnessing of it faithfully and fully, we will find that the path of obedience is the path of blessing. The attitude of prayer is the secret of power. Thus as our whole being is opened to the personal sway of the Spirit, there will flow from us rivers of living water, bringing life and blessing wherever we go.

One who is filled with the Holy Spirit will continually feel his need of the Spirit.

This may seem to be a paradox, but then the Christian life is made up of Paradoxes. When we are most satisfied, we are most thirsty—for the Lord's blessings, while they satisfy, create an appetite. When we are most conscious of the Lord's presence, we are most conscious of our weakness. We continually need the Holy Spirit to fit us for service. The lamps in the Tabernacle had to be trimmed and supplied with oil. The Bible says, "Command the children of Israel that they bring unto thee pure oil olive, beaten for the light, to cause the lamps to burn *continually* . . . Aaron shall order the lamps upon the pure candlestick before the Lord continually" (Leviticus 24:2, 4). So must we allow our Divine Aaron to come to us continually, with the supply of the Spirit for life and service, and to trim His "lamp" with the "snuffers" of the truth, that our life and labor may reflect Himself.

We continually need the Spirit to furnish us in service. The shew-bread was to be continually fresh, week by week—"every Sabbath Day he shall set it in order before the Lord *continually*" (Leviticus 24:8). So we must come week by week, not with the moldy bread of a past experience, but with the fresh bread made of the flour of truth. It has been ground in the mill of prayerful meditation and baked in the oven of a personal experience. It is warm with the fire of God's Spirit.

We need the Spirit to have the joy of the Lord in service. The Queen of Sheba said of the men who stood continually in the presence of Solomon, "Happy are thy men, and happy are thy servants who stand continually before thee" (2 Chronicles 9:7). Infinitely more, as we constantly recognize the presence and power of the Lord, and ever act as before Him, seeking His glory alone, shall we know what it is to have "joy and peace . . . in the Holy Spirit" (Romans 14:17).

To have fellowship with the Lord, by His Word, in service, we continually need the Holy Spirit. As Mephibosheth "did eat continually at the king's table" (2 Samuel 9:13), so must we continually partake of Christ in the Word. As Jeremiah has it, "Thy words were found, and I did eat them and thy word was unto me the joy and rejoicing of my heart" (15:16). It is only as we meditate on the Word that we are healthy in life, wealthy in experience, and helpful to others. The apostles felt this when they gave themselves to prayer and the ministry of the Word.

We continually need the Holy Spirit to inspire us to prayer in service. The

Lord Jesus felt the necessity for continuance in prayer—"He continued all night in prayer"—to be strengthened, to do the will of the Father, and to accomplish the work committed to His charge. How much we need to cry that the Lord should accomplish His own purpose in and through us! As the early Church continued in united, definite, earnest, believing prayer and supplication (Acts 2:42, 46) so we need to pray to Him for ourselves and to petition Him for others.

We continually need the Spirit for our life and service. As the mill-wheel needs continually the supply of water to keep it going, and as the body needs food to strengthen it, so we need the supply of the Spirit. In social life, in business life, in private life, and in church life, we need the supply of the Spirit. We are to pray in the Spirit, walk in the Spirit, work in the Spirit, worship in the Spirit, war in the Spirit, sow in the Spirit, praise in the Spirit, and love in the Spirit.

Filled with the Spirit, we will love the lost and long for their salvation, as did the Master. As He wept over sinners, so shall the Spirit of love, who sheds abroad the love of God in our hearts, cause us to weep.

Filled with the Spirit, we will have liberty in the Lord and be loosed from care and unbelief: for "where the Spirit of the Lord is there is liberty" (2 Corinthians 3:17).

Filled with the Spirit, we will love laboring with the Lord. His will shall be our will in life. His Word will be our weapon in conflict. His work will be our delight in service. The Spirit is the Oil of consecration and the uniting Power which enables us to have fellowship with Christ.

Filled with the Spirit, we will be lowly before the Lord, for as the Spirit is likened to dew which falls upon the ground, so He, filling us, will cause us to be filled with humility. The same mind which was in Christ will be in us.

Filled with the Spirit, there will be likeness to the Lord, for as the die on the soft wax leaves its impression, and the likeness of the seal is seen, so does the Spirit, who is the Seal, manifest Christ in the fruit which He produces.

Filled with the Spirit, we will ever be learning of the Lord. Knowing that the truths of Scripture are spiritually discerned, and only apprehended as we are under the direction of the Spirit, we will seek His instruction. This is why the disciples were delighted to ask Christ to explain His teaching.

Filled with the Spirit, we will listen to the Lord and long to see Him. In the last chapter of Revelation, Christ says, "Behold, I come quickly," and the Spirit in the Bride responds, "Come."

"Be filled with the Spirit" is the Divine and definite command of the Lord. It is not something we may choose or not: it is a command. Dare we grieve the Lord by disobedience? We *must* not, for we are not our own. We *dare* not, because it would be dishonoring Him.

This is the way one expressed himself when the command to be filled with the Spirit was brought home to him: "Yes! this is just what I want to be. The powers of the world are becoming intensely earnest, and I am feeling every day more keenly the great need of being possessed by an Almighty Spiritual Power, to enable me to witness, so that Jesus will be glorified in the salvation of men.

"For many years I have been sowing, sowing, sowing, scattering—as I supposed—bushels of precious seed, and only a solitary blade here and there, seems to be the outcome of all my labor. It ought not to have been so. Then am I only unfortunate? or am I guilty before God? Judged by my fruits, I have not been filled with the Spirit, and, as a consequence, I must have been dishonoring the Holy One. Yet I know, that, as a son of God, I have the Spirit of God dwelling in me, and my body is the temple of the Holy Spirit. But if this temple had been filled with the Holy Spirit, it would have been impossible that my past testimony should have been so fruitless.

"I believe that if I were filled with the Spirit, I should be as indifferent to self-interest as the Holy Spirit is Himself; the glorified presence of Jesus would be an abiding reality to my soul; I should be unceasingly satisfied in Him, and others would believe through my word. Then why is this not my experience, when the Spirit in all His fullness has been given me for this very purpose, that I may witness with Him of Jesus?

"I asked God again and again to fill me with the Spirit; yet I experienced no change. God commands me to be filled, and I want and ask to be filled, and yet I am not filled. What is the matter? Now, my soul, be honest before God.

"O Holy Spirit! here and now, I beseech You, show me everything that is in my heart displeasing to You, and by Your help I will cast it forth. My soul waits on You, O Lamb of God! search me . . . O what hideous forms are these rising up before me! Shall I hide my eyes from them? No. They are the revelations of the Holy Spirit. O blessed Spirit! I have been dishonoring You. I have been asking You to fill me, while at the same time I have been willingly consenting to Your enemies dwelling in Your temple. Bring them forth, that I may hew them in pieces.

"Yes, I have been proud, seeking the honor of men more than the honor of God. Yes, I have been envious, secretly sorry when others have been more successful than I. Yes, I have been worldly minded, having more pleasure in talking about preachers and churches than about the Person of Christ. Yes, I have been selfish, for I would rather speak about the good I have done, than the good others are doing. Yes, I have been uncharitable, for I have often attributed selfish motives to the actions of the benevolent.

"Yes, O my God! I acknowledge my sins before You; I am verily guilty and abhor myself in Your presence. But You have said that if we confess, You will forgive. I do confess my sins this day. O cleanse me from secret faults! O Jesus, my Redeemer, Your precious blood I claim to purge me this very hour from all these Spirit-grieving sins. And I entreat You, O my God, at any cost, to keep me ever humble at Your feet. Now, O God, I thank You that You have forgiven the iniquity of my sin, according to Your word. And now, O Holy Spirit, You who have come to fill the redeemed temple of my body, and to witness for Jesus through His temple, come now, take entire possession of me. I throw the door of my heart wide open unto You. O enter now, I surrender all to Your will. Henceforth Your mission shall be mine—to convince of sin, to witness for Jesus, to guide into truth, to keep self unseen, and to use, without wavering, the ungilded sword of God's naked Word."

9

The Discipler's Supply

The following report of certain structural alterations that had been carried out in a church building was announced in a religious periodical some time ago:

"Structural alterations have been effected in connection with the——church at——, producing many advantages, among which may be mentioned more room, more ventilation, more internal conveniences, and a much improved external appearance."

It occurred to me, in reading the above announcement, that what is said of this building in a material sense, would apply in a spiritual way to the believer in Christ. For is there not a need for "more room" in our hearts and lives for the love of God, that we may love Him and each other more? Is there not a need for "more ventilation" in our experience, that the pure air of the Spirit of God may make and keep us fresh? Is there not a need for "more light" from the holy lamp of God's truth, on every question that relates to the different spheres in which we move? Is it not true that we all want "more internal conveniences," or capacity for the development of Christ within us, that He may be "fully formed," and work unhindered through us? And if these wants were supplied, would there not be a "much improved external appearance" in our manner of life? As the hands of the watch indicate the working of the machinery within, so if our inner life is right, it must tell its own story in our walk without.

We cannot shut our eyes to the fact that the Church of God is not making the progress it should, in holy living and in zealous working. In a circular calling a Northfield Convention D. L. Moody wrote: "There are in the churches, stores of unconsecrated wealth, unused or misused talents, multitudes at ease in Zion, witnesses who bear no testimony for their Lord, workers without the Spirit's conquering power, teachers who speak without authority, disciples who follow afar off, forms without life, church machinery substituted for inward life and power."

What is the remedy for all this? Churches are made up of people. Thus we can seek to be individually right; and the way to accomplish this, is to see what grace has done for us; what the Lord is willing to do for, in, and with us; and to follow the directions of His Word. To this end, let us ponder the "MUCH MORES" of the Epistles, and seek to know the power of them by the Holy Spirit, so that our experience will have a new power in it, in that our spiritual life will be deepened, and thus our usefulness extended.

The Much More of Salvation

"*Much more* then, being now justified by his blood, we shall be saved from the wrath *[of God]* through him. For if, while we were enemies, we were reconciled to God through the death of his Son, *much more*, being reconciled, we shall be saved in His life" (Romans 5:9, 10, R.V., margin). There are two "much mores" in these verses. The first argues from the greater to the lesser, and the second, from the lesser to the greater. Being justified by the blood of Christ, thus freed from every charge brought against us, and accounted as righteous in the Righteous One, we need not fear that we shall be overtaken by the wrath of God. And not only so, but "if, while we were enemies, we were reconciled to God, *much more*, being reconciled, we shall be saved by His life"; that is, we are not only brought to God, but we are united to a living Savior, and energized in His life. As Dr. Brown says, "If that part of the Savior's work which cost Him His blood, and which had to be wrought for persons incapable of the least sympathy, either with His love or His labors on their behalf—even our 'justification,' our 'reconciliation,' is already completed; how much more will He do all that remains to be done, since He has it to do, not by death-agonies any more, but in untroubled life?"

I well remember being in the office of an orphan home when a poor, dirty child was brought in for admission. After the necessary inquiries were made, and the child had been given over to the friend of the waifs, Mr. Quarrier, the director, ordered him to be the next washed, clothed, and duly placed in the commodious and comfortable home. But what a contrast and a change from the old associations for the lad! If he had been interviewed after he had been in the home some time, and the interviewer had asked "Do you fear, my boy, that Mr. Quarrier will cease to care for you?" I think he would have replied, "I am sure that since Mr. Quarrier took me when I was filthy and needy, and made me what I am, he will continue to care for me." In like manner the believer can argue, "Since the Lord has reconciled me to Himself, justified me from every charge, and made me His own, therefore I am sure now, as He ever lives, and is unchanging, that He will keep me for Himself to the end."

Let us who are united to the Living Savior, evidence our union with Him, by being saved by His life, or, as the margin of the Revised Version gives it, "saved *in* His life." Let the knowledge of the preserving power of His life be made a practical power in our walk, and then we shall be saved from barrenness, even as the branch of the vine is saved from fruitlessness, because of its union with the vine.

The Much More of Supply

"For if by one man's offence death reigned by one; *much more* they which receive abundance of grace, and of the gift of righteousness, shall reign in life by One, Jesus Christ. . . . Moreover, the law entered, that the offence might abound. But where sin abounded, grace did *much more* abound" (Romans 5:17,

20, emphasis added). "For if the ministration of condemnation be glory, *much more* doth the ministration of righteousness exceed in glory . . . For if that which is done away was glorious, *much more* that which remaineth is glorious" (2 Corinthians 3:9, 11, emphasis added).

The one thought that predominates and permeates the above Scriptures is the excellent surpassing glory of the Gospel, whether it be in contrast to Adam's transgression, or the glory that was given by Moses. The glory of the law pales before the glory of the gospel, even as the stars fade away in the light of the sun. Whether it be our need as sinners, as saints, or as servants, there is abundant and sufficient supply in the grace of God. The light that streams from the sun is an illustration of the abundance of God's grace.

Sir Robert S. Ball, in his admirable book on *The Story of the Heavens*, in speaking of the superabundance of the light and heat that streams from the sun, says: "In all directions the sun pours forth, with the most prodigal liberality, its torrents of light and heat. The greater part of that light and heat seems quite wasted in the depths of space. Our earth intercepts only the merest fraction, less than the 2,000,000,000th part of the whole. Our fellow-planets and the moon also intercept a trifle; but what portion of the mighty flood can they utilize? The sip that a swallow takes from the river, is as far from exhausting the water in the river, as are the planets from using all the heat that streams from the sun." In the following abundant things, we have illustrated what the Lord says He will abundantly do for those who believe and abide in Christ.

Abundant grace.—"God is able to make all grace *abound* toward you" (2 Corinthians 9:8). As the prodigal confessed that the hired servants had bread enough and to spare, so there is more than sufficient in the grace of God to meet our need.

Abundant life.—"I am come that they might have life, and that they might have it more *abundantly*" (John 10:10). The abundant life of Christ is a vehement flame which burns up every sinful thing. The word rendered "more abundantly" is translated "vehemently" in Mark 14:31.

Abundant hope.—"*Abound* in hope, in the power of the Holy Spirit" (Romans 15:13 RSV) As the spring increasingly abounds in its supply of water, as the rain descends, so the believer is filled to overflowing, as the Lord ministers His grace.

Abundant love.—"I pray, that your love may *abound* yet more and more" (Philippians 1:9). As the battery charged with electricity communicates its power as it is applied, so if the love of God constrains us it leads us in holy devotion to Him, and in beneficent service to others.

Abundant glorying.—"That your glorying may *abound* in Christ Jesus in me through my presence with you again" (Philippians 1:26, R.V.) The glorying spoken of refers to the increased boasting in Christ there would be with the presence of Paul. All mercies should increase our boasting in Christ.

Abundant work.—"*Abounding* in the work of the Lord" (1 Corinthians 15:58). The work of the Lord is work received *from* the Lord, work done *in* the Lord, and work done *to* the Lord. To abound in such work is to work *as* the Lord, of whom it is said that He was "wearied" (John 4:6).

Abundant suffering and consolation.—"As the sufferings of Christ *abound* in us, so our consolation also *aboundeth* by Christ" (2 Corinthians 1:5). Mark the "as" and "so." The *as* of suffering makes us appreciate the *so* of sympathy. In the dark cloud of pain, there is the silver lining of Christ's presence.

Abundant prayer and an abundant answer.—"Praying exceedingly" (1 Thessalonians 3:10). "Able to do exceeding *abundantly* above all that we ask or think" (Ephesians 3:20). Dr. Pierson says upon the latter passage: "There is a word in the Greek which means *abundance;* add a participle, and it means *over-abundance;* add another, and it means the *excess of the superfluity of abundance,* and that is the word here." With such riches in Christ for us, how rich we should be in experience! There is no lack on the part of God. May there be no want of faith on ours.

It is said of two women who were going to a free soup kitchen that one took a comparatively small jug, and the other took a large container. These two women met on their way to the kitchen, when the woman with the small pitcher said, "You don't expect to get that jug filled, do you?"

"I mean to try," said the other woman, "for we were told to bring a jug, but the size was not stated."

When the women got to their destination, they both had their jugs filled.

"Well," said the woman with the small pitcher, "if I had known it, I would have brought a big one, too."

"Ah," said the other, "you have now to suffer for your unbelief."

How often do we lack because of our unbelief! "Shall not want any good," is the divine promise to the upright walker. Let us not limit the Lord, for all things are possible with Him, and to those who believe.

The Much More of Sanctification

"Wherefore, my beloved, as ye have always obeyed, not as in my presence only, but now *much more* in my absence, work out your own salvation with fear and trembling" (Philippians 2:12). While the apostle was at Philippi, he had looked after the saints, as a nurse cares for the children under her charge, and they had made progress in their spiritual life. Now that he is separated from them he urges them to be even more devoted in their obedience to Christ than when he was with them. In this "working out" of salvation one phase of sanctification is thus signified. There are two things implied in this exhortation, and these are: *first,* that we have the salvation to "work out." *Second,* that there is not anything between us and the Lord, so that He can work unhindered through us. For we can only work out as He works within, even as the engine can only do its work by the power of the fuel within it.

There is one Scripture which always seems to illustrate in a very practical and simple way, how we may work out our salvation. In 2 Peter 1:5-8, we are told by the Holy Spirit: "In your faith supply virtue; and in your virtue knowledge; and in your knowledge self-control (margin); and in your self-control patience; and in your patience godliness; and in your godliness love of the brethren; and in your love of the brethren love" (R.V.) I thought at one time that it meant here we were to add to our faith the different graces mentioned, as the bricks in a building are added, the one on the top of the other; but this implies that perhaps some one or more of the graces are lacking, if one is in the act of adding grace to grace. That is not what the Lord intended. He means that there shall not be lacking any one of the graces mentioned, even as the good baker sees that no ingredient is missing in the making of the cake. After supplying the flour, the baker supplies the butter; after supplying the butter, the sugar; and after supplying the sugar, the currants; and so till everything is added. Thus each ingredient goes to make up the whole.

I remember a good sister in Christ who had not had very much experience in cake-making. She thought she would see what she could do in that line, so she duly assailed the kitchen and commenced operations. After the cake was made, she asked one of the inmates of the home how she liked it, and the reply was, "It was very nice, but the plums were playing hi'dee." I am afraid that in the lives of many Christians, there are some of the graces lacking, and if this is the case with you, my reader, remember what the Lord has said, "He that lacketh these things is blind, and cannot see afar off." Let us see to it that the Lord works in us, then we shall be quite able and willing to work out our salvation in a truly saintly manner. And then, as the hands of the clock tell and keep the time, because every part of the works is in good order, and in union with the spring (the motive power) so the Holy Spirit will work unhindered and ungrieved in us; thus our whole inner life will be in submission to Him, and it will be evidenced that we are truly the saved of the Lord.

The Much More of Service

"And we have sent with them our brother, whom we have oftentimes proved diligent in many things, but now *much more* diligent" (2 Corinthians 8:22). "And many of the brethren in the Lord, waxing confident by my bonds, are *much more* bold to speak the Word of God without fear" (Philippians 1:14).

The one thought in each of these verses is increased activity on the part of those named. The nameless brother of whom Paul speaks had been diligent in service previously, but the apostle found him much more so when he knew the state of the Church at Corinth. Similarly, when the saints saw the apostle was imprisoned, they became much more bold in proclaiming the gospel. This is as it should be. Too often, circumstances retard workers in Christian service, instead of being a stimulus to greater zeal.

In speaking of the outcome of the trials and difficulties that he had passed through in the earlier experiences of his mission work at Tanna, Dr. John G. Paton said: "Oftentimes while passing through the perils and defeats of my first years, in the mission in Tanna, I wondered why God permitted such things. But on looking back now, I already clearly perceive that the Lord was thereby preparing me for doing greater things and providing me materials wherewith to accomplish the best work of all—being the instrument under God of sending out missionaries to the New Hebrides, to claim another island, and yet another, for Jesus. That work, and all that may spring from it in time and eternity, never could have been accomplished by me, but for first the sufferings, and then the story of my Tanna enterprise."

If workers are taken away, or circumstances arise that would seem to engulf the work, let us make these a means of grace, to spur us on to more zealousness of purpose, and diligent, prayerful, dependent service. I well remember one Christian worker who had a class of young women when she was called into the mission field in North Africa. The members of the class thought the class would decrease in numbers and interest. The cousin of the worker took it up with fear and trembling, but with prayerful trust in the Lord. Consequently the class trebled in size.

It is for us to remember that the work is the Lord's, and if He buries His workers, He carries on the work, for He is the Great Worker. For that reason He can do without any one of us. Think of some of the similes which the Lord uses in reminding us of our position in the Christian service. We are *witnesses* to tell what He has done, and what He is able to do. We are *ambassadors* who are sent forth with the message of the gospel, and with instructions from the Lord Himself as to its delivery. We are the *nets* to be used by the most skillful of all Fishermen. We are the *baskets* to carry the seed of the Word, that the Divine Sower scatters. We are *vessels* that contain the treasures of the gospel, which are carried by the best of Servants. We are the *instruments* that are to be taken up by the Lord to accomplish His purpose; and we are the *arrows* that the Heavenly Marksman takes, and puts to the bow of His Word in aggressive conflict against the enemies of truth and right. May we keep our right place, and then verily we shall not only work, but be in labors more abundant.

The Much More of Suffering

"That the trial of your faith, being *much more* precious than of gold that perisheth, though it be tried with fire, might be found unto praise and honor and glory at the appearing of Jesus Christ" (1 Peter 1:7). What a contrast there is between gold and faith! There is a difference in their *source:* the gold is from the earth, faith is of heavenly origin. There is dissimilarity in their *nature:* gold is material, while faith is spiritual. There is an unlikeness in their *endurance:* gold is perishable, while faith leads to eternal results. There is a disagreement in their *use:* gold debases if loved, while the greater our love for faith, the more our spiritual life increases. There is a distinction between gold and faith in their *outcome:* the former is enslaving, while the latter is liberating. And there is dissimilitude in their *testing:* gold is tested, and being found pure, there the matter ends; but faith, when tested, the believer enduring the trial, it puts to his account "honor and praise and glory," which shall be given when Christ comes. What a comfort this should be to God's suffering saints! It may seem to some that there is no brightness or newness in the future for them. It is simply the old suffering and weariness.

My suffering friend, remember there is a ministry of *suffering* as well as of active *service*. Call to mind the gain that the three Hebrew young men received as they were cast into the fiery furnace at Babylon. They lost their bonds, and found the company of Jesus. Do not forget that the *trial* of your faith is precious, and that the branch of the vine is never so near the farmer's hand when he prunes it. Therefore, suffering saint, sing upon your bed (see Psalm 149:5):

> "Is not the way to earthly gain through earthly grief and loss?
> Rest must be won by toil and pain. The crown repays the cross.
> As woods, when shaken by the breeze, take deeper, firmer root,
> As Winter's frost but makes the trees abound in Summer fruit,

So every heaven-sent pang and throe, that Christian firmness tries.
But nerves us for our work below, and forms us for the skies."

Many a tourist has found it difficult to ascend the Great Pyramid, but there is a pyramid of blessing which God has given His tried saints, not to tire them but to comfort them. It is found in 2 Corinthians 4:17. Here it is—

"Glory."
"Weight of glory."
"Eternal weight of glory."
"Exceeding and eternal weight of glory."
"More exceeding and eternal weight of glory."
"Far more exceeding and eternal weight of glory."

Now scale that height by faith (see verse 18), and see if it is not a means of consolation to you, and if it does not cause you to sing aloud on your bed. Ponder each word in the light of the Scripture: pray over each sentence, and take the whole verse by faith. In that way make it your very own by experience.

The Much More of Synthesis

The meaning of the word *synthesis*, is simply, "a putting together"; for instance, in surgery, it means the operation by which divided parts are united. In this relation the Divine Word is, "Not forsaking the assembling of ourselves together, as the manner of some is; but exhorting *one another:* and so *much* the *more* as ye see the day approaching" (Hebrews 10:25). Does not the Church of God as a whole, and in each gathering, need to carry out the above exhortation? Do we not find that there is unhappy division in the body of Christ, and that there is a need for the several members of the mystical body of Christ to be put together? The one thing that brought sickness, death, and the loss of spiritual power to the saints at Corinth was the division among them. When he neglects to attend the assemblage of God's people is that not an indicator of the spiritual state of anyone? The neglect is generally caused by one of the following: business, pleasure, secular education, a root of bitterness, or unbelief. Whatever it is, it means disobedience to our Lord, and more than that, it is treating Him with contempt. He has said: "Where two or three are gathered together in my name, there am I in the midst of them" (Matthew 18:20). If we don't come to meet Him, where is the evidence of our respect for Him, leaving out the question of love?

Ignatius has well said: "When ye frequently and in numbers meet together, the powers of Satan are overthrown, and his mischief is neutralized by our likemindedness in the faith." And besides, our meeting together for prayer, and remembering the Lord's death, is an illustration of our being together with the Lord when He comes again.

It is significant that the word which is translated, "*assembling of ourselves together,*" only occurs in one other place, and that is, 2 Thessalonians 2:1, which speaks of "*our gathering together* unto him." The assembling of ourselves together for Christian communion is an earnest of our being gathered together to Him at His appearing. In union there is strength; continual assemblings beget and foster *love* and give opportunities for provoking to good works by exhorting one another. Let us, therefore, stir each other up, that we may be in unison in worship and work, and the more so, for the day is approaching, and the coming of the Lord draws near.

The Much More of Severity

"See to it that you do not refuse him who speaks. If they did not escape when they refused him who warned them on earth, how much less will we, if we turn away from him who warns us from heaven" (Hebrews 12:25 NIV). The bleached bones of the children of Israel in the wilderness are a testimony as to the hardening power of unbelief, and the punishment that overtook God's people in consequence. We are warned of the evil effect of a heart of unbelief. We must not think we will escape punishment if we refuse to obey our Leader. We have a far greater than Moses, even Christ. Remember the warnings that Christ gave to the seven Churches, and how each message ends with, "He that hath an ear to hear, let him hear what the Spirit saith." If we refuse to obey what the Lord says in reference to pureness of heart (1 Peter 1:22), separation from the world (2 Corinthians 6:14-18), wholeheartedness in Christian life (Philippians 1:21), clearness in testimony of the truth (Jude 3), the filling with the Holy Spirit (Ephesians 5:18), prayerful dependence upon the Lord (Philippians 4:6), and humble submission to Himself (1 Peter 3:15, R.V.), then we place ourselves under His chastening hand (1 Corinthians 11:32). What we would not learn by prayerful obedience to His Word, we have to be taught by painful suffering.

Let us rejoice in these "much mores" of our risen, living, coming Lord, and live in the power of them, by abiding in communion with Him every day of our lives. Then it will be lit up with the indwelling presence of our Lord, and others shall be drawn to Him through us.

10

The Discipler's Theme

In his *Night Thoughts*, Edward Young says—

> "Thou, my All!
> My Theme! my Inspiration! and my Crown!
> My Strength in age! my Rise in low estate!
> My soul's Ambition, Pleasure, Wealth! my World!
> My Light in darkness! and my Life in death!
> My Boast through time! Bliss through eternity!
> Eternity, too short to speak Thy praise!
> Or fathom Thy profound of love to man!"

To the poet Christ is everything; and among the many things, He is his Theme. This is essentially and absolutely so for the true preacher of the gospel as well. He ever says with the apostle, "We preach not ourselves, but Christ Jesus the Lord" (2 Corinthians 4:5). This is illustrated in Peter's address on the Day of Pentecost, the subject matter of which is the Person of Christ as revealed in the Old Testament. And as Peter found that *Christ* was the Key to unlock the Old Testament, so shall we. None other can unlock the door of revelation but Christ. He has the key, and opens, and no man shuts; and shuts, and no man opens.

The late Professor William Morehead told of how he gave his children a jigsaw puzzle map. It was no small difficulty to place the map together; and so slow was the progress they made, that they had almost despaired of success. Then one of the children discovered that the other side of the puzzle bore the figure of a man, upon which she exclaimed, "If we get the figure of the man together, we have got the puzzle." So, reversing the puzzle, they set to work to supply the perfect figure, and having accomplished this, the map was complete. Thus it is with the Word of God: if we do not see Christ, we will be in a perfect maze. Only let us trace Him by the Spirit's power, and what were difficulties and mysteries, will vanish, as mist before the sun.

Peter's sermon in Acts 2 is full of Christ. The name "Jesus" is given three times in it—"Jesus of Nazareth," "this Jesus," "that same Jesus," in verses 22, 32, and 36. Jesus is the human name of Christ: it is "music in our ears." In the expression "Jesus of Nazareth" we are reminded of His humility as well as His humanity. As the ark of the covenant was made of shittim wood, the product of earth, so was Christ made in the likeness of sinful flesh. Dyer aptly puts it, "God made one Son like to all, that He might make all sons like to One."

Let us draw near and hear God's estimate of Christ, as He speaks through the Spirit-filled Peter on the Day of Pentecost.

Christ Was the God-approved Man

"A man approved of God" (verse 22). God had formerly said of Christ, "This is my beloved Son, in whom I am well pleased." Christ, in speaking of Himself, said, "Him hath God the Father sealed." As the sacrifices were marked and examined by the priest, he pronounced them fit for sacrifice. As they were free from blemish, so Christ, being sinless and well-pleasing to God, was sealed with the Holy Spirit. The Spirit of God was seen descending on Him, and *remaining* on Him—as John the Baptist testified (John 1:33), this was the mark, that He was fit to be offered up to God as a sacrifice for sin. His fitness is further demonstrated in the emblem used to describe the Spirit. He is "like a dove" (Matthew 3:16), the emblem of meekness and purity. He finds His counterpart in Christ, and abides with satisfaction on Him. By way of contrast, when the Spirit comes upon the disciples, the emblem used is "fire," because there is that in them which needs His purifying influence (Acts 2:3). Christ was sealed because of what He was in Himself; we are sealed, because of what we are in Him (Ephesians 1:13).

Christ Was the God-used Man

"A man approved of God among you by miracles and wonders and signs, which God did by him, in the midst of you, as ye yourselves also know" (verse 22). These words, "which God did by him," reveal to us the secret of the success of the *Man* Christ Jesus, as to His life and ministry. He had power to act from Himself, as He said (John 10:18), but He did not exercise it. In that God did these miracles by Him, we have proof sufficient that He was sent by God. Nicodemus was right when he said, "No man can do these miracles that thou doest, except God be with him." The disciples, in their testimony to the unknown Stranger on their Emmaus journey, also said, "Jesus of Nazareth, which was a Prophet mighty in deed and word before God" (Luke 24:19); what He did was in, and by God, for His glory. Then we have Christ's own testimony as to the power by which His work was done—and with what authority does He speak!—"I with the finger of God cast out devils" (Luke 11:20). Scripture testimony is full of how Christ acted in the power of the Spirit; but let these fifteen facts suffice:

1. Christ was *born* of the Holy Spirit as to His human nature (Matthew 1:18).
2. The Holy Spirit was the Father's promised *gift* to Christ (Matthew 12:18).
3. Christ was *sealed* with the Holy Spirit at His baptism (Mark 1:10).
4. Christ was *full* of the Holy Spirit as to His life (Luke 4:1).
5. The Holy Spirit was the *sphere* in which Christ moved (Luke 4:14).

6. Christ was *led* by the Holy Spirit (Matthew 4:1).
7. The Holy Spirit was the *power* by which Christ exercised His ministry (Luke 4:18).
8. The Holy Spirit was the *energy* in which Christ overcame the powers of Satan (Matthew 12:28).
9. The Holy Spirit was the *secret* of Christ's joy (Luke 10:21).
10. The Holy Spirit was the *anointing* which enabled Christ to go about doing good (Acts 10:38).
11. The Holy Spirit was the *strength* which enabled Christ to offer Himself as a sacrifice to God for sin (Hebrews 9:14).
12. The Holy Spirit was the *might* by which Christ was raised from the dead (Romans 8:11).
13. The Lord Jesus was the *Bestower* of the Holy Spirit to His disciples (John 20:22).
14. The Holy Spirit was the *authority* by which Christ gave His commands (Acts 1:2).
15. The Holy Spirit was the *justifier* of Christ (1 Timothy 3:16).

These fifteen facts are embraced in Peter's words at Cæsarea— "God anointed Jesus of Nazareth with the Holy Spirit and with power: who went about doing good, and healing all that were oppressed of the devil; for God was with Him" (Acts 10:38).

Christ Was the Separated Man

"Him, being delivered by the determinate counsel and foreknowledge of God" (verse 23). True, wicked men crucified Christ; but unwittingly they were carrying out the will of God. Trapp rightly observes, "The wicked's intense hatred carries on God's decree against their wills for while they sit backward to His command, they row forward to His decree."

As the paschal lamb was set apart four days before it was slain (being taken on the tenth day of the month, Exodus 12:3, and slain on the fourteenth, Exodus 12:6), so Christ was set apart from before the foundation of the world and was manifest in these last times (1 Peter 1:20). The work of Christ was no afterthought of God, but a divinely ordained and covenanted purpose, to be accomplished at a given time, at a given place, and for a given object. Christ was separated by the Father in the decree of His covenanted purpose; and Christ willingly separated Himself for the work in whole-hearted consecration. Like Abraham and Isaac, "they went both of them together" (Genesis 22:6), in the execution of the agreed plan.

Christ Was the Crucified Man

"Ye have taken, and by wicked hands have crucified and slain" (Acts 2:23). If the Jews could have had their own way, they would have stoned Jesus as they subsequently stoned Stephen to death. But why were they not permitted to do this? For the same reason that the Holy Spirit gives in connection with the Roman soldiers being restrained by God, but permitted to pierce His side, namely, "that the Scripture might be fulfilled." Type and Scripture demanded that not a bone of Him should be broken. The paschal lamb was a type of Christ our Passover, sacrificed for us; and of it, it is said, "neither shall ye break a bone thereof" (Exodus 12:46; Numbers 9:12). Had He been stoned to death, He could never have been beheld as the pierced One, as the following Scriptures foretold He would be—Psalm 22:16; Zechariah 12:10; John 19:37; Revelation 1:7. We have seen how type was fulfilled in not a bone of Him being broken; and Scripture was likewise fulfilled in one of the many Messianic Psalms—(34:19, 20)— *"He keepeth all His bones: not one of them is broken."* This we reckon among the "all things" referred to in Christ's own words to His disciples, "All things must be fulfilled, which were written in the law of Moses, and in the prophets, and in the psalms, concerning me" (Luke 24:44). Thus, we conclude that the "Righteous One," the "Afflicted One" referred to in Psalm 34 is the Lord Himself.

The Lord Jesus was crucified, then, that "Scripture might be fulfilled" (John 14:36, 37). But in addition to this, we must regard this fact: Christ Himself had again and again said that the manner of His death would be by crucifixion (Matthew 20:19; 26:2; Luke 24:7). Therefore, His death by crucifixion is another evidence of His deity; for as He looked on into the future, He saw what was before Him.

But the apostle Paul gives the reason of reasons why Christ was crucified; and he glories in the fact of His crucifixion thus: "We preach Christ *crucified*" (1 Corinthians 1:23)—"I determined not to know anything among you, save Jesus Christ, and Him *crucified*" (1 Corinthians 2:2). Paul gloried in Christ crucified, because it was "the Power of God and the Wisdom of God" (1 Corinthians 1:24, 25). "Christ crucified" tells us of the One who has borne the curse for, "It is written, Cursed is every one that hangeth on a tree" (Galatians 3:13). "Christ crucified" proclaims that the sins of those who believe in Him have been judged in Him, so that we can say, "who his own self bare our sins in his own body on the tree" (1 Peter 2:24). Even more, God reckons we have died with Christ, as the apostle says, "I have been crucified with Christ" (Galatians 2:20, R.V.), and hence we have crucified the flesh with all its affections and lusts (Galatians 5:24).

Christ Was the Slain One

"And slain" (verse 23). The Spirit of God has been very careful not to give the enemy a single loophole through which to creep. Notwithstanding this, Satan has tried to make some of his dupes believe, or at least state, that Christ did not die, that He simply swooned, and so His resurrection was a myth. The statement that Christ was *slain* gives the lie to such a notion; and besides, we have three most emphatic witnesses to the fact of Christ's death.

First witness—The Centurion. When Joseph of Arimathea came and begged the body of Jesus from Pilate, that he might bury it, Pilate marveled that He was already dead, and sent for the centurion to see if it were so; and "he asked him whether he had been any while dead. And when he knew it of the centurion, he gave the body to Joseph" (Mark 15:44, 45). Upon the testimony of the centurion that Christ was dead, Pilate gave orders for the entombment of Christ's body.

Second Witness—The Soldiers. When the soldiers came to break the legs of

Jesus, they found He was already dead. Thus they did not treat Him as they did the two thieves, who were crucified with Him. How clear the Scripture is! Listen! "The Jews . . . besought Pilate that their legs might be broken, and that they might be taken away. Then came the soldiers, and brake the legs of the first, and of the other which was crucified with him. But when they came to Jesus, and saw that He was dead already, they brake not his legs" (John 19:31-33).

Third Witness—The spear thrust and the blood and water which came out of the side of Christ (John 19:34). The blood and water coming out of the side of Christ may be accounted for in a natural way. At least it gives clear proof of His death. Some assert that the blood and water indicate death by a broken heart. Be this as it may, we believe His act of dying was supernatural, or by His own free will. Mark well what is said: "He cried with a loud voice," etc. "He bowed his head, and gave up his spirit." Trapp significantly remarks upon this: "He bowed His head and gave up the ghost; whereas other men bow not the head till they have given up the ghost. He also cried with a loud voice, and died, which shows that He wanted not strength of nature to have lived longer, if He had listed."

What the power and outcome of the death of Christ are, no mind can grasp, no tongue can tell; but the following nine facts are directly connected with that death of deaths.

1. *The necessity of His death.* "Christ died for our sins" (1 Corinthians 15:3). Justice demanded satisfaction from the sinner. Either he must be slain, or Christ. The sinner cannot give satisfaction. And Truth must see from the necessity of its nature the Word of God carried out, for it says, "The soul that sinneth, it shall die." Holiness cannot—and it would not if it could—pass over the sins of the sinner. Hence, Christ dies for us, and by that death Justice is satisfied; Truth is upheld; Holiness met; and God glorified.

2. *The death of Christ shows His obedience to the will of God, which was the Godward purpose of His death.* "Obedient unto *death*, even the death of the cross" (Philippians 2:8). Christ said, in speaking of Himself, "I lay down my life, that I might take it again. No man taketh it from me, but I lay it down of myself. I have power to lay it down, and I have power to take it again. This commandment have I received of my Father" (John 10:17, 18). If Christ had stopped one step short of the *death* of the cross, His obedience would have been faulty, His work incomplete, and His mission fruitless as to meeting man's need, and—above all, and highest of all—bringing glory to God.

3. *The object of Christ's death in its manward aspect was for ungodly ones.* "Christ died for the ungodly" (Romans 5:6). As when the nation of Israel was in Egypt, their need was expressed in their groaning and crying. Then God sent them a deliverer, so the very sinfulness and ungodliness of the sinner cried for someone to come and bear the punishment deserved on the part of the ungodly, and the One who came and died was the Son of God.

4. *Reconciliation to God is one of the many results of the death of Christ.* "Reconciled to God by the death of His Son" (Romans 5:10)—Christ died to reconcile us to God. "God was in Christ, reconciling the world unto Himself"

(2 Corinthians 5:19). God did not go away from the sinner: it was the sinner who went away from God. And God was the first to go after the sinner to bring him back to Himself. Now those who believe in Christ are reconciled to Him. Note this: it was the *death* of Christ which was the effectual cause of the reconciliation.

5. *The death of Christ shows us the power by which Christ overcame Satan and took away the authority which he had.* "That through *death* he might destroy" (*render powerless:* the same word that is here translated "*destroy*" is in Romans 4:14 translated *made of none effect)* "him that had the power of death, that is, the devil" (Hebrews 2:14). Satan was the strong man armed who kept his goods in peace, till the Stronger than he came. Christ took away from him that in which he trusted (Luke 11:21, 22). True, Satan wounded the heel of Christ, as it was said he would four thousand years before; but while he stooped to bruise the heel of Christ, Christ dealt him such a blow on the head, that he has never recovered, and never will (Genesis 3:15). Beyond doubt Christ has fulfilled the prophecy, "He shall divide the spoil with the strong": or, more correctly, as the Septuagint and Chaldee render it, "He shall divide the spoils *of* the strong" (Isaiah 53:22, comp. R.V.). Lowth remarks, "Christ shall turn Satan out of that kingdom, which he usurped over mankind, and assert His own right to it" (see John 12:31). By His death, He has been the death of death. He has overthrown the power of hell by coming under its power; He, "hell in hell laid low, and by dying, death He slew."

6. *The possession by Christ, by those who believe in Him, is the purchase of His death.* "For whether we live, we live unto the Lord; and whether we die, we die unto the Lord: whether we live therefore, or die, *we are the Lord's. For to this end Christ both died, and rose, and revived,* that he might be Lord both of the dead and living" (Romans 14:8, 9). Since we are the property of the Lord Jesus, purchased by Him with the costly price of His own death, we are responsible to Him to live before Him, and to do as He wills. He is our Lord and Master, and we are His servants. It is not for us either to question or quibble, as to which of His commands we shall obey. The command, "*Whatsoever* he saith unto you, *do it,*" will not be irksome if we recognize we are really His.

7. *Union with Christ is the outcome of His death.* Christ's answer to the request communicated to Him, "Sir, we would see Jesus," bears this out: "Verily, verily, I say unto you, Except a corn of wheat fall into the ground and die, it abideth alone: but if it die, it bringeth forth much fruit" (John 12:24). As the grain of wheat is alone until it is planted, when it rots and dies, and the germ of life manifests itself in the blade, the ear, and then the full corn in the ear with its many grains, so Christ went down into death alone. But the outcome of His death is that many are brought into union with Him, and thus He brings forth much fruit. By losing His own life, He has gained it in a fuller and higher sense.

8. *Holiness of life is the end of Christ's death, so far as the believer is concerned.* "He died for all, that they which live should not henceforth live unto themselves, but unto him which died for them and rose again" (2 Corinthians 5:15). Since Christ lived and died for us, we should live for Him—and be willing to die for

Him. "Unto Him who died we live" should be our motto; and as we live in the power of that motto, His will shall be our delight, His Word our study, His love our constraining power in service, His might our strength, His praise our glorying, His work our business, and His glory our aim in all things.

9. *The death of Christ is the guarantee that there will be a blessed reunion with all the loved ones who have fallen asleep, and a sharing together of His glory*. "If we believe that Jesus died and rose again, *even so* them also which sleep in Jesus will God bring with him" (1 Thessalonians 4:14). "Our Lord Jesus Christ *died* for us, *that*, whether we wake or sleep, we should live together with Him" (1 Thessalonians 5:9, 10). We believe Christ died and rose again for us; we are also cheered with the prospect of being sharers in His glory, forever. We shall "live together with him." "With Him!" Oh, how these words remind us of our oneness with Him in the past and present, for He says we have died, been quickened, and raised, and are seated with Him. The outcome of all this is: we shall be glorified with Him. Thus there is a chain of golden links in connection with the words, "with Him," one end of which is fixed by the staple of Christ's divinity to His cross, and the other end by the staple of His humanity to the throne of God.

Christ Was the Descending Man

"Thou wilt not abandon my soul to Hades" (Acts 2:27 RSV). "He spoke of the resurrection of the Christ, that he was not abandoned to Hades" (verse 31 RSV). Hades is the unseen world, the place of departed spirits, and is in the heart of the earth. That it is where we state may be gathered from the Old Testament. It is also borne out by Christ's own words and the inspired words of Paul. We are told that Korah and his followers went down "alive into the pit," or *sheol*, as the margin of the RSV of Numbers 16:30 renders it. *Sheol* in Hebrew corresponds to *Hades* in Greek. Note what is said of Korah and his followers, "The earth opened her mouth, and swallowed them up . . . they, and all that appertained to them, went down alive into the *pit* (margin R.V., *Sheol)*, and the earth closed upon them: and they perished from among the congregation. And all Israel that were round about them fled at the cry of them: for they said, Lest the earth swallow us up" (Numbers 16:32-34). Here we are distinctly told that the earth opened its mouth, and that the rebels went down alive into Hades.

Then we remember Christ's own words, "As Jonah was three days and three nights in the belly of the sea-monster" (see margin R.V.), "so shall the Son of man be three days and three nights *in the heart of the earth*" (Matthew 12:40). B. W. Newton says: "As the grave is regarded in Scripture as the prison-house of the body, so Hades is regarded as the prison-house of the disembodied soul, evidencing, consequently, the power of death. In order, therefore, to prove the completeness of His submission to the real power of death, and in fulfillment of His own words, respecting His being three days and three nights *in the heart of the earth*, the soul of our blessed Lord was in Hades, during the time that His body was in the grave. The text from the Psalms quoted by Peter in the Acts, 'Thou wilt not leave my soul in Hades,' unquestionably proves this. The same truth is likewise taught in Christ's words just quoted, respecting His being *in the heart of the earth*, for *heart of the earth* is not an expression that the Lord would apply only to the sepulchre in which His body was laid. If He had intended to refer only to the grave, He would no doubt have made special reference to His body, saying, 'The body of the Son of man shall be three days in the earth'; whereas His words are not so limited . . . 'in *the heart* of the earth'—words which cannot be understood so as to exclude reference to His soul, with which consciousness and feeling remained. Then again, the Apostle Paul, by the Holy Ghost, refers to Christ's descent into Hades in two places (Romans 10:7), 'who shall descend, into the deep?' (R.V. *abyss*), ('that is, to bring up Christ again from the dead,') and in Ephesians 4:9, 'Now that He ascended, what is it but that He also descended first *into the lower parts of the earth*.'"

The question naturally arises, What was His purpose in going to Hades, or, had He any purpose? Did He go to the place of lost spirits? No. Hades, as we gather from Luke 16 is divided into two—the place of the wicked, and the place of the righteous, where Christ went. Had Christ any purpose in going? Yes. Some have held that He went there to liberate the spirits of the Old Testament saints and take them to Paradise, which is the third heaven, according to 2 Corinthians 12:2-4. In connection with this, the marginal reading in Ephesians 4:8 is suggestive:—"When he ascended up on high he led *a multitude of captives*," while in Hebrews 12:23 we read that we are come "to the spirits of just men made perfect." Bishop Pearson says, "Some of the early Fathers thought that Christ descended to the place of Hades, where the souls of the faithful, from the death of righteous Abel to the death of Christ, were detained; and there, dissolving all the power by which, they were detained below, translated them into a far more glorious place, and estated them in a condition far more happy in heaven above."

Christ Was the Incorruptible Man

"Not let thy Holy One see corruption" (Acts 2:27 RSV). "Nor did his flesh see corruption" (verse 31 RSV). The body of Jesus did not need the spices and other things to preserve it. It was protected by God Himself, who had said by His servant David that He would not let His Holy or Beloved One see corruption or decay (Psalm 16:10, R.V.).

We fear lest we should attach to Scripture a meaning which it does not bear: with this reservation, we call attention to the reference which is made to the "*napkin*" in the burial of Lazarus and the entombment of Christ. In the case of Lazarus, "his face was bound about with a napkin" (John 11:44); but with Christ, "the napkin . . . was about His head" (John 20:7). Was the napkin over the *face* of Lazarus to hide corruption, while it was about the *head* of Christ, as if there was no corruption to hide?

Christ Was the Raised Man

"Whom God hath raised up" (Acts 2:24). "He (David) spake of the resurrection of Christ" (verse 31). "This Jesus hath God raised up" (verse 32). The resurrection of Christ holds an all-important place in Christianity. If Christ is not risen, we are indeed yet in our sins, and are of all men most miserable. The resurrection of Christ is the *heart* of Christianity: take this fact away and it is a lifeless thing. The resurrection of Christ is the *keystone* of the arch of truth: it is connected with every truth of the Bible, and secures the whole. The resurrection of Christ is the *foundation* of the Church, and no power of hell can overthrow it, because it is preserved, and protected by Him who is risen from the dead and is alive for evermore.

The resurrection of Christ is the *mainspring* of Christian activity. When He had accomplished His atoning work, the Father gave to Him all authority in heaven and on earth, so that He could send forth His disciples to preach the gospel to every creature, promising to be with them to the end of the age. This promise is experienced as we obey His commands.

The resurrection of Christ is the *lever* to move the world: this the men of the world owned to their rulers, in their account of the stir amongst them, saying, "These men that have turned the world upside down are come hither also."

The resurrection of Christ is God's *answer* to every one that would condemn the believer, or bring any charge against him. The resurrection of Christ is the *link* which binds believers together. Since we are risen with Him, our association with Him unites us one to another. The resurrection of Christ is the *life* that secures us, for since He is risen He is the One who is the Endless Life; and because He lives we shall live also.

O to know the power of His resurrection, to lift us above self, sin, and the world. Would that we could live in the power of which Lady Powerscourt spoke in thus describing a Christian: "A Christian is not one who is living on earth and looking up to heaven, but one who is living in heaven and looking down on earth." Living thus, it may be said of us (as of an honored servant of Christ), "He lives in heaven all the week, and then comes and tells us about it on the Sunday."

Christ Was the Joyful and Confident Man

"Therefore did my heart rejoice, and my tongue was *glad* . . . Thou shalt make me *full of joy* with thy countenance" (Acts 2:26, 28). And here is the cause of Christ's joy: "I foresaw the Lord always before my face, for he is on my right hand, that I should not be moved . . . Moreover also my flesh shall rest in hope: . . . Thou hast made known to me the ways of life" (Acts 2:25, 26, 28). It was the presence of God, the power of God, and the promise of God, which sustained the Lord Jesus as He looked on His earthly course. For the joy that was set before Him (of doing the Father's will and pleasing Him), "He endured the cross, despising the shame."

The Lord Jesus as the Man was ever conscious of the presence of God—He "foresaw the Lord always" before Him. Dependent as Jehovah's Servant on the Almighty strength, He could say, "He is on my right hand." Confident, too, was He of the Father's care, for He says, "My flesh shall rest in hope." And as the Obedient One, the Father told Him of the glory which awaited Him in the ways of life, and the fullness of joy from His own countenance.

The Lord Jesus is not spoken of as rejoicing very often. He rejoices over the sinner found, and repentant (Luke 15:6, 10). He rejoices at His Father's purpose in revealing heavenly things to the ignorant, who were yet wise unto salvation, and knew their names written in heaven (Luke 10:21). He rejoiced to be able to do the Father's will and to accomplish His work (Hebrews 12:2; Psalm 40:6-8; Hebrews 10:7, 9). Here He rejoices because God is with Him.

God promises to make Him full of joy, by raising Him from among the dead, and causing Him to behold His countenance.

Christ Is the Exalted Man

"Being by the right hand of God *exalted*" (Acts 2:33). This is one of the three references to Christ being exalted by the Father. Later we have such references as these: "Him hath God exalted . . . a Prince and a Savior, for to give repentance to Israel, and forgiveness of sins" (Acts 5:31); and in Philippians 2:9, "God also hath highly exalted him." In the first of these Scriptures, Christ has been viewed as exalted "by" or "with" the right hand of God; this is the *power* by which—not the *place* to which He has been exalted: Christ is seen simply as the Man, "Jesus of Nazareth." In the second passage, He is "Prince and Savior" (the words "*to be*" are in italics). The One whom the Father exalted is the Lord of glory, the Mighty to save, so that He can give repentance and remission. The "wherefore" in Philippians 2:9, gives us the reason of reasons why God has exalted Him; the preceding verses show us the seven steps in the humiliation of Christ, and taking the Revised reading, we have in striking contrast the seven steps to exaltation (see Philippians 2:7-11). Notice with me these seven steps in His humiliation.

1. "*He emptied himself.*" He who was rich, for our sakes became poor; He had no place to lay His head; no money to pay the tax; no colt to ride upon; no room in which to keep the passover; and no grave in which to be buried.

2. "*Taking the form of a servant*" (margin, "bond-servant"). Contrast this to "being in the form of God"; the Master taking the servant's place; He who was free became the bond-servant! As one has said, "His subjection to the law (Luke 2:21; Galatians 4:4), and to His parents (Luke 2:51); His low state as a carpenter and the carpenter's reputed son (Matthew 12:55; Mark 6:3); His betrayal for the price of a bond-servant (Exodus 21:32), and His slave-like death, to relieve us from the slavery of sin and death; and finally, His servant-like dependence as a man on God, whilst His divinity was not outwardly manifested (Isaiah 49:3, 7), all show His form as a servant."

3. "*Being made in the likeness of men.*" The Creator made in the likeness of men, and according to Romans 8:3, "in the likeness of sinful flesh." Note, not *in* sinful flesh, but in its *likeness*. There was no sin in Him; neither did He sin, nor know sin, but because "the children"—made such by adoption—"were partakers of flesh and blood, he also himself likewise took part of the same" (Hebrews 2:24).

4. "*Being found in fashion as a man.*" In no manifestation as the Angel of the Covenant to saints of former times did the Lord reveal Himself as man. But when He tabernacled among men, in His humanity, He did in very deed manifest Himself as such. Thus, He is described as "*this Man*" by friends and foes. "This man receiveth sinners" (Luke 15:2); "This man was the Son of God" (Mark 15:39); "This man hath done nothing amiss" (Luke 23:41); "Never man spake like this man," said His friends; while His foes retorted, "Why doth this man speak blasphemy?" (Mark 2:7).

5. *"He humbled Himself."* This is seen again and again if we call to mind how meekly He received the ill-treatment during His mock trial. His back was given to the smiters; His cheeks to them that plucked off the hair. His face was smitten; His cheeks polluted by the sinner's spittle. His eyes were bandaged; His brow lacerated with the cruel thorns. His hands and feet were nailed to the cross; and His body exposed to the unholy gaze of the ribald mob.

6. *"Obedient unto death."* In obedience to the Father's will, Christ gave Himself up to die for the disobedient (Romans 4:19; Hebrews 5:8). That obedience cost Him intense suffering and anguish, as we see Him in the garden of Gethsemane, in deepest anguish of soul and bitterness of spirit, while He beholds the cup He has to drink. Yet, though the burden of suffering presses sore upon Him, we hear, "Nevertheless, not as I will, but as thou wilt" (Matthew 26:39).

7. *"The death of the cross."* To die at all is shameful, for death is the offspring of sin; to die by the hand of robbers, who kill to plunder, is more shameful, for that is a cold-blooded deed; but to die a felon's death is most shameful, for it seems as if he who dies had done some deed worthy of such a death. Yet Christ took the most shameful place, although He "despised the shame" of it (Hebrews 12:2). For if He was not worthy of it, those for whom He died were; but He must be reckoned among the transgressors, if we are to be reckoned among the translated ones. (Compare Luke 22:37; Romans 4:5. The words "reckoned" and "counted" in these two passages represent the same word in the original.)

We have noticed the seven steps from the Throne to the Cross; we shall now consider the seven steps from the Cross to the Throne, and find an illustration of Christ's own teaching, "He that humbleth himself shall be exalted."

1. *"God hath highly exalted him."* Bengel says, "Christ *emptied* Himself: God exalted Christ as Man to an equality with God." As God, Christ had a glory equal with the Father—the essential glory of His Godhead; but by virtue of His accomplished work on earth, He is now "crowned with glory and honor"; hence He has an acquired glory as the Son of Man. Christ being made man identified Himself with those who were a little lower than the angels. But because Christ has glorified God, He occupies the highest place: "Far above all principality, and power, and might, and dominion, and every name that is named, not only in this world, but also in that which is to come" (Ephesians 1:22).

2. *"And given him a name which is above every name."* He not only occupies the highest place, but He bears the highest name. All other names are lost before it, as the stars pale before the rising of the sun. The name of Jesus—that name of which Bernard said, "It is as honey in the mouth, harmony to the ear, melody to the heart!" Anselm says regarding it, "It is a name of comfort to sinners when they call upon Him"; therefore he himself said, "Jesus, be my Jesus." Christopher Sutton says, "This name is above all names: *first,* that it was consecrated from everlasting; *second,* that it was given by God; *thirdly,* that it was desired of the patriarchs; *fourthly,* for that it was foretold of the prophets; *fifthly,* for that it was accomplished in the time of grace, magnified in the Apostles, witnessed of martyrs—acknowledged and honored shall it be of all

believers unto the world's end. This name Jesus is compared to oil poured forth; oil being kept close sendeth not forth such a savour as it doth being poured out; and oil hath these properties—it suppleth, it cherisheth, it maketh look cheerfully; so doth this name of Jesus—it suppleth the hardness of our hearts, it cherisheth the weakness of our faith, enlighteneth the darkness of our soul, and maketh man look with a cheerful countenance towards the throne of grace."

3. *"That at the name of Jesus every knee should bow."* Here we are told that every knee shall bow "at the name of Jesus." The believer right readily comes to God now, in the name of Jesus, in worship and adoration, for he knows that "whatsoever he asks in his name" the request will be granted. But while the child of God bends his knees in prayer and worship as Paul did (Ephesians 3:14), the unsaved shall bow the knee and acknowledge Christ as Lord, as the Egyptians did Joseph, when he was made ruler over Egypt (Genesis 41:43), and shall also submit to Him, however unwillingly, as Ahaziah's captain did to Elijah when sent by his master to him (2 Kings 1:13). For God has declared in righteousness that this shall be (Isaiah 45:23).

4. *"Of things in heaven."* The angelic host shall worship Him as the bearer of the highest name, for He is, as we have seen, "far above all principality, and power, and might, and dominion, and every name that is named." Seraphs with their fiery zeal, cherubs in their righteous service, principalities in their rule, powers in their authority, mights in their strength, dominions in their lordship, and angels in their song, all shall own Him Lord of all and chant His praises, as the angelic host did to the shepherds on Bethlehem's plains.

5. *"Things on earth."* When Christ was on earth some bowed the knee in mockery (Matthew 27:29), but when Christ is manifested in His glory all shall bow in reality. Israel will bow before Him in contrition and faith (Zechariah 12:10; John 19:37; Revelation 1:7); the unsaved will bow before Him in unwilling submission (Revelation 6:15); and the whole earth will be under His rule.

6. *"Things under the earth,"* or, as in the margin of the Revised Version, *"Things of the world below."* The wicked, the demons, the false prophet, the beast, and Satan, all will submit to Him, as the five kings had to submit to Joshua (Joshua 10:26). The wicked will own the justice of their punishment, the demons will tremble in dread before Him, the false prophet and the beast will He cast alive into the lake of fire, and Satan will be captured and never again be allowed to come out of his prison-house.

7. *"Every tongue should confess that Jesus Christ is Lord to the glory of God the Father."* No man now can call Jesus "Lord," but by the Holy Spirit (1 Corinthians 12:3). For there is nothing that would lead the natural man to acknowledge Him as such, since he sees no beauty in Christ. But in the coming day of Christ's glory, who and what He is will be revealed. The very shining forth of His glory will convince men of His Lordship and make them own that He indeed, the despised Nazarene, is the Lord from heaven. All this will redound to the glory of the Father who sent Him, loved Him, and acknowledged Him in His humiliation and humanity.

Now mark the contrast in these seven downward and upward steps:—

1. He emptied Himself; God highly exalted Him.
2. He took upon Himself the servant's form; God gave Him a name above every name.
3. He was made in the likeness of men; God causes every knee to bow to Him.
4. He was found in fashion as a man; God leads all heaven to acknowledge the Man.
5. He humbled Himself; God caused all on earth to own Him as the Exalted One.
6. He was obedient; God makes all the disobedient to submit to Him.
7. He died the death of the cross; every tongue confesses His Lordship.

Thus Christ is the Exalted Man. O that we may give Him the highest place in our affections!

Christ Was the Conferring Man

"Therefore, being by the right hand of God exalted, and having received of the Father the promise of the Holy Ghost, he *hath shed forth* this, which ye now see and hear" (Acts 2:33). John the Baptist had said that Christ would baptize with the Holy Ghost (John 1:33), and Christ Himself again and again said that He would send the Holy Ghost (see John 14, 16). They were told by Him to tarry for the bestowal of the Spirit (Luke 24:49), and in obedience to Him, they had done so, and had seen the promise fulfilled (Acts 2:2).

This gift was given to the believer for a threefold purpose—for *walk*, for *work*, and for *witnessing*. The gift of God to the world is Christ (John 3:26). The gift of the Father to Christ is the Church (John 17:6). And the gift of Christ to the believer is the Holy Spirit. Let us take Peter as illustrating the gift of the Holy Spirit received, and see the difference it made in him. Before Pentecost, Peter was very crooked in his walk: a servant-maid caused him to swerve from the straight path. Afterwards, however, note his devotion, even to the laying down of his life. As to his work before Pentecost, Peter went back to his old occupation—fishing; but after being filled with the Holy Spirit, he went steadily on with the work of the Lord. As to his testimony before Pentecost, he was ashamed to confess his Lord, but after, in the energy of the Spirit, he boldly witnessed for his Lord, confessing that all the wonderworking (whether it were in the manifestation on the day of Pentecost, or the healing of the lame man), was by the power of the Lord Jesus through the Holy Spirit.

Christ Is the Expecting Man

"The Lord said unto my Lord, Sit thou on my right hand, until I make thy foes thy footstool" (Acts 2:34, 35). Christ is seated at the Father's right hand at this time, waiting until He bids Him arise and overthrow His enemies, and take to Himself His great power and reign. That this will be so is prophesied in Psalm 110:1, quoted by Christ Himself in Matthew 22:41-46; the prophecy is again and again reiterated by the Holy Spirit, as in Hebrews 1:13; 10:13; and it is most strikingly symbolized in Daniel 2, where we have a panoramic view of "the times of the Gentiles" (Luke 21:24; Romans 11:25) in Nebuchadnezzar's colossal image. "The times of the Gentiles" cover a period of time from that of the then existing king of Babylon till Christ shall come. The image is very simply described. The head was of gold, the breast and arms of silver, the thighs and lower part of the body of brass; the legs of iron, and the feet and toes of iron mixed with clay.

The head of gold represented the Babylonian Empire; the breast and arms of silver, the Medo-Persian Empire; the lower part of the body of brass, the Grecian Empire; the legs of iron, the Roman Empire; and the feet and toes, the present time until Christ comes. We are about the *instep* of the feet, and under the Antichrist there will arise ten kings, as represented by the "ten toes," and in Daniel 7:7, 24, by the "ten horns." It is in connection with this that we read of a Stone which shall crush the image to pieces, and this Stone undoubtedly represents Christ putting down His enemies, of which we have a distinct account in Daniel 2:44, 45. (See also Daniel 7:13-27; Revelation 19:22 and chapter 22): "And in the days of these kings shall the God of heaven set up a kingdom, which shall never be destroyed; and the kingdom shall not be left to other people, but it shall break in pieces and consume all these kingdoms, and it shall stand for ever. Forasmuch as thou sawest that the stone was cut out of the mountain without hands, and that it brake in pieces the iron, the brass, the clay, the silver, and the gold; the great God hath made known to the king what shall come to pass hereafter: and the dream is certain, and the interpretation thereof sure."

Like Joshua's captains, who put their feet upon the necks of the five kings (Joshua 10:24), Christ and His people will put their feet upon His five principal foes, namely, the foes of Israel who had maltreated His chosen ones (Zechariah 14:1-3; Ezekiel 38, 39); the Antichrist who had dared to blasphemously personify Him (2 Thessalonians 2:4; Revelation 13:1-8); the false prophet, who aided the Beast (Revelation 13:11-18; 14:20); the harlot of corrupt Christendom, the devil's mimicry of the Bride of Christ (Revelation 17, 18); and that old serpent, the devil, who was at the root of all the mischief (Revelation 20:1-3).

Christ Is the Honored Man

"God hath made that same Jesus, whom ye have crucified, both Lord and Christ" (Acts 2:36). Here we are told of a double honor having been put on Christ by the Father. He is made *Lord*. Seven times the words "In the Lord" occur in the Epistle to the Ephesians, showing us the Lordship of Christ, and the attitude of submission and obedience in which we are always to stand before Him:

1. "Faith *in the Lord Jesus*" (1:15);
2. "Groweth unto an holy temple *in the Lord*" (2:21);
3. "Testify *in the Lord*" (4:17);
4. "Light *in the Lord*" (5:8);
5. "Children, obey your parents *in the Lord*" (6:1);
6. "Be strong *in the Lord*" (6:10);
7. "Tychicus . . . faithful minister *in the Lord*" (6:21).

Christ is Lord as the Sovereign of His people, to rule and govern them; the people of God are responsible to Him, to yield willing obedience to Him and His Word, to be ready for His work, to delight in His will, to recognize His claims, and to yield the members of the body as instruments of righteousness unto Him.

But Jesus is "Christ" as well as "Lord." Since He is Lord this reminds us of His right to us and His rule over us. But, as Christ, He is able to bless. This will be seen in the seven references to Him as "Christ" in Ephesians 5: 1) "Christ . . . loved us" (verse 2); 2) "Kingdom of Christ" (verse 5); 3) "Christ shall give thee light" (verse 14); 4) "Christ is the Head of the Church" (verse 23); 5) "The Church is subject unto Christ" (verse 24); 6) "Christ . . . loved the Church" (verse 25); 7) "Christ and the church" (verse 32). These passages, if read with "Jesus" for "Christ," would lose their force. "Christ" tells us of Him who is the channel of blessing for us, with whom we are forever identified. Thus we are taught our position is "in Christ," not "in Jesus." When our power for life and service is mentioned, it is *Christ in us:* "Christ liveth in me" (Galatians 2:20)—"that Christ may dwell in your hearts by faith" (Ephesians 3:17), but when it is our position and blessing we are said to be "in Christ."

Our position, then, is in Christ Jesus. We are "sanctified in Christ Jesus" (1 Corinthians 1:2). "Raised and seated in Christ Jesus" (Ephesians 2:6). "Now in Christ . . . made nigh" (Ephesians 2:13). "Blessed . . . in Christ" (Ephesians 1:3).

Peter's sermon on the day of Pentecost was a model one, for three reasons:

1. *It was full of Scripture.* Peter, according to our translation, which we take to serve our purpose, uses 531 words in his address; 218 of these are quotations from Joel 2:28-32; Psalm 16:8-11; Psalm 110:1; 91 words are used in reference to Scripture, and the remaining words have in them the aroma of Scripture, as the scent perfumes what it touches. Surely we cannot wonder at the blessing of God on such a sermon! It shows us that the Spirit manifests His presence, where the Word has free course; truly, we see that God-breathed utterances are effectual.

2. *The sermon was an unfolding of the Person of Christ.* There must be this, where there is a declaration of the truth of God, for Christ is the One Person of the revelation of God. As the leaf of the rose is a part of the rose, and has the fragrance of the rose, so every page of the Bible is a leaf of Him who has been called the "Rose of Sharon." There are no less than forty nouns and fourteen pronouns which refer to Christ, in this sermon of Peter's. The wheel of Peter's words revolves around and has the Person of Christ as its axis.

3. *The results that followed were remarkable.* There was *conviction* of sin, for men were pricked in their hearts, and said: "What shall we do?" (Acts 2:37). There was *conversion* to Christ, for "they received his word" (verse 41). There was *confession* of Christ, for they were baptized (verse 41). There was *communion* with the Lord's people, for those who believed were together, as the words "together"—"all"—"with one accord," in verses 41-46, plainly tell. There was *continuance*—no flash-in-the-pan conversions—"they continued steadfastly in the Apostles' doctrine and fellowship, and in breaking of bread, and in prayers" (verse 42). There was *consecration,* for they sold their possessions and gave to all as every man had need (verse 45). And then there was a fourfold consequence:

First, Godward—they were "praising" Him; *Second*, Manward—"having favor with all the people;" *Third*, Churchward—"the Lord added to the Church;" *Fourth*, Selfward—"those that were *being saved*" (verse 47 RSV)

Christian worker, if we work on the lines indicated and illustrated in the address of Peter, we will glorify God, exalt Christ, and honor the Holy Spirit. The results may not always be so manifest; but the Lord will be glorified. This, after all, is our main object.

11

The Discipler's Outlook

"I AM beaten out of good resolutions, and must look to Jesus alone"; so said one who had found the rotten plank of his own resolutions unable to bear him. He was forced to step upon the eternal Rock of Ages and rest on Him alone. We not only cause endless misery and mischief to ourselves by looking to fancied resources of our own, but we fill the heart of the Lord Jesus with grief and concern. One of our most talented writers tells of a dream of Christ which she once had, after a season of anxious care and questioning. She said His face looked so weary that she ventured to ask Him what made Him look so sad, and He answered: "Carrying your doubts and fears. It was easy to carry your sins and sorrows, but I cannot bear to have you doubt Me and question My love."

There are many things which come to those who look to Jesus, and the exercise fits the believer in every way for his Christian life and work. I am sure that while we should not look at our looking, but at Him who is the Object of our faith, yet we shall find that our looking to Jesus is the sinner's satisfier, the saint's inspirer, and the servant's safeguard.

The Sinner's Satisfier

How sad was our condition, and how low was our position, till we looked to Jesus! Sin as a burden weighed us down with intolerable depression and made us cry: "Mine iniquities are gone over mine head: as an heavy burden they are too heavy for me" (Psalm 38:4). The fever of fear was burning in the mind, and made us cry out in the delirium of doubt: "Oh, wretched man that I am!" The curse of a broken law was a rack to torture us. It made us shout with despair, "I am carnal, sold under sin." The ghosts of the misspent past haunted us, as they looked in at the windows of our being. They made us to be like Job when all his bones shook at the spectre he beheld (Job 4:14-16). The sight of sin's loathsomeness, as we saw its working within us, was like a foul leprosy. It made us confess with the patriarch, "I am vile." The black storm of God's wrath against sin, which we saw approaching, made us cry, like those in the book of the Revelation, for something to hide us from the indignation of the Lamb. As we caught a glimpse of the holiness of God, we were led to ask the question: "Who shall be able to stand?" Then it was we heard the still, small voice of the

Lord saying to us, in the music of His grace, "Look unto Me, and be ye saved." And as we, like Bunyan's pilgrim, looked to Jesus crucified for us, the burden of sin's load rolled from us. The wretchedness of fear departed, and the law's curse was removed. The ghosts of the past vanished, and the loathsomeness caused by sin was cleansed away by His blood. The holiness of God was our joy and safety, and the question of who would be able to stand in the Lord's presence, was answered. Being justified by faith, and thus having peace with God, we found we had access into the grace wherein we stood, and we could rejoice in hope of the glory of God.

Well may we look to Jesus crucified, for there is cleansing in His blood, life in His death, blessing in His curse, justification in His judgment, salvation in His loss, joy in His sorrow, ease in His suffering, welcome in His forsaking, heaven in His hell, gladness in His groan, and bliss in His ignominy.

The Saint's Inspirer

It was with a sad heart that Mary Magdalene wended her way to the sepulchre of Christ in the early hours of the resurrection morn. To her surprise, however, when she got to the tomb, she found it empty. With quickened footsteps, she ran and told Peter that the body of the Lord had been taken away. After Peter and John had satisfied themselves that the statement of Mary was correct, by going to the tomb and looking for themselves, they went home. Not so Mary; she stood outside the sepulchre. As she stood, she ventured to stoop down and look in, and to her surprise she saw two angels in white. The soul who stoops in humble enquiry is sure to see some angel of blessing. While in conversation with the angels, she suddenly saw their faces light up with an unusual expression. They looked past her as if they were gazing at some august presence. This made her look as well, and we know the sequel. The supposed gardener turned out to be her Divine Lord, and she exclaimed with grateful joy, "Rabboni!"

We can imagine what a lift it gave to her steps as she, in obedience to Christ's word, went to tell the disciples what she had seen and heard, that Jesus was risen. It was the Lord Mary wanted. Nothing else would satisfy her. The same is true of every true-hearted believer; it is Christ Himself we want, as Charlotte Murray suggests in the following lines:

"Do we know Him; not His doctrines,
  Not His wisdom, love, and power,
But *Himself*, the Friend unfailing
  In affliction's darkest hour?
To be with us as a Person,
  Not a presence—vague, unreal:
But a living, loving Savior,
  Who our every need doth fill?
Is He with us *now*, abiding?
  Is He chiefest, and the best?
Would our home be sad without Him?
  Have we each His perfect rest?
If we have, we know just dimly
  What the light of heaven will be;
But the joy will be the grander,
  For we then our Lord shall see."

The Bride in the Song of Solomon could speak of her Beloved with glowing utterance, because she knew His care and enjoyed His company. So shall it be with us. As we look at our Beloved, He will inspire us to sing His praises and declare His worth. As we glance at Him in the humility of His grace, in the compassion of His love, in the tenderness of His sympathy, in the dependence of His faith, in the unselfishness of His life, in the surrender of His will, in the thoroughness of His consecration, in the devotion of His work, in the endurance of His sufferings, in the beauty of His character, in the prayerfulness of His heart, in the readiness of His service, in the carefulness of His utterance, in the power of His testimony, and in the excellence of His God-glorifying life, we must be inspired to like conduct.

The Servant's Safeguard

The Christian worker is beset with a hundred and one dangers, any one of which may cripple him in his Master's service. But the cure for each is found in "looking unto Jesus."

Looking unto Jesus, we will not neglect the inner life. It was a sorry confession which the Bride in the Song of Solomon had to make, when she said: "They made me keeper of the vineyards, but mine own vineyard have I not kept" (Song of Solomon 1:6). Looking unto Jesus, we shall be able to say, "My own vineyard I have kept." Looking unto Him, we shall be clean ourselves, before we bring others to the Fount of cleansing. We shall have the lamps of our life trimmed, before we trim others. The incense of prayer shall rise from the altar of our holy place, before we urge others to pray. The grace of God in its seasoning power shall salt us, before we call on others to be salted with grace. The perfume of Christ's sweetness shall make us fragrant, before we exhort others to be sweet. The well of Christ's joy will be springing up in us, before we tell others to drink and be satisfied. The command of Christ, "Follow Me," will be obeyed before we say to others, "Come with us, and we will do you good," for what good can we do unless we bring others to the Source of all good?

Looking unto Jesus, we will not quarrel with our fellow-servants. The disciples began quarrelling amongst themselves because they took their eyes off Jesus and began to be occupied with their own fancied self-importance (Luke 9:46; 22:24). On one occasion, the mother of James and John asked Christ to favor her sons by allowing them to sit in the choice places on either side of His throne. This request filled the other disciples with indignation. Why? Because they wanted the places themselves. They wanted the places and were occupied with them; hence their indignation against the two others. If they had been occupied with Jesus, they would have said, "Lord, we don't care what place we occupy, so long as we are with You." Why does the servant in the parable begin to strike his fellow-servants? He says, "My lord delayeth his coming" (Matthew 24:48); he gets his eyes off his Master and His return. Then he begins to hit them. This will not be so if we are looking to Him, for looking to Him we shall see that He loves us dearly, cares for us tenderly, watches us carefully, pleads for us earnestly, chides us gently, speaks of us hopefully, talks to us graciously, and tends us faithfully, and we will act in like manner to our fellow-men,

Looking unto Jesus, we will not be deterred in testimony for Christ. One of the brightest examples of faithful service we have in the New Testament is Stephen. Of him it is said, "He was full of the Holy Spirit," and "full of faith and power." Such being the case, we do not wonder his enemies were not able to "resist the wisdom and spirit by which he spake," and that his face was like an angel's (Acts 6:5, 8, 10, 15). But the secret of his sustainment is given to us when he said, "I see the heavens opened, and the Son of Man standing on the right hand of God" (Acts 7:56). That heavenly vision was the ballast which kept him steady, amid the storm of persecution that howled around him. It will be the same with us; if we can look our Savior in the face with an uncondemning heart, we will not fail to look into the faces of men with unflinching courage.

Looking unto to Jesus, we will not be inflated with pride and self-importance. After Isaiah had seen the Lord in His holiness, he exclaimed, "Woe is me . . . for mine eyes have seen the King" (Isaiah 6:5). There are three little words of telling importance in connection with the humiliation of the prophet, and they are—

The "Woe" of condemnation.
The "Lo" of cleansing.
The "Go" of commission.

And the truth contained in these words always comes in the above order. Confession of sin first, cleansing from sin second, and then consecration in service. There must be the withering work of the Holy Spirit, to blast our pride and self-sufficiency, before there can be the winning work of His grace to bring others to Himself. We must know what it is to lie low before the Lord, before there can be fitness for His service. The crucifixion of self must precede the communication of Pentecost.

The same truth is borne out in Job's experience. He could justify himself till he saw the Lord in His glory, then he said, "I have heard of thee by the hearing of the ear: but now mine eye seeth thee. Wherefore I abhor myself, and repent in dust and ashes" (Job 42:5, 6). When he had come to an end of himself, the Lord could use him in blessing to his friends, and give him free deliverance; for it was when he prayed for his friends that his own captivity was turned, and he received double at the Lord's hands for all he had lost (Job 42:10).

Looking unto Jesus, we will not use bad material in the Lord's work. There are two men in the Bible who stand out prominently for the carefulness of their work and for their fidelity to the instructions given to them: namely, Moses and Paul. Both these servants were men who had a heavenly vision. I especially call attention to the first.

Before Moses was entrusted with instructions regarding the construction of the tabernacle and its vessels, he had to have audience with God. There, face to face with Jehovah, he received his instruction. Every detail of the tabernacle, as to the material to be used, the manner of the making, the men who were to make the things, and the positions of the vessels when they were made was given. Again and again do we find the Lord reminding Moses that everything was to be carried out according to the pattern given (Exodus 25:9, 40; 26:30; 27:8). There were seven principal vessels in the tabernacle, which, in their special significance, may be taken to illustrate the kind of material we should use in the Lord's work. The vessels were: the altar of burnt offering, the laver, the lampstand, the table of shewbread, the golden altar, the golden censer, and the ark of the covenant. Looking to Jesus, we will see they all represent Him in the multiplicity of His work:

The altar—His all-sufficient atonement for sin.
The laver—His life-giving and cleansing truth.
The lampstand—His sevenfold illuminating grace.
The table of shewbread—His all-satisfying love.
The golden altar—His all-glorious priestly service.
The golden censer—His all-fragrant intercession.
The ark of the covenant—His all-comprehensive glory.

Looking unto Jesus, we will not mind what work we do, so long as He gives it. Whether it be abiding by the stuff, or being in the front of the battle; watching the sick, or rejoicing with the healthy; alone on some isolated Patmos, or in the midst of sympathetic friends; in the drudgery of life, or in the ease of it; so long as we are working for Him, we will be happy.

There is a beautiful legend told of a shepherd who was kept at home watching a fevered guest on the night that the angels came with the announcement of the birth of Jesus. The other shepherds saw the heavenly host, heard their song, and beheld the glory. Returning home, their hearts were wondrously elated. All the night, the shepherd Shemuel sat alone by the restless sufferer and waited. His fellow-shepherds pitied him in that he missed the vision and the glory that they had seen. But in his lowly service, Shemuel had blessing and reward of his own. Indeed, he missed the splendor of that night in the fields, but in his service he gave his own life, and then he saw a more wondrous glory than that which his fellow-shepherds saw.

"Shemuel by the fever-bed,
Touched by beckoning hands that led,
Died, and saw the Uncreated;
All his fellows lived and waited."

He had waited by the sickbed, while they saw the glory; now they waited amid earth's dull scenes while he witnessed the glories of the eternal. Let us do all duties as to Christ, and we will have our reward. The Lord does not want service done, if it means the neglecting of home duties and life, but He will bless us in those duties. Whatever the need of our life, whatever the trials or temptations, they will be dispelled by "looking unto Jesus."

12

The Discipler's Trait

The gifts of 1 Corinthians 12 are capped with the grace of love in 1 Corinthians 13, like the snow-capped mountain summit upon which the sun is shining with reflective glory. As the mighty St. Lawrence Seaway has many tributaries and lakes, which go to make up its grand volume of water, so the many traits which are given of love's character reveal its power and perfection.

Patience of Love

"Love is patient . . ." (verse 4 RSV) Love is an enduring grace. When the love of God burns within the soul, hate cannot kill it, persecution cannot destroy it, nor envy stamp it out. The noble army of martyrs down through the centuries illustrate the endurance of love. The young men in the fiery furnace in Babylon, the faithful Christians hunted to death in Rome, the steadfast Huguenots in France, the unswerving believers in Spain, the unflinching Ridley and Latimer in England, and the true and stalwart covenanters in Scotland, are a few illustrations of love's steadfastness. Love is like Jacob, laboring for Rachel (Genesis 29:20); it can brave disappointment. Love is like Nehemiah, when the enemies were sneering at his work; it pushes bravely on, undeterred by opposition (Nehemiah 4:1-6). Love is like Eliezer, carrying out Abraham's commission (Genesis 24:66); it never sits down till the task is completed. Love is like the gold that was used for the vessels of the tabernacle, which were hammered into shape (Exodus 25:21); it is beautified by the trials through which it passes. Love is like Rizpah, watching the dead bodies of her sons (2 Samuel 21:10); it will not be driven from its post. Love is like Joseph (Psalm 105:17-20); it can suffer long and patiently wait till its cause is vindicated. And love is like Stephen, when being stoned to death (Acts 7:60); it will not give up its cause, but remains faithful to Christ to the end.

Practice of Love

"And is kind" (verse 4). Love is an active grace; it has the heart of Mary, and the hands of Martha, without her cumbering. Love is as the fragrance of the flowers; it brings satisfaction to others, like Mary of Bethany, when she anointed the Savior with the costly spikenard (John 12:3). Love is as the fruit of the trees, which brings refreshment to man, like Jonathan, who, out of love to David, sacrificed all to him (1 Samuel 18:1-4). Love is as the warmth of the sun; it awakens dormant powers in the heart like the woman in the Gospel, who, out of love to Christ, washed His feet with her tears and wiped them with the hairs of her head (Luke 7:47). Love is as the shining of the moon which lights the weary traveler on his homeward journey, like Barnabas at Antioch who encouraged the young believers to cleave to the Lord with purpose of heart (Acts 11:23). Love is as the incoming tide, which cleanses the shore and removes the refuse, like Moses when he prayed to be blotted out of God's Book for Israel's sin (Exodus 32:32). Love is as the stored-up electricity in the motor which moves the machinery to its work, like the apostle Paul when he tells us the secret of his joyful sufferings and faithful service (2 Corinthians 5:14). And love is as the purling stream which brings gladness and refreshment wherever it flows, like the good Samaritan who came to the aid of the man who fell among the thieves (Luke 10:33).

The kind activity of love is well illustrated in the following incident:

A well-known Christian was working in a certain neighborhood, during a terrible epidemic of cholera and small-pox. There was one case of awful despair, a poor dying woman who refused to listen to any words of the mercy of God, saying only: "Too late, too late!" To her the man devoted much care and many prayers. It seemed as though no impression could be made upon her. Her repeated cry was: "Too late, too late; too late for me!" But his tender fervor to bring her to faith and trust in her Savior prevailed at last. Christ's servant said: "But you do believe in the love of those around you, now that Jesus sends it to you?" With what seemed the last effort of her life, she raised herself, clasped her arms round the neck of the sister who was attending to her, and answered: "Yes, it is love." The last struggle followed almost immediately, and she was heard to say: "Jesus, save me!"—the words she had been entreated to use. So prayer had been heard. She died in hope and faith.

It was love that conquered this woman's obstinacy and despair, a love which had its origin in the Savior's dying love and which had been fed by the Spirit's grace.

Purity of Love

"It does not envy" (verse 4 NIV) Envy is as cruel as the grave and as dark as hell. The beacon light of God's Word shines out upon the black waters of envy and reveals its sunken reefs upon which many have made soul-shipwreck. Envy is the cause of persecution (Acts 5:17: 13:45), the mother of division (1 Corinthians 3:3), the companion of jealousy (Acts 7:9), the sign of unbelief (Acts 17:5), the child of the devil (James 3:14, 15), the worker of mischief (James 3:16), and the work of the flesh (Galatians 5:21). Love will have nothing to do with envy; it keeps separate from it. Like Phinehas with the Israelite and the Midianite woman, love will kill it if it dares to come in the camp of the soul's presence (Numbers 25:1-8).

> "Base envy withers another's joy,
> And hates that excellence it cannot reach."

Not so love—

> "True love welcomes another's joy,
> And seeks that excellence it cannot reach."

Love has no irritating thorn in its hand, nor jealous look in its eye, nor depreciating words on its lips, nor sore feeling in its heart. Love sees the best in others and the worst in itself. Love will wash another's feet and think it is honored by so doing.

Peacefulness of Love

"It does not boast" (verse 4 NIV). Love ever takes a back seat and is willing to work unseen. Love is like the harpstring struck by the musician. Its vibrations cause it to vanish but its music is heard and appreciated. The music of love is appreciated by heaven though not acknowledged by man. It is said that when some young pastors once paid a visit to one of the great ministers of the past generation, they found him preparing to go to a meeting, where a strong debate was expected. He was reading the thirteenth chapter of the first Epistle to the Corinthians, and then praying that its teaching might guide his conduct. He felt he needed the restraining hand of grace and the calming power of love, lest he should be rash in speech. David said in his haste that all men were liars (Psalm 116:11). He would not have been so rash if he had spoken in the calm moments of leisure.

Pufflessness of Love

"Is not puffed up" (verse 4). Puffery (or pride) is not worth much anywhere. It is suggestive of smoke, unreality, uncertainty, ill-health, wind, and self-seeking. The Holy Spirit had to chide the church in Corinth with their being puffed up. The word "*puffed up*" only occurs seven times in the New Testament. In six out of the seven, it occurs in connection with the Church in Corinth. It was because there were those who were puffed up that the apostle had so much trouble with them. Because they were puffed up by self-assertiveness and pride, division abounded among the Corinthians (1 Corinthians 4:6, 18, 19; 5:2; 8:1). There is only one thing that can kill this spirit of pride, and that is love. Love is content with what God gives and allows, and says—

> "Can I be stem, and another be wheat?
> Can I be shell, and another be meat?
> Another be head, while I am feet?
> If God will."

It was said of Charles Lamb: "Whether he had won for his greedy listener only some raw lad, or a charmed circle of beauty, rank, and wit, who hung breathless on his words, he talked with equal eloquence; for his subject, not his audience, inspired him."

Thus when the love of God is the force that inspires us, like the "subject" did Lamb, we shall not be puffed up with pride in order to self-aggrandisement, but we will be humble in heart and lowly in life.

Politeness of Love

"It is not rude" (verse 5 NIV). "Politeness has been defined as love in trifles. Courtesy is said to be love in little things. The one secret of politeness is love." The meaning of the word "gentleman" is a gentle man, one who does things gently and in love. There are many who spoil a good deed by the rude manner in which they perform it. Love is the *file* that removes the roughness of uncouthness, the *oil* that banishes the squeakiness of uncourtesy, the *knife* that cuts out the cancer of inconsiderateness, the *instrument* which takes away the blight of rudeness, and the *plane* which is careful to smooth away with the coarseness of evil appearance. Love looks well to see that the house of the heart is kept pure, sweet, and clean, but it is also careful that the outside of the house is beautiful, as well. Unseemly speech, uncomely actions, and unkind words are not in the educational code of love. Love, like Abigail in the gifts for David, not only gives its best, but gives it in the best possible way.

Preference of Love

"It is not self-seeking" (verse 5 NIV). There are three characteristics of love, namely, it does not think of itself, it does not save itself, it does think of others. *Love does not think of itself.* Wilberforce was asked one day by a friend how his own soul fared in the midst of so much business, entailed upon him by his efforts to free the slaves. His reply was significant: "I forgot I had a soul." *Love does not save itself.* One of the true things said of Christ in derision, was: "He saved others; himself he cannot save." He did not save Himself, for He desired to save others. Love ever acts in this self-sacrificing way. "An engineer on a locomotive recently saw a train with which he must collide. He resolved to slow up his train and stand at his post for there were passengers behind. The engineer said to the fireman: 'Jump! One man is enough on this engine. Jump!' The fireman jumped, and was saved. The crash came. The engineer died at his post." Thus love ever acts. It acts for others, and not for itself. *Love thinks of others.* It looks on the things of others (Philippians 2:4). "I have been a member of your church for thirty years," said an elderly Christian to his pastor, "and when I was laid by with sickness, only one or two came to see me. I was shamefully neglected."

"My friend," said the pastor, "in all these thirty years, how many sick have you visited?"

"Oh," he replied, "it never struck me in that light. I thought only of the relation of others to me, and not of my relation to them."

Love's unconscious action is ever for others' good, at the expense of itself.
Love's song is, "Not my own, I'm purchased by the blood of Christ."
Love's work is "Not my own labor, I am but an instrument to be used in Christ's service."
Love's aim is, "Not my own pleasure, I seek to please my Lord."
Love's desire is, "Not my own ambition, I'm constrained by the love of Christ."
Love's testimony is, "Not my own words, it is the message of Christ."
Love's ministry is, "Not my own honor, it is for the glory of Christ."
Love's seeking is, "Not my own way. I follow in the steps of Christ."

Love never says these things of itself, but its actions say them. Love, like the face of Moses, is unconscious and unconcerned about its own shining.

Provokelessness of Love

"Is not easily provoked" (verse 5). It will be seen that the Revised Version is more emphatic than the Authorized. The word "easily" is omitted from the former. As long as love holds the reins of the soul, there is no danger of its being provoked to anger or to spiteful action, which leads to sin; and yet love may be provoked in the Lord's service as it beholds that which is wrong. The apostle Paul himself is a case in point. Twice in the Acts of the Apostles, we find him keenly provoked. When he saw the idolatry of the Athenians, his spirit was "*stirred,*" or "provoked," for the word "stirred" is the same as rendered "*provoked*" in 1 Corinthians 13:5. Again, Paul was provoked at the action of Barnabas when he insisted on taking John Mark with him; for we read that the "*contention* was *so sharp*" (the same word rendered "*contention so sharp*" is "*provoke*" in Hebrews 10:24), "that they departed asunder one from the other" (Acts 15:39). It seems Barnabas was wrong in wanting to take Mark with him. It is not without meaning that Barnabas is never mentioned again in the Acts of the Apostles. The Lord Himself was provoked with the unbelief of Israel in the wilderness (Hebrews 3:15, 16). The meaning undoubtedly is, love is not provoked *to sin,* and is never moved without some justifying cause.

Preclusion of Love

"Thinketh no evil" (verse 5). The Revised Version has it, "Taketh not account of evil." Rotherham renders the words: "Imputes not that which is base." The word "*thinketh*" would be better rendered "*imputeth.*" It is thus given in Romans 4:8, 11, 22, 23, 24. Love never condemns on mere suspicion nor imputes evil without evidence, An old writer says: "Love delights to think well and speak well of others. She talks well of their good actions, and says little or nothing, except when necessity compels her, of their bad ones. She does not look around for evidence to prove an evil design, but hopes that what is doubtful will, by further light, appear to be correct. She imputes no evil as long as good is probable. She leans on the side of candor rather than that of severity. She makes every allowance that truth will permit. She looks to all the circumstances which can be pleaded in mitigation; suffers not her opinion to be formed, till she has had opportunities to escape from the midst of passion, and to cool from the wrath of contention. Love desires the happiness of others, and how can she be in haste to think evil of them?"

Propriety of Love

"Rejoiceth not in unrighteousness" (verse 6, R.V.) The word *adikia* is generally rendered "*unrighteousness.*" Love does not, like Balaam, "love the wages of unrighteousness" (2 Peter 2:15); nor has it "pleasure in unrighteousness," as the followers of anti-Christ will have (2 Thessalonians 2:12); nor will it yield its members as "instruments of unrighteousness unto sin" (Romans 6:13); nor will it have fellowship with unrighteousness (2 Corinthians 6:14). Love prays to be cleansed from all unrighteousness (1 John 1:9), and, in consequence, departs from it (2 Timothy 2:19). Anything that departs the straight path of honesty, love discards, and keeps straight onwards, like the kine who were yoked to the cart on which was the ark of the covenant: they "took the straight way to the way of Beth-shemesh" (1 Samuel 6:12). Love in action says: "In business I give thirty-six inches to the yard, sixteen ounces to the pound. No two prices for one article sold under the same conditions. Everything is sold for what it is said to be. No cotton-wool goods sold for only wool. In the home I seek to be true in utterance and right in action; in the Church I seek to love all; and in the world I endeavor to do to others as my Lord would wish."

Pleasure of Love

"Rejoices in the truth" (verse 6 NIV). The difference between the Revised "in" and Authorized Version "with" is important. One may rejoice "*in*" the truth, in admiring its suitability, its inspiration, and the fruits it produces, and yet not know the power of the truth in the life, even as a man may assent to a given proposition as being the right thing to follow, and yet not practice its teaching. To rejoice *with* the truth means that we have fellowship with it, in carrying out its teaching. In six other places in the New Testament, the same expression occurs, and in each instance there is the thought of fellowship. The neighbors and cousins of Elizabeth "*rejoiced with her*" (Luke 1:58) at the birth of John the Baptist. The good shepherd, when he had found the lost sheep, and the woman, when she discovered the lost piece of silver, both called their friends together, and said, "*Rejoice with me*" (Luke 15:6, 9). All the members of the Body of Christ, as they are in sympathy with the Head, "*rejoice with*" any one member that rejoices (1 Corinthians 12:26). There was a mutual joy between the apostle Paul and the saints in Philippi; hence he says, I "*rejoice with* you," and you "*rejoice with* me" (Philippians 2:17, 18). Thus, to rejoice with the truth means to have fellowship with it.

Paths of Love

There are four paths in which love walks. (1.) "*Beareth all things*." Love is never quick-tempered. The same word as rendered "*beareth*" is translated "*suffer*" in 1 Corinthians 9:12, and "*forbear*" in 1 Thessalonians 3:1, 5. Love is like Issachar—willing to be the burden-bearer for others (Genesis 49:14, 15). (2.) "*Believeth all things*." The same word as "*believeth*" is rendered "*trust*" in 1 Thessalonians 2:4, and "*committed*" in Galatians 2:7. Love is not suspicious. It has confidence and looks on others with the glance of faith. (3.) "*Hopeth all things*." The cheery smile of hope lights up the countenance of love. Love is like the lark: it loves to soar high and sing in the blue of heaven. (4.) "*Endureth all things*." Love is never tired—or if it is weary *in* the work, it is never weary *of* it. Paul is one of love's examples (2 Timothy 2:10), and Christ is *the* Example (Hebrews 12:2, 3).

Permanence of Love

"Love never fails" (verse 8 NIV). The word *ekpipto*, translated "*fails*," means to fall, or fall away, as when the stars fall from heaven (Mark 13:25), or one falls from grace (Galatians 5:4), or the passing away of the flower's beauty (1 Peter

1:24) but love ever keeps and shines in her orbit, keeps her place, and retains her beauty.

The permanence of love is further emphasized when we are told it "abides." The word "abides" means to remain, continue, dwell, endure. The Greek word "*meno*" is applied to the Word of God, which "*abides* forever" (1 Peter 1:23), to Christ, who in His High Priestly office "*continues* forever" (Hebrews 7:3), to the fruit of the believer, which "*should remain*" (John 15:16), to the Holy Spirit, of whom Christ said, "He dwells with you" (John 14:17); and the word is also rendered, "*might stand,*" in calling attention to God's purpose of electing grace. Further, the word "*meno*" rendered "*abideth,*" is the one which is generally used when the believer is exhorted to *abide* in Christ (John 15:4, 5, 6, 7, 9, 10), and in describing the believer's dwelling in God, and God's dwelling in the believer (1 John 3:17, 24; 4:12, 13, 15, 16). From this we gather that love is no fickle flame which soon dies out, but a permanent steady one, which burns like the light of the golden lampstand, continually (Leviticus 24:2).

"Alexander, Ceasar, Charlemagne, and myself," says Napoleon, "founded great empires; but upon what did the creations of our genius depend? Upon force. Jesus alone founded His empire upon love, and to this very day millions are ready to die for Him." Where are the empires of Alexander and Ceasar today? We look upon their ruins, and in those ruins we behold that what is gained by might and not by right, will work out its own destruction. What was the end of Napoleon's achievements? The artist's pencil has well depicted it, in the solitary figure, who, with bowed head and sorrowful countenance, paces up and down in his confinement on St. Helena. On the other hand, where love has acted, the name of the actor lives. The names of Howard, the prisoner's friend; Florence Nightingale, the soldier's nurse; Wilberforce, the slave's emancipator; Muller, the children's benefactor; Moffatt, the ardent missioner; Spurgeon, the faithful preacher; and Carey, the devoted missionary, live on with honor, and will live on, for their deeds were wrought *in* love, and prompted *by* love; therefore, they being dead are yet speaking.

Pre-eminence of Love

"The greatest of these is love" (verse 13). Love is the greatest of all graces, for it is that which makes the rest of the graces graceful; we may even say, every other grace is an expression of love.

What is *mercy* but love compassionate toward the guilty? What is *kindness* but love ministering to the needy? What is *pity* but love's thoughtfulness for the suffering? What is *faith* but love's confidence in the Savior? What is *hope* but love's expectation of her Lord? What is *courage* but love's fortitude in conflict? What is *righteousness* but love's conformity to God's law? What is *holiness* but love's imitation of the Divine? What is *joy* but love's exultation in the Savior? What is *peace* but love's repose in the Redeemer? What is *patience* but love's endurance in the race? What is *meekness* but love's unselfishness in giving way to others? What is *prayer* but love's supplication for the aid of the Almighty? What is *worship* but love's offering of praise? What is *penitence* but love bewailing her shortcomings? What is *justice* but love paying her dues? What is *beneficence* but love distributing her bounties? What is *faithfulness* but love's fidelity in performing her promises? What is *zeal* but love's ardor in fulfilling her trust? What is *testimony* but love telling out the glory of the gospel? What is *fruit* but love's life manifesting itself? What is *work* but love's employment in serving the Lord?

So might every trait of Christian life and labor be summarized. Love is the *backbone* of truth, the *lever* of grace, the *heart* of the gospel, the *summary* of Christianity, the *motor* of true service, the *meaning* of the Cross, and the *nature* of God; therefore, it must have the pre-eminent place and be like the Beloved, the chiefest among ten thousand, and the altogether lovely.

Pursuit of Love

"Follow after love" (1 Corinthians 14:1, R.V.). Here love is made to be a person, whom we are to follow. Where can such an One be found? Only in Christ. Therefore, He is the *Expression* of love's traits, as brought before us. Think then of Christ, in pondering the characteristics of love, for no one except He answers to them fully:

Christ's Suffering Love—"Suffereth long."
His Compassionate Love—"Is kind."
His Pure Love—"Envieth not."
His Abasing Love—"Vaunteth not itself."
His Humble Love—"Is not puffed up."
His Wise Love—"Does not behave itself unseemly."
His Unselfish Love—"Seeketh not her own."
His Patient Love—"Not provoked."
His Unsuspicious Love—"Thinketh no evil."
His Holy Love—"Rejoiceth not in iniquity."
His Truthful Love—"Rejoiceth in the truth."
His Forebearing Love—"Beareth all things."
His Expectant Love—"Hopeth all things."
His Trustful Love—"Believeth all things."
His Enduring Love—"Endureth all things."
His Unending Love—"Never faileth."
His Excelling Love—"Greatest of these is love."

Thus our thoughts are led along the "more excellent way" (1 Corinthians 12:31), to the *Most Excellent One*. Let us follow HIM, for as we do so, we must catch His spirit. Follow Him as Ruth did Naomi, *tenaciously* (Ruth 1:26.28); follow Him as the Levites did Moses, *faithfully* (Exodus 32:26.28); follow Him as the 300 men did Gideon, *earnestly* (Judges 7:17); follow Him as Ittai the Gittite did David, *consecratingly* (2 Samuel 15:19, 22); follow Him as Elisha did Elijah, *determinately* (2 Kings 2:1-6); follow Him as Peter did the angel, *obediently* (Acts 12:8); and as Israel did Ehud, *triumphantly* (Judges 3:28).

Power of Love

Our study would be incomplete if we were to stop without calling attention to the secret cause of all true loving, i.e., the moving power of Christ's indwelling presence. When we think of the power of love, we refer not to the influence which emanates from those who love, but rather to the power which makes us love in truth, and to love truly, that is, to Him whose name is Love.

Some years ago, a well-known professor brought out a booklet entitled, *The Greatest Thing in the World*, in which he sought to show that *man's love to God* was the greatest thing in the world. But surely this was a misnomer, for is not *God's love to man* the greatest thing in the world? Therefore to say the former is, is to cause the thoughtful Christian to endorse what the late kindly Archbishop Tait said, when he called the treatise, *The Strangest Thing in the World*. Our love to God is but the reflection of God's love to us even as the moon reflects the glory of the sun. Our love to God is but the outcome of God's love to us even as the rain is but the result of the sun's exhalation of the moisture from the earth. Our love to God is but the result of God's love to us even as the fruit is the result of the growth of the tree. Our love to God is the flowing forth of God's love through us even as the stream is the flowing forth of the spring.

William Tyndale, the translator of the Scriptures, had many enemies who persecuted him with cruel hatred. To them he bore the tenderest charity. It is recorded that to some of them he said one day: "Take away my goods, take away my good name! Yet so long as Christ dwelleth in my heart, so long shall I love you not a whit the less." In these words, Tyndale gives us the secret of all loving. Christ the loving One must indwell us if we are to love as He directs. Otherwise we shall be driven to despair, like the Brahmin, who, when he heard Dr. Duff read the 1 Corinthians 13, exclaimed: "Who can act up to that!" Who, indeed! There is only One who can, and that is the One who has already lived out every trait of Love's character.

Let us but trust Him, and Christ will do it. If we delight in Him with a simple faith, He will demonstrate through us His sanctifying love. There will be no doubt of this, if we can say with the poet,

"As the bridegroom to his chosen,
As the king unto his realm,
As the keep unto the castle,
As the pilot to the helm,
So, Lord, art Thou to me.

"As the fountain in the garden,
As the candle in the dark,
As the treasure in the coffer,
As the manna in the ark,
So, Lord, art Thou to me.

"As the ruby in the setting,
As the honey in the comb,
As the light within the lantern,
As the father in the home,
So, Lord, art Thou to me.

"As the sunshine to the heavens,
As the image to the glass,
As the fruit unto the fig-tree,
As the dew unto the grass,
So, Lord, art Thou to me."

13

The Discipler's Study

PART 1

Bacon says, "Studies serve for delight, for ornament, and for ability. The chief use for delight is in privateness and retiring; for ornament is in discourse; and for ability is in judgment and disposition of business." Bacon practically says that study is a means of enjoyment in privacy, a means of illustration in testimony, and a means of determination in business. In other words, study is what luscious fruit is to the thirsty traveler, refreshment; it is what windows are to the building, illumination; and it is what knowledge is to the experienced mariner, safety. Study is of vital importance in any position in life, if one is to gain success. It is of equal, if not of more pressing importance, for the Christian disciple. There is one Book which occupies the chief Place, and that is the Word of God. Therefore, in directing attention to the Discipler's Study, we would call special attention, in the first instance, to the disciple's treatment of his Bible in marking it. As he carefully marks it, it will be a source of enjoyment to himself, a means of help to others, and a trusted teacher to guide in the way of peace.

There are three points to which I call your attention.

First, *Meditation*—The Prelude to marking the Bible.
Second, *Method*—The Plan in marking the Bible.
Third, *Materials*—The Plant for marking the Bible.

Meditation, the Prelude to Marking the Bible

Imitation may be good, that is, copying into our Bibles what others have gathered from it; but the more excellent way is to gather our own fruit. There is a great difference between the strawberries which are bought at the shop and those which are gathered and eaten direct from the plants in the garden. There is as much difference between the truth which is found as the result of personal and prayerful research, and that which we receive through the medium of another.

There are two things, among others, which we should do in relation to the Scriptures. They are found in connection with the words, "search," "meditate."

1. *Search*. We read of the Jews in Berea, that they "*searched* the Scriptures daily" (Acts 17:11). The word which is rendered "*searched*," is translated "*discerned*" and "*judged*" in calling attention to the fact that "the natural man receiveth not the things of the Spirit of God; for they are foolishness unto him; neither can he know them, because they are spiritually *discerned*. But he that is spiritual *judgeth* all things" (1 Corinthians 2:14, 15).

The significance of the word in each case is this: to examine carefully as when a judge examines a prisoner. The word is thus given in Luke 23:14, where Pilate says to the rulers about the Lord Jesus, "I, having *examined* him before you, have found no fault in this man touching those things whereof ye accuse him." This implies a qualification to examine. Not every man is qualified to act as a judge, neither is everyone fitted to examine the Scriptures. It is "he that is spiritual," who judges (discerns) all things.

A writer in the *Contemporary Review*, in calling attention to the fact that titmice will find out a piece of meat which is hidden, while sparrows cannot, quoted the following words of Longfellow—

> "Never stoops the soaring titmouse
> On the bacon-rind or suet,
> But another titmouse watching,
> Wonders what he's got and follows,
> And a third pursues the second,
> First a speck, and then a titmouse,
> Till the place is full of titmice."

"How do the titmice find out the meat? The robin seems to be the only bird that shares the faculty with them, and it appears to me that it distinctly marks off these two birds as carnivorous, and possessed of 'a meat-sense' for which our own senses afford no better explanation than they do of the bee's 'honey-sense.'" As the titmice have a sense which enables them to discover the secreted bacon-rind, so the one who has spiritual life, and is living in the Spirit, has the divine sense and spiritual faculty to discern and understand spiritual things.

Having the spiritual sense, we are called upon to carefully evaluate the things revealed in the Scriptures, that all our decisions may be in accordance with them.

There is another expression rendered "*search*," which we find in connection with the study of the truth. That is found in 1 Peter 1:10, 11, where we are told that "the prophets have enquired and *searched diligently*, who prophesied of the grace that should come unto you: *searching* what, or what manner of time the Spirit of Christ which was in them did signify, when it testified beforehand the sufferings of Christ, and the glory that should follow." The use of the word is very suggestive; it is used to describe a lioness tracking a man who has robbed her of her cubs; of dogs following the scent of the game; and of spies exploring a country. The same Greek term is found in a variety of connections in the Septuagint version of the Old Testament: To search in a sack as when the steward of Joseph searched in the sacks of Joseph's brethren to find the hidden cup (Genesis 44:12). To search a house as when the King of Syria threatened to search the house of Ahab (1 Kings 20:6),

Coleridge says, "There are four kinds of readers. The first class may be compared to an *hour-glass*, their reading being as the sand; it runs in and runs out, and leaves not a vestige behind. A second class resembles a *sponge*, which imbibes everything and returns it in nearly the same state, only a little dirtier. A third class is like a *jelly-bag*, which allows all that is pure to pass away, and retains only the refuse and dregs. The fourth class may be compared to the *slave of Golconda*, who, casting aside all that is worthless, preserves only the pure gems."

We will resemble the slaves of Golconda if we consistently practice what we know, for the one who does His will shall know of the doctrine; we will discover fresh gems of God's grace and the precious jewels of His truth as we *meditate* upon the Word of His love. There were two things that characterized the clean animals upon which Israel could feed, namely, the divided hoof and the chewing of the cud; so we must have the divided hoof of a holy walk in separation *from* evil and in separation *to* God; and also the chewing of the cud in meditating upon the truths of God's Word, and in contemplating the Living Word as He is revealed within it.

2. *Meditate.* Paul, in writing to Timothy by the Holy Spirit, urges him to "give attendance to reading, to exhortation, to doctrine," etc.; and says, "*meditate* upon these things; give thyself wholly to them" (1 Timothy 4:13-15). The meaning of the term meditate is to think upon anything, so as to be able to perform it. It comes from the same root as the term "careth," when we are told that the "Lord *careth*" (1 Peter 5:7). The Lord not only thinks of us, but He thinks to a purpose, namely, to help. Christ uses the word in a negative sense when He charges His disciples not to "*premeditate*" what they shall say when they are brought before magistrates (Mark 13:11). To premeditate in this case means to think in order to act. Timothy was not to be in a listless and dreamy mood, with no practical end in view, but he was to think in order to act. This is further brought out when Paul uses the expressions, "give attendance," and "give thyself wholly to them." The latter suggests an ardent student, and the former a diligent servant.

"I put my soul into it," was the reply of one, who had risen from the position of an errand boy to be the head of a large business, when he was asked for the secret of his success; and there is no success in anything without the soul is put into it. This is specially true with regard to meditating upon God's Word. There are two things always to remember—first, to get the precious gems of God's truth, there must be patient, persistent, and careful study; and second, we must put to use by prayerful practice what we get, or else it will be like the manna which was not eaten. It will only breed worms. In other words, merely knowing the truth and not practicing it will puff up, while practicing what we know will build us up and make us strong and healthy in soul.

We have been looking at and pondering God's Word, mainly from the human standpoint. There is one essential thing we must always remember, and that is the illuminating presence of the Holy Spirit. In the dusk of the evening we go into some grand cathedral with a friend. The friend begins to describe the beauty of the colored windows, but owing to the absence of light no beauty is to be seen. The following day, at noon, we go again to the cathedral, when the sun is shining into the place, and lighting up the scenes depicted upon the windows.

This makes them stand out in unmistakeable splendor. What has made the difference? We had the power of seeing before, but there was no illumination around. What the sun was to the windows, the Holy Spirit is to the prayerful student of God's Word. He *illuminates* it. When He gives the *inner* illumination, namely, the spiritual sense to see; and the *outer* illumination, namely, the unveiling of the truth, as in Jesus, then we see light in His light.

Let us take an illustration of the fitness and fullness of the Word in noting a few of the appellations which are applied to it.

The Word is the Word of the Lord to *reveal* (1 Thessalonians 4:15).
The Word of Christ to *inspire* (Colossians 3:16).
The Word of the Gospel to *gladden* (Acts 15:7).
The Word of Reconciliation to *communicate* (2 Corinthians 5:19).
The Word of Salvation to *deliver* (Acts 13:26).
The Word of Grace to *invigorate* (Acts 20:32).
The Word of Faith to *assure* (Romans 10:8).
The Word of Truth to *arm* (2 Corinthians 6:7).
The Word of Righteousness to *feed* (Hebrews 5:13).
The Word of Life to *attract* (Philippians 2:16).
The Word of God to *command* (Hebrews 4:12).

These designations of God's Word are not given in a haphazard way, neither can the terms be interchanged. There is a distinct and definite thought associated with each. Let us take the last by way of illustration, namely, "The Word of God." The Word of God is said to be, "Quick (living) and powerful"; hence, where the Word of God is spoken of as such, one of these thoughts will be found in connection with it. The following instances, where the expression occurs, will illustrate:

Powerful, to create.—"The worlds were framed by the *Word of God*" (Hebrews 11:3).

Powerful, to beget.—"Begotten again, not of corruptible seed, but of incorruptible, through the *Word of God*" (1 Peter 1:23).

Powerful, to implant.—"Faith cometh by hearing, and hearing by the *Word of God*" (Romans 10:17).

Powerful, to command.—"Ye received the *Word of God,* which ye heard of us, ye received it not as the word of men, but as it is in truth, the *Word of God,* which effectually worketh also in you that believe" (1 Thessalonians 2:13).

Powerful, to keep.—"The *Word of God* abideth in you, and ye have overcome the wicked one" (1 John 2:14).

Powerful, to sanctify.—"Sanctified by the *Word of God*" (1 Timothy 4:5)

Powerful, to make way.—"The *Word of God* is not bound" (2 Timothy 2:9).

The one practical result that flows out of the searching of God's Word is that it makes us like it as we feed upon it, for it communicates its nature to us. It is a well-known scientific fact that birds are changed by the food they eat. Seagulls which feed upon fish, if confined and fed upon grain, have had their stomachs entirely changed. "Hunter, for example, in a classical experiment, so changed the environment of a seagull by keeping it in captivity, that it could only secure a grain diet. The effect was to modify the stomach of the bird, normally adapted to a fish diet, until in time it came to resemble in structure the gizzard of an ordinary grain-feeder, such as the pigeon. Holmgrén again reversed this experiment by feeding pigeons for a lengthened period on a meat-diet, with the result that the gizzard became transformed into a carnivorous stomach. Mr. A. R. Wallace mentions the case of a Brazilian parrot which changes its color from green to red or yellow when fed upon the fat of certain fishes." I have seen canaries which had a red hue about their yellow feathers, and on asking the cause, was informed that it was the result of giving cayenne pepper to them when moulting. What is true in the natural world is also true in the spiritual realm; that is, we become like the thing upon which we feed. The Word of God is holy in its nature, powerful in its utterance, living in its composition, pure in its character, righteous in its structure, Christ-honoring in its revelation, separating in its tendency, God-glorifying in its aim, inspiring in its working, and consecrating in its influence; and as that Word lives in and operates through us, we shall be holy in nature, powerful in utterance, living in God's purpose, pure in heart, righteous in action, Christ-honoring in life, separate from evil, God-glorifying in conduct, inspiring in service, and consecrated to God.

Materials, or the Plant for Marking

It may seem unnecessary to say what I am about to say, as the suggestions should be obvious without the saying. But my experience has taught me that they do not occur to all. There are several things that are essential in Bible marking:

A clean, fine-pointed pen; a ruler; a Bible on whose sheets one may write; a notebook for making notes; a discriminating eye.

Method, or Plan in Marking

Don't mark the Bible for the sake of marking. The facing page will illustrate what I mean (see page 131).

There are three things to which attention is directed in the sketch before us.

First, *Railways*. Certain similar expressions can be connected, such as—

"Rejoice in the Lord" (verse 4).

"I rejoiced in the Lord" (verse 10).

And if the connected words are pondered, it will be seen that in the first we have Paul's injunction, and in the second his experience, telling us that he practiced what he preached.

"The peace of God" (verse 7).

"The God of peace" (verse 9).

In the first, we find the blessing of peace, but in the second we discover the Blesser Himself. The former is what comes from Him, but the latter is what He is Himself.

"Be careful for nothing" (verse 6).

"My God shall supply all" (verse 19).

PHILLIPIANS 4

4 Rejoice[a] in the Lord alway: *and*
again I say, ~~Rejoice.~~ *farewell.*
5 Let your moderation[c] be known
unto all men. The Lord[d] is at
hand.
anxious 6 Be careful[e] for nothing; but in
every thing by prayer and
supplication, with thanksgiving,
let your requests be make known
unto God.
7 And the peace[g] of God, which
passeth all understanding, shall
Deut. keep your hearts and minds
32:10 through Christ Jesus.
8 Finally, brethren, whatsoever
things are true,[h] whatsoever things
are [T]honest, whatsoever things *are*
just,[j] whatsoever things *are* pure,[k]
what-soever things *are* lovely,[l]
whatsoever things *are* of good
report;[m] if *there* be any virtue,[n] and
if *there* be any praise,[o] think on
these things.
9 Those things, which ye have
both learned, and [T]received, and
1 Cor. heard, and seen in me, do: and
11:1 the God[p] of peace shall be with
you.
10 But I rejoiced in the Lord
greatly, that now at the last your
care of me[q] hath flourished again:
wherein ye were also careful, but
ye lacked opportunity.[r]
Heb. 11 Not that I speak in respect of
5:8 ~~want:~~ for I have learned in
whatsoever state I am, *therewith* to
be content.[s]
12 I both how to be abased, and
I know how to abound: every
where, and in all things, I am
instructed, both to be full and to
be hungry, both to abound and to
suffer need.
~~13~~ I can do all things through[b] *Zech. 10:12*
Christ which strengtheneth me. *Num. 13:30*
14 Notwithstanding, ye have
well done that ye did communi-
cate with my afflictions. *Heb. 13:6; Acts 20:35*
15 Now ye Philippians know
also, that in the beginning of the
gospel, when I departed from
Macedonia no[t] church communicated with me as concerning giving and again unto my necessity.
16 For even in Thessalonica ye
sent once and again unto my *Heb. 13:7*
necessity.
17 Not because I desire a gift; but *2 Cor. 9:10*
I desire fruit that may abound to *Col. 1:6-10*
your account.
18 But I have all, and abound, I
am full, having received of *Eph. 5:1*
Epaphroditus the things *which*
were sent from you, an odour of a
sweet smell, a sacrifice[u]
acceptable wellpleasing to God.
19 But my God shall supply[v] all *Deut. 31:23*
your need, according to his *Is. 45*
riches[w] in glory by Christ Jesus. *2 Cor. 12:9*
20 Now[x] unto God our Father *be*
glory forever and ever. Amen.
21 Salute every saint in Christ
Jeus. The brethern which are
with me greet you.
22 All the saints salute you,
chiefly they that are of Caesar's
household.
23 The grace of our Lord Jesus
Christ *be* with you all. Amen.

A.D. 64

a chap. 3:1
b John 15:5 2 Cor. 12:9
c 1 Cor. 9:25
d Rev. 22:7, 20
e Matt. 6:35 1 Pet. 5:7
f 2 Cor. 11:8, 9
g Is. 28:3 Jn. 14:27
h Eph. 4:25
T or, memorable
i 2 Cor. 8:21
j De. 16:20 Isa. 26:7
k Ja. 3:17 1 Jn. 3:3
l 1 Cor. 13
T or, have received
m Col. 4:5 Heb. 11:2
n 2 Pet. 1:3, 4 Prov. 13:3
o Heb. 13:16
r Heb. 13:20
s Ps. 23:1
T or, is received
u Rom. 16:27
v 2 Cor. 11:9
w Heb. 13:5

Phil. 2:19 trust in the Lord
Phil. 2:24 trust in the Lord
Phil. 2:20 receive Him
Phil. 3:1 rejoice in the Lord
Phil. 4:4 rejoice in the Lord
Phil. 4:10 rejoice in the Lord
Phil. 4:1 stand fast in the Lord

Phil. 3:10 Exemplified in the family of Bethany
That I may know Him– Martha– Luke 10:38
The power of His resurrection– Lazarus– John 11:44
The fellowship of His sufferings– Mary– John 12:3

In the first, we have the command not to worry, and in the second we have the reason. There is no cause for anxiety, since the Lord cares and supplies.

"I have learned" (verse 11).

"I am instructed" (verse 12).

The instructed man is the one who has learned. He who has the experience speaks with authority.

"Glory unto God" (verse 20).

"Grace with you" (verse 23).

In these sentences we have Paul's doxology and desire, or what he would give to God, and what he wished from God.

The above will suffice to indicate what I mean by *railways*. Sometimes it may be a given word that is of frequent occurrence, as the words "joy" and "rejoice" in the Epistle to the Philippians; or it may be a thought that is railwayed, as the threefold action of love in 1 John 4:9-17, where we read of

"Love *toward* us" (verse 9).

"Love *in* us" (verse 12).

"Love *with* us" (Margin, verse 17).

Second, *Notes*. To refer again to the illustrative page, it will be seen that there are two notes of Bible readings at the bottom. The one on Philippians 3:10 is illustrated by the three characters in the home at Bethany. If Martha had known the Lord better, she would never have found fault with her sister Mary, as Christ indicates in His gentle rebuke (Luke 10:38-42). Lazarus illustrates the power of "His resurrection," for he experienced Christ's raising power, while Mary illustrates the "fellowship of His sufferings," for she was the only one who comprehended that He came into the world to die; hence she anointed Him for His burial, and thus had fellowship with Him in His sufferings.

Third, *Marginal References*. Again referring to the illustrative page, if the attention is turned to verse 11, it will be seen that the words, "I have learned," are connected with an arrow which points to the margin, in which is found the reference, "Hebrews 5:8," and if this Scripture is turned up, it will be discovered that Christ is our example in learning. Again, the words, "I can do all things," in verse 13, are connected in the printed margin with John 15:5, where Christ says, "Without me ye can do nothing"; and in the opposite blank margin, references are given to Zechariah 10:12, and Numbers 13:30; in the former Scripture, we have a promise to strengthen, and in the latter we have an example of one who was strengthened by the Lord, and hence, in the face of great difficulties, was able to say, "We are able."

The Discipler's Study

PART 2

There are two "Take heeds" which Christ gives us in speaking of the Word of God, and these are, "Take heed *what* ye hear" (Mark 4:24); and "Take heed *how* ye hear" (Luke 8:18). The first has reference to the *object* of our hearing—the Word of God; and the second, to the *method* of our hearing—our treatment of the Word of God. It is this second point to which we direct attention in further considering the Discipler's Study, for as we are to take heed how we *hear*, so we should take heed how we *study* God's Word.

There are different ways in which we may study God's Word. We shall confine our study to the following points: Geographically, Geologically, Grammatically, Topically, Comprehensively, Comparatively, Concentratingly, Critically, Textually, and Practically.

Geographically

What we mean by studying the Word of God in a geographical sense is to read through a Gospel or an Epistle and ponder it, in order to get the main drift of its unfolding. For instance, the first Epistle of John presents Christ to us as the Word, the Divine Logos, who unfolds God as Light, Love, and Life. The whole Epistle may be summed up:

In chapter 1:1-4, Christ is seen as the Word, in His oneness with the Father in the past eternity, and His manifestation in human form in time, as the Revealer of the Father.

Chapters 1:5 to 2:11 show God as the Light, God in His holy nature and character.

Chapters 2:12 to 5:3 reveal God as Love. In Christ's life and death we see what God is.

Chapter 5:4 to 5:21 reveals God as the Life. We see God in Christ as the Source and Sustenance of Life Eternal.

From the above brief outline, it will he seen that the first section presents

Christ as the Life, and this is presented first, because life is what we need; but before life can come to us, Light and Love must act for us. Therefore, Light is the claim of Love. Love meets the claim of Light; and Light imparts the life of Love.

Light is the claim of Love, for God in His holiness makes known His claim in His law, which is that man should love Him with all his heart, and his neighbor as himself.

Love meets the claim of Light, for God in His grace has given His Son to die, "to be the propitiation for our sins," and this propitiation meets the height of God's throne in His demand, and the depth of man's need in his extremity.

Light imparts the life of Love. That is, God in His righteousness can now bestow the provision of His love in giving to man eternal life through faith in His Son, thus making the believer one with Christ and Himself.

The main thought running through the first Epistle of John is *fellowship*. The following outline illustrates this:

I. Prelude to Fellowship (1:1, 2)
   1. Christ's manifestation to us
   2. Listening to Christ
   3. Receiving Christ

II. Partners in Fellowship (1:3)
   1. The Father
   2. The Son
   3. Believers

III. Joy of Fellowship (1:4)
   1. Word of God

IV. Place of Fellowship (1:5-7)
   1. Announcement of it (1:5)
   2. Essential to it, not walking in darkness (1:6)
   3. Character of it, "Light" (1:7)
   4. Keeper in it, "The Blood" (1:7)

V. Hindrances to Fellowship (1:8, 10)
   1. Assertion of sinlessness (1:8)
   2. Self-righteousness (1:10)

VI. Restoration to Fellowship (1:9; 2:1, 2)
   1. Confession of sins (1:9)
   2. Cleansing from unrighteousness (1:9)
   3. God's Faithfulness (1:9)
   4. Christ's Advocacy (2:1, 2)
   5. Christ's propitiation (2:1, 2)

VII. Safeguards to Fellowship (2:1-6)
   1. Not sinning
   2. Keeping His commands
   3. Keeping His Word
   4. Abiding in Him
   5. Walking as He walked

VIII. Results of Fellowship (2:7-14)
1. Shining for Christ
2. Loving like Him
3. Helpful to others
4. Not hating the brethren
5. Rejoicing in sins forgiven
6. Knowing the Father
7. Overcoming the evil one
8. God's Word abiding within us

IX. Enemies to Fellowship (2:14-19)
1. The evil one
2. The world's trinity of evil
3. The antichrist
4. False brethren

X. The Power of Fellowship (2:20, 27)
1. Anointing of the Holy Spirit

XI. The Law of Fellowship (2:21-26)
1. The truth
2. Knowing the truth
3. Truth abiding in us
4. Abiding in Christ

XII. Blessings of Fellowship (2:28—3:3)
1. Confidence in the Lord (2:28)
2. Recognition in Him (2:29)
3. Knowing His love (3:1)
4. Future eradiated (3:2)
5. Life purified (3:3)

XIII. Evidences of Fellowship (3:4-22)
1. Comprehending what sin is (3:4)
2. Knowing Christ's purpose (3:5, 8)
3. Not sinning (3:6, 9)
4. Doing righteously (3:7, 10)
5. Loving each other (3:11, 14, 16-19, 23, 24)
6. Hated by the world (3:12,13, 15)
7. Uncondemning heart (3:20, 21)
8. Answered prayer (3:22)

XIV. Character of Fellowship (4:1-21)
1. Must be in the truth (4:1-6)
2. Must be in the love of God (4:7-21)

XV. Essentials in Fellowship (5:1-12)
1. Faith in Jesus as Christ (5:1)
2. The New Birth (5:1)
3. Love to God (5:1)
4. Love to the brethren (5:1)
5. Keeping God's commands (5:2, 3)

6. Overcoming the world (5:4, 5)
7. Believing the Spirit's witness (5:6-12)

XVI. Helps in Fellowship (5:13-21)

1. Believing God's Word (5:13)
2. Prayer (5:14-17)
3. Kept by Christ (5:18. R.V.)
4. Assurance (5:19, 20)
5. Separation (5:21)

Generally speaking, one should keep the five following points in mind in reading any section of God's Word: Who, Where, When, What, Why it was written. Apply these points to John's Epistle.

Who wrote the Epistle? John, the Beloved Disciple.

Where was the Epistle written? It is supposed to have been written in Ephesus.

When was the Epistle written? It is supposed to have been written when the Apostle was aged; hence, the frequent expression, "My *little children*" (2:1, 12, 13, 18, 28; 3:7, 10, 18; 4:4; 5:2, 21).

What was the Epistle intended to do? To combat the gnostic antichristian error, that Christ did not actually come and suffer in the flesh (2:21, 22; 4:1, 2; 5:1; 2 John 7-11); and to declare the evidences of life which are seen in those who are born again (2:29; 3:9; 4:7; 5:1, 4, 18).

Why was the Epistle written? The two main reasons are given in connection with the words, "*These things*" (1:4; 5:13). See also as to details, the words "*write*" (1:4; 2:1, 7, 8, 12, 13), and "*written*" (2:14, 21, 26; 5:13).

As the keynote in a piece of music governs the whole of it, so we find that fellowship with God, in Christ, by the Holy Spirit, and evidenced by oneness with believers, is the pitch of this Epistle, and every note accords with this main theme. Let us ever endeavor, whenever we come to any one portion of God's truth:

> "To know the Word, perceive its plan,
> To feel its force, and learn its scope."

Geologically

Geology deals with the structure of the earth's crust and the substances which compose it. The geologist endeavors to understand the composition of the earth. When we state, therefore, that we want to study the Word of God from a geological standpoint, we mean to examine words and phrases in order to know their derivation, meaning, and use. Let us take two words by way of illustration, one from the Old Testament, and one from the New. They are "*Atonement*" and "*Power*."

"ATONEMENT."—Many preachers have called attention to the syllables of the word, at-one-ment, as making them to explain the meaning of the word. This will not bear the light of Scripture, for reconciliation, to bring at one two offended parties, is rather a result of the atonement, than the atonement itself.

Besides, this explanation reflects on the character of God, for the expression is generally, "to make an atonement" (Leviticus 8:34; 15), which would signify that something was done to reconcile God to man, whereas, He never went from man, but man came from Him; hence, we find "God was in Christ reconciling the world unto himself" (2 Corinthians 5:19)—not Himself to the world. The fact is, the word atonement means *to cover*, or *shelter*. Canon Girdlestone, in his *Synonyms of the Old Testament*, says upon this word, "The Hebrew word whereby this doctrine is universally set forth in the Old Testament, is CAPHER, the original meaning of which is supposed to be to cover, or shelter. A noun formed from it is sometimes used to signify a village as a place of shelter. Another form of this word, namely, COPHER, usually rendered ransom, is translated '*camphire*' in Song of Solomon 1:14. In Genesis 6:14, the verb and noun are used where God is represented as telling Noah to '*pitch*' the ark within and without with '*pitch*.'"

The question will naturally be asked, "How is the average reader of the Bible, who does not understand Hebrew and Greek, to find out the use, derivation and meaning of Bible words?" Easily enough, if the "average reader" will go to a little expense and pains. We will suppose for one moment he possesses an Englishman's Hebrew Concordance and Strong's Exhaustive Concordance. He takes the former first, and looks in the index for the word "atonement," and he finds that the word "CAPHAR" is translated "*Pitch*" in Genesis 6:14; "*Appease*" in Genesis 32:20; "*Cleansed*" in Numbers 35:33; "*Merciful*" in Deuteronomy 32:43; "*Pardon*" in 2 Chronicles 30:18; "*Purge away*" in Psalm 79:9; "*Disannulled*" in Isaiah 28:18; "*Pacified*" in Ezekiel 16:63.

The word "COPHER," rendered "*atonement*," is translated "*Pitch*" in Genesis 6:14; "*Sum of money*" in Exodus 21:30; "*Ransom*" in Exodus 30:12; "*Satisfaction*" in Numbers 35:31, 32; "*Villages*" in 1 Samuel 6:18; "*Bribe*" in 1 Samuel 12:3; and "*Camphire*" in Song of Solomon 1:14.

Having seen how the word is translated, he will then take Strong's Concordance, see the number given against the word "*atonement*," and then look up the number in the Lexicon at the end of the book. He will find under CAPHAR, this comment—"A primary root, meaning to cover. To appease, or condone; to placate or cancel." And under COPHER this note is given—"From Caphar. A cover, *i.e.*, a village (as covered in); bitumen (as used for coating); and the henna flowers (as used for dyeing)."

From the above, it will be seen that the primary meaning of the word "atonement" is to cover. When Jacob sent the present to "*appease*" his brother, he sought to hide himself behind it, that his past conduct might not be seen. Thus is it with the atonement of Christ. It is that which completely covers the claim of God and gives Him satisfaction; and it absolutely covers the believer's sinfulness and makes him exclaim with the Psalmist, "Blessed is he whose . . . sin is covered" (Psalm 32:1).

"POWER."—There are five words rendered "*power*" in the New Testament, and these are "*Arkee*," "*Exousia*," "*Iskus*," "*Dunamis*," and "*Kratos*." To use these words indiscriminately is to fail in rightly dividing the word of truth.

"*Arkee*."—This word signifies that which is principal, first, the head, or the beginning of anything. It is used of the spies who were watching Christ to deliver Him to the "*power*" (Luke 20:20). The word is rendered "*Principality*" and "*Beginning*" in calling attention to Christ's exalted position (Colossians 2:10), and to Him as the commencement of things (Revelation 21:6) and it is also used of the wicked angels, who "kept not their *first* estate" (Jude 6). The word is mainly associated with a *position of power*; hence, the believer is exhorted to "hold the *beginning*" (Hebrews 3:14) of his confidence, and not be like the Church in Ephesus, which left its first love; nor like Samson, who lost his power in having the symbol of Nazariteship cut—his hair.

"*Exousia.*"—This word means the right, or liberty, to act; hence, those who have washed their robes, have the "*right*" to the Tree of Life (Revelation 22:14); and the apostle uses the word when he calls attention to his not being chargeable to the saints, "not," he says, "because we have not *power*" (2 Thessalonians 3:9). He had the right, but he did not use it. Christ used this word when He said He had "*power*" to lay down His life (John 10:18), and when He called attention to the "*authority*" which His Father had conferred upon Him (John 5:27; 17:2). Again He uses the word when He promises to the overcomers, "*Power* over the nations" (Revelation 2:26). This word is also applied to us as believers when we are told of the "*right*" which God gives us to become His children (John 1:12, margin). Thus, as Robert Chapman says, "We are children of God by right, and not by sufferance."

Iskus.—This word is expressive because of its inherent force. It points to the internal quality of any given thing. It indicates the character of a person, or the quality of an action. It is translated "*mighty*," and "*might*" in speaking of God's power (Ephesians 1:19; 6:10), and it is used in speaking of the "*ability*" which God gives to those who minister in His Name (1 Peter 4:11). Shakespeare says, "The devil hath power to assume a pleasing shape," but he lacks that personal sanctity which is born of the holiness of God, hence his influence must always tend to what he is in himself—evil; he has no power to raise to the higher and holier things.

"*Dunamis.*"—The word dynamite comes from this word, hence, its signification is power in action, or the transference of power from one body to another. It is translated "*violence*" in Hebrews 11:34; "*virtue*" in Luke 6:19; "*strength*" in 2 Corinthians 12:9; "*might*" in Ephesians 3:16; and "*power*" in Romans 15:13, and 1 Corinthians 2:4. The first passage speaks of the "violence of fire," and, therefore, it illustrates power in action. In each of the other places there is the thought of the transference of power, as illustrated in the healing of the woman by Christ, in His strengthening of Paul, and in the efficiency which is supplied by the Holy Spirit to the believer. This power makes the believer say, with Whittier:—

> "In God's own might
> We gird us for the coming fight,
> And, strong in Him whose cause is ours,
> In conflict with unholy power,
> We grasp the weapons He has given,—
> The Light, and Truth, and Love of Heaven."

"*Kratos.*"—This means the manifestation of power, or the strength which is requisite in order to perform any given action. It is translated by the words *"strength," "dominion,"* and *"power,"* in speaking of God's power in action (Luke 1:51; 1 Peter 4:11; Jude 25; Ephesians 1:9; Colossians 1:11); and it is also rendered *"mightily"* in Acts 19:20, when reference is made to the widespread influence exerted by the effective working of the Word of God. When applied to the believer, the word is used to describe what God does in him (Colossians 1:11). In every other case in the New Testament excepting one, it is used in an objective sense, in calling attention to what God has and does. There is an exception in Hebrews 2:14. There attention is called to the power which Satan had before Christ by His death nullified his dominion. Does not the use of this word in the New Testament demonstrate to us beyond any question that God alone is the One who has the requisite strength to perform any given thing in the spiritual realm of grace? The late Princess Alice, in reply to one who asked who she was, said, "I, myself, am nobody, but my mother is the Queen of England." So every loyal-hearted Christian worker says, "I am nothing in myself, but my Savior is the King of Glory. Therefore, to Him be all the glory and dominion."

Much more might be written to illustrate the geological study of God's Word, but the above will suffice to show the pleasure and profit of it, as well as its importance; for, as Addison says, "Words are the transcript of those ideas which are in the mind of man." So we say of the words of the Bible, "They are the transcript of those ideas which are in the mind of God."

Grammatically

What is one of the first things a missionary would do to acquire the language of an aboriginal race to whom he wished to preach? Does he not get to know the names of objects, thus making himself familiar with the nouns of the language? Then he seeks to know what the various objects *do* in order to learn his verbs. In the next place, it would be necessary to ascertain the relation which one object bears to another, and thus get the prepositions. We may take our cue from the above as to how we may study the Word of God in an elementary way from the grammatical stand-point.

In thinking of the nouns of Scripture, our thoughts will cluster around the three most important names and titles of Christ, i.e., Lord, Jesus, Christ. In studying the verbs, we will call attention to the verb to love; and in pondering the prepositions, we will note one out of the many which are used in the New Testament.

Paul's reply to the jailer's anxious enquiry, as to what he must do to be saved, was, "Believe on the Lord Jesus Christ." To believe on the Lord Jesus Christ is to believe in Him as such. As Lord, He is the Sovereign *over* us (1 Peter 3:15, R.V.); as Jesus, He is the Savior *for* us (Matthew 1:21); and as Christ, He is the Sanctifier *within* us (Galatians 2:20). These names are not used in an indiscriminate manner. The Holy Spirit never says "Jesus" when He means "Christ," and He never says "Lord" when He means "Jesus." Let us take an example illustrating each.

LORD.—It is of peculiar interest to note that Judas never called Jesus "Lord." When Christ told His disciples that one of their number would betray Him, they all, except the traitor, said, "Lord, is it I?" But Judas exclaimed, "Master, is it I?" (Matthew 26:12, 25). The eleven used a word which means Ruler, or Owner, therefore, the one who has the right to exercise lordship. Only Judas gave to Christ the title of Master, or Teacher. Not without significance is it revealed that when the other Judas calls Christ "Lord," the Holy Spirit distinctly states it was "not Iscariot" (John 14:22). We are not surprised at this, for "No man can say that Jesus is the Lord, but by the Holy Spirit" (1 Corinthians 12:3). When we are told that the last supper is the "Lord's Supper," it is such because He has told us to remember Him in this way. We have no choice but to obey Him in the matter. Again we are exhorted to "rejoice in the Lord"; by implication, it says we are walking in obedience to Him, thus joy comes in consequence. When the believer is told to "marry in the Lord," it means he is not only to marry a believer (that would be marrying in Christ), but he is to take the one the Lord wishes him to have.

JESUS.—Jesus is the name which is associated with Christ's humiliation. In the record of His earthly life, as brought out in the Gospels, it occurs 566 times; while Christ, or "the Christ," only occurs 36 times; but the name is not only associated with His humiliation but with His exaltation. For all things in heaven, earth, and hell are to bow to Him as bearing the name of Jesus (Philippians 2:10). We must not forget though that His exaltation is because of what He accomplished in His humiliation. Remembering this, it gives additional interest when we discover that the name Jesus occurs eight times in the Epistle to the Hebrews, in connection with His present service and High Priestly glory. As Jesus He is seen as—

The Exalted Man (2:9).
The Appointed High Priest (3:1, R.V.)
The Gracious Forerunner (6:20).
The Sure Bondsman (7:22).
The Efficient Opener (10:19).
The Living Example (12:2).
The Holy Mediator (12:24).
The Loving Sanctifier (13:12).

CHRIST.—Drummond says, "He lives who dies to win a lasting name." Jesus, as the Christ, especially illustrates this saying. As the Anointed of God, who was known by the title Christ in the Gospels, He has had given to Him, because of His life and death, the title "Christ" as a proper name. Thus we are told that God has made the despised Jesus the Christ of His throne (Acts 2:36).

The Christship of Jesus is a most interesting subject, for it illustrates the progressiveness of revelation. Thus in the *Gospels* we have *Christ personally*, and as such He is the Anointed and Sent One of God (John 1:41; 4:25). He is the Builder and Foundation of His Church (Matthew 16:16-18; Mark 8:29).

In the *Acts* we have *Christ officially*, in His exaltation and power, hence, the burden of the apostle's preaching is, "Jesus is the Christ" (Acts 5:42; 8:5; 9:22; 17:3; 18:5, 28, R.V.). In the *Epistles* we have *Christ mystically* (1 Corinthians 12:12), as the Head of the Church; hence, believers are always said to be "in Christ" as to their position (2 Corinthians 12:2; Ephesians 2:6, 10, 13; 3:6), and Christ is said to be in them as to their power of life (Galatians 2:20). This topic alone illustrates the importance of carefully pondering the teaching of the Holy Spirit and of following Him, as He leads by the torch of His Word into the wondrous cavern of truth. Thus we see its ever-increasing beauty.

THE VERB LOVE.—There are two words which are rendered love in the New Testament—*Agapeo* and *Phileo*. The former, when applied to God's love to man, signifies the *grace of love* in compassionating him, as when we read, "God so loved the world . . ." (John 3:16). When it is used of the Father's love for Christ, it means the *esteem of love*—"The Father loveth the Son" (John 3:35). When used of Christ's love for His people, it signifies the *care of love*—"Having loved his own . . . he loved them unto the end" (John 13:1). When used to express the believer's love for the Lord, it denotes the *reverence of love*—"We love him because he first loved us" (1 John 4:19). When used of the believer's love to fellow-believers, it indicates the *sympathy of love*—"That ye love one another, as I have loved you" (John 13:34). When used of the believer's love to the world, it expresses the *help of love*—"Love your enemies" (Matthew 5:44); and when used in a prohibitive sense, it shows forth the *regard of love*—"Love not the world" (1 John 2:15).

Phileo is used in a bad sense, as well as in a good one, and denotes in a general way fondness for anything, and may be summarized as follows: *Endearment of love*—"The Father loveth the Son" (John 5:20). *Ardor of love*—"Behold how he loved him!" (John 11:36). *Passion of love*—"He that loveth his life shall lose it" (John 12:25). *Profession of love*—"Whomsoever I shall kiss" *[phileo]* (Matthew 26:48). *Desire of love*—"Love the uppermost rooms" (Matthew 23:6). *Kinship of love*—"the world would love his own" (John 15:19). *Fondness of love*—"Greet them that love us" (Titus 3:15).

These two words are used together in one incident in the life of Christ, and that is, in His personal interview with Peter, after His resurrection. In Christ's first and second questions to Peter, "Lovest thou me," He uses the word *agapeo*, but Peter replies, "Thou knowest that I love thee" each time, using the word *phileo*. He, evidently, after his backsliding, is not prepared to use the word which is expressive of fidelity to his Master, and yet, notwithstanding his failure, he is fond of Him. After this repeated expression of fondness, Christ uses Peter's own word, "Lovest thou me" (art thou fond of me?), and he replies, "Lord, thou knowest all things, thou knowest that I love thee" (John 21:15-17).

THE PREPOSITION EK.—It may be well to state, although the majority of our readers know it, that a preposition shows the relation of one word to another. We can only call attention to one of the many prepositions used in the New Testament, and that one is *ek*. Let us note three of the connections in which it is found. The new birth, resurrection, and separation.

The New Birth.—In John 1:13 *ek* occurs four times and is translated *of*. This does not give the full force of its meaning. It is better rendered as in several places in the Gospel according to John by the words *out of* (John 1:46; 2:15; 4:30, 47; 7:38; 10:28, 39; 13:1; 15:19; 17:15).

Remembering that its meaning is *out of*, gives added force and interest to the words of John 1:13 where we are told from whom the new birth is not, and from whom it is. It is not "*out of*" blood, that is, not by natural descent; not "*out of*" the will of the flesh, that is, it is not obtained by the power of man's own will;

and it is not *"out of"* the will of man, that is, it is not the bestowment of one man to another; but it is *"out of"* God. He alone is the Imparter of spiritual life.

Resurrection. The Jews believed in the resurrection *of* the dead, but when the disciples began to preach the "resurrection *from (ek)* the dead," they were grieved (Acts 4:2). This was something new, but they clearly understood that it meant the separation of a certain class from among the dead ones, and that class of people were Christ's own, for since He has risen *from* (out from among) the dead, He has become the firstfruits of them that sleep in Him (1 Corinthians 15:20).

Separation. A believer is not only saved *by* Christ, but he is separated *to* Him. We cannot go into the subject in detail, but the following points will indicate its comprehensiveness:

1. Separation by covenant. "The men which thou gavest me *out of* the world" (John 17:6).
2. Separation by calling. "Called you *out of* darkness into his marvellous light" (1 Peter 2:9).
3. Separation by redemption. "Who gave himself for our sins, that he might deliver us *out of* this present evil world" (Galatians 1:4, R.V.)
4. Separation by faith. "He that . . . believeth on Him . . . hath passed *out of* death into life" (John 5:24, R.V.)
5. Separation by power. "Keep them *out of* the evil" (John 17:15, R.V., margin).
6. Separation by command. "Come out *from* among them" (2 Corinthians 6:17).
7. Separation by dedication. "Arise *from* the dead" (Ephesians 5:14).

Topically

The Bible abounds in topics and it is rich in veins of definite thought. Such subjects as repentance, faith, grace, love, redemption, holiness, and glory run like the four rivers in Genesis 2, in all directions through the country of God's truth. We give but one subject, and that is the practical one of keeping ourselves, by way of illustrating the topical study of God's Word.

One of the things which is an abomination to the Lord is a false balance (Proverbs 11:1); while, on the other hand, "a just weight and balance" are specially said to be "the Lord's" (Proverbs 16:11). It is of pressing importance to recall and dwell upon the Lord's gracious promises of preservation, such as we get in Psalm 121; but it is of practical importance that we should keep ourselves, for the water of God's power is meant to move the mill of our being in obedience to the Divine Word. And it is only as we allow the water of God's power to move the wheel of our obedience that we have the corn of blessing in the mill of our being.

1. A *sure test*. "If you love me, you will *keep* my commandments" (John 14:15 RSV) We know we have the life of the Spirit as the pulse of love is throbbing in us. The galvanism of profession may move the dead body of ceremonialism, but it requires the breath of holy obedience to demonstrate the reality of love. Sounding brass betrays itself on the counter of heaven's truth, but sanctified lives ring out their worth in loving deeds.

2. *An Assured Faith.*—"Hereby we do know that we know him, if we *keep* his commandments" (1 John 2:3). There are two words rendered *"know"* in John's first epistle. One meaning, as in 1 John 2:29 (the first word), that which has come within a person's observation; and the other word signifies a true relation between two parties, as the second *"know"* in 1 John 2:29. One means to know *about,* and the other means to be personally acquainted *with.* The word *"know"* in 1 John 2:3, is the latter one. It indicates the ground of assurance as to whether we are personally acquainted with the Lord Jesus. The knowledge of observation is the mere knowing about a certain thing, as when one knows about a feast that is to be given at a certain place; but the knowledge of obedience is the personal acquaintance with anything, as when one is invited to the feast and partakes of it.

3. A *Separated Walk.*—*"Keep* himself unspotted from the world" (James 1:27). Often it is difficult to know what the world is. Generally speaking, the world is anything, or anyone, who takes the place of the Lord. It may be the gold coin of covetousness, the evil root of bitterness, the tinsel of unnecessary apparel, the black heart of unbelief, the rock of error, the polluting hand of the flesh, the green eye of jealousy, the big head of pride, the tumor of conceit, the cancer of doubt, or the paralysis of laziness. Whatever it is, the man who is in the path of pure and undefiled religion keeps himself unspotted from it, as one would keep from a plague-stricken district.

4. A *Holy Charge.*—"If a man love me, he will *keep* my words" (John 14:23). We can quite understand how the parent prizes the dying words of some beloved child. They are mulled over, meditated upon, and spoken about. They are treasured in the casket of the memory, and again and again they are brought out to be weighed. How much more should we ponder and prize the words of the Lord Jesus! They should be as a *fire* to warm us in coldness (Jeremiah 20:9), as a *spring* to refresh us in weariness (Isaiah 1:4), as a *spur* to move us in sloth (Psalm 119:154), as a *rule* to square us in life (Psalm 119:133), as a *magnet* to attract us in prayer (Jeremiah 1:4-10), as a *cordial* to soothe us in sorrow (1 Thessalonians 4:15), and as a *staff* to stay us in trial (Psalm 130:5).

5. A *Faithful Service.*—"I have *kept* the faith" (2 Timothy 4:7). Paul had faithfully traded with the pound of the gospel (Luke 19:12-26). He had kept the treasure of the truth. He had watched the camp of the church with holy diligence. He had been no hireling, for he had labored incessantly night and day. There was no mere routine with him, for he had suffered for the gospel, as his lacerated body testified; and he wept for the gospel, as his tears evidenced. The slave Onesimus, the prayerful Epaphras, the physician Luke, the worldly Demas, the helpful Timothy, the praiseful Silas, the consecrated Barnabas, and the soldiers at Rome could all testify to the truth of the apostle's faithful service.

6. A *Safe Environment.*—*"Keep* yourselves in the love of God" (Jude 21). What the air is to the bird, and what the water is to the fish, the love of God is to the believer. It is the element in which we are to live and move. The word "environ" only occurs once in the Authorized Version of the Bible, and that is in Joshua 7:9, although the same Hebrew word is translated "compass" in the

previous chapter seven times. Joshua, in his prayer to Jehovah regarding the defeat of Israel at Ai, said the Canaanites would get to hear of it, and "environ" them round and cut them off. An adverse power would surround Israel to their detriment. The love of God is a power to surround us for our safety, for it is a wall of fire to protect us from hatred, a hedge to keep out the robbers of sin, a fence to keep out the foxes of doubt, an element to keep us warm with sympathy, an atmosphere to make us pure in heart, and a sphere where evil cannot touch us.

7. A *Stimulating Promise.*—"If ye *keep* my commandments, ye shall abide in my love" (John 15:10). This promise of Christ gives us the crux of the whole situation. There is no royal road to any one of the blessings enumerated in the Bible. They all come through obedience. This is the door through which we enter into the King's garden of delights. The key to unlock the treasure house of Christ's unlimited fullness is obedience to His commandments. By that means, the treasures in the treasury are revealed to us for our use and enjoyment.

Comprehensively

As there was an unseen bar which shot through all the boards of the tabernacle, as they rested on their foundation (Exodus 36:33), so there are definite lines of truth which run through all the Word of God. One such truth is this: all blessing from God, and all approach to Him, are based upon sacrifice. The skins with which our first parents were clothed testify to it in the book of Genesis. And the great multitude, who stand in heaven's glory, who have washed their robes and made them white in the blood of the Lamb, herald forth the same truth (Revelation 7:9-14).

There are many complete circles of truth which illustrate the comprehensiveness of God's Word. Perhaps one of the most concise is the feasts mentioned in Leviticus 23. These typify the order of events from Christ's baptism, onward to the judgment at the end of the millennium.

The Sabbath (Leviticus 23:1-3) is typical of God's rest in Christ, as expressed in the Spirit of God abiding (resting) on Him, and the Father's acknowledgment of Him, as the One in whom He was well pleased (Matthew 3:16, 17; John 1:33).

The Passover (Leviticus 23:5) is typical of Christ's death for sin, and is expressive of the protection there is in Him who was "sacrificed for us" (1 Corinthians 5:7; Romans 8:1-4, R.V.)

The Feast of Unleavened Bread (Leviticus 23:6) represents the outcome of faith in Christ. He, by His indwelling presence, purged out the leaven of legality (Galatians 5:9), malice and wickedness (1 Corinthians 5:7, 8).

The First Fruits (Leviticus 23:9-14) is typical of Christ's resurrection from the dead, as the first fruits of those who sleep in Him (1 Corinthians 15:20).

Pentecost (Leviticus 23:15-21) is typical of the coming and dispensation of the Holy Spirit (Acts 2:1), as He is gathering out from Jew and Gentile (two loaves) those who shall make up the mystical body of Christ (1 Corinthians 12:12; Ephesians 2:16).

The Feast of Trumpets (Leviticus 23:23-25) is typical of the time when the trumpet of Christ's return shall be heard as He gathers His own people to

Himself in the glory (1 Thessalonians 4:13-18; 1 Corinthians 15:52).

The Day of Atonement (Leviticus 23:26-32) is typical of Christ's manifestation to Israel as their Messiah when they shall look upon Him whom they have pierced (Zechariah 12:10; Revelation 1:7).

The Feast of Tabernacles (Leviticus 23:33-34) represents the millennium, when the scene on the Mount of Transfiguration (Mark 9:2-7) shall be known over the whole earth, for the Glory of the Lord will cover it (Habakkuk 2:14).

The Vintage (Leviticus 23:39) is typical of the vintage of God's wrath, the judgment after the millennium (Revelation 20:11-15), before the final conclusion of things before the eternal blessedness of the new heaven and new earth.

When Satan was tempting Christ, in a moment of time he brought before Him the kingdoms of the world and the glory of them (Luke 4:5); but in the feasts of Jehovah we have given us in a comprehensive panoramic view, the purpose of God, stretching from the cradle of Christ's incarnation to the throne of His judgment.

Comparatively

One of the injunctions of the Holy Spirit is, we are to be "comparing spiritual things with spiritual"* (1 Corinthians 2:13). Godet says, "The verb strictly denotes the act of bringing two things together to compare them and fix their relative value." There are many lines of truth which may be taken, as we compare the Old Testament with the New. What a difference between God's demand under law and His bestowments under grace. Look, for instance, at the different treatment the prodigal received! Under the law, the prodigal was stoned to death (Deuteronomy 21:21), but under grace he is compassionated and honored (Luke 15:20-24).

The three Psalms which treat of what Christ *was*, what He *is*, and what He *will be*, make a profitable comparative study. The following points of contrast will indicate.

PSALM 2	PSALM 23	PSALM 24
Christ, "a worm"	Christ, the Shepherd	Christ, the King of Glory
The Cross with its Shame	The Crook with its care	The Crown with its glory
The Good Shepherd in death	The Great Shepherd in Power	The Chief Shepherd in Glory
Christ's yesterday of suffering	Christ's today of grace	Christ's forever in splendor
Christ dishonored	Christ honoring	Christ honored
Christ brought low	Christ bringing home	Christ at home
Strengthless	Strengthening	Strong
His Cry	His Comfort	His Claim

* Godet's translation is the more correct, as the context shows: "The Spirit teacheth, appropriating spiritual things to spiritual men."

Another comparative study is the difference between Aaron as a high priest and Christ as the High Priest. There are many points of resemblance, but the differences are most pronounced.

Aaron entered the holiest of all on the great day of atonement with the blood of the slain animals, but Christ entered into heaven by means of His own blood; therefore there is a difference as to the basis of priestly service (Hebrews 9:12).

There is a difference in the persons who fill the office. Aaron was an imperfect man, compassed with infirmity. Christ is the "Perfect man"—"holy" in His devotion, "harmless" in His conduct, "undefiled" in His personality, and "separate" in His walk (Hebrews 7:26, 27).

There is a difference as to the place of priestly service. Aaron's sphere of service was in the tabernacle on earth. Christ's is in the presence of God in heaven (Hebrews 8:4; 9:24).

Aaron's priesthood passed to his son, and so from sire to son; but Christ's priestly office has no end. He did not receive it from man, nor does it pass to another. Therefore there is a difference in the *order* of the priesthoods (Hebrews 7:24, 25).

Again, there is a difference in the continuance of the priesthoods. Death put the high priest out of office again and again, but Christ in His priesthood is unchangeable, because He lives in the power of an endless life, therefore He is a Priest forever (Hebrews 7:3, 16, 17, 21-25). Yet one other difference we note, namely, the difference in the outcome of the priesthoods. The work of the high priest could never bring cleansing and satisfaction to the conscience. His work was only transient. But Christ, by His work, and in His office, has obtained cleansing to the conscience and eternal redemption for us (Hebrews 9:11-14).

Concentratingly

As the burning glass exposed to the rays of the sun collects them to a focus, and thus concentrates the heat to the combustion of the material upon which it is centered; so, what we mean by the concentrative study of the Scriptures, is the focusing of a number of passages upon a given one, in order that they may illustrate it and amplify its meaning. Let us look at two sentences of Scripture by way of demonstration. One is associated with the believer's action to the Lord, and the other with Christ's office as Shepherd.

Unto the Lord. Among other things of which we read in connection with the believers at Thessalonica, is this: they "turned to God" (1 Thessalonians 1:9). In their turning unto the Lord, we have suggested the principal law in the believer's life, namely, all we do is to be Godward. We become believers by turning to the Lord (Acts 9:35; 11:21), and we show we are such by doing all things to Him (Colossians 3:23). The following seven Scriptures focused upon the latter point bring out its fulness: 1) Cleaving unto the Lord is the law of the believer's faith (Acts 11:23). 2) Living unto the Lord is that law of the believer's life (Romans 14:8). 3) Making melody unto the Lord is the law of the believer's worship (Ephesians 5:19). 4) Service done to the Lord is the law of the believer's work (Colossians 3:23). 5) Ministering unto the Lord is the law of the believer's ministry (Acts 13:2). 6) Commending unto the Lord is the law of the believer's sympathy (Acts 14:23) and 7) giving unto the Lord is the law of the believer's consecration (2 Corinthians 8:5).

Christ as Shepherd. The Psalmist, in speaking of the Lord as to what He was to him, says, He "is my Shepherd" (Psalm 23:1). His Shepherd character may be illustrated by referring to the seven shepherds mentioned in the Old Testament, namely, Abel, Abraham, Isaac, Jacob, Joseph, Moses, and David. 1) Abel, the providing shepherd. He is said to be a feeder (margin) of sheep (Genesis 4:2). 2) Abraham, the parting shepherd. He separated himself from Lot, he would not quarrel with him about the pasture for their flocks (Genesis 13:9). 3) Isaac, the peaceful shepherd. He would not quarrel with the herdmen of Gerar about the well he had dug (Genesis 26:19-22). 4) Jacob, the purchasing shepherd. He purchased the cattle which he possessed by his service (Genesis 30:31; 31:40, 41). 5) Joseph, the prophetic shepherd. When he was feeding the flock with his brethren, he foretold his coming greatness (Genesis 37:2). 6) Moses, the protecting shepherd. He is said to have kept the flock which was committed to his care (Exodus 3:1). 7) David, the powerful shepherd. He defended his father's sheep from the ravages of the lion and the bear (1 Samuel 17:34, 35). At once it will be seen that these seven shepherds are types of Christ the Shepherd, for He provides for us in His ministry (Hebrews 8:6), He parts us from sin by His Spirit (Galatians 5:16), He calms us by His presence (Exodus 33:14), He claims us by His atonement (1 Corinthians 6:20), He assures by His promise of His coming glory (John 14:2), He keeps by His power (1 Peter 1:5), and defends us by His might (Romans 8:14).

Further, Christ as the Shepherd is variously described: 1) He is God's Shepherd, as His equal (Zechariah 13:7). 2) He is the Good Shepherd in giving His life for the sheep (John 10:11). 3) He is the Great Shepherd in resurrection power (Hebrew. 13:20). 4) He is the One Shepherd over the one flock (John 10:16). 5) He is the Chief Shepherd in His coming glory (1 Peter 5:4). 6) He is to be Israel's Shepherd to gather Israel back to Jehovah and their own land (Ezekiel 34:12-33). 7) He is the Believer's Shepherd, for he can say, "The Lord is *my* Shepherd" (Psalm 23:1).

Yet a further line of thought can be followed in thinking of what Christ does for His sheep. He feeds (Isaiah 40:11), leads (John 10:4), keeps (John 10:28), knows (John 10:14), calls (John 10:3), marks (John 10:27), and separates (Matthew 25:32).

Critically

When we speak of the critical study of God's Word, we do not mean that we are to find fault with it, or to judge it, but rather to study it, to find out the Spirit's meaning.

The word "critic" is a Greek word *(Kritikos)*, and only occurs once in the Bible, and it is not without significance in this day, when men are judging the Word of God, that it should be found in describing what it is. We read in Hebrews 4:12, "The Word of God . . . is a discerner *(Kritikos)* of the thoughts and intents of the heart." The Word of God is capable of judging the thoughts and intents of the heart. When our minds are subject to the authority of God's Word, then the Holy Spirit can lead us into the hidden meaning of His truth (1 Corinthians 2:9-14).

We often find a looseness in referring to sentences of Scripture. For instance, a Principal in one of the Colleges in Scotland, in referring to the inspiration of the Bible, said, "I wish to say, that belief in an infallible book is just as enervating to the spiritual intelligence as belief in an infallible Church, or an infallible person. An immense amount of mischief has resulted in the past from bondage to the letter of the Scripture, and neglect of Paul's warning, that while the spirit giveth life, the letter killeth." The question naturally arises, "Is the construction which the Principal puts upon Paul's words a correct one?" He makes Paul say, the letter of God's word is of small importance, so long as you get the spirit of it. The apostle is not referring to the Word of God as such when he says, "The letter killeth, but the Spirit giveth life" (2 Corinthians 3:6). He is contrasting the law, which he calls the "ministration of death," and "of condemnation" (2 Corinthians 3:7, 9), and the gospel, which is the "ministration of righteousness" and "glory" (2 Corinthians 3:9, 18). The law always brings death to man, because of his inability to fulfil it (Romans 8:3). The gospel brings life to those who are dead in trespasses and sins (Ephesians 2:1; John 5:24, 25). The Word of God is living (Hebrews 4:12), for it is the incorruptible seed "which liveth and abideth for ever" (1 Peter 1:23).

One verse of Scripture may be critically considered in its relation to another, or to its context. In Romans 6 we have two questions relating to the believer and sin. In verse one we read, "Shall we continue in sin, that grace may abound?" And in verse 15, we read, "Shall we sin, because we are not under the law, but under grace?" Many have thought that the questions are the same. In verse one the question is, Shall a justified believer still go on in His old manner of life, in order that grace may abound? This is shown to be an impossibility, as the old associations with sin are cut off through being baptized into Christ's death. The question in verse 15 narrows itself down to this, "Shall a sanctified believer commit a single act of sin?" The answer is the same, "By no means."

Professor Godet puts the whole case very clearly. He says, "The question is no longer, as in verse 1, whether the justified believer will be able to continue the life of sin which he formerly led. The answer has been given in verses 1-14. But the matter in question is whether the new dominion will be strong enough to banish sin *in every particular case*. Hence the form of aorist subjunctive: *Should we commit an act of sin?* Could we act thus voluntarily in any single instance? And in point of fact, a believer will not easily say: By grace I shall remain without any change what I have been till now. But he will find himself only too easily regarding some particular leniency toward sin as admissible, on account of the freeness of pardon. The gradation between the question of verse 1 and that of verse 15 makes itself felt in the form of the motive alleged in favor of unfaithfulness. The Apostle does not say now: '*that* grace may abound,' words which could only come from a heart yet a stranger to the experience of faith; but he says here: '*because* we are under grace.' The snare is less gross in this form. Vinet one day said to the writer of these lines: 'There is a subtle poison which insinuates itself into the heart of the best Christian; it is the temptation to say: Let us sin, not *that* grace may abound, but *because* it abounds?'"

Textually

There is one text in the Gospel of John which we may examine as illustrating the textual study of the Scriptures, John 3:16. The central theme of this verse is love, and the words of the verse suggest a sevenfold aspect of God's love.

1. His love is *expressive in its action*. The height, depth, length, and breadth of His love are suggested in the words, "For God so loved." The height of love for "*God*" is its source; the depth of love for man's necessity is suggested in the conjunction "*for*" connecting with the words of John 3:14, 15; the breadth of love is discovered in the "*so*," for who can comprehend its magnitude? And the length of love is made known in the "*loved*," for who can measure the longitude of Him who is Love itself?

2. God's love is *extraordinary in its choice*. The marvel is that God should love "the world!" The world whose mind is enmity against God; whose course is evil; whose sin is self-pleasing; whose heart is wicked; whose trend is sinward; whose will is perverse; and whose god is the devil.

3. God's love is *expensive in its sacrifice*. Who can sound the deeps of such a sentence as—"that he gave his only begotten Son"? Abraham gave tithes to Melchizedek, Eliezer jewels to Rebekah. Joseph gave his brethren a change of raiment, Caleb gave Achsah the upper and nether springs, Boaz gave Ruth six measures of corn, and Jonathan gave up his right to the kingdom to David. But what are these givings compared with God's gift of Christ? These stars all pale in the light of this sun. Think *for whom* Christ was given, *to what* He was given, and then estimate the expensiveness of the sacrifice by Gethsemane's terrible agony, Gabbatha's shame, Golgotha's suffering, heaven's blackness, earth's convulsions, law's curse, death's sting, and sin's judgment.

4. God's love is *extensive in its offer*—"Whosoever." *Love's eyes* look upon the need of all. *Love's voice* invites all to come to Christ. *Love's heart* of compassion beats for all. *Love's hands* are ready to save all. *Love's feet* run to meet all returning prodigals. *Love's ears* listen to all who call upon Him; and *Love's will* is to bless all.

5. God's love is *exclusive in its bestowment*—"Believeth on him." Faith is the *eye* which looks to Christ and obtains life from the Lord; faith is the *hand* which receives God's gift to the enrichment of the believer; faith is the *ear* which heeds Christ's call and obeys His voice; faith is the *foot* which runs at Christ's invitation and follows in His steps; and faith is the *will's* response to God's Word of direction. The *giver* of faith is the Holy Spirit, the *ground* of faith is God's Word, the *Object* of faith is the living Christ, the *outcome* of faith is holiness of life, the *end* of faith is salvation, the *nature* of faith is trust, and the *companion* of faith is love. God's blessings are only promised to faith.

6. God's love is *exceptional in its work*—"Should not perish." These words express the exceptional work of love. Who can understand the word "*perish*"? In it we hear the groans of the damned, we have the depth of misery, the despair of the lost, the outer darkness of the unsaved, the doom of the wicked, the failure of the sinner, and the nature of hell. When man believes on Christ, love saves from this doom.

7. God's love is *eternal in its blessing*—"Have everlasting life." Eternal life! What does it mean to possess it? Or rather to possess Him (1 John 5:12)? It means we are saved in an eternal salvation, comforted with eternal consolation, liberated by eternal redemption, kept for an eternal inheritance, secured in an eternal covenant, possessed by the eternal Spirit, and loved with eternal love.

Dr. Alex. Dickson gives a good illustration of textual study in the following outline on Acts 1:25: "Judas by transgression fell that he might go to his own place. 1. Here is sin represented as a fall. First, faster and farther; secondly, no self-recovery possible, as in a falling body; thirdly, ultimately fatal; and yet fourthly, responsible because caused by transgression. 2. Every soul goes to his own place. First, every soul has his own place; secondly, makes his own place; thirdly, finds his own place; fourthly, feels that it is his own place when he gets there." The above outline is all evolved from the text. There is no importation. It is all exportation and thus illustrates the true textual study of God's Word.

Practically

The Christian worker must apply himself wholly, by earnest meditation, if he is to understand God's Word, and he must also pray that the Word may be wholly applied to him by the Spirit's power, if he is to be a spiritual man and have spiritual power.

The one simple essential is to say to the Lord, when He speaks to us in His Word, "Yes, Lord." The "Yes" being, not merely the yes of assent, but the yes of obedience. We must be like the blind men when Christ asked them if they believed He was able to give them sight. They immediately replied, "Yes, Lord" (Matthew 9:28). They abandoned themselves to Him, and as a consequence, they received their sight.

There are twelve "I will's" in Isaiah 41, which we may take by way of illustration. Let us briefly look at each and see how they work out as we put "Yes, Lord" against each.

1. *The I will of strengthening in weakness by His grace*. "I will strengthen thee" (verse 10). "Yes, Lord." Then we are strong in Him.
2. *The I will of equipping in conflict by His aid*. "I will help thee" (verse 10). "Yes, Lord." Then no foe can defeat us.
3. *The I will of upholding in walk by His power*. "I will uphold thee with the right hand of my righteousness" (verse 10). "Yes, Lord." Then there can be no fainting or falling.
4. *The I will of assurance in fellowship by His love*. "I the Lord thy God will hold thy right hand, saying unto thee, Fear not" (verse 13). "Yes, Lord." Then, since His word assures me of His presence, I may count upon His loving care.
5. *The I will of sustainment in trial by His aid*. "I will help thee" (verse 13). "Yes, Lord." Then His grace will be sufficient, whatever happens.
6. *The I will of preservation when fearful*. "Fear not, thou worm Jacob . . . I will help thee" (verse 14). "Yes, Lord." Nothing can haunt, and no hate can harm with such a word.
7. *The I will of efficiency in service by His making*. "I will make thee a new

sharp threshing instrument having teeth" (verse 15). "Yes, Lord." Then, since He is the Worker, and I am the instrument, His will must be done, and His work accomplished.

8. *The I will of encouragement in prayer by His declaration.* "I the Lord will hear them" (verse 17). "Yes, Lord." Then I may count upon His faithful answer to my petition.
9. *The I will of supply in need by His abundance.* "I will open rivers in high places, and fountains in the midst of the valleys" (verse 18). "Yes, Lord." Then there can be no famine or failure with such resources.
10. *The I will of conversion in life by His grace.* "I will make the wilderness a pool of water, and the dry land springs of water" (verse 18). "Yes, Lord." Then all my barrenness and nothingness are but so many empty reservoirs for His fulness.
11. *The I will of implanting in the heart with His graces.* "I will plant in the wilderness the cedar, the shittah tree, and the myrtle tree, and the oil tree" (verse 19). "Yes, Lord." Then since He plants within me the graces of His Spirit, I will let Him cultivate the same.
12. *The I will of bestowment for usefulness by His blessing.* "I will set in the desert the fir tree, and the pine, and the box tree together" (verse 19). "Yes, Lord." Then I must be a blessing to others, since He blesses me.

As we thus apply the Word of God to ourselves, it will impart its secrets to us. And we shall find, as the reformers did, that the Word of God is what it is said to be in the following lines. This poem appeared in many editions of the translations of the Bible, such as Miles Coverdale's, and others:

Here is the spring where waters flow,
To quench our heat of sin;
Here is the tree where truth doth grow,
To lead our hearts therein.

Here is the Judge that stints the strife,
Where men's devices fail,
Here is the bread that feeds the life
That death cannot assail.

The tidings of salvation dear,
Come to our ears from hence;
The fortress of our faith is here,
And shield of our defence.

Then be not like the hog, that hath
A pearl at his desire;
But takes more pleasure in the trough,
And wallowing in the mire.

Read not this Book in any case,
But with a single eye;
Read not, but first desire God's grace
To understand thereby.

Pray still in faith with this respect—
To fructify therein;
That knowledge may bring this effect
To mortify thy sin.

Then happy thou, in all thy life,
What so to thee befalls;
Yea, doubly happy shalt thou be,
When God by death thee calls.

14

The Discipler's Accuracy

One of the most important things in Christian work is accuracy in relation to the Scriptures for a careless reader of the Bible lacks a close walk with God and an efficient work for Him. Every businessman knows that attention to details is one of the essential things in a successful business. "Trifles make perfection, and perfection is no trifle," replied Michelangelo, when one remarked to him that he seemed to be occupied with trifles because he paid such minute attention to a statue which he was making. With equal or greater force this same principle applies to our use of the Scriptures.

As the title of the chapter suggests, it is most important for the Christian worker to be accurate in his use of Scripture, to avoid two common mistakes: to misquote the Scriptures in attempting to quote them, and to misrepresent them in referring to them.

Mistakes in quoting the Scriptures

In misquotation, three common mistakes are: *addition*, saying more than is written; *subtraction*, taking from what is written; and *altering*, misrepresenting what is written. Eve, in the garden of Eden, did all three of these. She added to the word of the Lord, took from it, and altered it. Let us briefly note her mistakes.

Subtraction: The Lord's command was as follows: "And the Lord God commanded the man, You are free to eat from any tree in the garden" (Genesis 2:16).

Eve's answer to the serpent's tempting question was: "We may eat fruit from the trees in the garden" (Genesis 3:2).

It will be seen that the woman left out of God's direction the word *"free,"* and by doing so, she not only took from His word, but cast a reflection upon His character.

Addition: God made one exception to the trees from which our first parents were to eat, and that exception was the tree of knowledge of good and evil. His command was: "but from the tree of the knowledge of good and evil, you must not eat for when you eat of it you will surely die" (Genesis 2:17).

Eve's reply to the tempter was as follows: "But God did say, 'You must not eat fruit from the tree that is in the middle of the garden, and you must not touch it, or you will die'" (Genesis 3:3)

Eve added to the words of God, by saying, "and you must not touch it." The Lord did not say anything about *touching* the tree. His command was that they were not to eat of the fruit of it.

Alteration: The consequence of disobedience was stated very clearly and emphatically. The Lord said, ". . . you will surely die" (Genesis 2:17). But Eve altered the words to "or you will die" (Genesis 3:3) thus minimizing the sharp and pungent words, ". . . you will surely die."

Subtraction

It has been said, "We shall lose heaven by *neutrality* as well as by *hostility*, by wanting oil, as well as by drinking poison. An unprofitable servant will be as much punished as a prodigal son. Undone duty will undo our souls." To omit any of the words of the Bible subtracts from its value and mars its worth.

A well-known evangelist once remarked to a number of ministers that he would give a new Bible to the first one who could quote a single passage of Scripture correctly. One of the ministers accepted the challenge, and said, "God so loved the world that he gave his only begotten Son, that whoever believes in him shall not perish, but have eternal life." "You are wrong," replied the evangelist; "you have left out the first word of the verse, the word *for*." A very important omission, as may be seen, by looking at the reason of the conjunction. It may seem to be an unnecessary remark to make, "John 3:14, 15, comes before John 3:16," but its importance is easily discovered when we read the three verses together. They read as follows—"Just as Moses lifted up the snake in the desert, so the Son of Man must be lifted up that everyone who believes in him may have eternal life. For God so loved the world that he gave his one and only Son, that whoever believes in him shall not perish but have eternal life."

In verse 14, the Lord Jesus states the absolute necessity of His atoning death—the Son of Man *must* be lifted up; and then in verse 16 He brings out the great and glorious fact that the sacrifice which He makes is the expression of God's love for the world; thus the importance of the conjunction "*for*."

Many Christians have found consolation in the hour of death, power in the time of conflict with evil, and joy in the moment of doubt, as they have remembered that "the blood of Jesus Christ cleanses from all sin." Nothing should be done to discourage any of God's people in obtaining stimulus and strength from any given word of God, but, on the other hand, we must not take any words of grace out of their context for to do so is like removing the hub from a wheel, which thus makes the spokes useless. The connection of the above words which refer to the Blood of Christ is seen at once if the preceding words are pondered. The Scripture is, "But if we walk in the light, as he is in the light, we have fellowship with one another, and the blood of Jesus, his Son, purifies us from all sin" (1 John 1:7). The truth of the verse is that the atonement of Christ continually meets the sin of which we are unconscious while we are walking in the light and having fellowship with the Lord. The highest form of Christian experience is described to us as walking in the light and having fellowship with the Father and the Son and yet, while we are there, we still need the precious Blood of Christ to keep us clean for we need Him not merely as our Substitute to bear our sins (1 Peter 2:24), but also as our Great High Priest to bear the iniquity of our holy things (Exodus 28:38).

There are many who believe in what is known as Universalism, who base their belief on a sentence of Scripture, "Restore everything." Without any explanation, the words are wrested from their setting in Scripture and, as the cruel Inquisition often made Christians say things when they were tortured on the rack, so these words are taken as a basis upon which to build the theory that all men will be saved irrespective of faith and character. Even the devil himself is ultimately to enjoy the felicity of heaven. The restoration to which reference is made is limited in its application, as may be gathered from the words that follow, which are, "as he promised long ago through his holy prophets" (Acts 3:21). The times of restoration point onward to that period of universal blessedness and peace, which is described in Isaiah 11 and 65.

One of the most striking examples of subtracting from the Word of God is found in connection with the words, "Work out your own salvation." While we recognize that these words are often misquoted and made to mean "Work *for* your own salvation," we must also guard against the mistake of stopping at all after the word "salvation," for the scripture is, ". . . work out your salvation with fear and trembling, for it is God who works in you to will and to act according to his good purpose" (Philippians 2:12, 13). Merely to emphasize the words which direct us to work out our own salvation is to throw us back on our own resources and to land us in the bog of despair. If we recognize the fact that it is God who both wills and works in us, however, it makes us move in glad and swift obedience, removes all friction, and helps us face every difficulty with fortitude and power, even as a ship can move on in the face of the storm by reason of the motive power which propels it along.

Addition

We now come to those mistakes which are made by adding to what the Lord has said. We have an instance of this in the latter part of Ephesians 4:21, which is usually quoted, "The truth as *it* is in Jesus." By the misplacement of the "*as*," and the addition of the "*it*," we have a comparative statement which makes truth to reside in others as well as in the Lord; whereas we know that he Himself is the embodiment of all truth. Bacon, in his Essay on Truth, begins thus: "'What is truth?' said jesting Pilate, and did not wait for an answer." Christ Himself is the answer for He said: "I am the Truth." This is the thought in the passage before us, the correct reading of which is, "The truth that is in Jesus." The statement is an exclusive one for it makes truth to center in Christ and in Him alone, and it is also a conclusive one for there is no court of appeal when He is in question.

Some Christians, when they wish to draw attention to the fact that God must deal in judgment with those who refuse to receive Christ, seek to emphasize this judgment by saying that "God, *out of Christ*, is a consuming fire." The text to which they refer is, "for our God is a consuming fire" (Hebrews 12:29). The exhortation with which it is connected is to the children of God, pointing out to them the manner in which they are to serve, i.e., "with reverence and awe"; and then comes the reason why they are to serve Him thus: "for *our* God is a consuming fire."

The declaration has often been made from the pulpit, "Without shedding of blood is no remission *of sins*." The desire is to show that the blood alone is that which removes the sins from the sinner's conscience. While this may be rightly inferred from the text, yet a great deal more may be found in it if we take it as it is without the addition of the words *"of sins."* Adding *"of sins"* limits the fulness of the text. While the Greek word *"Aphesis"* is translated *"forgiveness"* in Acts 5:31 in speaking of sins, it is also rendered *"liberty"* and *"deliverance"* in Luke 4:18. We may, therefore, rightly say that its meaning is not merely the pardoning of offenses, but the discharge of all penalty and deliverance from that power which led the sinner to commit the sins.

Among the instructions which the Lord gave to Moses in connection with the tabernacle in the wilderness was a direction with regard to the loops, clasps and pegs (Exodus 36:12, 13; 38:20). It may be said that these were things of no importance, and yet they were all important in their own places. The greater things often depend upon the smaller ones. Attention to details is one of the main factors leading to success. Mortar holds the bricks together which make the house, and pivots, nuts, and screws are indispensable in the machinery of the factory.

What is true generally is especially so in connection with the little words of the Bible—they make or mar its meaning.

Bishop Westcott has said that the whole force of revelation is contained in the two letters of the Greek preposition *"en,"* which is generally translated "in." Its force and fulness can easily be gathered as it is found in connection with Christ. To be *in* Him is to be in the sphere of His saving grace and His sanctifying influence. To be *out* of Him is to be beyond the pale of His redemption.

While it is necessary to recognize the little words which are used by the Holy Spirit, we must be equally careful to guard against interpolations. There is a common mistake made in quoting Hebrews 9:27. It reads: "And as it is appointed unto men once to die, but after this the judgment"; but it is often quoted out of context. "It is appointed unto *all* men once to die," etc. With the misquote a definite statement is made, that death and judgment are the portion of all men. If we look at the context, we find that there is a contrast given in the *"as"* and *"so."* The whole passage is as follows: "And *as* it is appointed unto men once to die, but after this the judgment: so Christ was once offered to bear the sins of many; and unto them that look for him shall he appear the second time without sin unto salvation." Death and judgment are the common lot of humanity because of sin. For the believer, however, Christ has died the *death* and borne the *judgment*, so that the believer is looking for neither *death* nor *judgment*, but is expecting Christ to return and complete his salvation. We have the definite statement of the apostle Paul that "We shall not all sleep" (1 Corinthians 15:51).

Again we find there is all the difference between taking *of* a thing, and taking the thing itself. We are exhorted to "take the Water of Life freely" (Revelation 22:17), not as is often quoted, "Take *of* the Water of Life freely." It is not merely something *of* Christ that the Holy Spirit urges us to take; it is Christ Himself, as the Water of Life, who satisfies the thirsty soul with His salvation and blessing. A great stumbling block to believers is becoming occupied with some blessing which Christ gives and losing sight of Christ Himself in whom all blessing dwells (Ephesians 1:3). The devil's motto is, "Anything but Christ, even blessing." The Holy Spirit's direction is, "Looking unto Jesus," and to Jesus alone (Hebrews 12:2).

At times addition to the words of the Lord reflects upon His goodness or takes away from His power. Ephesians 3:20 is often quoted, "Now unto him that is able to do exceeding abundantly above all that we *can* ask or think, according to the power that worketh in us." By the addition of the "*can*," the thought is suggested that God can just go beyond what we can ask or think when there is really a positive and emphatic statement that "He is able to do exceeding abundantly above all that we ask or think."

We are distinctly warned in the Scriptures against adding to what God has said for He says: "Add thou not unto his words, lest he reprove thee, and thou be found a liar" (Proverbs 30:6).

Alteration

Some of the alterations which are made in scholastic establishments are rather amusing, and it might not be out of place to call attention to a few of them.

It is most important that we should put first things first, because, if we make God's first things our chief study, we shall be in the line of His care and blessing. Furthermore, we must be careful not to take more than He has pledged Himself to give. Christ's command, "Seek ye first the kingdom of God, and his righteousness, and all these things shall be added unto you," is often misquoted, in that "*all other things*" is put in the place of "*these things*" (Matthew 6:33). "These things" to which Christ makes reference are food and raiment, and to make His promise read "all other things" is to claim what God has never pledged Himself to give.

"There is a flaw in it, hence it is not so valuable as it would be," said one friend to another, in speaking of an amethyst, for in looking at the back, there was a distinct mark, which indicated its imperfection. As the flaw took from the value of the stone, so those who alter Scripture in quoting it, by their misquotation take from its worth; for instance, the passage which speaks of "judgment" in connection with the ministry of the Holy Spirit, is often quoted "judgment to come," whereas the whole passage is, "Of judgment because the prince of this world is judged" (John 16:11). The future condemnation of the wicked is not in question; it is the Spirit's message, which tells of Christ's triumph over the god of this world, in His death on the cross, by depriving him of his power (Hebrews 2:14).

One of the glad features of the Gospel is its simplicity, but one must take care in selecting which passages are used to illustrate this simplicity. For example, Habakkuk 2:2 is often quoted: "Make it plain, that he that runs may read," the thought being that the gospel is so plain that no effort is needed on the part of the observer; he can read as he runs. In reality the thought in the passage is the very opposite, "Write the vision, and make it plain upon tables, that he may run that readeth it"—thus the correct thought is that the man reads and the reading makes him run, not that he reads while he runs.

By altering some of the promises of God, a great deal of their meaning and blessing are taken away. The following is a case in point: I was staying with a friend in Scotland, and noticed an illuminated text hanging up in his dining room, which was as follows: "My God shall supply all your need out of His riches in glory by Christ." The correct reading is not *"out of,"* but *"according to"* His riches in glory by Christ Jesus (Philippians 4:19). Perhaps the difference of the two readings may be best gathered by a simple illustration. Suppose a millionaire meets a beggar in the street who asks him for a few coppers to meet his necessity. The millionaire gives the beggar *out of* his riches as he drops sixpence into his hand, but if he took him to his home and adopted him as his son, made him his heir and treated him as such, he would be giving him *according to* his riches. In like manner, when the Lord blesses us, He does not bestow upon us the driblets of His grace, but He gives us a deluge of blessing. His blessing is *according to* the "riches of His grace" (Ephesians 1:7). His power to us-ward is according to what He wrought in Christ when He raised Him from the dead (Ephesians 1:19, 20), and the measure of the Spirit's strengthening and Christ's indwelling is *according to* the riches of His glory (Ephesians 3:16, 17).

Mistakes that are made in referring to Scripture

It is an absolute necessity to be accurate in all our references to the Book of books, and we must not under any circumstances take anything for granted, but look things up for ourselves.

A learned judge made the solemn declaration from the bench [in calling attention to man's tenacity to life], "We have the highest possible authority for saying, 'All that a man hath will he give for his life.'" I presume the judge meant to say that this was what the *Lord* said to man. The passage of Scripture states, however, "*Satan* answered the Lord, and said, 'Skin for skin; yea, all that a man hath will he give for his life'" (Job 2:4). I am sure Satan would not be credited as "the highest possible authority," if it had been known he was the speaker. The judge took it for granted the Lord was the speaker and blundered in consequence.

A common mistake made in connection with Absalom is that he was caught in the oak by his hair and hanged to his death as a result. The fact is, Absalom was killed by Joab "while he was yet alive in the midst of the oak" (2 Samuel 18:14).

A similar mistake is often made with regard to Elijah for we frequently hear, that he went up to heaven in a *"chariot of fire."* The Scripture says, "There appeared a chariot of fire, and horses of fire, and parted them both asunder; and Elijah went up by a *whirlwind* into heaven" (2 Kings 2:11).

There are many instances of most remarkable blunders which have been made by Oxford undergraduates in the Scripture examination, which they must undergo before taking their degree. The following are a few among many: One was asked who was the first king of Israel. Either by accident or real knowledge, he readily answered, "Saul." Then, wishing to give a little additional Scripture information, he added, "Saul, afterwards called Paul." Another undergraduate was asked which were the two instances in the Bible where we have the record of the lower animals having spoken; he at once replied, "Balaam's ass." "Yes," said the examiner, "that is one; now the other." The young man answered after a slight hesitation, "The whale! The whale said unto Jonah, 'Almost thou persuadest me to be a Christian.'"

While we should always be careful in dealing with the Word of God, above all things we should be accurate in our own heart and life by seeing that the actions of our conduct correspond to God's Truth. Scripture charges us to keep our hearts with diligence (Proverbs 4:23), to bridle our tongue with caution (James 1:26), to concentrate our gaze with attention (Hebrews 12:2), to watch our ways with vigilance (1 Peter 5:8), to separate all pollution from our inner life (2 Corinthians 7:1), and to set our affection on things above (Colossians 3:2). Then we can pray—

"Oh, let me give
Out of the gifts Thou freely givest;
Oh, let me live
With life abundant, because Thou livest;
Oh, make me shine
In darkest places, for Thy light Is mine;
Oh, let me be
A faithful witness for Thy truth and Thee."

15

The Discipler's Sharpener

"Quicken Thou me according to Thy Word" (Psalm 119:25).

Many similes about God are used in the Scriptures to elucidate its intrinsic value, its inherent virtue, and its inspiring vitality. We may call the Word of God a whetstone to sharpen. As every mechanic knows the value of a whetstone to sharpen his tools, so every believer in Christ realizes the importance of sharpening the graces of the spiritual life with the Word of Truth.

God's people, in all ages, know they can lose ground in the Christian life. The intensity of love to Christ may be slackened by the love of other things. The glow of zeal may be dampened by discouragement. The grip of faith may loosen its grasp by self-occupation. The brightness of testimony may be tarnished by the breath of the world. The bloom of consecration may be rubbed off by the hand of inconsistency. The voice of prayer may be hushed by the paralysis of doubt; and the cord of unity may be snapped by the rude force of discord and neglect of the means of grace.

One half of our freedom from failure in the Christian life is to know our danger. When we imagine we are safest, we are in the greatest peril. When we think we are strongest, we are most weak. The Church at Laodicea is a case in point; they thought they were all right when they were altogether wrong. When we are deeply conscious of our utter weakness, our complete sinfulness, and constant need of grace, we cast ourselves the more upon the Lord. John Newton puts it well when he says, "Alas! My experience abounds with complaints. He is my Sun; but clouds, and sometimes walls, intercept Him from my view. He is my Friend; but on my part there is such coldness and ingratitude, as no other friend could bear. He is my Strength, yet I am prone to lean upon reeds. But still He is gracious and shames me with His repeated multiplied goodness. Oh, for a warmer heart, a more simple dependence, a more active zeal, a more sensible deliverance from the effects of this body of sin and death." So prays every true child of God.

Then there is another danger. In looking to our inability, we fail to see God's ability; the sense of our insufficiency does not make room for God's sufficiency, and our weakness so overpowers us that we do not let God's power possess us.

The one and only safeguard is to keep in touch with the Lord through His Word, and if we do this, the soul of our love will be true, the grip of our faith will be strong, and the cry of our prayer will ever be, "Quicken me according to Thy Word."

In calling attention to the fact that the Word of God is a whetstone to sharpen us in the many-sidedness of our Christian life, I want to call attention to the frequency with which the Psalmist pleads the prayer, "Quicken me," in Psalm 119. The Hebrew word translated "quicken," occurs no less than sixteen times. Nine times the term is rendered "*quicken*" and "*quickened,*" and five times "*live.*" The same word is translated "*revive*" in 1 Chronicles 11:8 (margin); Nehemiah 4:2; Psalm 138:7; Habakkuk 3:2. The word occurs in three relations in Psalm 119:

1. There is the Psalmist's testimony as to what the Lord has done in the past (verses 50, 93).
2. The Psalmist's prayer for present revival (verses 17, 25, 37, 40, 77, 88, 107, 116, 149, 154, 156, 159, 175).
3. The Psalmist's confidence as to what the Lord will do (verse 144).

Does not the Psalmist's desire to be revived according to God's Word give us the reason why so few are intense in their love to Christ and wholeheartedly devoted to Him? Many would like a revival, but it must be according to their fancy, or their methods, or their senses. True revival is always according to God's Word. When there is a revival according to God's Word, it will be a revival indeed.

Let us see how the Word of God is as a whetstone to sharpen us.

The Word of God is a whetstone to sharpen us in prayer

Among the many promises that Christ has given us is this: "If ye abide in me, and my words abide in you, ye shall ask what ye will, and it shall be done unto you" (John 15:7). Christ's words dwelling in us not only give us the authority to pray and direct us as to the petitions we should make, but also give us the incentive to prayer. When we come in the spirit of faith to the Word of God, it sharpens our desires and makes us turn what we read into prayer.

Listening to the Lord as He speaks to us in His Word makes us pray for the blessings of which He speaks. When Christ spoke to the woman of Samaria about the Living Water, she exclaimed, "Give me this water."

Pondering the promises of God's Word makes us bold to plead them in petition. When Elijah on Mount Carmel called upon Jehovah as the "God of Abraham, Isaac, and Israel," he claimed the covenanted promises given to the fathers that God would care for His people and vindicate their cause against all the Lord's enemies.

Feeding upon the holy sayings of Christ which refer to His death, makes us say prayerfully with Thomas, "Let us . . . die with him" (John 11:16), die to sin, to self, to the flesh, to the world, and all that is associated with the old man and his deeds.

Dwelling upon the commands of Christ as He bids us follow Him, abide in Him, believe in Him, rest upon Him, suffer with Him, look to Him, and testify of Him stirs in our hearts the longing to show our love for Him by our obedience to Him, and we cry with the Psalmist, "Help me, O Lord my God'" (Psalm 109:26).

Thinking of the power of Christ, as the Spirit of God tells us that Christ is the Power of God, excites in us the longing to come in contact with Him as the woman did who touched the hem of Christ's garment and into whom flowed the power of Christ. We pray with the apostles that the Spirit of Power may rest upon us that we may boldly proclaim the sufficiency of Christ as the Savior of the world.

We hear the Savior speaking of the coming glory in His gracious promise, "I will come again and receive you to Myself," and His pointed declaration, "Behold I come quickly, and My reward is with Me, to give to every man according as his work shall be." As we walk with Him our hearts gladly respond, "Come, Lord Jesus, come quickly." Thus the Word of God is a whetstone to sharpen the soul in prayer.

The Word of God is a whetstone to sharpen us, in separating from us things contrary to the mind of God

There is one incident recorded in the Acts of the Apostles which illustrates in a remarkable manner the separating influence of the Word of God—when it is believed—upon the life. The apostle Paul met with great success in his preaching at Ephesus. One result of his mission was that many who had used cunning arts burnt all their books; and the cause of this is put down to the working of God's Word for, in speaking of the burning of the books, it says, "So mightily grew the Word of God and prevailed" (Acts 19:20).

"The Swedish Nightingale," Jenny Lind, won great success as an operatic singer, and money poured into her purse. Yet she left the stage when singing her best and never went back to it. She must have missed the money, the fame and the applause of thousands, but she was content to live in privacy.

Once an English friend found her on the sea shore, with a Bible on her knee, looking out into the glory of a sunset. They talked and the conversation drew near to the inevitable question. "Oh, Madame Goldschmidt, how is it that you ever came to abandon the stage at the height of your success?"

"When every day," was the quiet answer, "it made me think less of this (laying a finger on the Bible) and nothing at all of that (pointing to the sunset), what else could I do?"

As the laver in the tabernacle was given that the priests might wash their hands and feet therein and the defilement they had contracted might be removed, so the Word of God will separate from us the dirt of worldliness, the slime of unbelief, the mud of superstition, the filth of lust, the dust of conceit, the spots of jealousy, and the ashes of pride.

The Word of God is the whetstone to sharpen us in our spiritual life

When the apostle Paul was leaving the Church in Ephesus he said, "I commend you to God, and to the word of His grace, which is able to build you up" (Acts 20:32). The Holy Spirit says a great deal in relation to the Christian life in connection with the little word "*Up*." The following are a few of the directions the Lord has given in the word of His grace as to the *up-grade* of faith:

The *attitude* in our spiritual life is to be *looking up*. As the Psalmist says, "In the morning I will direct my prayer unto thee, and will look up" (Psalm 5:3), for, as the mirror reflects the image of the person who is looking into it, so the believer reflects Christ as he looks at Him.

The *strength* of our spiritual life is to *gird up* the loins of our mind with the truth of God. We read in 1 Peter 1:13: "Gird up the loins of your mind," for as the girdle strengthens the loins in walking, so the truth of God ministers to us its power, and we are girded with it.

The *exercise* of our spiritual life is to *stir up* the fire of grace which the Lord has kindled in our hearts. Paul says in writing to his son Timothy, "Stir up the gift of God, which is in thee" (2 Timothy 1:6), for, as the fire in the grate will burn the brighter when it is stirred, so the Divine life will glow when stirred by the truth of God.

The *place* of our spiritual life is the presence of the Lord. "Go *up* to Bethel, and dwell there" (Genesis 35:1) was the command of God to Jacob. We, too, have our Bethel (Bethel means the House of God), namely, abiding in Christ. As certain plants will only grow in a warm atmosphere, so our spiritual life will only flourish in the warm environment of His presence.

The *responsibility* of our spiritual life is to *take up* our cross daily as Christ took up the cross for us. His word is calm and clear as He bids us follow Him. "Take up the cross" (Matthew 16:24). Cross-bearing always precedes crown-wearing. There was no ascension glory before Calvary's cross.

The *secret* of our spiritual life is to *grow up* into Christ in all things (Ephesians 4:15). The secret of all growth is Christ. Winning Christ, knowing Christ, and apprehending Christ are the causes that make us advance in grace even as the child grows in stature as it is fed with good food.

The *solidarity* of our spiritual life is to be *built up* with the strengthening of God's truth. The stamina of faith, the steadfastness of love, the sturdiness of zeal, the solidity of service, the stalwartness of witnessing, and the stabilizing in the truth are all born of the cementing power of the Word of Grace.

The story is told of a great bell which was made to vibrate by the note of a slender flute. The flute had no influence upon the bell, except when a certain note was sounded. Then the great mass of metal breathed a responsive sigh. Thus, when our hearts and lives are in unison with the flute of God's Word, there sounds forth from the bell of our conduct a corresponding action. When the Thessalonians received the Word of God, the bell of faith sounded forth from them, in that they turned to God from idols, to serve the living and true God, and to wait for His Son from heaven.

Let us, morning by morning, like the Master (Isaiah 1:4, R.V.), sharpen our spiritual faculties by the whetstone of the Truth for it will give edge to our testimony (Acts 2:37), keenness to our vision (Acts 17:11, 12), courage to our ministry (2 Timothy 2:15), intensity to our love (Acts 16:14, 15), alertness to our faith (Acts 16:33, 34), tone to our spiritual life (Psalm 1:2, 3), and equipment for our service (2 Timothy 3:16, 17).

16

The Discipler's Toil

Some years ago, a sister in Christ said to me, "Have you noticed that the four things which the Shunammite woman provided for the prophet Elisha are illustrative of the four things which the worker for Christ needs?"

"No," I replied, "I have not."

She said, "The four things were a bed, a table, a stool, and a candlestick" (2 Kings 4:10). The bed is the symbol of rest which is found in Christ by coming to Him and in being yoked in God's will with Him (Matthew 11:28, 29). The table is the symbol of fellowship with Him for He spreads a table before us in the presence of our enemies (Psalm 23:5), and bids us 'come and dine' (John 21:12). The stool is the symbol of instruction from Christ for we must sit at His feet and learn of Him if we would be initiated into the secrets of His will (Deuteronomy 33:3; Luke 10:39). The candlestick is the symbol of testimony for Christ for He says we are the light of the world and His witnesses to testify of Himself (Matthew 5:14; Acts 1:8)."

It seems to me that not only are these four things illustrative of what the Christian worker needs, but the order in which they are given is also important. Rest in Christ by being yoked with Him in the will of God is essential in order to have fellowship with Him; fellowship with Him is the qualification for instruction from Him; and instruction from Him is the precursor of effective testimony for Him.

As those who are called to bear witness to our Lord, we esteem it a high privilege to be fellow-toilers with God. I prefer to render the passage, "Fellow-workers with God" (1 Corinthians 3:9, R.V.), "Fellow-*toilers* with God" for the word *toil* suggests *hard* labor. There are plenty of workers so called but few *toilers*. If anything is to be got first hand, it means hard work. As Ruskin says, "If you want knowledge, you must toil for it; if pleasure, you must toil for it. Toil is the law. Pleasure comes through toil, and not by self-indulgence and indolence. When one gets to love work, his life is a happy one."

There are six different words in the New Testament associated with labor. The first word describes the laborer himself; the second word is associated with motive in labor; the third word is used in connection with those with whom we labor; the fourth word indicates how the work is to be accomplished; the fifth word illustrates the fervor of the labor; and the sixth word speaks of the exhaustion which is the consequence of such labor.

The Toiler

The first word associated with Christian labor describes the toiler himself. The word used is illustrative of his occupation and the wages he receives, and thus characterizes one who lives by his labor. Christ employs the word when He urges us to pray that laborers may be thrust into the harvest field (Matthew 9:37, 38). The Holy Spirit also uses it when He says "the laborer is worthy of his reward" (1 Timothy 5:18), and when He says to Timothy through Paul, "Study to show thyself approved unto God, a workman," or laborer (it is the same word) "that needeth not to be ashamed" (2 Timothy 2:15). The spiritual thought lying under the surface is, the toiler in Christian labor ministers to his own necessity in ministering to others even as the workman maintains himself and his home by his occupation.

As there are four requisite things for health of body, namely, fresh air, good food, frequent ablutions, and temperate exercise; so there are four things necessary for health of soul, namely, the fresh air of prayerful dependence on the Lord, the good food of meditation in the truth of the Lord, the cleansing of the walk by the operation of the cleansing of the Holy Spirit, and healthy exercise by being about the business of the Lord.

Attention is directed to the last. He who will not work shall not eat, says the apostle. There are a great many of God's people who are nearly starved spiritually, and it is because they will not work. They complain about their leanness when they should be confessing their laziness. It is absolutely necessary for our spiritual welfare that we should be engaged in Christian work. We get in giving. We obtain help in helping. The muscular arm of the blacksmith is obtained by the constant swinging of the hammer. The smart appearance and the skilled display of the soldier are the outcome of the incessant drill through which he has passed. The skill of the gardener, as seen in the prize plant at the flower show, is an evidence of careful attention in the garden. The thrilling music from the violin, as the musician handles the instrument, is the result or years of practice in solitude. The correct borings of the engineer demonstrate his careful and minute calculations beforehand. All the above are rewarded in consequence of their toil. The blacksmith has gained strength of arm, the soldier has gained his perfect poise, the gardener has won his prize, the musician has obtained his honor, and the engineer has received his certificate, but all as the result of their careful work.

The same is true in the Christian life. As we study to feed others with the Bread of life, we feed ourselves just as the widow found food for herself as she ministered to the prophet Elijah (1 Kings 17:14). As we labor in prayer that others may be blessed, we oil the wheels of our own spiritual nature, just as Epaphras did in praying for the saints at Colosse (Colossians 4:12). As we endeavor to keep the unity of the Spirit, we keep our own minds calm just as Paul did in seeking the oneness of others (1 Corinthians 3:3-9). As we trim our neighbor's hedge in kindly service, we clip our own, just as Daniel's faithfulness to the king brought him honor from the king (Daniel 6:1-4). As we minister the oil of love to make the lamp of another's life burn brighter, we give light to ourselves, even as the lamp in the holy place also not only lighted up the other vessels of the sanctuary but also gave light over against itself (Numbers 8:2, 3). As we give the word of encouragement to our brother, we banish discouragement from our own dwelling, just as David found when he befriended the poor Egyptian, who had information which led to the recovery of David's lost property (1 Samuel 30:10-18). As we lend our being to the Lord's service, we shall find abundant blessing as Peter found for it was after he had lent his ship to Christ that he received such a draught of fishes through Christ (Luke 5:37). As we follow Christ and deny ourselves even by death to self, we shall find our life in the "much fruit" of the afterward (John 12:24-26).

The Toiler's Aim

As the electric current runs through the wire connected with the battery, so the spiritual thought of God's truth is found in the words which the Holy Spirit employs in expressing to us God's will. Thus the second word associated with Christian labor gives us the true aim in service. It is found in 2 Corinthians 5:9 where the apostle says, "We *labor* . . . that we may be accepted of Him," or, as the Revised Version gives it, "We make it our *aim*. . . . to be well-pleasing unto Him." The same word occurs in two other places in the New Testament. In Romans 15:20 it is translated "*strived,*" in speaking of the apostle's aim to preach Christ where He had not been named before. In 1 Thessalonians 4:11 it occurs when Paul exhorts the saints to "*study,*" or to make it their aim to be quiet. The meaning of the word is to have a purpose in all one does; thus, it signifies one who labors with an end in view and, as a consequence exerts himself out of love to the object. The end the Christian has in view is, as the apostle indicates, to be well-pleasing unto the Lord. The Christian does not labor as Diotrephes to get a name, nor as Judas to obtain money, nor as Balaam at the dictation of man, nor as Saul to please the people, nor as Aaron to quiet the clamoring voice, nor as the Athenians for some new thing, but as Christ labored for the Father, namely, because He loved Him.

A lady once said to the late William Burns, the missionary, "I presume you are going to China to win souls?"

"No, madam," he replied, "I am going there to glorify God." The man with such a motive and an end in view will take little heed of what men think of him for it is his aim to be right with heaven.

It is said the Lacedaemonions used to stir themselves to heroism by the thought, *What will they say of us in Sparta?* Such a spirit will actuate the true laborer. What does my Lord think? What will He say? What does He desire? What is pleasing to Him? What will call forth His "Well done?" are questions which arise in the mind of those who desire to honor the Lord.

Fellowship in Toil

One special feature of the boards of the Tabernacle was that they were closely connected with the foundation and also with each other. The silver foundation upon which the boards rested is typical of the redemptiveness of Christ's atonement (Exodus 36:24; 1 Peter 1:18) and suggests our identification with Him in His death (2 Corinthians 5:14, R.V.). The boards being united to each other sets forth the fact that believers are members of each other by virtue of their union with the Head of the Church (1 Corinthians 12:12, 13).

This thought is shown forth in the third word associated with Christian service. The thought of fellowship is distinctly wrapped up in it. The word *Sunergos* is variously rendered, but wherever it occurs, fellowship is brought out. We find it rendered *"Laborers together with,"* in 1 Corinthians 3:9 in calling attention to the fact that the Lord's servants are associated with Him in His labor. Paul uses the word in speaking of Urbane as a "*Helper* in Christ" (Romans 16:9), of Epaphroditus as a "*Companion* in labor" (Philippians 2:25), and of the *"fellow-laborers"* whose names are in the book of life (Philippians 4:3). The words suggest a twofold dependence, dependence upon God and dependence upon fellow-believers. There is no man who illustrates in such a remarkable manner this twofold dependence as the apostle Paul. Let us ponder the apostle's dependence on the Lord.

Dependence on God. Paul recognized he was at work for God and that God Himself was the great Worker. *Prayer to God* was the habit of his life and the secret force which propelled him in all his actions; thus, we find him saying, "I bow my knees unto the Father" (Ephesians 3:14), and more than once he is found in the attitude of prayer (Acts 20:36; 21:5).

The *presence of God* was the apostle's stay. He was independent of man because he was so absolutely dependent on the Lord. The Lord's presence was his joy in sorrow, his peace in persecution, his power in testimony, his courage in conflict, his comfort in trial, his supply in service, and his consolation in suffering and loneliness. When in a time of trial and suffering and he had no one to stand with him, he could confidently say, "All forsook me . . . notwithstanding the Lord stood with me" (2 Timothy 4:16, 17).

The *power of God* was the electric current which charged the being of Paul with such mighty energy that it made his service effective in its influence wherever he went. But it was *God's* power, and not Paul's preaching, which was the effective instrument as he himself confesses, "His working which worketh in me mightily" (Colossians 2:29).

The *love of God* was the inspiring motive which caused the apostle to move with such glad and quickened footsteps in his Lord's service. He says, "The love of Christ constraineth us" (2 Corinthians 5:14). The love of Christ was an inward fire in his heart and an enclosing force in his life as the word *"constraineth,"* which is rendered *"taken with"* in Luke 4:38 in speaking of Peter's wife's mother being "taken with" a fever, and the same word is given *"throng,"* in calling attention to the fact that the people were "thronging" the Lord Jesus (Luke 8:45).

The *Word of God* was always the message which was dropping from Paul's lips like sweet smelling myrrh. Never does he say "I think" but always "God says." Listen to him as he speaks at Antioch: "To you is the word of this salvation sent" (Acts 13:26), and, in referring to his ministry at Ephesus, he declares, "I have not shunned to declare unto you all the counsel of God" (Acts 20:27). His constant court of appeal was to "Thus saith the Lord," and this was the secret of his manifold blessing to others.

The *grace of God* was the tent of blessing under which Paul sheltered as he pled that his thorn in the flesh be removed; and yet he glories in his infirmities when he finds the grace of God is sufficient, for he says "that the power of Christ may rest upon me'" (2 Corinthians 12:9), or as the sentence might be translated, "The power of Christ to tabernacle upon me" so that he would be entirely enveloped by it, as the disciples were by the cloud on the mount (Luke 9:34).

The *glory of God* was ever before the apostle. The pole star which ever guided him was how he might glorify God. One of the greatest things which brought the greatest satisfaction to Paul's heart was when he could say, "They glorified God in me" (Galatians 1:24).

Dependence on fellow believers. Now, on the other hand, we find the apostle was dependent upon fellow believers. He desired that they should work with him and he with them. There are little touches which bring out his dependence. He is glad when he knows others are preaching the truth although he is not in sympathy with some of the methods adopted (Philippians 1:18). He is thankful for the temporal assistance given to him by Epaphroditus (Philippians 2:25). He is comforted by the fidelity of Timothy and speaks of him "as dear to me" (Philippians 2:20, margin). He is encouraged by those who had helped in the Gospel (Philippians 4:3). He is cheered by the presence of Luke and says Mark is "profitable to me for the ministry" (2 Timothy 4:11). He is dependent upon Timothy for little acts of kindness and asks him to bring the cloak which he left behind at Troas (2 Timothy 4:13). And he asks Philemon to refresh him by being kind to Onesimus (Philemon 20). All these touches go to show how Paul recognized the oneness of the body of Christ. It was this fact that evidently led him to write: "Christ, from whom the whole body fitly joined together, and compacted by that which every joint supplieth" (Ephesians 4:16). While every joint has direct communication with the head, each joint is the means of supplying the other joint; thus, while all are supplied from one source, each in turn is a means of mutual communication.

Diligence in Toil

Among other things in relation to the love of God, we are exhorted to behold the manner of it (1 John 3:1). Not merely are we to know the fact of God's love, but the way it acts. The same thing may be said of the believer's service for Christ: we are not only told to labor, but we are urged to "*labor*" in order to enter God's rest. The same word as translated "*labor*" in Hebrews 4:11 is rendered "*was forward to do*" in Galatians 2:10 when Paul speaks of his remembrance of the poor; "*endeavored*" in 1 Thessalonians 2:17 when the apostle speaks of his endeavor to see the face of the Thessalonians; and the same word is given "*diligent*" in Titus 3:12. The meaning of the word is diligence, earnestness, zeal, to make haste. The King's business requires haste; there must be no loitering on the way. Those who loiter on the Lord's business are sure to meet with some disaster as the man of God out of Judah found when he turned aside from the direction of the Lord at the invitation of the old prophet of Bethel (1 Kings 13). However, there is a haste which is not after God, but contrary to Him. How are we to know when we are acting in unison with God? We know when we obey His word. Paul in writing to Timothy says "*Study*" (or be diligent, it is the same word as in Titus 3:12), "to show thyself approved unto God" (2 Timothy 2:15). When the soul is in communication with the Lord, it must do the Lord's work in a becoming manner for to be listless where He is concerned would be to show our want of love to Him.

Fervor in Toil

There are some Christian workers who never get to the boiling point in the Lord's work. They are always afraid lest they should blunder in some way. Spurgeon used to say, "A blundering horse is better than a dead one."

It is only when our own hearts are all aglow that we will make others so. Burning for God comes through musing upon Him (Psalm 39:3; Jeremiah 20:9). Thomas Watson says, "Meditate till thou findest thy heart grow warm. If when a man is cold you ask how long he should stand by the fire? Sure, till he be thoroughly warm, and made fit for his work. So, Christian, when thy heart is cold, stand at the fire of meditation till thou findest thy affections warmed, and thou art made fit for spiritual service. David mused till his heart waxed hot within him." As we thus muse and become warm, we will become fervent in prayer and enthusiastic in service.

The fifth word rendered "labor" occurs in Colossians 4:12 in speaking of the fervency, frequentness, and fulness of the prayers of Epaphras. The word is also rendered "*strive*" (Luke 13:24), and "*fight*" in 1 Timothy 6:12. It comes from the same root as "*agony*," which is used to describe Christ's sufferings in Gethsemane. The word means to struggle, to *contend* with an adversary, to compete for a prize, to endeavor to accomplish anything.

There are forces all around which are opposed to us, and there are forces within us which would drag us down, but the man of God must be like his Master and set his face against them and in the glow cf the Holy Spirit determine to rise above them. No one ever yet accomplished anything who was not in earnest about it, and this is especially true with reference to the Christian life.

Thank God, it is easy to be saved because Christ by His death has removed the hindrance (Hebrews 9:26), but it is not an easy thing to live as a Christian (1 Peter 4:18). There is a *battle* to be fought (1 Timothy 6:12), a *trust* to be kept (2 Corinthians 5:18), a *talent* to be used (Matthew 25:14, etc.), an *enemy* to overcome (1 Peter 5:8, 9), a *watch* to maintain (Mark 13:37), a *ministry* to fulfill (John 13:14), and a *prize* to win (Philippians 3:14).

To accomplish all these we must be under the power and presence of the Holy Spirit. He is only known in power as we look to Him in prayer, prayer which is fervent and full of faith. As Bishop Hamilton says, "No man was likely to do much good in prayer who did not begin to look upon it in the light of a work, to be prepared for, and persevered in with all the earnestness which we bring to bear on subjects which are most necessary and interesting."

Exhaustion in Toil

One of the features of Gideon's faithful 300 was they were careless of their comfort in that they did not put themselves in the same position of ease to drink as the others (Judges 7:5, 6). Are there not Christian workers who are so concerned about their own comfort, convenience, and reputation, that they never go out of their way to do anything extraordinary in the service of Christ, much less become tired in His service? They have little sympathy with Elijah under the juniper tree, because they have never been strung up to his pitch, nor done so nobly and fearlessly in witnessing for God. All who have done anything for God, in serving Him, have known what it is to be tired out, exhausted. This thought is brought out in the sixth word rendered labor.

This word means to be spent out through hard work, to be weary and faint. The word is translated weary in describing Christ being *"wearied"* with His journey when He must needs go through Samaria and sat on Jacob's well (John 4:6). The word is also translated *"laboring"* in Acts 20:35; *"labored"* in 1 Corinthians 15:10; and *"laboreth"* in 2 Timothy 2:6. Next to the Lord Jesus, we instincitively turn to the apostle Paul as an example. He certainly illustrates in a peculiar manner the truth embodied in the word before us. Of him it is said he "hazarded" his life (Acts 15:36), and when he wrote to the Corinthians he said to them, "I will very gladly spend and be spent for you" (2 Corinthians 12:15). I want to call attention to the three words, "Hazarded," "Spend," "Spent."

"Hazarded." To hazard one's life means to give it over to death. The same word occurs three times in Romans 1:24, 26, 28 and is there rendered *"gave up,"* and *"gave over."* Every true Christian worker is careless of his own ease. Lady Edgeworth, in the days of King Charles II, had suddenly to defend the old castle at Lissom in the absence of her husband. In doing so she had to go down and fetch powder from the castle vaults. On her return she said to the woman who had gone with her, "Where did you put the candle?" "I left it stuck in the barrel of black salt." Then did that glorious woman go down to the spot where the candle was burning into the powder and put her hand round it like a cup, lift it up and take it out, and so, at the hazard of her own life, saved the lives of others. Sinners are like that candle burning into the powder of their own destruction. Who is willing to deliver himself over to death, if needs be, in order that they may be saved? We shall be if we recognize that Christ was delivered (the same word as rendered "hazarded") for our offenses.

"Spend and be *spent."* The word "spend" means to *"consume"* as is translated in James 4:3. The same word is given *"spent all"* in Mark 5:26 and Luke 15:14 where we read the woman who spent all she had in trying to be freed from her disease and of the prodigal who spent all in riotous living. The word *"spent"* signifies to be *"exhausted."* Thus we may paraphrase the apostle's words, "I am willing to spend all my resources, and I am willing to exhaust myself in order to benefit you." Such a spirit should characterize all workers. The lighted candle preaches a sermon to us for it says, "I give to others, and I am consumed in doing so."

17

The Discipler's Sanctifier

One of the seven "As he's" of John's first epistle is "As he is, so are we" (1 John 4:17). May we not apply these words to the subject before us? For what was true of Christ in reference to the Holy Spirit is also true of us who are believers in Him. As He was *born* of the Holy Spirit (Luke 1:35), so are we (John 1:13); as He was *sealed* with the Holy Spirit (Luke 3:22), so are we (Ephesians 1:13); as He was *led* by the Holy Spirit (Luke 4:1), so are we (Romans 8:14); as He was *anointed* with the Holy Spirit (Luke 4:18; Acts 10:38), so are we (2 Corinthians 1:21); as He *acted* in the power of the Holy Spirit (Luke 4:14-19), so should we (Acts 1:8); as He *offered* Himself as a sacrifice for sin to God by the Holy Spirit (Hebrews 9:14), so should we be sacrificing ourselves in order to be well pleasing to Him as His children and servants (Romans 15:16); and as He was *raised* from the dead by the Spirit (1 Peter 3:18), so shall we be quickened (Romans 8:11).

The scriptural meaning of the word "sanctification" is separation or dedication. Believers are separated *to* God, *in* Christ, *from* the world, and as such they are to dedicate themselves unreservedly *to* God, *for* Himself and His service, *by* the power of the Holy Spirit.

We shall take up a few Scriptures in reference to the Holy Spirit and the believer and seek to bring out the practical side of the truth as illustrating the Spirit's operation in His sanctifying grace.

As sinners, we are quickened by the Holy Spirit

"Except a man be born of water and of the Spirit, he cannot see the kingdom of God" (John 3:5). What is the evidence that we are born of God? We have the question answered in John's first epistle. (1) *"Ye know that every one that doeth righteousness is born of Him"* (2:29). The meaning of the word "righteousness" is straightness. Uprightness of life and straightness of conduct are evidences of the new birth even as the growth of the plant is evidence of its being alive. (2) *"Whosoever is born of God doth not commit sin,"* etc. (3:9), that is, does not willfully or habitually do it. God has made no provision for us to sin although if we do sin, Christ's advocacy provides for our restoration (1 John 2:1). It is the nature of a sow to wallow in the mire but if a sheep gets into the mire it is not in its element and seeks to get out of it. The unsaved delight in sin, but the Christian, while he may be tripped up through sudden temptation, can never be happy in sin, even as the normal condition of the electric wire is to transmit the electric current although there may be a temporary cessation through some intervening obstacle. The normal condition of the child of God is that he is no longer in the servitude of sin nor has he any desire to do the biddings of the old master. (3) *"Every one that loveth is born of God"* (4:7). We love Him because He first loved us; we love all who are His although we cannot always love some of their ways; and, being constrained by His love, we love those who are perishing. True love always does two things: it gives its best, like Mary with her costly box of spikenard (John 12:3); and it does its utmost, like Jonathan in his plan to benefit David (1 Samuel 18:4). (4) *"Whatsoever is born of God overcometh the world"* (5:4). There is victory over the lust of the flesh, the lust of the eyes, and the pride of life, as we trust in the Lord. We ignore the flesh as Joseph did (Genesis 39:9) by remembering we are crucified with Christ (Galatians 2:20). We look to the Lord as Abraham did (Genesis13:14-15), and thus keep our eyes from beholding vanity (Psalm 119:37). We let the Spirit work in us the mind of Christ (Philippians 2:1-5), and follow His humble example, and thus kill the evil weed of pride.

As saints, we are sealed with the Holy Spirit

"Grieve not the Holy Spirit of God, whereby ye are sealed unto the day of redemption" (Ephesians 4:30). All the sacrifices of old upon being found without blemish, were sealed or a mark was put upon them as attesting the fact that they were fit for sacrifice. Christ was sealed because of what He was in Himself (John 6:27; Luke 3:22); we are sealed because of what we are in Him (Ephesians 1:13). The Spirit as the Seal is God's mark upon us that we are His for "if any man have not the Spirit of Christ, he is none of His"; and also that we are accepted in the Beloved, the Spirit by the Word telling us that in Him, having believed, we were sealed with the Holy Spirit of promise (Ephesians 1:13, R.V.) When a seal is pressed upon the melted wax, there is the impression of the die left. The Spirit being within us, He writes God's law on our hearts and minds so that we not only keep the letter of the moral law, but the spirit of it; and the impression of His presence is seen in the life in the fruit of Himself which is "love, joy, peace, long-suffering, gentleness, goodness, faith, meekness, temperance."

As children of God, we have the witness of the Spirit

"The Spirit Himself beareth witness with our spirit, that we are the children of God" (Romans 8:16, R.V.; Galatians 4:6). The Lord witnesses to us by His Word for "he that believeth on the Son of God hath the witness in him." The witness is this, that the Lord has given unto us eternal life (1 John 5:10-13, R.V.), and we know it because He tells us so in the Word. He has given to us the possession of the Spirit whom He has sent into our hearts and who cries there "Abba Father." This "witness" is twofold. There is the witness *from God to us*, that we are the children of God, which He gives to us in His Word and which He makes true in our experience; and then there is the witness *from us to God*, which is born of our obedience to Him through the Spirit's power, which has its resting-place in an uncondemning heart (1 John 3:20-24).

As priests, we are anointed with the Holy Spirit for worship, work, and walk

"Now He which stablisheth us with you in Christ, and hath anointed us, is God" (2 Corinthians 1:21). "And ye have an anointing from the Holy One" (1 John 2:20, 27, R.V.). All God's children are priests. We are a holy priesthood and a royal priesthood. A "holy priesthood to offer up spiritual sacrifices acceptable to God by Jesus Christ" (1 Peter 2:5). We are to yield our bodies as a living sacrifice to God (Romans 12:1). We are to offer up the sacrifice of praise to God continually (Hebrews 13:15). We are not to forget to do good to others for with such sacrifices God is well pleased (Hebrews 13:16; Philippians 4:18). These sacrifices are all to be offered up in the name of the Lord Jesus and by the power of the Holy Spirit for it is by Him we have access through Christ to the Father (Ephesians 2:18). And it is only as we are working in the Spirit that the work is pleasing to God (Galatians 6:8).

Again, we are a royal priesthood that we should show forth the praises, or virtues, of Him who has called us out of darkness into His marvelous light (1 Peter 2:9). Here we see our individual responsibility to glorify God in our walk in the midst of a crooked and perverse generation. Being in the light, the light is to be in us through our habitual walk in it. Then the light of God's love and grace radiates from us even as it did in the case of Moses after He had been in the presence of the Lord forty days, and the people knew it for his shining face was an unmistakable argument (Exodus 34:35).

As members of the Body of Christ, we have the baptism of the Holy Spirit

"For by one Spirit are we all baptized into one body" (1 Corinthians 12:13). It is not merely a judicial fact but a living reality that we are united to the Lord Jesus by the Holy Spirit; thus, we are also united to one another. This union, as we abide in Christ and His words abide in us, causes us to experience the risen life of Christ and to know in very deed that the law of the Spirit of Life in Christ Jesus has made us free from the law of sin and death. The practical outcome of this is the fulfillment of the eleventh commandment which is "loving one another." How is it Christians do not realize the keeping and energizing power of the Spirit? Why do they not fervently love each other with pure hearts? Because the channels of communication between God and the soul are not clear. When the cable was being laid down between England and America, there was something that stopped the communication. So they had to take the cable up and remove the hindrance. If there is any known sin or doubtful thing in the life or an evil heart of unbelief, let the Master remove it. Then shall we realize His almighty power. As we, by the Spirit, manifest the disposition of Christ, we realize more of the Spirit. We often ask for more grace and more of the Spirit's power; what we really need is that God should have more of us, and then we should possess more of Him. Let us acknowledge to the Spirit His right to possess us and in faith pray—

> "Thine is the throne-room of the soul!
> Its Ruler, break each barrier down;

As with full tide o'erflood the whole,
Self overborne by Thee alone . . .
Spirit of Truth, of Holiness.
We cry not '*enter*,' but '*possess*.'"

As heirs of God, we have the Spirit as the Earnest of our inheritance

"The Holy Spirit of promise, which is the earnest of our inheritance" (Ephesians 1:13, 14). The Spirit is the earnest of our inheritance; the Pledge of our resurrection or of our being changed at the coming of Christ; and the Token—or as our Scotch friends would say, "the Arles"—of our sharing the coming glory with Christ. We are brought to God and to heaven by the work of Christ for us; but God and heaven are brought to us by the Spirit as Christ lives in us as the Hope of Glory. What is Heaven? Heaven is emancipation from a body humiliated by sin (Philippians 3:21); conformation to Christ's image (Romans 8:29); satisfaction in the Lord's presence (Revelation 7:15-17); reflection of God's glory (Revelation 21:11); and communion with Christ in His glory (John 17:24). We have a foretaste of these blessings now (John 8:36; 1 John 3:3; Psalm 103:5; 1 Corinthians 1:9), even as Israel had a foretaste of the fruitfulness of Canaan in the fruit which the spies brought back from the land (Numbers 13:23-25). We are a heavenly people, and, while in the world, we are not of it; as strangers we do not belong to it, as foreigners we are not at home in it, and as pilgrims we are hastening through this world to our heavenly fatherland.

As temples of God, we have the presence of the Spirit

"Know ye not that ye are the temple of God, and that the Spirit of God dwelleth in you" (1 Corinthians 3:16)? The Dagon of the flesh must fall before His presence (1 Samuel 5:3). The things of earth, the love of money, self-glorifying, self-seeking, self-love, and self-esteem must all be cleared out before Him even as Christ cleared out the money changers from the temple. Then He will come and fill His temple with His glory so that self will not be able to stand, even as Moses in the tabernacle and the priests at the dedication of Solomon's temple could not stand before the glory of the Lord. Then shall it be said, "Every whit of it uttereth" (margin) "His glory" (Psalm 29:9).

There may be some who hesitate to allow the Lord to cleanse out every defiling thing. This hesitation elicits the grave question: are they the Lord's at all? Surely one result of being His is the desire to do as He wishes. Cleansing will mean unspeakable blessing. When Mahmoud, the conqueror of India, had taken the city of Gujarat, he proceeded, as was his custom, to destroy the idols. There was one, fifteen feet high, which its priests and devotees begged him to spare. He was deaf to their entreaties, and seizing a hammer he struck it one blow; when, to his amazement, from the shattered image there rained down at his feet a shower of gems, pearls, and diamonds—treasure of fabulous value, which had been hidden within it! Had he spared the idol he would have lost all this wealth.

Let us not spare *our* idols. It is to our interest to demolish them. If we shatter them, there will rain upon our hearts the very treasures of Heaven, the gifts and graces of the Holy Spirit; but if we spare our idols we shall miss riches unspeakable as well as desecrate the temple of the Holy Spirit and place ourselves under the chastening hand of God.

As believers, we need the daily renewing and supply of the Holy Spirit

"And when they had prayed . . . they were all filled with the Holy Ghost" (Acts 4:31). We need this renewing for our spiritual growth in grace, for our *downward* growth in the truth, for our *upward* growth into Christ, and for our *outward* growth in usefulness. We need this renewing for daily walk, for every detail in every day life, and for victory over self, for if we "walk in the Spirit, we shall not fullfil the lusts of the flesh" (Galatians 5:16). We need this renewing for our work so that we are abounding by the power of the Spirit. Yesterday's manna will not do for today. Yesterday's success will not answer for the present. Yesterday's filling and power for service will not avail now. The apostle Peter illustrates this: he was "filled with the Holy Ghost" on the day of Pentecost (Acts 2:4), and yet we find him with the others again filled at a later period (Acts 4:31). He needed a fresh equipment for new service. As the cistern is filled with water again when it is drawn out through the action of the ball-tap allowing the supply to enter, so as we keep in fellowship with the Lord, He meets the recurring need by the supply of the Spirit.

How are we to get this renewing? (1) *By waiting upon God in prayer.* "They that wait upon the Lord shall renew their strength; they shall mount up with wings as eagles" (Godward), "they shall run and not be weary" (in the Lord's commands, and through the world), "and they shall walk and not faint" (as we live in the Spirit). (2) *By searching the Word.* Read Psalm 119 where in nearly every verse we have a reference to the Word of God, and notice its practical results. (3) *By faith.* How often we hear Christians say, "I cannot do this, and I do not realize that." Is it not because of unbelief? The Master is saying, "Believe ye that I am able to do this?" Faith responds, "Yes, Lord."

As we do the *trusting*, He will do the *keeping:* as we do the *yielding*, He will do the *filling*; as we do the *obeying*, He will do the *empowering*; as we do the *submitting*, He will give the *victories*; and this He will accomplish by the *indwelling*, *inflowing*, and *outflowing* of the Holy Spirit; for

> "Every virtue we possess,
> And every victory won,
> And every thought of holiness,
> Are His alone."

18

The Discipler's Winning

"He that winneth souls is wise" (Proverbs 11:30).

William Arnot says, on soul-winning, "To win an immortal soul from sin and wrath to hope and holiness—this is honorable and difficult work. It is a work for wise men, and we lack wisdom. On this point there is a special promise from God. Those who need wisdom, and desire to use it in this work, will get it for the asking. The wisdom needed is very different from the wisdom of men. It is very closely allied to the simplicity of a little child. Much of it lies in plainness and promptness. Those who try to win souls must not muffle up their meaning; both by their lips and their lives they must let it be seen that their aim is not to make the good better, but to save the lost." Thus, tersely, does Arnot put the whole subject, and yet we may look at it in detail, as the architect does, when he has not only the ground plan of the house but the detailed plans as well.

He who would win others to Christ must be won himself

The Revised Version reverses the order of the text and says, "He that is wise winneth souls." The Authorized Version may mean one of two things, namely, either the winning of souls demonstrates the wisdom of the winner or that he becomes wise by so doing; but the Revised Version makes it plain that it is the wise man alone who wins souls.

Who is the wise man? There are at least three things which demonstrate his wisdom. (1) The wise man is one who knows the Embodiment of all the Wisdom of God, namely, Christ Himself (1 Corinthians 1:24). To know Him is to trust Him (Psalm 9:10), to possess eternal life (John 17:3), and to be at peace (Job 22:21). (2) The wise man is one who is in touch with the Spirit of Wisdom (Acts 6:3, 10). As it is the wisdom of a moving army to keep their communications open with headquarters that supplies may not be cut off, so the believer in Christ knows that the secret of all prosperity in spiritual life and power in service is found by living in constant touch with the Holy Spirit by an obedient faith. (3) The wise man is one who is instructed by the Word of Wisdom. The

Scripture makes one "wise unto salvation" by assuring us we are delivered from condemnation, and it also makes us wise unto salvation in instructing us so as to avoid the deceitfulness of sin, the allurements of the world, and the craft of the evil one.

From what we have stated, it is essential that we be wise unto salvation. In other words, be won by Christ and to Him. It is a sorry thing that any who are not saved themselves should seek to save others. "First be trimmed thyself, and then adorn thy brother," say the Rabbins. And, as Gregory says, "The hand that would make others clean must not itself be dirty." The priests were fitted for their service before they entered upon it; and that preparation was a threefold application, namely, they were cleansed by water, consecrated by blood, and anointed with oil (Exodus 29:4-21). These applications must have their counterpart in our experience. Cleansing by water is typical of the application of Christ's atonement by the Holy Spirit to the believer whereby he is cleansed from condemnation and an accusing conscience (Hebrews 9:14; 10:10). Consecration by blood is typical of the cleansed one's separation to God for His fellowship and service, by the death of Christ (Hebrews 13:13, 20, 21; 2 Corinthians 5:15); and the anointing is typical of the power which is to rest upon the believer that he may be equipped for the service to which he is called (Luke 4:18; 1 John 2:27; 2 Corinthians 1:21).

Richard Baxter puts the whole case in his *Reformed Pastor*, when he says, "Many a tailor goes in rags who makes costly clothes for others; and many a cook scarce licks his fingers when he has dressed for others the most costly dishes. Believe me, God never saved any man for being a preacher, nor because he was an able preacher; but because he was a justified, sanctified man, and, consequently, faithful in his master's work. Take heed, therefore, to yourselves first, that you be that which you persuade others to be, and believe that which you daily persuade them daily to believe, and have heartily entertained that Christ, and that Spirit, which you offer to others. He that bade you love your neighbor as yourselves did imply that you should love yourselves, and not hate and destroy both yourselves and them."

He who would win others must win Christ

One of the seven "that I may's" in Paul's epistle to the Philippians is, "That I may win Christ" (Philippians 3:8). The word *win* signifies to acquire as gain as when the merchantman gains wealth by his trade, the scholar gains knowledge by his study, the athlete gains strength by his exercise, the miner gains gold by his labor, the fisherman gains fish by his fishing, the farmer gains the harvest by his toil, and the employee gains promotion by his attention to his employer's business. Thus the believer wins Christ by whole-hearted devotion to Him, by believing prayer in Him, and by prayerful study of Him through the Word.

From whatever aspect we look at the subject, we find it absolutely essential that we should first know the truth in our own experience before we pass it on to others. The disciples must receive the bread from the hand of Christ before they could give it to the multitude (John 6:11). The Water of Life must be springing up in our inner being as the well of the Spirit's abiding grace before it can flow out from us as rivers of blessing bringing refreshment to others (John

4:14; 7:37). We must cultivate the garden of the inner life before we endeavor to put the vineyards of other people in order, for should we fail to do this, we will have to make the sorry confession, "My own vineyard have I not kept" (Song of Solomon 1:5).

It is essential that we should exercise the priesthood which is holy before we exercise the priesthood which is royal for we are a holy priesthood to offer up spiritual sacrifices, and we are a royal priesthood to show forth His praises (1 Peter 2:5, 9). The strength to run in the way of the Lord's commandments is obtained by waiting upon God for "They that wait upon the Lord shall renew (change) their strength" (Isaiah 40:31). From this verse we gather that there is no running without first waiting upon God. The shining face of Moses, as seen by men, was the outcome of his private communion with God. The mantle of Elijah was obtained by Elisha's persistence in following his master. The commission of Isaiah was preceded by his cleansing. Paul found Christ's strength all-sufficient through his tarrying at the throne of grace. All this goes to prove that the inner life which is fed by winning Christ is required, in order to make the outer life effective in winning others.

The late Dr. A. A. Bonar summarizes the whole subject as follows: "If a man wins Christ, and gets at His unsearchable riches, there is no question but he will discover much about himself and sin. The prophet Isaiah, when he saw the King, the Lord of Hosts on the throne, in a moment felt self was withered into nothingness. And just as little doubt is there that a man who wins much of Christ's riches, will win souls. Who has not observed that when those who conduct meetings, and have been at the first greatly blessed, afterwards lose their power, it is almost without exception because they have not been winning Christ. They have been giving out what they once had, just the same thing over and over again, but making no advances, getting no fresh insight into Christ; and so their words have begun to fall without power. The audience, though they cannot define what the difference is, soon know that there is a difference. There never can be the same unction and power when a man is not winning Christ, bringing out fresh ore from the mine, and laying it down before the hearer. If, therefore, we would be more useful, there is no other way but by winning Christ. This is the shorthand method. Win Christ every day, and the Holy Spirit will bless what you tell of Him, for He delights to glorify Christ."

He who would win others must be consistent

The most potent influence which a godly wife can exert in winning her ungodly husband to Christ is, as the Holy Spirit says, a "chaste manner of life coupled with fear" (1 Peter 3:1, 2, R.V., margin). It is not what she *says* but what she *is* which tells, as the Word puts it, "They may without the word be won," or as Bengel renders it, "without word"; that is, without saying anything. Thus, the consistent life of the godly one is the means of the conversion of the ungodly one. There is no speech so powerful as the action which is after godliness, as someone has said, "Unspoken acting is more powerful than unperformed speaking." How careful we should be that our life is consistent for we can never tell the influence we exert nor the souls we may win through the Spirit's operation. And a soul converted, as Archbishop Leighton says, "Is gained to itself, gained to the pastor, or friend, or wife, or husband, who sought it, and gained to Jesus Christ; added to His treasury, who thought not His precious blood too dear to lay out for this gain."

Let us remember that consistency is essential and indispensable in soul-winning. To say well and do ill is to bring upon us the censure that was once passed upon an inconsistent minister who had an eloquent tongue but a lying life. It was said that when he was in the pulpit he ought never to come out again, and when he was out of it, he ought never to enter again. Bishop Reynolds had made some weighty and timely remarks upon the subject before us. He said, "The star that led the wise men to Christ, the pillar of fire which led the children of Israel unto Canaan, did not only shine, but went before them. The voice of Jacob will do little good, if the hands be the hands of Esau. In the law, no person who had any blemish was to offer the oblations of the Lord. The priest was to have in his robes, bells and pomegranates; the one a figure of sound doctrine and the other, of a fruitful life. The Lord will be sanctified in all them that draw near unto Him (Isaiah 52:11). The sins of the priests made the people abhor the offering of the Lord (1 Samuel 2:17); their wicked lives do shame their doctrine, as St. Austin says, 'With their doctrine they build, and with their lives destroy.'"

He who would win others must be used by Christ

Among the many "I will's" of promise which Christ gives to His disciples is "I will make you fishers of men." There are three things necessary for successful fishing: we must go where the fish are; we must fish with the right materials; and we must fish in the right manner.

1. *We must go where the fish are.* On two occasions when Christ brought a miraculous draught of fishes to His disciples' nets, He indicated where the fish were to be found. On the first occasion He said, "Launch out into the deep" (Luke 5:4), and on the next He said, "Cast the net on the right side of the ship" (John 21:6). We must be acting under the direction of Christ, and as we do so, He will lead us to where we will catch men for Him. In Acts 16, we find that Paul and Silas were "forbidden of the Holy Ghost to preach the word in Asia," and when they "assayed to go into Bithynia," He again stepped in and "suffered them not" (Acts 16:6, 7). On the other hand, when Paul saw in a vision a man of Macedonia beseeching him to help, he took it as an indication that the Lord wished him to go to Macedonia as he says, "Assuredly gathering that the Lord had called us for to preach the gospel unto them" (Acts 16:10). All this goes to show that we not only need to pray, "Lord, *what* wilt Thou have me to do," but we need to pray, "Lord, *where* wilt Thou have me to go?"

2. *We must fish with the right materials.* No one knows better than the skilled angler how essential it is for him to have the right hooks baited with suitable bait. The same thing holds good with reference to deep-sea fishing. The seine net will do for a shoal of fish near the land, but for deep-sea fishing there must be the drag net. If we would catch men for Christ we must see that we use the gospel net for it alone will catch men. The iron net of the law will only frighten. The silken net of ordinances will break, and the wide net of sociology will not

avail for its meshes are too large. The gospel net will catch and keep. We have abundant evidence of its effectiveness to catch people for Christ no matter what kind they are, or how great sinners they have been. In the sixteenth chapter of the Acts of the Apostles, we have an account of three conversions of cultured Lydia, the demonized damsel, and the cruel jailer. The same Lord of the gospel brought blessing to each although the action was different in dealing with them. The Lord opened the heart of Lydia to her conversion; the power of the name of Jesus brought deliverance to the possessed damsel; and the same Savior brought salvation to the jailer and his house.

3. *We must fish in the right manner*. There are many graces which the Christian worker needs that his manner may be winning. He should be compassionate in heart, earnest in purpose, zealous in work, patient in method, holy in life, Scriptural in testimony, single in aim, and pure in motive. But all these things have their rise in the person of Christ even as the waters of Ezekiel's temple shall have their rise from under the threshold of the house and by the altar (Ezekiel 47:1). Christ's compassion shall make us compassionate in heart even as the oil of the lampstand made it burn (Exodus 35:14). Christ's earnestness shall make us earnest in utterance even as the word of the Lord in Jeremiah made him speak (Jeremiah 1:7). Christ's zeal shall make us intense in our interest, even as the Spirit of the living creatures moved the wheels and made them go wherever He went (Ezekiel 1:19-21). Christ's patience shall make us endure in labor, even as Paul testified, "I labored more abundantly than they all: yet not I, but the grace of God which was with me" (1 Corinthians 15:10). Christ's holiness shall make us consecrated in life even as the glory of God sanctified the tabernacle at its consecration (Exodus 40:34). Christ's word shall make us faithful in testimony even as Moses who did all the work of the tabernacle according to the word of the Lord (Exodus 40). Christ's direction shall make us single in aim, even as the oxen took the straight way to Beth-shemesh when the ark was restored by the Philistines to Israel (1 Samuel 6:12). His love shall make us pure in motive, even as Jonathan's affection for David was without guile (1 Samuel 18:1; 20:31, 32).

He who would win others must have a message

We are not left in the dark as to what the message is; our Lord's word is clear and emphatic, "Go and preach the gospel" (Mark 16:15). There are many things to which the gospel may be compared. The following three fairly cover the ground. The gospel is a stethoscope to reveal the state of man; a telescope to manifest the love of God; and an electroscope to indicate God's power.

1. *The gospel is a stethoscope to reveal the state of man*. Many a doctor, in applying the instrument to the chest of his patient, has found the lungs unsound and the heart diseased. There are two incidents in the life of Christ which illustrate that the gospel, directly or indirectly proclaimed, brings home to the sinner his individual state before God. Christ's conversation with the woman of Samaria about Himself as the Water of Life in its cleansing, satisfying, and inspiring influence, not only convinced her of her need, but revealed to her, her past life in all its uncleanness, for when she got back to the village she said,

"Come, see a man who told me all things that ever I did: is not this the Christ?" (John 4:29).

The other case is that of the dying thief. Like his companion, he was also railing at Christ (Matthew 27:44); but afterwards a distinct change came over him. What caused that change? It must have been as he listened to Christ pray in accents of pained love, "Father, forgive them; for they know not what they do" (Luke 23:34). Christ's words were a gleam of heaven's light which penetrated into the dark dungeon of the mind of one of the thieves for we find him directly afterward crying, "Lord, remember me." And further, he gave proof of the change which had come over his inner being for, when his companion continued to rail at Christ, he said to him, "Dost thou not fear God, seeing thou art in the same condemnation? And we indeed justly; for we receive the due reward of our deeds: but this Man hath done nothing amiss" (Luke 23:40, 41). The gospel which Christ made known in His wondrous prayer of love was that which revealed the thief to himself in all his sinfulness.

2. *The gospel is a telescope to manifest the love of* God. "The Gospel of God" is one of the many titles which is given to the Gospel (1 Thessalonians 2:2, 8, 9). It has been happily said, "The thought you make of God is the thought that makes you." It is important for us to have a clear conception of the gospel's origin. If we say that Christ came to make God love us, we misrepresent both Him and God. The fact is, Christ came *because* God loved us. This is the gospel as taught by Christ for He Himself has said, "God so loved the world that he gave his only begotten Son." As one gazes upon the force and flow of the mighty Niagara Falls, one is led to ask, where is the mighty source from whence these waters come? The answer is, from the distant mountains.

> "Through the meadows, past the cities, still the brimming streams are rolled,
> Now in torrents, now expanding into silver lakes and gold,
> Wafting life and increase with them, wealth and beauty manifold.
>
> "Whence descends the ceaseless fulness, ever giving, never dry?
> Yonder, o'er the climbing forest, see the shining cause on high—
> Mountain-snows their watery treasures pouring everlastingly."

Similarly as we gaze upon the beautiful life, the satisfying atonement, and the mighty resurrection of Christ and know the blessings which flow from Him, we discover that He is not an isolated individual acting on the authority of His own personality, but that "God was in Christ reconciling the world to himself." As we take up the telescope of the gospel and look through it at the glorious arc of the Divine nature, there is not a single star of blessing but what is stamped with the name of God. The blood that atones is the blood of God (Acts 20:28); the grace that saves is the grace of God (Ephesians 2:8); the salvation which emancipates is the salvation of God (Acts 28:28); the love that satisfies is the love of God (1 John 3:1); the peace that calms is the peace of God (Philippians 4:7); the power which keeps is the power of God; and the heaven which fascinates is the glory of God (1 Peter 1:5).

3. *The gospel is the electroscope to indicate God's power*. As an electroscope is an instrument for observing the existence and power of free electricity, the

gospel declares and defines the power of God; the gospel is "the power of God unto salvation" (Romans 1:16). The character of that power is defined in many ways. Its operation may be summed up under the words "Displacement" and "Placement."

1) *Displacement*. The one peculiar and pertinent feature of Christianity is that it is pregnant with life. Wherever it goes it brings life, light, and liberty. The dead leaves of bad habits are thrown off by the living sap of the gospel as it courses through the one who has received Christ; the Ephesians, who believed in Christ immediately threw off the old sinful pursuits of witchcraft. They "showed their deeds . . . so mightily grew the Word of God and prevailed"; thus, the Holy Spirit describes the cause and effect of the gospel's working. When the morning light kisses the distant hills, and the sun bathes the valleys with its glow and beauty, then the darkness and the shadows flee away. The same is true of the gospel's displacing power for as its light of knowledge and warmth of love enter the human mind, the darkness of sin and the shadows of unbelief pass away. When the gospel came in power to the Thessalonians, they immediately turned to Him who is Light and Love, abandoned their idols, and henceforth walked in the ways of holy service, and were filled with a longing expectancy to see the Savior they loved (1 Thessalonians 1:5-10).

The nineteenth century abounds with evidences of the displacing power of the gospel as we think of its influence upon communities. The slavery of America, the cannibalism of the New Hebrides, the barbarism of Fiji, the cruelty of Madagascar, the beastliness of many places in Central Africa, the idolatry of the Sandwich Islands, and the degradation of the Falkland Islands have all been displaced by the gospel of Jesus Christ.

2). *Placement*. The gospel of God is not merely a *negative* power, removing the evil, but it is a *positive* power, placing us in a new sphere in which we find unlimited supplies for all things that pertain to life and godliness.

The epistle to the Ephesians is one of the richest mines of the New Testament, and there we find many precious jewels of blessing. We can only indicate what some of these blessings are by the following alphabetical list. Each one of these is found in connection with the Greek preposition "*en*."

Acceptance. "Accepted *in* the beloved" (Ephesians 1:6).
Blessing. "Blessed us with all spiritual blessings . . . *in* Christ" (1:3).
Chosen. "He hath chosen us *in* Him" (1:4).
Dwelling. "Christ may dwell *in* your hearts" (3:17).
Enduement. "Strong *in* the Lord" (6:10).
Filling. "Be filled *in* the Spirit" (5:18, R.V., margin).
Growth. "Groweth unto an holy temple *in* the Lord" (2:21).
Heritage. "*In* whom also we have obtained an inheritance" (1:11).
Instruction. "Taught *in* Him even as truth is *in* Jesus" (4:21, R.V.)
Joined. "*In* whom ye also are builded together" (2:22).
Kindness. "His grace *in* kindness toward us *in* Christ Jesus" (2:7, R.V.)
Light. "Light *in* the Lord" (5:8).
Might. "His mighty power which He wrought *in* Christ . . . and you" (1:19, 20; 2:1).

Nearness. "Made nigh *in* the blood of Christ" (2:13, R.V.)
Oneness. "To make *in* Himself of twain, one new man" (2:15).
Power. "The power that worketh *in* us" (3:20).
Quickened. "Quickened us together *in* Christ" (2:5, R.V., mar.)
Redemption. "*In* whom we have redemption" (1:7).
Sealing. "*In* whom . . . ye are sealed" (1: 13).
Translation. "Made us sit together *in* heavenly places *in* Christ Jesus" (2:6).
Unity. "*In* whom all the building fitly framed together" (2:21).

In the multiplicity of the above Scriptures, it is impossible to take more than one by way of illustrating the position in which the gospel places the believer, and that one "Light in the Lord." "There were two artists, close friends, one of whom excelled in landscape painting, and the other in depicting the human figure. The former had painted a picture in which wood, and rock, and sky, were combined in the artist's best manner. But the picture remained unsold—no one cared to buy it. It lacked something. The artist's friend came and said, 'Let me take your painting.' A few days later he brought it back. He had added a lovely human figure to the matchless landscape. Soon the picture was sold. It had lacked the interest of life." Thus, when Christ comes into the life, we are found in Him, and He in us; He lights us up by His presence. The light of His knowledge illuminates the understanding (2 Corinthians 4:6); the light of His love warms the heart (Psalm 27:1); the light of His joy gladdens the spirit (Esther 8:16); the light of His grace strengthens the soul (2 Samuel 23:4); the light of His Word guides the feet (Psalm 119:105); the light of His countenance encourages the life (Psalm 89:15); and the light of His presence satisfies the mind (Revelation 21:23).

19

The Discipler's Wisdom

Astronomers tell us that many of the stars, which seem to us to be single suns, are double when examined through a powerful telescope. For instance, the star known as Castor is a double one, although to the naked eye it appears to be a single star. Another feature about these stars is this: they are so intimately related to each other that the one influences the other. Something similar may be said with regard to the Discipler's Wisdom in winning souls. It is a double subject. There is the Divine side to it, and there is the human side; there are certain conditions which the believer has to fulfil; and there are certain promises which God has pledged Himself to keep as the believer keeps to those conditions. Let us look at the subject before us from these two standpoints.

The Human Standpoint

There are five things to which we call attention, and these are: self-abnegation, singleness of aim, simplicity of utterance, stalwartness of faith, and steadfastness in labor.

1. *Self-abnegation.* A lad who was fishing on the banks of a stream and who was very successful in his operations was asked by a gentleman what rules he observed. The boy's reply was, "I observe three rules: I keep myself out of sight; and second, I keep myself further out of sight and third, I keep myself further out of sight still." These rules are absolutely essential in the Divine art of fishing for human souls. Unless self and all selfish interests are kept out of the work of the Lord, it will be marred and tarnished.

A Chinese fable tells of a potter who had received an order from the emperor to make for him a porcelain set of vases. He tried again and again but he failed to make anything to his satisfaction. At last in utter despair he flung himself into his furnace that this self-sacrifice might give to the vases the luster he desired. The fable says his end was achieved, for there came out of the furnace such wares of marvelous beauty that they excited the admiration of all. The moral of the fable is plainly seen. When there is self-abandonment, self-effacement, and self-abnegation, then there is the luster of praise which brings glory to God.

In what the enemies of Christ said to Him when He was on the cross a great principle is illustrated. They said, "He saved others, Himself He cannot save." The fact is, He was able to save others *because* He did not save Himself. This is a truth which runs through the whole of the Word of God. "He that loseth his life shall find it." If we seek to conserve our life, however, we consume it. The only way we can be of use in the Lord's service is as we are dead to self. If we engage in Christian work because others are occupied by it (or because we are asked to do it, or take it up merely as a hobby) then it resolves itself into self-effort alone and will be an absolute failure in that deeper and God-glorifying sense. But if the work is for Christ, and Christ is in the work, it will be a success, for labor in the Lord can never be in vain (1 Corinthians 15:58).

When Ignatius was placed in the amphitheatre waiting for the lions who were to kill him, he said, "I am grain of God, I must be ground beneath the lions' teeth to make bread for His people." It was a noble example: he was willing to be sacrificed to encourage God's people. We are not called to lay down our lives in this way but the principle is the same, for the Word of the Lord is: "Hereby know we love, because he laid down his life for us: and we ought to lay down our lives for the brethren" (1 John 3:16, R.V.) This self-abnegation is no light matter. It will cost many a heart pang, for self is like our shadow. It follows us wherever we go, and it is only Christ who can cope with it.

Someone has said "the number of the beast is not 666, but number one." We can only overcome self as we remember we are crucified with Christ and as we reckon we are identified with Him. We may illustrate this by the transposition of the letters of the words "Himself" and "Christ." If we take away *H-i-m* from *Himself*, we have nothing left but *self*; but when we put *Him* before *self*, then *self* is swallowed up in *Him*. Or, to put the same thing another way, if we take the fourth letter in the name *Christ*, we have nothing but *I*, which is suggestive of proud "I," as may be seen in the case of Nebuchadnezzar when he said, "Is not this great Babylon which *I* built." Or the letter I speaks of self-will as is illustrated in the words of Naaman when he said, "*I* thought the prophet would have done some great thing," but when *C-h-r* is put in front of the letter *I*, and *s-t* behind it, then *I* is lost in *Christ*. Let us look away to Christ when self would intrude itself, then all shall be well; for as we lose sight of our shadow in looking to the light, so we shall be able to deny self itself, as we look away to Him.

2. *Singleness of aim*. The late Dr. A. A. Bonar once sat down to analyze modern zeal in Christian work, and the result of his analysis was as follows:

Personal ambition	23 parts
Love of praise	19 parts
Pride of denomination	15 parts
Pride of talent	14 parts
Pride of authority	12 parts
Bigotry	10 parts
Love of God	4 parts
Love of man	3 parts
	100 parts

According to this calculation, 93 parts of modern zeal are carnal, and only seven spiritual. How different from Christ who could say, "I do always the things that please my Father." What the aim of the worker should be, was clearly stated by the apostle Paul when he said, "We make it our aim . . . to be well-pleasing unto him" (2 Corinthians 5:9, R.V.) The son of Confucius once said to his father, "I apply myself to every kind of study with diligence and neglect nothing that could render me clever and ingenious; but still I do not advance." "Omit some of your pursuits," replied Confucius, "and you will get on better. Among those who travel constantly on foot, have you ever observed any who run? It is essential to do everything in order, and only grasp that which is within the reach of your aim; for otherwise you give yourself useless trouble. Those who, like yourself, desire to do everything in one day, do nothing to the end of their lives, while others who steadily adhere to one pursuit find that they have accomplished their purpose." "This one thing I do," says the apostle. Yes, and he who has one thing to do, and does it, will, as Confucius said to his son, do more than he who attempts many. Thus, the Christian worker who remembers he has one thing to do in all his life and labor, namely, to please his Lord, will accomplish more than those who endeavor to please themselves, or please men, for those who seek to please others or themselves, only tease themselves to their own hurt, and blight and blur all they touch.

3. *Simplicity of utterance*. One of the many things which impressed the hearers of the late C. H. Spurgeon was the simplicity of his language. If he referred to a donkey, he would not speak of it, as "that quadruped which has elongated appendages"; nor would he call any two names given to any two things, "an illustration of the *binomial theorem*"; nor would he, in speaking of the number of quarters necessary to make up ten dollars, say, "It was a demonstration of the theory known as *differential calculus*." It may sound well enough to call a spade "an agricultural implement," but it would be meaningless to a simple countryman. If a spade was spoken of as "a shovel," he would know what was meant at once. We need to be simple in telling out the gospel message so that the most ignorant may understand.

In His ministry the Lord Jesus used the simplest possible language, and brought surrounding objects to illustrate and enforce truth. By doing so, He was able to bring to the people the claims and teaching of the truth of God. He is our Example in this as in everything else.

It is related of Sir Astley Cooper on a visit to Paris that a certain surgeon asked him how often he had performed a certain type of surgery. He replied he had performed the operation thirteen times.

"Ah, but, Monsieur, I have done it one hundred and sixty times."

"How many times did you save the life?" continued the curious Frenchman, after he had looked in blank amazement into the Englishman's face.

"I," said Sir Astley Cooper, "saved eleven out of the thirteen. How many did you save out of the one hundred and sixty?"

"Ah, Monsieur, I lose dem all, but the operation was very brilliant."

The same may be said of some Christian workers. Their speech is eloquent, their elocution perfect, and their rhetoric magnificent, but the spiritual results are *nil*, for the simple reason, that while the preacher is admired, the truth is ignored, because it is smothered by flowery language. Let us in our speech be like the apostle Paul who said, "And I, brethren, when I came to you, came not with excellency of speech or of wisdom, declaring unto you the testimony of God. For I determined not to know anything among you, save Jesus Christ, and him crucified. And I was with you in weakness, and in fear, and in much trembling. And my speech and my preaching *was* not with enticing words of man's wisdom, but in demonstration of the Spirit and of power: That your faith should not stand in the wisdom of men, but in the power of God" (1 Corinthians 2:1-5).

4. *Stalwartness of faith*. As the roots of the oak take hold of the earth in which it is growing, so faith takes hold of the promises and abides in them; thus the believer is strong and steady amid the storms and stress of life. This is what the Old Testament saints did. We read of them: "These all died in faith, not having received the promises, but having seen them afar off, and were persuaded of them, and *embraced* them, and confessed that they were strangers and pilgrims on the earth" (Hebrews 11:13). They took the promises to themselves, and made them their own. Faith always does this, for the ground of all faith's action is, "Thus saith the Lord." When we have God's "Go forward" we may be sure that every Red Sea of difficulty will roll back before us.

"When Mr. Webster, at the laying of the Bunker's Hill shaft, besought the crowd to 'stand back,' lest the concourse of people should break the speaker's platform down, at the peril of life and limb, the answer was, 'It is impossible!' 'Impossible!' thundered the American Demosthenes, 'nothing is impossible at Bunker's Hill.' And when we remember who gave us our marching orders, and who left us the pledge of His perpetual presence—when we stand beside that cross on which He bore our sins, we dare not talk of impossibilities. In the lexicon of the Christian life, there is not, and there should not be, such a word as fail. Nothing is impossible at Calvary."

The one thing that shall make our faith strong, and give backbone and spring to it, is simple and whole- hearted faith in the Word of God. When we have the authority of God's Word, then we can speak with authority. The inwrought conviction of the truth of God's Word will tell in our testimony in working upon others. The lamp of truth must be shining in the dwelling of our own being before it can shine upon others to their illumination. The reason why the gospel came in power to the Thessalonians was that it had first come home in power to Paul himself.

When believers look at things from God's standpoint and keep in touch with Him by doing so, then faith is stalwart; but when they fail to do this then faith is feeble and weak-kneed. Things which are small and insignificant when faith is strong look large and important. Was this not so in the case of the children of Israel? They looked at the sons of Anak and the walled cities of Canaan, and the consequence was they thought of themselves as "grasshoppers," and shut themselves out of the land by their unbelief; whereas if they had looked at things from God's standpoint, they would have seen that the sons of Anak were but "grasshoppers" (Numbers 13:33 Isaiah 40:22), and they would have entered the land.

5. *Steadfastness in labor.* Some Christian workers have an up and down experience in the Lord's work; they are like the gas which comes through a meter which needs water. They bob up and down. We should be like a dry meter, which does not require the application of any local agent between it and its source of supply. The secret of steadfastness in every department of the life of faith is given to us in Isaiah, where we read of Christ saying in prophecy, "He wakeneth mine ear to hear as they that are taught." Then directly afterwards He says, "The Lord God will help me; therefore have I not been confounded: therefore have I set My face like a flint" (Isaiah 50:5, 7, R.V.) The fulfillment of this prophecy occurs in Luke 9:51, where we read, "He steadfastly set his face to go to Jerusalem." He knew what awaited Him there. Gethsemane with its agony, Gabbatha with its shame, and Golgotha with its awful death, were before Him; but for all this, He kept steadfastly on His way. A like spirit should characterize us. As Ruth was steadfastly minded to go with Naomi (Ruth 1:18), so we should be steadfastly minded to follow in the steps of Christ in following His example of persistency in work.

The Divine Standpoint

What we have dwelt upon relates to *our* attitude toward God. Now we come to *His* attitude toward us. This latter presupposes receptivity and response on our part. As the leaves of the apple tree are in spirals of five, so there are five thoughts to this branch of our topic, namely, the interpenetration of the Holy Spirit, the instrument of the Spirit, the intercession of the Spirit, the illumination of the Spirit, and the inspiration of the Spirit.

1. *The interpenetration of the Spirit.* The Lord wants the Spirit to penetrate every part of our nature. As the light is diffused by the atmosphere, so it should be with the Spirit and us. He should penetrate every part of our nature. When Gideon asked for a sign from God, he prayed that the fleece might be saturated with dew while all around was dry. This illustrates what the condition and the position of the child of God should be. The world is dry and barren all around, but we should be filled with the dew of the Spirit, that our Divine Gideon may press out from us the grace and love of the Spirit to the refreshment and blessing of others (Judges 6:33-40).

Christ refers to this in His promise to the believer, "Out of you shall flow rivers of living water" (John 7:37). Chrysostom says upon this, "Rivers, not river, to show the copious and overflowing power of grace; and living water, *i.e.*, always moving; for when the grace of the Spirit has entered into, and settled in the mind, it flows freer than any fountain, and neither fails, nor empties, nor stagnates." The well of water must be springing up in our inner life, before there can be the flowing out in effective testimony.

When the electricity of the Spirit charges every part of our spiritual nature, then His power will touch others as they come in contact with us. Bishop Webb tersely puts the whole subject when he says, "The Holy Spirit not only dwells in the Church as His habitation, but also uses her as the living organism whereby He moves and walks forth in the world, and speaks to the world, and acts upon the world. He is the Soul of the Church, which is Christ's body." This implies that the measure of our influence upon the world is gauged by the influence we allow the Spirit to exercise upon us.

2. *The instrument of the Spirit*. The believer in Christ is the instrument which the Spirit of God uses in His service. All God's servants are sons, and as such, the Lord says to each, "Son, go work today in My vineyard"; but as sons, they are not to act apart from the Lord, not even as agents, for the true position of every child is that of an instrument to be used by the Lord. The Great Worker is the Holy Spirit. This is strikingly brought out in the Acts of the Apostles, or, to be more correct, "The Acts of the Holy Spirit through the Apostles." The disciples spoke, "As the Spirit gave them utterance" (Acts 2:4). When the people wonder at the peculiar phenomena on the Day of Pentecost, Peter at once repudiates any personal power but attributes the working to the Spirit, saying, "This is that which was spoken by the prophet Joel; and it shall come to pass in the last days, saith God, I will pour out of my Spirit" (Acts 2:16, 17). Disputants were not able to resist the burning words of Stephen, for this simple reason: the wisdom and power in which he spoke were by "the Spirit" (Acts 6:10).

The Spirit was the One who directed Philip to go and speak to the eunuch, and the same Power caught Philip away when his work was done (Acts 8:29, 39). The Spirit was the Speaker who told Peter there were three men waiting for him and that he was to go with them to Cesarea; and who also told the Church at Antioch to separate Paul and Barnabas for the work of the ministry (Acts 10:19; 11:12; 13:2). The Spirit was the Power which proclaimed through Agabus, and Esaias, events which were to happen in the future (Acts 11:28; 28:25). The same Spirit gave Stephen spiritual vision to see Christ at the right hand of God and enabled Paul to detect imposture, and also prevented him from preaching in Asia and Bithynia.

The Holy Spirit directed Paul to preach the gospel in Macedonia and foretold that the apostle would suffer at Jerusalem, and the same Spirit was the Appointer of the Elders at Ephesus (Acts 7:55; 13:9; 16:6, 7, 10; 21:4, 11; 20:28). The one thought running through the whole of these passages is that the Holy Spirit is the Operator. We are not to call in God to help us to carry out our plans, but we are to be instruments in His hands for Him to execute His plan through us.

3. *The Intercession of the Spirit*. "The Spirit maketh intercession" (Romans 8:26) is the Divine utterance as to the secret of effectual prayer, for the Spirit-begotten prayer is always the answered prayer. We pray *to* the Father as the Granter of our petition; we pray *through* the Son as the Medium of our approach, and we pray *by* the Spirit as the Power which inspires. Praying in the Spirit is our responsibility, for that means the fulfillment of the conditions to answered prayer; but the Holy Spirit praying in us is the inspiration in prayer. Sometimes we cannot voice our petitions. We are burdened with the weight of our inward necessity. The deepest prayers are often those which "cannot be uttered." The sightless eyeballs of the blind beggar and the muteness of the dumb are the most pathetic appeal.

One of the impressive features of the ministry of the Lord Jesus was His meeting the need of people when there was no direct appeal made to Him. The disciples toiling in rowing (Mark 6:48), the hungry multitude in their need (John 6:5), the bowed woman in her infirmity (Luke 13:12), the widow in her sorrow (Luke 7:13), Peter's wife's mother in the fever (Matthew 8:14), the woman in her sin (Luke 7:44), Zaccheus in his curiosity (Luke 19:1, etc.), and Mary Magdalene in her grief (John 20:11) are a few of the many instances where Christ blessed people without any direct request being made to Him.

Andrew Murray says: "In the life of faith and prayer, there are operations of the Spirit in which the Word of God is made clear to our understanding, and our faith knows how to express what it needs and asks. But there are also operations of the Spirit deeper down than thoughts or feelings, where He works desires and yearnings in our spirit in the secret springs of life and being which only God can discover and understand." There are experiences which cannot be voiced in prayer; but it is then the Spirit, in a special way, appeals to heaven in our voiceless need. The Christian worker, burdened with a sense of responsibility, or his passing through some Gethsemane of suffering, or the spirit stirred at the inroads of sin, or the inward desire to please the Lord, all are the outcomes of the Spirit's working within. All this leads us to see that it is not those who say most, who necessarily pray most, but they pray best who learn to keep "silent" before the Lord (Psalm 62:1, R.V.), who "muse" with the psalmist (Psalm 143:5), who "wait" with the disciples (Acts 1:4) and who "tarry" as the Lord directs (Luke 24:49).

4. *The illumination of the Spirit*. "Eye hath not seen, nor ear heard, neither have entered into the heart of man, the things which God hath prepared for them that love him. But God hath revealed them unto us by His Spirit" (1 Corinthians 2:9, 10). The quick eye of man's keen observation, the attentive ear of man's care to the voice of tradition, and the intellectual grasp of man's intuitive inspirations are not capable of mastering the things of the Spirit. The eyes of the heart must be opened by the Holy Spirit before the things of God can be seen. Worldly wisdom was, and is, aptly summed up in the dying words of Professor Clifford; he said, "My researches have revealed to me a soulless universe looked down upon by a godless heaven." Such men need to learn the lesson of Mrs. Prosser's simple parable: "See how much they think of me!" said a lantern to some dips that were hanging on a nail close by. "The master says he doesn't know what he should do without me these dark nights." "No doubt," said the candles; "but he'd sing a different song if it weren't for one of us inside of you. Did it ever occur to you, friend, that you wouldn't be of the least use to anybody if our light didn't shine through you?" The lantern of our being, however great its intellectuality, would be of no use without the Spirit's inner shining.

The following seven things which the Spirit does will give some little apprehension of the enlightening character of His ministry. The Holy Spirit is the Spirit of Truth to unveil to us the personal glory of the Lord Jesus and to show us things to come (John 16:13, 14); He is the Spirit of Life to communicate to us the wonderful grace and glory of the Gospel (2 Corinthians 3:6-18); He is the Spirit of Wisdom to enable us to apprehend the three "What's" of the Lord's possessions in us and His power for us (Ephesians 1:17, 18); He is the Spirit of Prophecy to give us to understand the trend of the times and what we may expect in these last days, for upon these things He speaks "expressly" (1 Timothy 4:1); He is the Spirit of Bestowment to qualify believers to exercise the gifts which are given (1 Corinthians 12:3-7); He is the Spirit of Revelation to disclose to us the glory which awaits the Church and the doom reserved for the "ungodly" (Revelation 1:10; 4:2; 17:3; 21:10); and He is the Spirit of Searching to instruct in the deep things of God (1 Corinthians 2:10).

5. *The inspiration of the Spirit.* The word "inspiration" only occurs twice in the so-called "authorized version" of the Bible—once in the Old Testament, and once in the New. The passage in the New Testament refers to the inspiration of the Scriptures (2 Timothy 3:16); and the verse in the Old Testament is found in relation to the speech of Elihu where he speaks of the "spirit in man" and the "inspiration of the Almighty giveth them understanding" (Job 32:8). The meaning of the word "inspiration" is to in-breathe. The word, as applied to the Scriptures, gives to them a significance which makes them to be different from all other writings. As one has well said, "I am satisfied only with the style of Scripture. My own style, and the style of all other men, cannot satisfy me. If I read only three or four verses, I am sure of their divinity on account of their inimitableness. *It is the style of the heavenly court.*" As the inspiration of the Bible makes it different from any other book, so the inspiration of the Spirit makes the servant of God a different man from any other. Adolphe Monod aptly sums up the whole case when he says, "All in Christ; by the Holy Spirit; for the glory of God. All else is nothing." "All is nothing." Yes, all our efforts are nothing, all our organizations are nothing, and all our plans are nothing; only as they are the outcome and working of the Holy Spirit. In his translation of 1 Corinthians 2:13, Darby renders the latter part of the verse which speaks of "comparing spiritual things with spiritual," as follows:

"Communicating spiritual things by a spiritual medium." What is that spiritual medium? It is the Spirit of God. He alone is competent to communicate the things of God to us, and through us to others.

This inspiration of the Spirit is what the insight given to Elisha's young man was (2 Kings 6:17); it enables us to see things we should not otherwise comprehend. The inspiration of the Spirit empowers us to do what we cannot accomplish without it, as Gideon experienced when "clothed" with the Spirit (Judges 6:34, margin). The inspiration of the Spirit will form the character in godliness, so that its influence will be felt by others, as may be seen in the testimony of Pharaoh to the consistency of Joseph (Genesis 41:38). The inspiration of the Spirit will cause us to exercise such care and bestow upon us such wisdom that we shall fulfil the will of God in His Word, as Bezaleel did in making the tabernacle according to God's plan (Exodus 31:3). The inspiration of the Spirit will energize us so that we will have strength to overcome our enemies, even as the Spirit of the Lord empowered Samson to defeat those who came against him (Judges 14:6, 9; 15:14). The inspiration of the Spirit will embolden us to faithfully deliver the message of God without fear or favor, as it did Azariah when he went to "meet Asa" (2 Chronicles 15:1-8); and the inspiration of the Spirit will fill our hearts with an overflowing gladness and make us to praise the Lord with acceptance (Ephesians 5:18, 19).

There is undoubted truth in the statement which is sometimes made, namely, "It is unscriptural to pray for the Holy Spirit and to Him." Yet there is one hymn which seems to voice the need, promise, and work of the Holy Spirit which might be voiced by all for the simple reason that it takes in the whole of our need as sinners, saints, and servants. I refer to the hymn of Joseph Hart, written over a hundred years ago. He prayed then, and may we not pray?

"Come, Holy Spirit, come,
Let Thy bright beams arise:
Dispel the darkness from our minds,
And open all our eyes.

"Convince us of our sin,
Then lead to Jesus' blood,
And to our wondering view reveal
The secret love of God.

"Show us that loving Man
That rules the courts of bliss,
The Lord of Hosts, the mighty God,
The eternal Prince of Peace.

"'Tis Thine to cleanse the heart,
To sanctify the soul,
To pour fresh life in every part,
And new-create the whole.

"Dwell, therefore, in our hearts,
Our minds from bondage free;
Then we shall know, and praise, and love,
The Father, Son, and Thee."

20

The Discipler's Privilege

The greatest privilege which a child of God possesses, is the God-given right of prayer. The new life has its origin in prayer, its growth is dependent upon it, and the believer's last petition is, "Receive my spirit." Every lack in the life may be traced to the want of prayer, while, on the other hand, he who waits upon God shall not want any good.

Prayer is the sin-killer. When Josiah began to pray to the Lord, then he put away the abominations which had defiled and damaged the nation (2 Kings 23:3-8). *Prayer is the strength-obtainer*. Paul found this out when the Lord assured him, in answer to his thrice-repeated cry, that His grace was sufficient to enable him to glory in his infirmity (2 Corinthians 12:8, 9). *Prayer is the help-giver*. Peter experienced its power, when the Church prayed, and brought the angel of deliverance to him while he was in prison (Acts 12:5). We, too, may find help, by coming to the throne of grace (Hebrews 4:16).

Prayer is the holiness-promoter. Paul recognized this when he referred to the fervent prayers of Epaphras that the saints might stand perfect and complete in all the will of God (Colossians 4:12). *Prayer is the soil in which the plant of holiness ever grows*. *Prayer is the power-conductor*. The power of the Holy Spirit came upon the early disciples, while they "continued with one accord in prayer and supplication" (Acts 1:14). When the wood of our earnest plea is placed on the altar of consecration, then the fire of the Holy Spirit ignites it in an effectual blaze to the warmth of others. *Prayer is the love-inspirer*. The "great grace" that was upon the early church which showed itself in the mutual love the saints had for each other was the outcome of the earnest pleading which had gone before (Acts 4:33). *Prayer is the supply-receiver*. There is an abundance in the larder of God's grace for the supply of all and for the need of each. The only requisite is to bring the key of believing prayer to unlock this larder of love; then the riches of His provision will meet our every requirement, as Nehemiah found when he made his "prayer unto God" (Nehemiah 4:9).

We will consider two things in thinking of the believer's privilege in prayer, namely, the power of prayer and the prayer of power.

The Power of Prayer

The best commentary on the Bible is the Bible itself. This is strikingly illustrated in the subject of prayer. In answer to Abraham's prayer, God permitted Ishmael to live before Him (Genesis 17:18). Prayer stayed the hand of God for a time from inflicting judgment upon the cities of the plain (Genesis 19). Prayer was the magnet which drew Eliezer and Rebekah together (Genesis 24:12). Prayer was the transforming power that changed the name of Abram to Abraham, and of Jacob to Israel (Genesis 17:3-5; 32:28).

Prayer was the messenger which brought the Lord to the help of Israel in Egypt, delivering them from the tyranny of Pharaoh (Exodus 2:23). Prayer was the hand that grasped the arm of justice as it was raining the plagues upon Egypt (Exodus 9:28). Prayer was the magic wand that caused a way to be opened through the Red Sea when the enemies of Israel were pursuing them (Exodus 14:10, 15). Prayer was the angel of mercy that brought the antidote to heal the bitter waters of Marah and to make them sweet (Exodus 15:25). Prayer brought from heaven the manna which sustained the thousands of Israel for forty years in the wilderness (Exodus 16:3, 4; Joshua 5:12; Nehemiah 9:20, 21).

Prayer was the conduit which brought the water to thirsty Israel and satisfied their need (Exodus 17:4). Prayer was the secret of Israel's victory over Amalek (Exodus 17:11). Prayer was the advocate which caused God's anger to abate, when Israel sinned in making the golden calf (Exodus 32:11). Prayer was the glass which caused Moses to see the glory of God (Exodus 33:13-23).

Prayer was the evangelist that brought healing mercy to the poisoned Israelites (Numbers 21:7, 8). Prayer was the detective which discovered Achan in his sin (Joshua 7:7). Prayer was the hand which stayed the sun and moon while Joshua gained the victory over the Amorites (Joshua 10:12, 13).

Prayer was the inspiration that nerved Gideon to hew down the groves of Baal and to gain the decided victory over Midian (Judges 6, 7). Prayer was the mantle of power that gave Samson his lost strength (Judges 16:28).

Prayer was the means of Samuel's birth as his name implies, "Asked of God" (1 Samuel 1:11, 20, margin). Prayer winged the stone that killed Goliath (1 Samuel 17:45, 49). Prayer was the oil which caused the life of David to run in the lines of truth, as seen in his inner life in the Psalms.

Prayer was the obtainer of the wisdom which graced Solomon (1 Kings 3:5-14). Prayer was the healing power that restored Jeroboam's withered hand (1 Kings 13:6). Prayer was the restorer of life in the hand of Elijah, when he raised the widow's son from the dead (1 Kings 17:20, 22).

Prayer was the instrument which stopped the supply of rain for three years and a half, in the days of Ahab (James 5:17). Prayer was the censer which brought the consuming fire to the sacrifice on Carmel's mount (1 Kings 18:36). Prayer increased the cloud, no bigger than a man's hand, to one which covered the heavens, and its waters satisfied the thirsty land (1 Kings 18:42). Prayer was the conductor of life to the Shunammite's son (2 Kings 4:33). Prayer was the eye-salve which caused the young man to see the Lord's army, protecting Elisha and himself (2 Kings 6:17). Prayer was the dust which blinded the eyes of Elisha's enemies when they were sent to capture the prophet (2 Kings 6:18).

Prayer was the savior of Jehoahaz, bringing deliverance from the king of Syria (2 Kings 13:4). Prayer was the angel that smote Sennacherib, giving Hezekiah signal victory (2 Kings 19; Isaiah 37). Prayer was the physician who added fifteen years to the life of Hezekiah and caused the shadow to go back ten degrees (2 Kings 20:3, 11).

Prayer was the power that opened the floodgates of prosperity to Jabez (1 Chronicles 4:10). Prayer was the dynamite which scattered the forces of the Ethiopian (2 Chronicles 14:11, 12). Prayer was the connecting band which gave Jehoshaphat the power of God to overthrow the combined forces of Ammon and Moab (2 Chronicles 20). Prayer was the key that unlocked the prison-house of Manasseh and gave him deliverance from Babylon (2 Chronicles 33:11-13). Prayer was the stimulant which nerved Nehemiah to proceed with the building of the wall of Jerusalem in the face of determined opposition (Nehemiah 4:9).

Prayer was the muzzle on the lions' mouths when Daniel was in the den; it was also his keeper and deliverer (Daniel 6). Prayer was the key which delivered Jonah from his three days' and nights' imprisonment (Jonah 2:1, 10).

Prayer was the expression of faith which procured cleansing to the leper from the Divine cleanser (Matthew 8:2-4). Prayer showed the reality of Blind Bartimaeus' faith when sight was given (Mark 10:47). Prayer revealed the strong faith of the Syrophoenician woman in the power of Christ to expel the demon from her daughter (Matthew 15:22). Prayer was the balm that soothed the bereaved sisters at Bethany (John 11:32). Prayer was the harbor where Christ in His weariness found rest (Matthew 14:23). Prayer brought joy to the heartbroken father when he saw his son freed from Satan's power (Matthew 17:15).

Prayer was the power which brought the hand of the Lord to save sinking Peter (Matthew 14:31). Prayer was the carriage which brought Christ to the ruler's house to raise his daughter (Matthew 9:18, 19). Prayer brought the earthquake which caused the prison at Philippi to shake to its foundations (Acts 16:26). Prayer was the heavenly messenger which brought Peter out of prison (Acts 12:12). Prayer was the opener of the door at Pentecost when the Holy Spirit was poured out (Acts 1:14); and prayer was the means of emboldening the disciples so that they fearlessly witnessed of Christ (Acts 4:31).

These are some instances of the power of prayer, or of what God did in answer to prayer, as recorded in His Word. Those who have been men of power in the service of God have always been men of prayer, as Mary Queen of Scots confessed: "I fear John Knox's prayers more than an army of ten thousand men."

The Prayer of Power

Would we have the prayer of power? Then we must recognize the following conditions:

1. *The name of Jesus is the plea in the prayer of power*. "Whatever you ask in my name, I will do it, that the Father may be glorified in the Son; if you ask [me] anything in my name, that will I do" (John 14:13, 14 RSV). To use a person's name generally means that we are authorized to do so and that there is some advantage to be gained. "Mention my name," says a friend in writing to another, when he wants to get a certain article for a given purpose. The signature on the

check means that he who signs it is ready to pay the amount stated. Petitions must not be in our name for we have no account in the bank of heaven. But Christ has, and His name holds good for the amount. Look at the pyramid of blessing in Ephesians 3:20:

"*Ask*."
"*All* that we ask."
"All that we ask or *think*."
"*Above* all that we ask or think."
"*Abundantly* above all that we ask or think."
"*Exceeding* abundantly above all that we ask or think."
"*Able to do* exceeding abundantly above all that we ask or think."

2. *An uncondemning heart marks the state of soul in the prayer of power*. By this we shall know that we are of the truth, and reassure our hearts before him whenever our hearts condemn us; for God is greater than our hearts, and He knows everything. "Beloved, if our hearts do not condemn us, we have confidence before God; and we receive from him whatever we ask, because we keep his commandments and do what pleases him" (1 John 3:19-22 RSV). If there is anything between our souls and God, any enmity or root of bitterness, any malice or uncharitableness—we have no confidence in prayer, for these sins will obscure our vision and will be like spectres. They will haunt us when we draw near to the throne of grace. It was vain for Joshua to pour out his complaint regarding the defeat at Ai, while Achan lay unexposed, but as soon as the sin was judged God was ready to work with His people. Our hearts must be right with God before He can regard our petitions and reward our pleas.

3. *The prayer of faith is the repose of the soul in the God of power*. "Without faith it is impossible to please him. For whoever would draw near to God must believe that he exists, and that he rewards those who seek him" (Hebrews 11:6 RSV). We do not attach any merit to prayer, as some seem to do when they say, "Pray for me," as if there were special merit in the person whose prayers are asked. But we do need the *prayer of faith*. Very often we pray and do not expect an answer. We are like the gathered disciples praying for the release of Peter, who were much astonished when he, in person, sought admission to their company. Like many today, too often we ask and ask and expect no answer; and when the Lord graciously answers, we are taken by surprise. We need to learn from the psalmist, who says, "Morning by morning, O Lord, you hear my voice and wait in expectation" (Psalm 5:3 NIV); as much as to say, "I shall be on the lookout for the answer, and wait until it arrives."

4. *The Holy spirit is the effectual cause of the prayer of power*. "Likewise the Spirit helps us in our weakness; for we do not know how to pray as we ought, but the Spirit himself intercedes for us with sighs too deep for words. And he who searches the hearts of man knows what is the mind of the Spirit, because the Spirit intercedes for the saints according to the will of God" (Romans 8:26, 27, RSV). "Praying in the Holy Ghost" (Jude 20).

The following quotation from Andrew Murray's *Spirit of Christ* is a fitting summary of the chapter on "The Spirit of Prayer," where these Scriptures are dealt with:

"Now we can understand how the Lord, in the last night, could give us those wonderful prayer-promises, with their oft-repeated '*What ye will.*' He meant us to have the Holy Spirit praying in us, guiding our desires and strengthening our faith. He expected us to give our whole being to the indwelling of the Spirit, that He might have free scope to pray in us, according to God. Let us take up the holy calling, and give ourselves to the Holy Spirit to pray in us. 'We know not how to pray as we ought': how often this has been a burden and a sorrow! Let it henceforth be a comfort. Because we do not know, we may stand aside, and give place to One who does know. We may believe that in our stammerings, or even sighs, the mighty Intercessor is pleading. Let us not be afraid to believe that within our ignorance and feebleness the Holy Spirit is hidden, doing His work. 'As we ought.' The great *ought* of prayer is faith. The Spirit is the Spirit of faith, deeper than thought. Let us be of good courage, our faith is in the keeping of the Spirit. Here, as elsewhere, all leads up to one point: the Holy Spirit's indwelling must be our one care. In faith that holds the promise, in tender watchfulness that waits for and follows His leading, in the entire surrender of the flesh to the death, that He alone may rule and lead, let us yield ourselves to our beloved Lord to fill us with His Spirit: the Spirit will do His work."

5. *Abiding in Christ is the secret of the prayer of power*. "If you abide in me, and my words abide in you, ask whatever you will, and it shall be done for you" (John 15:7 RSV). What does it mean to "abide in Christ"?

There are at least seven evidences given to us which prove our abiding in Christ.

First: *Abiding in Christ brings freedom from the power of sin and from the love of it*. "No one who abides in him sins; no one who sins has either seen him or known him" (1 John 3:6 RSV). To be kept from consciously sinning is true Christian experience as Dr. Saphir says: "Why is it that, when we possess a Savior whose love and power are infinite, we are so often filled with fear and despondency? We are wearied and faint in our minds, because we do not look steadfastly unto Jesus, the Author and Finisher of faith, who is set down at the right hand of God—unto Him whose Omnipotence embraces both heaven and earth, who is strong and mighty in His feeble saints.

"While we remember our weakness, we forget His all-sufficient power. While we acknowledge that apart from Christ we can do nothing, we do not rise to the height or depth of Christian humility, 'I can do all things through Christ which strengtheneth me.' While we trust in the power of the death of Jesus to cancel the guilt of sin, we do not exercise a reliant and appropriating faith in the Omnipotence of the living Savior, to deliver us from the bondage and power of sin in our daily life. We forget that Christ worketh in us mightily, and that, one with Him, we possess strength sufficient to overcome every temptation. We are apt either to forget our nothingness, and imagine that in our daily path we can live without sin, that the duties and trials of our everyday life can be performed and borne in our own strength; or we do not avail ourselves of the Omnipotence of Jesus, who is able to subdue all things to Himself, and to keep us from the daily infirmities and falls, which we are apt to imagine an inevitable necessity. If we really depended in all things, and at all times, on Christ, we should in all things, and at all times, gain the victory, through Him whose power is infinite, and who is appointed by the Father to be the Captain of our salvation. Then all our deeds would be wrought, not merely before, but in God. We should then do all things to the glory of the Father, in the all-powerful name of Jesus, who is our Sanctification. Remember that unto Him all power is given in heaven and on earth and live by the constant exercise of faith in His power. Let us most fully believe that we have and are nothing, that with man it is impossible, that in ourselves we have no life which can bring forth fruit; but that Christ is all, that abiding in Him, and His Word dwelling in us, we can bring forth fruit to the glory of the Father."

Second: *Abiding in Christ means the keeping of the Lord's commands*. "All who keep his commandments abide in him, and he in them" (1 John 3:24 RSV). There is one word which sums up the Christian life and that word is obedience. When the heart throbs with love to Christ, it shows itself in ready response to His directions. "Obedience is the key to every door," the solution to every difficulty, the killer of every doubt, the lifter to every good, the obtainer of every blessing, the measure of all power, and the proof positive that we are abiding in the Lord.

Third: *Abiding in Christ shows itself in fruit borne*. "He that abideth in me, and I in him, the same bringeth forth much fruit" (John 15:5). Bringing forth fruit to God is far more than working for Him. Many who are busy about the Lord's work are not bearing fruit to His glory. Fruit-bearing has to do with the personal character. We are told in Galatians 5:22, 23, what the "fruit of the Spirit" is. The "love, joy, and peace" are the God-ward features of the fruit-bearing. Love to Him, joy in Him, and peace with Him. "Long-suffering, gentleness, and goodness" are the things which should characterize the child of God in his dealings with others: enduring under trial, gentle under provocation, and helping those who are in need. "Faith, meekness, and temperance" are what the believer is to have in his personal life: personal confidence in the Lord, personal likeness to the Lord, and personal control through the Lord. These are the fruits the Lord loves to come and gather in His garden (Song of Solomon 4:16) and which demonstrate we are in living union with Himself.

Fourth: *Abiding in Christ manifests itself in love*. "God is love and he who abides in love abides in God, and God abides in him" (1 John 4:16 RSV). "He who loves his brother abides in the light" (1 John 2:10 RSV). "If we love one another . . . By this we know that we abide in him" (1 John 4:12, 13 RSV). God plainly tells us that we can only show our love to Him by the sympathy we have for each other. Carlyle was not far off when he defined love as "a discerning of the Infinite in the finite, of the Ideal made real." Love is like the sun. It paints the flowers of earth with the glories of heaven and they in turn throw off their fragrance on all around. The language of love is one that needs no interpreter. It reveals itself in its actions.

Fifth: *Abiding in Christ means walking as Christ walked*. "He that saith he abideth in him ought himself also to walk, even as he walked" (1 John 2:6). He walked submissive to truth, dependent on the Spirit, humble in heart, prayerful in life, loving God's will, doing His work, and living for the glory of His Father. Following Him, we will in some measure be like Him even as the child seeks to imitate the parent it loves.

Sixth: *Abiding in Christ, we will continue in His Word.* "If you continue in my word, you are truly my disciples" (John 8:31 RSV). Ruskin says, "He only is advancing in life whose heart is growing softer, whose blood is warmer, whose brain is quicker, whose spirit is entering into living peace." Advancement is the very soul of continuance. If we are not moving forward, we are going back. A Christian is like one on a bicycle—if he does not go on he will fall down. How can we continue in Christ's Word? By believing it fully, by obeying it unhesitatingly, and by loving it supremely.

Seventh: *Abiding in Christ we shall be faithful to God's truth.* "If what you heard from the beginning abides in you; then you will abide in the Son and in the Father" (1 John 2:24 RSV). "Any one who goes ahead and does not abide in the doctrine of Christ does not have God; he who abides in the doctrine has both the Father and the Son" (2 John 9 RSV). The above Scriptures have one thought in them, namely, remaining in the truth of God. The truth is the mold in which the character is formed and the magnet by which people are attracted from the haunts of sin to the heart of God. If anyone goes ahead past the truth he will place himself beyond the influence of truth, and thus lose the formative power which makes one like Christ; and he will cease also to ply the instrument which the Holy Spirit uses to bring men to the Savior.

6. *The prayer of power follows the rules of the Word of* God. "This is the confidence we have in him, that if we ask anything according to his will he hears us. And if we know that he hears us, in whatever we ask, we know that we have obtained the requests made of him" (1 John 5:14, 15 RSV). Christ did not merely say, "If ye abide in me . . . ye shall ask what ye will"; He also said, "and my words abide in you" (John 15:7). It is by the Word of God that we know the will of God. Watson has well said, "The tree of promise will not drop its fruit unless shaken by the hand of prayer." This is true: only let us take care that we shake the tree of promise and not the tree of our own fancies. Prayer according to the Word is, as Charnock remarks, "Nothing else but a presenting God with His own promises, desiring Him to work that in us and for us which He has promised to us." If the promises of God are dwelling in us, we will have enough to pray about, and we will pray aright, for the prayer will be according to the words of Jesus, and thus shall it be in us as a bubbling spring, manifesting itself in earnest supplication.

7. *The glory of God is the only aim in the prayer of power.* "You ask and do not receive because you ask wrongly, to spend it on your passions" (James 4:3 RSV). Many prayers are for selfish ends. We look on our own plans and want them blessed. We have an eye to our interests and ask God to bless us. But will God answer our prayers for this end? I believe not. The one thought in Christ's promising to answer prayer is, "That the Father may be glorified in the Son" (John 14:13). Let us not ask wrongly, that is, crave our own petitions for our desire's sake, but for the Lord's glory alone. Then we shall find that what is for the Lord's glory must be for our good.

As we thus pray the prayer of power, we will prove the power of prayer. Then we can say with the poet Alfred Lord Tennyson:

"More things are wrought by prayer
Than this world dreams of. Wherefore, let thy voice
Rise like a fountain for me night and day.
For what are men better than sheep or goats,
That nourish blind life within the brain;
If, knowing God, they lift not hands of prayer
Both for themselves and those who call them friend?
For so the whole round world is every way
Bound by gold chains about the feet of God."

21

The Discipler's Isolation

The Lord commanded the prophet Ezekiel, "Go shut thyself within thine house" (Ezekiel 3:24). The prophet was prohibited from speaking any further to the rebellious house of Israel. He was to seclude himself. This command may be taken as applying to the Christian life as indicative of the Lord's desire that His children should spend much time alone with Him. He is continually saying to us, "Let me see thy countenance, let me hear thy voice; for sweet is thy voice, and thy countenance is comely" (Song of Solomon 2:14).

We have not only the desire of the Lord in His expressed command that we should dwell in the secret place of His presence, but there are unnumbered blessings which come to us in so doing. In this chapter we will focus the line of our thought upon some of the

SHUT DOORS OF SCRIPTURE

as illustrating and bringing out some of these blessings.

The Shut Door Is the Place of Safety

When Lot was in danger of being brutalized by the Sodomites, the angels pulled him into the house and shut to the door (Genesis 19:10). Being in the house he was safe from the unholy hands of the men of Sodom. The discipler is also in danger amid the dust and din of life, lest the world should pull him down into the dirt of worldliness and thus soil the garments of his spiritual life. Lot would never have been in the position of danger if he had kept in the place of separation, but he had allowed himself to drift with the tide of worldliness. As a consequence, he found himself in the place of defilement from which he had to be rescued by the angels. Something similar happens in the lives of God's children at times. Through willfulness or compromise with some truth, or hesitation at some specific command, they find themselves in places of peril from which they have to be rescued by the Lord's gracious intervention.

Please take special note of this: it was not till Lot was behind the shut door that he was safe. The men of Sodom would have attacked him if he had been outside. The lesson for us is this: when we find ourselves in danger of contamination from worldly association, through carelessness, the only place of safety and restoration is to shut ourselves in with the Lord, confess the wrong, and abide with the Lord in secret prayer. Unless we keep in communion with Him we will find the world will entrap us. I well remember a Christian worker telling me that in his endeavor to rescue one from a life of shame, he was placed in a very awkward and trying position. His safety in not yielding to temptation was found in dropping on his knees and praying aloud. His action in so doing proclaimed the fact that he was in touch with the Lord. He was living behind the closed door of the Lord's presence; hence, he was preserved from evil.

The Shut Door Is the Place of Searching

In the thirteenth and fourteenth chapters of Leviticus there are certain directions given as to people who showed signs of leprosy. In an unmistakable case of leprosy these directions did not apply, but where there was mere suspicion of leprosy they did, whether it was an individual (Leviticus 13:1-46), a garment (13:47-59), or where there seemed to be indications of leprosy in a house (14:33-57). Let us take the case of the individual: he was to be shut up for seven days. For instance, if the spot on the man was no deeper than the skin, and the hairs had not turned white, he had to be shut up for seven days to see if there was any development. On the seventh day the priest was to examine the man, and if he found the "plague was at a stay," then the man had to be shut up seven days more, and on the fourteenth day if the priest found "the plague spread not in the skin," then the priest pronounced him clean, for the spot was only "a scab" (Leviticus 13:1-6).

The one thing to which reference is made, is this: all the while the man was shut up it was a time of testing. We can quite understand what heart-searchings and fears he would have. We may take this as illustrative of what the believer will find in the secrecy of the Lord's presence. We need not fear this searching process, for it will mean growth in grace.

When the Lord touches our self-will and makes us conscious of our weakness, it is but to make Israels of us, having power with Himself. When the Lord makes us conscious of our sins of omission and leads us to cry out with Isaiah, "I have been dumb, therefore I am a man of unclean lips," it is that we may be better fitted for future service. When the Lord allows some bodily affliction to assail us and we cry out for the removal of the thorn, we find, as we wait upon Him, that He Himself has "given" us the thorn. Through it He wants us to prove in our experience the reality of His all-sufficient grace and to know the joy which comes in having fellowship with Him in the Gethsemane of suffering.

When the Lord comes with the pruning knife and cuts away the superfluous growths which have come through our association with the gospel, it is that we may know that the Christian life in its very blessedness exposes us to peculiar temptations. He seeks only to remove from us the hindrances to our fruitfulness when He uses the rod of chastisement. He desires us not to go away from Him, nor to be discouraged by His dealings, but rather to remember that the reason for His action is found in His heart of love; for in every blow He gives, He has some lesson to teach, some gift to bestow.

When He turns the searchlight of His holiness upon us and reveals us to ourselves, it is that we may see our defects and remedy them by allowing Him to adjust us. When He tells us the truth about ourselves, He always bids us buy the gold of His blessing; and when He rebukes our self-confidence, as He did in Peter's case, it is but to make us confident in Himself. All these things are happily learned in the secret of His presence. Unless we get there, despondency, murmuring, and complaining will fill our hearts to our detriment and grief.

Alone with the Lord, Jacob found out His crookedness and the patience of God's grace. Alone with the Lord, Daniel discovered his ugliness, and the ravishing beauty of God's glory. Alone with the Lord, Job was made conscious of his vileness and the almightiness of God's power. Alone with the Lord, Moses realized his unfitness for God's service and the secret of His plans. Alone with the Lord, Isaiah had revealed to him his uncleanness and the sufficiency of God's atonement.

Alone with the Lord, Peter owned His self-confidence and learned the blessedness of God's love. Alone with the Lord, John saw the evil of man and the grandness of God's purposes.

George Müller, in unfolding the secrets of a life of sanctity and service, said: "There came a day when *I* died utterly. First, to George Müller; and second, to my fellow men." So saying, he bowed himself down almost to the ground, expressing by his attitude what he sought also to express by word. He added: "Not till I became totally indifferent to what George Müller thought, desired, and preferred; to George Müller's opinions, tastes, purposes; and also to the blame and praise, the censure or applause of my fellow men; and determined henceforth I would seek no approbation but that of God, did I ever start on a life of happiness and holiness; but from that day until now, I have been content to *live alone with God.*"

The Shut Door Is the Place of Supply

The widow came with her complaint to Elisha and told him that her sons were likely to be made slaves because she could not meet the creditor's claim. One of the first things he asked her was, "What do you have in your house?" At once she responded, "Your servant has nothing there at all, except a little oil." She had something, but it was not sufficient to meet her own need, leaving out the obligation of her liability. How like many of God's people. They have the oil of God's grace within them, but even that has not been sufficient to satisfy them, for they have such a scanty supply. They are like the saints at Corinth, they "are sanctified in Christ," for that is a matter of God's grace, but they are babes in the spiritual life when they ought to be men; and as such they are occupied with minor things, and neglect the major ones.

Yes, the widow with the pot of oil, but unable to meet her liabilities, is a picture of many believers today. They have the oil of God's grace and the presence of the indwelling Spirit, but they do not meet the obligations resting upon them, nor have they sufficient to satisfy their own need. It is not until they have learned to wait upon God in secret that they will have satisfaction in their hearts, or give what the world's need is asking for.

These were the directions of the prophet to the widow: she was to get all the empty vessels she could, and then shut herself in her house with her sons and pour out from the pot of oil she had. What did the woman do? She "shut the door" and did as Elisha told her (2 Kings 4:2-6 NIV). As a consequence, she not only had sufficient to meet her own liabilities, but she and her sons had a source of supply for the time to come. She met her liability *without*, by the supply she got *within*. In this she illustrates the main principle of the Christian life, the measure of our giving out is circumscribed by the quantity we take in.

Oil was used for many purposes in the East, but without going into the manners and customs there, we may note one reference to oil in Scripture, namely, "oil for the light." The "oil for the light" in the Tabernacle was to feed the seven-branched golden lampstand, that it might give light in the holy place (Exodus 35:14). This may be taken as typical of the Spirit's indwelling presence in the believer, as his Source of supply to enable him to shine for the Lord. Christian character must be formed and fed from the supply of the Spirit's grace and power. The command of the Lord is, "Let your light shine before men, that they may see your good deeds, and praise your Father in heaven" (Matthew 5:16 NIV). If we are to shine before men in public, we must wait upon God in private.

"The connection is lost," remarked one friend to another as they were riding in an electric car in the North of England. The car had suddenly stopped and the lights went out. As soon as the car was disconnected from the source of supply, there was no light and no power. The same thing is true in the lives of God's people. As long as they are in secret communion with the Lord, they have the power to shine before men, but let anything interrupt the communion with Him and they are as helpless as shorn Samson in the lap of Delilah. They are as useless as Jonah when he fled from the Lord, and as helpless as the unbelieving disciples when they could not cast out the demon from the stricken child.

One thing should be apparent to every prayerful and careful reader of the New Testament. It is what we might call the *inness* of the spiritual things which feed and fashion the spiritual life. Notice just a few. The *sphere* of the believer's walk is "in the light" (1 John 1:7) of God's holy presence and truth, for as there are three properties in the rays of sunlight, namely, illumination, healing, and warmth, so as we walk in the light we are warmed by God's love into obedience, healed by His gracious word to our improvement, and enlightened by His truth to our knowledge.

The *soil* in which the believer grows is "*in* grace" (2 Peter 3:18). Grace is to the child of God what the soil is to the plant; it nourishes and strengthens it. As the plant keeps in the soil, lays hold of it, and draws in its nutriment, the soil imparts its properties to it so it is with us as we lay hold of the grace of God. It infuses its nature into us, till men have to say of us, as was said of Stephen, we are "full of grace" (Acts 6:8 RSV).

The *secret* of the believer's safety is to be "kept *in* the power of God" (1 Peter 1:5). The Greek preposition "*en*" should be translated "*in*," and not "*by*." The power of God is not a power which keeps us as a prisoner is kept in a cell, but rather as the earth, which is kept habitable because of the atmosphere which surrounds it. The power of God keeps us insofar as we keep ourselves in it.

The *source* of the believer's fruitfulness is found as he abides in the Divine Vine (John 15:4). This abiding is finely expressed as "all who keep his commandments" (1 John 3:24 RSV). Obedience to the Lord is abiding in Him, and as we do so, the sap of the Divine life courses through our spiritual being, and manifests itself in the fruit of the Spirit.

The *spring* of the believer's action is known as he keeps himself "*in* the love of God" (Jude 21). What a difference may be seen in two persons as they walk along the street. The lethargic person moves with languid step, which proclaims a torpid liver or a shortage of energy. The other person, by his alertness of manner and elasticity of step shows his healthfulness and energy. Thus is it with the Christian life. When the love of God moves the heart, the walk of faith and the labor of love are prominent in their activity.

The *sanctifier* of the believer's heart and life is the truth of God, for as one moves in it, he will answer Christ's prayer that he may be sanctified "*in* the truth" (John 17:17 RSV). The tropical plant languishes and dies in a cold atmosphere. But if it remains in its native surroundings, it will flourish and bloom. Similarly is it the case with the child of God being born again by the truth of God; he makes progress in grace insofar as he keeps in the truth.

The *supply* of the believer's need is ever met as he is "praying *in* the Holy Ghost" (Jude 20). This last is the secret of all the rest, for the only way to know the inness of the former things is as we abide in the attitude of prayer. Praying in the Holy Spirit will keep us in the secret of the Lord's presence, press us into the soil of His grace, preserve us in the Lord's keeping, keep us in the flow of the Divine life, cause us to move with holy energy, encircle us with God's truth, and enable us to rejoice in the supplies of heaven's blessing.

The Shut Door Is the Place of Intercession

The story of the Shunammite woman and her son is most touching in its details. Without going into the minutiae of the story, we concentrate our thought upon the woman as she kneels before Elisha, sharing her grief in the death of her God-given son. In response to the woman's pleading, Elisha tells his servant to go and put His staff upon the dead boy; but the woman is not satisfied with the servant's mission, she wants the master's presence. The prophet grants the woman's request, but when he arrives at the house he will not allow anyone in the room with him. He must be alone with God and the dead body. Alone with God he prays and stretches himself upon the dead body. He pleads and he prays till the body is warm, and the child sneezes seven times. Then his task is done and he is satisfied (2 Kings 4:28-37).

Personal consecration is essential if we are to prevail in intercession for others. At first the prophet sends Gehazi to place the staff upon the dead child, but there is no result as the servant confesses, "The child is not awakened." Gehazi is a type of those who, while they are acquainted with the exterior of the things of God, know nothing of their inward power and reality. They can handle the prophet's staff, but they do not possess the prophet's power.

Further, the prophet's staff is useless in itself. It is only when the power of God courses through the man of God, and from him, to and through the staff, that it becomes an instrument of blessing. The isolated staff, lying on the dead child, is an illustration of the utter insufficiency of religious organization and church machinery, apart from the power of God. The staff of dead formalism will never quicken those who are dead in trespasses and sins.

Elisha, the man of God, is the one who is qualified to pray and prevail in bringing life to the dead. He is an illustration of those who are wholly consecrated to the Lord. Elisha's previous experience (and the meaning of his name) may be taken to illustrate the prerequisites to consecrated intercession. The meaning of the name Elisha is, "The salvation of God." Elisha had left all to follow Elijah (1 Kings 19:20, 21). In 2 Kings 2 we have a detailed account of Elisha's tenacity and devotion to Elijah. He would not leave Elijah, however much he might seem to discourage him. Elisha went with him from Gilgal to Bethel, from Bethel to Jericho, from Jericho to Jordan, and from Jordan till he received the double portion of his spirit.

All this may be taken as typical of the experience of every consecrated worker. First, we must know the spiritual significance of Elisha's name in being partakers of God's salvation, in being saved by His grace through faith in the atoning Savior (Ephesians 2:6). Second, we must leave all to follow our Divine Elijah in the paths of sanctification and service (Romans 12:1). Third, we must separate ourselves from the Egypt of the world, through the Gilgal of Christ's death (Joshua 5:9; Galatians 6:14). Fourth, we come to the Bethel of communion with the Lord (Genesis 28:12-19; 1 Corinthians 1:9). Fifth, we understand that the Jericho of the world is under the curse of God, hence we can have no fellowship with its evil aims (Joshua 6:26; 1 John 2:15-17), but keep ourselves from the "accursed" place (Joshua 6:17, 18; 2 Corinthians 6:17). Sixth, then we apprehend that the old self-life is dead in the death of Christ and that we are identified with Christ in resurrection power, even as the twelve stones which were placed in Jordan. The twelve stones which were taken out of the Jordan represented Israel's death to the old life in Egypt and their new life in Canaan (Joshua 4:1-9; Romans 6:3-5). Seventh, after we have passed through the Jordan of Christ's death, then we receive the baptism of power for service. Like Christ, we must go through the Jordan of death before we can receive the enduement of the Spirit's enabling (Luke 4:1, 18). Such are the workers who are qualified to plead for those who are dead in sins, and *they* shall not plead in vain.

Personal identification with those who are dead in sins follows intercession. "He went up and lay upon the child" (2 Kings 4:34). There is a legend in the Greek Church about her two favored saints, St. Cassianus, the type of monastic asceticism and individual character; and St. Nicholas, the type of genial, active, unselfish, laborious Christianity. St. Cassianus entered heaven and Christ said to him, "What hast thou seen on earth, Cassianus?"

"I saw a peasant floundering with his wagon in a marsh."

"Did'st thou help him?"

"No."

"Why not?"

"I was coming before Thee, and I was afraid of soiling my white robes."

Then St. Nicholas entered heaven, all covered with mud and mire. "Why so stained and soiled, Nicholas?" said the Lord.

"I saw a peasant floundering in the marsh," said St. Nicholas, "and I put my shoulder to the wheel and helped him out."

"Blessed art thou," answered the Lord; "thou did'st well; thou did'st better than Cassianus." And He blessed Nicholas fourfold.

The legend teaches us this one thing, that the Lord views with special approval those who go out of their way to help their fellows. The way to help our fellows is to identify ourselves with them in order to help them.

There are many illustrations given in the Word of God of this personal identification in helping others. When Peter bade the lame man, "In the name of Jesus Christ rise up and walk," he did more than utter those words. "He took Him by the right hand and lifted him up" (Acts 3:6, 7).

When Ananias greeted Saul of Tarsus, he not only said to him, "Brother Saul," but he put "his hands on him" (Acts 9:17); and when Christ healed the leper, He put forth His hand and touched him.

There must be the placing ourselves alongside of of the needy if we would reach and win them to Christ. The stand-off-ish-ness of patronage, and the put-on-ed-ness of pride will never interest, impress, and lead to the Savior. But where there is the look of sympathy, the warm touch of help, and the ready aid of love, then there is sure to be the quickening into life of those who are dead in trespasses and sins.

One of the most striking illustrations of the power of this identification was seen in the life of the late F. W. Crossley of Manchester. In his biography, the writer seemingly addresses one who had been helped by him, in the following words: "You, sister H., do you remember the power that drink had over you, and how you came into the Star Hall one day after your husband, and had enough sense to know that you were too drunk to sit with him, and went into a corner and sat down where you thought no one could see you? You are well saved today, and a follower of the Lamb; but do you remember how Brother Crossley came down from the platform that day, and came to you and said: 'Sister H., Jesus loves you,' and took you by the hand. And someone said, 'Eh! no; if He does, He is the only One who does.' Which wasn't quite true, considering that there was someone helping the Lord in the business? And do you remember how he kept your hand, and went on saying, 'Sister H., Jesus does love you,' until someone went home with the thought in her heart that led her to salvation in spite of the devil and the drink? And as we are telling of love being stronger than the drink, and stronger than all sin, you won't be likely to forget that when you were sick, Brother Crossley visited you himself and brought you the jugs of soup in his own hands; and when your eyes were bad, he went home and fetched a lotion for you and washed your eyes with it himself. You are like the rest of us in having learned a lot of what you know about the love of God by what you saw in Brother Crossley."

The Shut Door Is the Place of Manifestation

When the disciples were gathered together in the upper room, on the morn of the resurrection, they not only closed the doors but they made them fast. Rotherham emphasizes this fact in rendering the words relating to their action, "The doors having been made fast." The locked doors were to keep the Jews out, but they could not keep Jesus out, for He came and stood in their midst, greeting them with peace, gladdening them with joy, and quickening them by the in-breathing of the Holy Spirit.

This manifestation of Christ to His disciples illustrates what comes to those who patiently wait upon the Lord in prayer and meditation. Christ manifests Himself in at least four characters, namely, as the Peace-Giver, as the Joy-Inspirer, as the Service-Sender, and as the Power-Bestower.

1) *Christ manifests Himself as the Peace-Giver*. His greeting, "Peace be unto you," is more than an eastern salutation; it is the bestowment of the living Christ, the calm which comes into the spirit from being personally reconciled to God through His death. The peace which comes to the believer is like the summer breeze warmed by the setting sun, after everything has been stirred and drenched by the thunderstorm.

Christ not only said to them "Peace" once, but He said to them again, "Peace be unto you" (John 20:19, 21). When Christ uses the word "Again," it is either in the way of emphasis, as when He reminded the Jews that He had already said He was going away (John 8:14, 21); or the word is used in speaking of something in addition, as when He says, "I will come again" (John 14:3). In this latter sense Christ uses this salutation. He has an additional and deeper blessing to bestow. He not only gives the peace of conscience, which He procured by the death of His cross; but He gives peace of heart in the storms of life when we allow Him to live and rule in our hearts. Christ's peace, like the garments of the virtuous woman (Proverbs 31:21, marg.), is double.

There are many of the Lord's people who have "peace *with* God" (Romans 5:1), but do not enjoy "the peace *of* God" (Philippians 4:7). The former is bestowed by God's grace through faith in the Christ; but the latter is conditional on prayerfulness in everything, anxiety about nothing, and thankfulness for anything. Many things tend to disturb us. The *ague of fear* would make us shake with fearfulness as did the disciples when tossed on the storm-troubled lake. They cried out: "We perish." The *terror of doubt* would frighten us out of our faith, as when Peter, dismayed at the wind and waves, exclaimed, "Lord, save me." The *fret of anxiety* would prey upon our minds, and fill us with forebodings, as it did Hezekiah when he thought he was sick unto death, so that he said, "He will cut me off with a pining sickness."

The *nightmare of our sinful past* would disturb us with its spectral presence as the spirit which appeared to Eliphaz and made his hair to stand on end. The *worm of discouragement* would gnaw into the success of our service and make us free from our work for God, as it did in the case of Elijah when he ran away from his post and laid himself under a juniper tree, praying for death. The *root of bitterness* would embitter us with its foul growth and fill us with its rankling presence as it did the disciples who quarreled among themselves, as to which should be the greatest; and the foul presence of some besetting sin would color our life as worldliness did the life of Demas.

The cure for all disturbing and peace-killing events is to live in the calm and holy presence of Christ. "The Earl of Dundonald fought with his solitary ship a line of formidable forts in South America, whose fire proved so raking that his men could not stand to their guns. Calling to his wife, he asked her to fire one of the guns and show these men how to do their duty. She did so. Instantly they returned, burning with shame, to their posts, and soon the victory was theirs. The lady, in rehearsing the circumstances, said the thing which was felt by her to be most terrible was not the din of battle, not the raking fire, but the awful calmness that sat fixed on her husband's countenance as it seemed to carry in itself the sure presage of victory." In a far grander, deeper, and more realistic sense, we look into the calm, true, sweet, holy, gentle, firm, and loving face of our Lord Jesus Christ. Through abiding in unbroken communion with Him we catch His spirit and His peace fills our hearts.

2) *Christ manifests Himself as the Joy-Inspirer*. "Then were the disciples glad when they saw the Lord" (John 20:20). The Greek word *kairo* is variously rendered. The following places where the word occurs will indicate some feeders of the believer's joy. We are *"glad"* in the Father's gladness in being welcomed to His heart and home (Luke 15:32). We *"rejoice"* that our names are written in heaven (Luke 10:20). We are going on our way *"rejoicing,"* having found the Lord as our Sin-Bearer (Acts 8:39). We *"rejoice"* when we are called to be "partakers of Christ's sufferings" (1 Peter 4:13; Matthew 5:13; Acts 5:41). We are *"rejoiced"* when we see others walking in the truth (2 John 4); and when the gospel blesses the lives of others we are *"glad"* (Acts 11:23). But that which makes our gladness joyful comes, when like the disciples, we behold the glorious person of our adorable Savior.

The action of Christ in showing His hands and side to His disciples convinced them that it was He Himself in their midst. It produced joy in their hearts in consequence. Johnson once said to Boswell, "You have only two subjects—yourself and myself—and I am sick of them both." Something similar the believer says of himself, the more he knows of the sinfulness of his own heart and the loathsomeness of iniquity. But this is not so with Christ. The more we know of Him, the better we trust Him, and the better we trust Him, the more ardent will be our love to Him.

The riven side of Christ reveals a heart of love which has poured out its life's blood to benefit us; a heart of sympathy which beats in tender feeling for us; a heart of regard which aches for our sufferings; a heart of mercy which feels compassion for us, while it makes no excuse for our weaknesses; a heart of grace which ever thinks how best to help us; and a heart of care which is ever planning to serve us.

The hands of Christ are studded with the jewels of blessing. They are so because they have been pierced by the cruel nails of the cross. The ordinary observer would not see anything peculiar in the hands of Christ, but the believer says:

"His hands were rough, and His hands were hard,
For He wrought in wood, in Nazareth town;
With naught of worship, with no regard.
In the village street He went up and down.

"His hands were rough, but in them was light,
As they lay on the eyes of him born blind;
Or struck sick folk in their healing might,
And ministered joy to the hearts that pined.

"His hands were hard, but they spiked them fast
To the splintering wood of the cursed tree;
He hung in sight of the world, at last,
In His shame. And the blood trickled so free."

Yes, and because "the blood" has "trickled free" from those hands, they are strong to save, as Peter found (Matthew 14:31); potent to heal, as the leper experienced (Matthew 8:3); almighty to create, as the Psalmist states (Psalms 95:5 102:25; 119:73); sufficient to supply, as David testifies (Psalm 104:28); tender to bless, as the children knew (Mark 10:16); strong to uplift, as the bowed woman felt (Luke 13:13); and mighty to keep, as the Lord Jesus assures (John 10:28). The hands of the Lord do all these things, and a great deal more, and *all*—let it be repeated—*all* because those hands were once gory with His blood of atonement. There is only one letter more in the word glory than gory, and that letter is the initial letter for love, the letter *L*. So that we may say, the *gory* cross is the Christian's *glory*, for it tells out in unmistakable language the provision *Love* has made for us in the propitiation of Christ.

"Look at the wounds of Christ," said Staupitz to Luther. Looking at those wounds, we find a *mirror* to show us the evil of sin, a *microscope* to reveal the purpose of God, a *magnet* to attract to consecrated service, a *motor* to move us in loving consideration for others, a *motive* to cause us to please God, a *means* of grace to enable us to endure suffering, a *might* to strengthen us in our conflict with evil, and *music* which will make our whole being glad in the Lord's presence.

3) *Christ manifests Himself as the Service-Sender*. In thinking of Christ's sending forth His disciples the main thing to note in thinking of Christ's sending forth His disciples, is, the correspondingness of it as brought out in the "*as*" and "*so*." "As my Father hath sent me, even *so* send I you." He says, in so many words, "What I have been, while I have been with you, you are to be when I am absent. As I have manifested My Father's character in fulfilling His will, you are to henceforth manifest My character to the world." This is a great privilege and a grave responsibility. Christ did His Father's service in blessing mankind; we follow His will in doing the same.

As we bring the sensitive plate of prayerful inquiry to the scene of Christ's life, what are the special traits which the sun of God's truth photographs upon it? *The might of His service* was the Holy Spirit. He ever filled the censer of His ministry with fire from the altar of God's power. *The manner of His service* is well expressed in the frequent references to His compassion. The love of God was the secret force which caused Him to act in pity, mercy, and grace. *The music of His service* is aptly expressed in His Gethsemane prayer, "Not my will, but thine be done." *The harmony of His life* is found in that key-note. There were no false notes of self-will and self-seeking in His life. *The message of His service* was to tell men of the Father's heart of love, the Father's hearth of grace, and the Father's home in glory. They said of His speaking, "Never man spake like this man"; may we not further say, "Never man had a message like this Man"?

The majesty of His service is unfolded in the great aim of His life, which was to bring glory to His Father. The gem of His perfect life only flashed out with greater contrast as the unholy light of the world's glitter played upon it. Thus we see that Christ is the Model for our action in service. All this is implied in the authoritative utterance of His commission. As He was sent forth by the Father, and represented Him, so He sends us forth to represent Him. But to fully and faithfully do this, we must be much alone with Him, for how can we freshly manifest Him to others if we are not continually receiving manifestations from Him?

4) *Christ manifests Himself as the Power-Bestower.* "He breathed on them, and saith unto them, Receive ye the Holy Ghost" (John 20:22). The actions of Christ, as well as His words, are profoundly significant and suggestive. When He groaned in spirit at the grave of Lazarus, it showed the intensity of His feelings. When He lifted up His eyes to heaven, before He voiced that memorable prayer for His disciples, as recorded in John 17, He showed His unswerving confidence in His Father. When He broke the bread at the institution of the Lord's supper, it was typical of the breaking of His body in death on the cross. When He gave the disciples the bread at the feeding of the 5,000, it was symbolic of His greater gift of Himself to benefit humanity.

When He looked at Peter after his denial of Him, it was a searching reminder of what Christ had already told him he would do. When Christ touched the polluted leper, His act expressed His gracious sympathy; and now, when He breathes upon His disciples, it proclaims the absolute power He possesses.

The question arises, how are we to understand the words which refer to the Holy Spirit? Was its bestowment equivalent to the gift of the Holy Spirit on the Day of Pentecost, or does it refer to some gift of power bestowed to qualify for service? I think the latter, and for the simple reason that there is no definite article in the Greek, as Rotherham points out. He renders the sentence, "Receive ye Holy Spirit." There are three things suggested by these words, namely, *impartation* of abundant life, *illumination* of the understanding, and *infusion* of power for service.

Impartation of abundant life. Breathing is equivalent to life. In vindicating himself to his friends, Job, among other things, refers to his dealings with the owners of the land he possessed, and imprecates himself if he has caused "the owners thereof to lose their life" (Job 31:39). Again, at the creation of man, God "breathed into his nostrils the breath of life" (Genesis 2:7). Yet one other illustration, when the prophet saw the valley of dead bones he cried to the Spirit of Life to come in the words, "Come from the four winds, O Breath, and breathe upon these slain, that they may live" (Ezekiel 37:9).

The disciples had spiritual life, but lacked vitality. Their testimony needed grit, their love wanted glow, their temper lacked grace, their service needed go, their faith called for grip, their spirits needed gladdening, and their whole nature needed grounding. Christ, in resurrection power, seeks now to supply the need, for His blessing will mean their betterment.

Until we know Christ in resurrection power, we will never rise above the petty annoyances of life; but when we know Him, and the power of His resurrection, then the morning of our life will glow with the sun of His love and grace. Living in the consciousness of His in-breathing power and living presence, we cannot do anything mean, selfish, worldly, unrighteous, or fleshly. "When Frederick Arnold was writing the life of F. W. Robertson, he went to Brighton to talk to Robertson's friends, to find incidents for his biography. Among other places, he went to a bookseller's shop, and learned that the proprietor had been a constant attendant upon Robertson's ministry, and had in his parlor a picture of the great preacher. The bookseller said to Mr. Arnold, 'Do you see that picture? Whenever I am tempted to do a mean thing, I run back here and look at it. Then I cannot do the mean thing. Whenever I feel afraid of some difficulty, or some obstacle, I come and look into those eyes, and I go out strong for my struggle.'" If the face of a dead friend inspired the man to such a degree as he states, how much more should the living presence of our Divine Lord! It will, if we only recognize that presence.

Illumination of the Understanding. The Hebrew word rendered *"breathed"* in Genesis 2:7, is given "bloweth" in Isaiah 54:16, in speaking of the smith who "bloweth the coals in the fire." Often the fire of the understanding burns low because the breath of the Lord's quickening is not allowed to blow upon it Govett says, "I understand those words, 'Receive ye Holy Spirit,' to be parallel with the words in Luke relating to this scene, 'Then opened he their understandings that they might understand the Scripture' (Luke 24:45). It was a gift of inspiration in relation to the Old Testament Scriptures; and it was by virtue of this inspired intelligence that Peter acted in the first of the Acts, according as the Psalm directs—that another apostle should be chosen in the place of Judas. It did not make needless the descent of the Holy Ghost at Pentecost, of which our Lord in this Gospel had abundantly testified as the near hope of the disciples."

If we are shut in with the Lord, this always follows: a deeper insight into the things of God. Those who dwell deep in communion with God are sure to be initiated in the deep things of His purpose. The late F. W. Crossley relates a similar experience which he had to that of the disciples. He says: "I was praying, when the Lord filled me with a new kind of faith and joy—a faith and a consciousness of cleansing *(somewhat wavering, but quite different from any previous sense)*. I felt and feel loosed from my infirmity to testify . . . . The beginning of the matter was a quite new appetite for His Word. I hungered for it and ate it up as never exactly before, then to prayer, and then this blessing." The study of the Word led him to prayer, but what was it that led him to study the Word? It was prayer, too; this gave him the appetite for the study of the Word. How often have we heard it said, "The Bible has been a new book to me since I have been filled with the Spirit"?

Infusion of power for service. The power which equipped Bezaleel for service is tersely expressed in the following words of Jehovah: "I have filled him with the Spirit of God, in wisdom, and in understanding, and in knowledge, and in all manner of workmanship" (Exodus 31:3). The Hebrew word for spirit in some places is translated "breath." So that we might read, "The Breath of God" for "The Spirit of God," especially where the gracious influence is referred to. Yet we need to guard against a misapprehension, for the Holy Spirit is as much a person as the Father and the Son. The one practical thought for the believer is this: we require supernatural power to serve God. There is a striking illustration of this in the Epistle to the Corinthians. The lowest status of society in the apostle's day was that of a slave. The natural advice men would give to such an one would be, "Make every effort to get out of the position you are in." Does the apostle give this advice? No. He says, "Brethren, let every man, wherein he is called, therein abide with God" (1 Corinthians 7:24). This statement turns the drudgery of the slave into the service of the saint. Godet put it finely when he said, "This is what raises the humblest duties it can impose on him to the supreme acts of worship . . . In fact, this principle has been of incalculable importance in the development of the Church. It is by the means of it that Christianity has been able to become a moral power, at once sufficiently firm and sufficiently elastic to adapt itself to all human situations, personal, domestic, national, and social. Thereby it is, that, without revolution, it has worked the greatest revolution, accepting everything to transform everything, submitting to everything to rise above everything, renewing the world from top to bottom, while condemning all violent subversion."

Such a thought gives new meaning to service for God. It proclaims the fact that the duties of earth done to the Lord Himself cause them to reflect the glory of heaven. It is not without reason that the common duties of life follow the command to "be filled with the Spirit," for it is only as we are filled with *Him* that we can fulfil *them*.

Out of all this there comes a sweet contentment with one's lot, which makes one acquiesce to the sentiment expressed in the following lines:—

"Do what you can,
Being what you are;
Shine as a glow-worm,
If you cannot be a star;
Work like a pulley,
If you cannot be a crane;
Be a wheel-greaser,
If you cannot drive a train.

"Be the pliant oar,
If you cannot be the sailor;
Be the little needle,
If you cannot be the tailor;
Be the cleaning broom,
If you cannot be the sweeper;
Be the sharpened sickle,
If you cannot be the reaper."

In the biography of George Müller, the following incident is related: "On April 20th, Mr. Müller left for Bristol. On the journey he was dumb, having no liberty in speaking for Christ, or even in giving away tracts, and this led him to reflect. He saw that the so-called work of the Lord had tempted him to substitute *action for meditation and communion*. He had neglected that still hour with God which supplies to spiritual life alike its breath and bread. No lesson is more important for us to learn, yet how slow we are to learn it—that for the lack of habitual seasons set apart for devout meditation upon the Word of God and for prayer, nothing else will compensate." We are too apt to forget that we need the polishing by the pierced hand of our Redeemer in secret, to reflect more effectually His glory in public.

The importance of entering into the closet for communion before going forth in service is repeatedly emphasized in God's Word. The exercise of the holy priesthood in offering up spiritual sacrifices is the forerunner of the qualification for the royal priesthood to show forth God's praises (1 Peter 2:5, 9) even as the High Priest on the Day of Atonement entered the Holiest of All, wearing the holy linen garments (Leviticus 16:4) before he came forth to bless the people, having on the garments of glory and beauty (Exodus 28:43). The holy garments of a consecrated life, as formed through fellowship with the Lord, must be worn before the royal robes of a faithful testimony.

We must tarry in prayer before we can testify in power. The early disciples moved God by their prayer of faith. God in response moved them by His Spirit. And they in turn moved the people (Acts 4:23-32). The shining face of Moses was not obtained by looking into the faces of men, but was the result of being alone with God in the glory (Exodus 34:29).

Waiting upon God is the way to obtain strength to walk after Him in obedience. Running well in obedience to the Lord's directions, mounting high in the Divine life, and an untiring walk in love, are all consequent upon the strength obtained in secret from the Lord's presence. Before David conquered Goliath in public, he had learned to overcome the lion and bear in secret. The required skill to overcome our enemies is the result of long and patient practice in secret.

To have the tongue of the taught we must have the willing ear of attention (Isaiah 50:4, R.V.). Before Moses could be the leader of Israel, he must spend forty years at the back side of the desert. In his self-evolved zeal he could smite the Egyptian, but the Lord had to but Him on the grindstone of His training to remove the encrustations of impatience. Moses learned his lesson well, for afterwards he did everything according to the word of the Lord (Exodus 40:16), except in striking the rock when the Lord told him to *speak* to it (Numbers 20:12).

To have effective Martha service, we must have the humble posture of Mary, and also her teachable spirit (Luke 10:39). The secrets of the Master are not received while we are in the hurry of work. They are obtained while quietly listening to His voice as He speaks to us in His Word. The Mary spirit precedes all true, real, and effective service. There would be less tartness in our testimony if there were more tarrying in His presence.

As we abide in the Lord's presence we will better understand many of the Lord's negative responses to our petitions. Three times Paul asks the Lord to remove the thorn in his flesh. His prayer was not granted as he desired. The Lord did not remove the thorn but He told His servant, "My grace is sufficient for thee." From that interview with the Lord Paul learned that he had a greater blessing *with* the trial than if he had been *without* it. He found that the messenger of Satan brought a gift from heaven.

Prayer to the Lord was the feeder of the consistent life of Daniel. The king suffered no damage because Daniel did not suffer his spiritual life to be hurt. He demonstrated the saying, "The soul of all prosperity is the prosperity of the soul." When we receive the plan of our conduct from God's Word, as Moses received the plan of the tabernacle, the glory of the Lord's grace will shine out from the tabernacle of our character even as the glory of the Lord filled the tabernacle of old (Exodus 40:34).

There is one chapter in the life of F. W. Crossley of Manchester which is most suggestive. It is called *"Machinery and Religion,"* and in the chapter, it is repeated again and again that he would not engage in any business transaction which was not straightforward. He would not send out a faulty engine. His religion was in His machinery. The reason of this is not far to seek, for all who knew him testify to the thoroughness of his consecration to Christ and the spirituality of his life. This is so true that his biographer speaks of his conscience as a "Franciscan conscience." All this goes to prove that they who live for God live best before men. The secret of a consistent life is a consecrated one.

22

The Discipler's Walk

In Proverbs 6:13 we read that the wicked man "speaketh with his feet." From this we gather the meaning of the word "walk," for as the wicked man speaks by his life, and tells us which way he is going, so the Christian should as plainly indicate by his manner of life whom he serves. The term "walk" in the Word of God refers to the whole tenor of the life. Looking back upon the past, we are reminded in Ephesians 2:2, 3 what was the tone and tendency of our walk—even "following the course of this world, following the prince of the power of the air, the spirit that is now at work in the sons of disobedience. Among these we all once lived in the passions of our flesh, following the desires of body and mind, and so were by nature children of wrath, like the rest of mankind" (RSV).

The believer's walk is spoken of in different ways, such as walking with God, before Him, and after Him. We shall confine ourselves to the first:

Walking with God Means Companionship with Him

"Can two walk together except they be agreed?" (Amos 3:3). Sin thrust man out from the presence of God. Christ came to reconcile man to God. It was man who went away from God, and not God from man. Now God is beseeching the sinner to be reconciled to Himself; and the moment he is reconciled by faith in Christ, the difference is removed, his sins are forgiven, he is made a child of God, and all the value of the person and work of Christ is reckoned to him; and God is well pleased, for He sees the believer in Christ. In Eden, God walked and talked with Adam, but sin severed the communion. Now grace restores man to the companionship of God: hence, we are called to have fellowship with Him and with the Lord Jesus.

Walking with God Implies Acquaintance with Him

The question asked long ago, "How can man be just with God?" (Job 9:2; 25:4), is answered in Romans 5:1, "Being justified by faith we have peace with God, through our Lord Jesus Christ." When we believe in Christ, we become acquainted with God, and thus we are at peace (Job 22:21). There is no longer opposition on our part; we comply with His conditions, and we accept His invitation to be reconciled. Thus there is agreement as to our salvation, as there was with Israel, when, in obedience to the command of God, they took the lamb and slew it, and sprinkled its blood on the doorposts and lintels. Then God went with them out of Egypt.

Walking with God Means Agreement with Him

In speaking of Job's friends and referring to what Job had said, Elihu spoke thus: "He hath said, It profiteth a man nothing that he should delight himself with God" [or, as the margin of the R.V. has it, "consent with God"] (Job 34:9). What the Lord says is our law, and what He wills, we love. We are one with Him and have all in common with Him. As God says of the wicked, "When thou sawest a thief, then thou consentedst with him, and hast been partaker with adulterers" (Psalm 1:18), so now we consent with *His* plan and partake of His provision.

Walking with God Suggests Achievement with Him

In the history of Israel under King Saul, we find that on one occasion when the Israelites were fighting against the Philistines Saul had commanded the people not to eat until the evening. The one who disobeyed was to die. Jonathan, however, had not heard of the command of his father, and he in returning from the slaughter of the enemy had put his spear into a honey-comb and eaten. Because of this act Saul said that Jonathan should die. But the people protested and said, "God forbid: as the Lord liveth, there shall not one hair of his head fall to the ground, for he hath wrought with God this day" (1 Samuel 14:24, 27, 28, 29, 43, 45). The point to which we call attention is this, what Jonathan and his armor-bearer did, they accomplished with God. Their achievements came because the Lord Himself was with them. Similarly, in our defensive action against the wiles of the enemy, and our offensive achievements in pulling down the strongholds of Satan, it is only as the Lord is with us, and as we are with Him, that He gives us the victory.

Walking with God Speaks of Allegiance to Him

In contrasting the condition of Israel and of Judah, the Lord says, "Ephraim has surrounded me with lies, the house of Israel with deceit. And Judah is unruly against God, even against the faithful Holy One" (Hosea 11:12 NIV). As the soldier shows he is loyal to his sovereign and country by his faithful obedience, and as the governor of an institution shows he is with those who placed him in the position he occupies by ruling according to their desire, so we evidence our walking with God by obeying His Word and observing His will.

Walking with God Denotes Abiding with Him

In giving directions as to what action the Christian was to take in reference to his worldly occupations, the Holy Spirit says, "In whatever state each was called, there let him remain with God" (1 Corinthians 7:24). Walking with God, there will be no hasty step taken, but a calm, patient waiting upon Him, and an acquiescence with His will. If there were always this calm abiding with

God, what mistakes would be avoided and what blunders prevented, and yet what readiness to do His will. When He bids us "go forward," we may be sure that it must mean to be with Him! It was because Levi and Phinehas were walking with God that the one was afraid before the name of Jehovah, and the other was not afraid to slay the Israelite and the Midianite woman, when they brought sin into the camp (compare Malachi 2:5, 6, with Numbers 25:6-14). If we know what it is to look into the face of God, we will not be afraid to look into the face of man. Abiding with God, we shall be in the right place.

Walking with God We Will Be in Activity with Him in Christian Work

"My Father is working still, and I am working" (John 5:17 RSV), said Christ; and the apostle Paul, in speaking of himself and his fellow-laborers, says, "We are God's fellow workers" (1 Corinthians 3:9). Here we are reminded of our dignity and duty. "Who would not labor in such sweet company?" So says an old Puritan. All believers are "saved to serve," as a friend wrote on his photograph in placing his autograph upon it. But let us remember that there may be activity without walking with God. Peter was very active when he cut off the ear of the servant of the high priest, but Christ was not with him in the action. Only what is done with God counts, and we are only truly active when we keep step with Him.

Walking with God, There Will Be Acknowledgment by Him

We read that the angel said to Mary, "You have found favor with God" (Luke 1:30 RSV); and also of Jesus it is stated, in speaking of Him as to His humanity, He "increased in wisdom and in stature, and in favor with God and man" (Luke 2:52 RSV). Enoch, of whom it is said that he "walked with God," gives us the clue to obtaining the favor or pleasure of God, in that it is said of him, "he *pleased* God" (Hebrews 11:5). How? By simply walking with Him. Walking with God does not mean that we shall be acknowledged by men, but this to the true heart is of little importance as long as he knows that walking with God will bring acknowledgment from Him.

What are some of the results of walking with God? We have already implied in some measure what they are, but there are seven distinct results mentioned in the Word:

1. *Joy in God.* As Enoch pleased God by his walk, and that meant joy to him, so will it be with us, for as we accompany Him, we have the joy of His strength as our support, the joy of His salvation as our song, the joy of His presence as our stay, the joy of His countenance as our delight, the joy of His service as our success, and the joy of His Word as our study.

2. *Endurance in God.* "Noah walked with God" (Genesis 6:9). In Hebrews 11:7, we are told how he walked with God. The Lord told him to build the Ark and he simply obeyed. We may imagine what he had to endure—the opposition, the persecution, and the sneers which he would encounter, and how discouraging, humanly speaking, to preach all those years without any fruit! (See 1 Peter

3:20.) But he endured because he was with God, and being with Him, he understood the Divine plan. Many suffer from the disease of fits and starts in Christian service. This is because they do not have the remedy—walking with God. Those only endure who walk with the Enduring One.

3. *Knowledge in the ways of God.* God "made known his ways unto Moses, his acts unto the children of Israel" (Psalm 103:7). Israel only knew the ways of God by His *acts*, but Moses knew the *ways* before the acts. And we shall know the ways of God as we walk with Him. He will instruct us, and we will be able to enter into His mind, respecting His people, His purpose, His love, His will; for while the things that are of God "have not entered into the heart of man," yet He will reveal them to us by His Holy Spirit, through the Word, as we walk with Him (1 Corinthians 2:9, 10).

4. *Courage in God.* Phinehas was courageous, quick to discern evil, and zealous for the honor of God, because he was in fellowship with Him (Malachi 2:6; Numbers 25:6-15). The fear of man will not be known by us if we are looking into the face of God. The face of Jesus was "set" like a "flint" (Isaiah 50:7), as He steadfastly went to Jerusalem (Luke 9:51); and if we would have the face of flint, we can only obtain it through the light and strength which comes from communion with God. If we receive not from the Divine Source the firmness of courage we need, we will be like the soft wax that yields to the lightest impression.

5. *Confidence in the Lord.* David could calmly sing, "I will fear no evil: for thou art with me" (Psalm 23:4). Enemies surround him, and their shadows were flitting across his path as he was walking through the valley, but the Lord was with him. Therefore he had a good Defense and an able Deliverer, and he could confidently boast in the Lord. Whom need we fear, if we are walking with God? No man on earth, nor any of Satan's hellish band.

6. *Rest in the Lord.* The Lord Jesus gives us the clue to this, when He says, "Take my yoke upon you, and learn of me, for I am meek and lowly in heart, and ye shall find rest unto your souls" (Matthew 11:29). Yoked with Christ, we walk with Him and hold sweet conversation. What is the yoke of Christ? It is simply the will of God. And as we are in His will, we walk with Him, for this is His will. Thus we enjoy His own rest. Rest in service. Freedom from care and worry. Liberty from self by resting in Him. Deliverance from care by casting all upon Him.

7. *Zeal kindled by the Lord.* "Did not our heart burn within us, while he talked with us by the way, and while he opened to us the Scriptures? And they rose up the same hour, and returned to Jerusalem, and found the eleven gathered together, and them that were with them, saying, The Lord is risen indeed" (Luke 24:32-34). For those disheartened disciples on their way to Emmaus, Christ opened their understanding, as He opened to them the Scriptures while they were walking together. Then He made Himself known to them as He lifted up His hands to bless the evening meal. Thus were their hearts warmed and their souls stirred, as with swift feet they went to make known to the rest what had happened. What was it that caused the change in them from sadness to gladness, from faint-heartedness to heartiness? It was their *walk with Christ*.

Let us walk with Him, and thus be separate from the world. Then we shall find that in His presence there is fullness of joy, perfect peace, the comfort of His promises, the assurance of His truth, the strength of His arm, and the supply of His hand.

23

The Discipler's Worship

Worship and work both have their place, but in these days of restless activity it is necessary to watch lest worship be neglected. Work done for God, unless done in the spirit of worship, is not of much account in God's sight. When service is done with a heart overflowing with adoration, it is acceptable to God and profitable to man. There are four principal words which are associated with worship in the New Testament. The understanding of each answers the question as to what worship is. These may be summed up under the following points: Submission, Ascription, Consecration, and Service.

Submission

The Greek word "*proskuneo*" signifies the act of worship. It means to kiss, like a dog licking its master's hand as it crouches before him; hence, its signification is to reverence and adore. Satan uses the word when he urges Christ to "fall down and worship" him (Matthew 4:9), but Christ reminds him that there is only One who is worthy of that act. He says, "It is written, thou shalt worship the Lord thy God, and him only shalt thou serve" (Matthew 4:10). A further illustration of the word may be found in the thirteenth chapter of the Revelation. There we find that the anti-Christ causes the dragon to be worshipped, and he in turn is worshipped too, for the false prophet causes the anti-Christ to be worshipped, and if there are any who will not worship him they are put to death (Revelation 13:4, 8, 12, 15). Taking the word in its widest and most spiritual application, it will be seen that the word submission sums it up. We find seven illustrations of this aspect of worship in the Gospel according to Matthew, in persons who rendered homage to Christ. Suppose we take the passages as illustrative of the deeper meaning of the subject before us and call attention to the leading thought in each case:

Submission to Christ's Rule. When the wise men saw the infant Christ they "fell down, and worshipped him" (Matthew 2:11). It was the King (Matthew 2:2) they came to seek, and when they had found Him, they gladly paid Him homage, and gave Him the best they had. When Christ rules in our heart by His love, dominates our mind by His truth, sanctifies our being by His Spirit, empowers our inner nature by His indwelling, leads our lives by His example, inspires our testimony by His Word, and influences our giving by His claim, then we worship Him and crown Him Lord of all. Unless we crown Him Lord *of all*, we do not crown Him Lord *at all*.

Submission to Christ's Cleansing. When the leper came to Christ for cleansing, he "worshipped Him" (Matthew 8:2). There is a cleansing which all God's children know, that is, the cleansing of the conscience by the atoning blood of Christ from the condemnation of sin; but there is another cleansing, namely, the cleansing from the indwelling contamination of sin. This twofold cleansing is referred to in 1 John 1:7, 9. The blood of Christ cleanses us from all sin as to its guilt; but He Himself cleanses us from "all unrighteousness" as to its government. It has been said that some Christians are like well-supplied cruet bottles. Tip them upside down and you will get something peppery or vinegary. The Lord can cleanse us if we will. He can remove the defilement of an impure heart. He can take away the tartness of an unholy temper. He can remove the black desire of couvetousness. He can take away the root of bitterness. He can cut out the ill-humor of pride. He can kill the weed of jealousy. He can conquer the swagger of self-will. But we must plan our part as did the leper; we must ask in faith believing before there can be the communication of Christ's cleansing power.

Submission to Christ's power. "There came a certain ruler, and worshipped him, saying, My daughter is even now dead: but come and lay thy hand upon her, and she shall live" (Matthew 9:18). Jairus had unswerving faith in the power of Christ to raise his daughter from the dead, and his faith was rewarded. We too must have faith in the power of Christ to quicken those who are dead in trespasses and sins, for it is only as we submit to His power that we have any power. What Dr. Maclaren says of the Holy Spirit applies here. "The Holy Ghost is the only real Power for service. Why have we not got this power? Because we are not willing to be made invisible by the investure." That's it, the invisibility must precede the investment. In other words, submission to Christ's power goes before the operation of that power through us. When we give ourselves wholly to it, it will give itself wholly to us, even as the electricity in the motor communicates itself to the wire the moment it is in connection with it.

Submission to Christ's Deity. "Then they that were in the ship came and worshipped him, saying, Of a truth thou art the Son of God" (Matthew 14:33). The Deity of Christ is not only a doctrine to be believed, in the sense of assenting to its validity. It is also a truth to be known in all its vitality. The one thing which convinced the disciples of the deity of Christ was His power to calm the troubled waters; and the argument which will convince the world of the reality of the Christian faith will be as Christ shall calm the storm of sin's passion and exhibit the calm of His own holy grace in us. In speaking of what Christ did for the early Christians, Justin Martyr says: "Those who were lately the slaves of sensual passion, as was the case with myself, have now no ambition other than to lead pure and holy lives; those who were but yesterday given to the practices of sorcery and the art of magic, are today consecrated to the service of the eternal and unbegotten God; those who, as Pagans, prized wealth above everything else, as Christians distribute all they have to the poor; those who formerly despised persons of any other nationality but their own, ridiculed their customs, and would hold no conversation with them, live, since the birth of Christ in their souls, in peace with their enemies, and offer prayers and do other kind offices for those who hate and persecute them." From what source were such changes effected? From Him who was "declared to be the Son of God with power."

If we submit to Him as the Son of God, then we shall know the blessedness and power of His Sonship as brought out in the seven references to it in the first Epistle of John, for they who know Him in truth, confess Him as the Son of God (4:15), have the witness that they possess eternal life (5:10), know it through His assuring word (5:13), live a life of faith upon Him (5:13), have a personal acquaintance with Him (5:20), overcome the world (5:5), and know that He was manifested to destroy the works of the devil (3:8).

Submission to Christ's Word. "Then came she and worshipped him, saying, Lord, help me" (Matthew 15:25). The Canaanite woman never for one moment questioned the words of Christ. Even when He discouraged her, she clung all the more to Him. Thus it is ever with faith. Whittier says of faith:

> "Through the dark and stormy night
> Faith beholds a feeble light,
> Up the blackness streaking;
> Knowing God's own time is best."

Yes, not only is "God's own time best," but His *way* is best, too. Faith says, "I'll go where He wishes, I'll do what He tells me, I'll take what He gives, I'll follow where He leads, I'll deliver the message He bids, I'll lie where He puts me, and I'll keep low in His presence in humble and adoring worship."

Submission to Christ's right. "Then came to him the mother of Zebedee's children with her sons, worshipping him, and desiring a certain thing of him" (Matthew 20:20). The request she made was a wrong one. But she recognized the power of Christ in doing so, although the particular favor asked had to come from His Father. Still He granted her some favor, in promising that her sons should be identified with Him in suffering. We may often have a right posture in worship, but put in a wrong plea. We may be perfectly honest and yet be blundering in our requests; hence, the very best answer to our prayers is denial. We recognize His right to give, and He exercises His right in not giving. But if we truly worship Him, it will be quite sufficient that He refuses, for we know that He must have the best of reasons for doing so. In that case His withholdings are the best blessings.

Submission to Christ's glory. "As they went to tell his disciples, behold, Jesus met them, saying, All hail. And they came and held him by the feet, and worshipped him . . . And when they saw him, they worshipped him" (Matthew 28:9, 17). Christ in the glory of His risen power met the women and the disciples. The glory of Christianity is Christ—the living Christ, with His saving grace, holy influence, warm sympathy, touch of power, lowly love, sufficient atonement, encouraging word, enabling strength, and lasting and unchanging personality. We say as we think of Him,

"Subtlest thought shall fail and learning falter,
Churches change, forms perish, systems go;
But our human needs, they will not alter,
Christ no after age shall e'er outgrow.

"Yea, Amen! O changeless One, Thou only
Art life's guide and spiritual goal;
Thou the light across the dark vale lonely,
Thou the eternal haven of the soul."

We may well bow before the lowly, loving, lightening, liberating, and lasting Christ, in adoring worship, and pray that the glory of His personality may penetrate every part of our nature, and that all other glories may pale before His all-glorious person.

Ascription

The word *"Doxa"* is rendered *"worship"* in Luke 14:10. It speaks of the man who takes the lowest place at the wedding feast, but who is called by the governor to occupy a higher one. In being thus honored, he is said to "have *worship* in the presence" of the rest of the guests. The meaning of the word will at once be seen. It signifies the giving of honor to anyone, as when the cleansed leper gave *"glory"* to God for his cleansing, and when the living creatures give *"glory"* to the Throne-sitter (Luke 17:18; Revelation 4:9, 11; 5:12, 13). The word has a wide application and refers to the honor in which anyone is held by another. When applied to God it is generally found ascribing praise to Him, in connection with the sentence, "To whom be *glory*." Where this sentence occurs, we find that some special trait of God's character is referred to. This calls forth the ascription of praise. Let us note seven of these references.

Praising God as the Source, Sustainer, and End of all things. "For of him, and through him, and to him, are all things: to whom be *glory* for ever" (Romans 11:36). The keys to unlock this passage of Scripture are found in the prepositions *"of," "through,"* and *"to."* In the Greek they are *"ek," "dia,"* and *"eis." "Ek"* means, *"out of,"* as illustrated in the stream coming out of the mountain, or the light coming forth from the sun. *"Dia"* signifies *"by means of,"* as the electricity is transmitted by means of the wire, or the athlete is made proficient by means of training. *"Eis"* means *"unto,"* as denoting the purpose for which anything is made, as when we are told believers are called *"unto* the fellowship" of Christ (1 Corinthians 1:9). From the meaning of the prepositions, we may gather that God is the Source of all things, for from Him come all things; He is the Holder-together of all things, or He is the Law of Gravitation which keeps everything in its place; and He is the End of all things, for as Hodge says, "The highest end for which all things can exist and be ordered is to display the character of God." When we think of what we owe to God, of all that comes to us through Him, of the end He has in view, can we do anything else than praise Him?

Praising God for His wisdom. "To God only wise, be *glory* through Jesus Christ for ever" (Romans 16:27). The apostle is speaking of the wisdom of God in the revelation of the gospel, and the manifestation of that wisdom in the wondrous display of the grace of God in making dirty sinners into bright saints. It is to this display of the wisdom of God that the apostle refers when he speaks of the manifold wisdom of God being made known to the angelic host by the church (Ephesians 3:10).

In the early morning, the traveler in Switzerland could often see the Alps appear under a sky still dark, their summits cold and lifeless. At the base of the mountain range a lake lies motionless, in which is mirrored the pale rays of a setting moon, making it look weird and death-like. A few hours later, the whole scene would change. The sun had risen and lit up everything with its glowing splendor. The mountain peaks, with their snow-capped summits, now glow in their virgin whiteness. The glaciers are reflecting the beauteous sunlight, the streams are singing in their onward course, the lake is quivering in its blueness, the birds are twittering in their gladness, the trees greet the refreshing breeze with a seeming murmur of gratitude, the flowers open and give forth their fragrance, the cattle graze with satisfaction, and the bells around their necks tinkle in discordant harmony. All nature is alive and seems to be praising the Lord of Life and Glory. A transformation has taken place and all this is brought about by the glorifying of the sun.

Something similar takes place when the light of the glorious Gospel shines into the heart of the believer, for then it reflects the light of love, and grace, and holiness, to the praise and glory of God; and as the angels see the variegated glory of God manifested in us, they wonder, and learn, and praise. So with us, they too adore the manifold grace of God.

Praising God for His inworking. "Unto him be glory in the church" (Ephesians 3:21). The purpose of God's blessing to the believer is not for his own comfort, but for the glory of God. The glory of God in the church is the outcome of, and is measured by, "the power that worketh in us" (Ephesians 3:20). When the temple of our being is garlanded with the graces and the beauty of the indwelling Christ, and the realm of our nature is under the absolute sway of the Holy Spirit, then we praise the God of our salvation. Madam Guyon used to say, "There are only two truths, the nothingness of the creature and the all of God." It is only as we are nothing that God can make something of us. Our very impotence makes room for the display of His omnipotence, even as the rich soil can manifest itself in the fruitfulness of the tree which is planted in it.

Praising God for Christ's sacrifice. "Christ who gave himself for our sins, to deliver us from this present evil age, according to the will of our God and Father; to whom be the glory for ever and ever. Amen" (Galatians 1:4, 5 RSV).

When the Scotch fought the English and were defeated, James the Fourth of Scotland, the flower of the Scotch nobles, perished on the field of Flodden. The Provost and the Town Councillors at Edinboro' were waiting throughout the night for news of the battle. Murray came up to the city gates at midnight, but the news was too heavy for him to tell to any until he was able to reach the City

Hall. There he stood in the presence of the Provost. As he held in his hand the banner, he said to the Lord Provost and the Councillors:

> "Ay! ye may well look upon it—there is more than honor there,
> Else, be sure, I had not brought it from the field of dark despair.
> Sirs, I charge you, keep it holy, keep it as a sacred thing,
> For the stain ye see upon it was the life-blood of your king."

The Holy Spirit speaks to us in similar strains, for He charges us to keep "the blood-stained banner of the cross." In it He says to us—

> "I charge you, keep it holy, keep it as a sacred thing,
> For the stain ye see upon it was the life-blood of your King."

And as we keep in remembrance His death for "our sins," we must "keep it as a sacred thing," for the fire of our grateful praise is kindled from the altar of God's sacrificing grace; and as our praise is perfumed with the merit of the Savior's worth, it ascends to God as a sweet-smelling savor. Let us ever say to "our God and Father," to His praise and glory:—

> "No subject so glorious as He,
> No theme so affecting to us."

Praising God as the Need-Supplier. "Now unto God and our Father be glory for ever and ever" (Philippians 4:20). The apostle had been thanking the saints at Philippi for the help they had sent him in ministering to his need. He assured them that it had gone up to God as a sweet-smelling savor, and he cheered them by reminding them that He would supply every need of theirs, according to His riches in glory. Then Paul caps his words by this ascription of praise. Samuel Rutherford, in speaking of spiritual blessing in Christ, says, "How little of the sea can the child carry in his hand! As little do I take away of my great sea, the boundless love of Christ. I am pained with wondering at new opened treasures in Christ. Our best things have a worm in them; our joys, beside God, in the inner half, are but woes and sorrows. Christ, Christ is that on which our love and desires can sleep sweetly, and rest safely upon. Christ hath made me content with a borrowed fireside, and it casteth as much heat as my own. How sweet is the wind that bloweth out of the earth where Christ is. Every day we may see some new thing in Christ. His love hath neither brim nor bottom. Oh, that I had help to praise Him!" Such a spirit of praise must fill the heart of every believer as he contemplates the fullness of blessing in Christ for him. As we see the ocean of blessing in God's provision, it constrains us to bring the bucket of our gratitude and pour out its contents as an offering of praise to God. This is what David did with the water obtained from the well at Bethlehem at the risk of the lives of three of his mighty men (1 Chronicles 11:18). The ascription of praise is the language of spiritual instinct, which cannot be repressed.

Praising God as the Savior. "Now unto the King eternal, immortal, invisible, the only wise God, be honor and glory for ever and ever. Amen" (1 Timothy 1:17). As Paul looked at what he was, and what the grace of God had made him, it stirred his heart to its very depths. It made him exclaim as he did in grateful praise to God. When thankfulness is enthroned in the heart, praise will be on the lips. The experiential knowledge of God's grace leads us to praise our Lord to His glory. The doxology of our praise ascends to our heavenly Father because the benediction of His favors has first descended into our lives. The Lord compasses us with songs of deliverance" (Psalm 32:7), and we praise Him with our songs of thanksgiving (Nehemiah 12:46). He crowns us with "loving-kindness and tender mercies" (Psalm 103:4), and we cast the crowns of our gratitude at His feet (Revelation 4:10).

Praising God as the Preserver. "The Lord shall deliver me from every evil work, and will preserve me unto his heavenly kingdom: to whom be glory for ever and ever. Amen" (2 Timothy 4:18). With martyrdom staring him in the face, his professed friends deserting him, and very little sympathy around him, Paul could look up and praise God, for he was confident He would preserve him unto His heavenly kingdom. As Paul confidently thinks of this, it touches the spring of gratitude and at once praise leaps from his heart and lips.

"You see that finger! As long as that can move, I will put you down," so said the burgomaster of Hamburg to Oncken the pioneer missionary in Germany. Upon which, Oncken replied, "Sir, I see your finger; but I also see an arm, which you do not see, and so long as that is stretched out, you cannot put me down." With the right hand of God's power around us to protect, and the left hand of His love to caress (Song of Solomon 2:6), we need not fear anyone or anything, for His love will comfort on the one hand, and His power will keep on the other. We may well, therefore, lie back with content in the everlasting arms and praise our Father. Yes, we must praise Him for whatever comes, and in whatsoever we do, for His word is, Whatsoever ye do, *do all to the glory of God*" (1 Corinthians 11:31). As we live in this spirit we will enter into the spirit of the following lines of Kate V. Carpenter:

"Praise God! Praise God!"
We smilingly say,
With peace within our dwelling,
When love-light beams along our way,
And joy the heart is swelling.

" Praise God! Praise God!"
We murmur low,
When wealth and friends forsaking,
Make dearer still the hearts we know
Still true to us, though breaking.

"Praise God! Praise God!"
With faltering tone
We breathe o'er loved ones, lying
Beneath His rod, whose touch alone
Changed living into dying.

"Praise God! Praise God!"
If from our grasp
He forced a long-sought treasure,
'Tis but to grasp with loving clasp
Some safer, purer pleasure.

"Praise God! Praise God!"
Of all bereft
That makes life sweet and pleasant;
Seeking the only refuge left,
We find our Helper present.

"Praise God! Praise God!"
With sobbing breath,
Low on our knees we pray it,
And ask for grace, defying death,
Triumphantly to say it.

Consecration

A writer of fiction in referring to one of her characters, an artist, makes reference to a picture which she had produced. It attracted the special attention of the art world. The idea reproduced by the picture is given in the following quotation: "It was a fine picture, strongly painted, and was a representation of the Black Country, with its mingled gloom and glare, and its pillar of smoke always hanging over it. In the foreground were figures of men, women, and children looking upwards to the pillar of cloud; and, by the magic spell of the artist, Elizabeth had succeeded in depicting on their faces, for such as had eyes to see it, the peace of those who knew that God was with them in their journey through the wilderness. They were worn, and weary, and toil-worn, as they dwelt in the midst of the furnaces; but, through it all, they looked up to the overshadowing cloud, and were lightened, and their faces were not ashamed. In the far distance there was a glimpse of the sun setting behind a range of hills; and one felt, as one gazed at the picture, and strove to understand its meaning, that the pillar of cloud was gradually leading the people nearer and nearer to the far-off hills, and the land beyond the sunset; and that there they would find an abundant compensation for the suffering and poverty which had blighted their lives as they toiled here for their daily bread."

There is one thought, at least, found in the picture. God is seen in the protection of His presence, in the smoke of the common duties of life, yes, that very smoke is the symbol of His presence. The same thought is found in connection with the third word rendered worship, the word *eusebeo*. It is translated *"worship"* in Acts 17:23, where Paul calls attention to the ignorant and empty worship of the Athenians; and it occurs in one other place, namely, 1 Timothy 5:4, where it is rendered *"to shew piety."* The New International Version has it: "to put their religion into practice." The meaning of the word is to be devout, and, in the spiritual sense, signifies to be pious towards God. In these two instances where the word is used we have a suggestive explanation as to the difference between the world's conception of worship and God's thought about it. Man's thought about worship very often is a religious ceremony irrespective of character; but God's conception of worship is *practical godliness associated with grateful adoration*. The one is aptly summed up, "An altar with this inscription, To the unknown God"; while the other is epitomized, "Learn to show piety at home." The connection of the last passage is most suggestive, for in it we find two principles which are abundantly illustrated in the pages of God's Word. The verse reads as follows: "But if any widow have children or nephews (RSV, 'grandchildren'), let them learn first to shew piety at home, and to requite their parents: for this is good and acceptable before God" (1 Timothy 5:4).

Real consecration is shown in the fulfilment of the personal obligations resting upon us in the home-life. The one practical and definite direction given by the apostle is this: children and grandchildren should compensate those who have cared for them. This they were to do by their willing obedience, by their dutiful reverence, and the giving of their monetary help. But we want to look at the Scriptural principle as applying to all believers.

By way of illustration, let us look at seven things in the tabernacle as indicative of what we, as Christians, should be in the home.

1. *The fire of a holy love should be burning on the altar of our heart*. When the citadel of the heart is right, then the outworkings of the life will correspond.

The altar of God's earthly dwelling place was kindled by the fire of heaven. So the love which is to burn on the altar of the believer's heart is not of earth's igniting, it is the flame of the love of God. The apostle John has been called "the beloved disciple," and he has been rightly named. But he was so called not because of his love to Christ, but because of Christ's love to him. He is said to be the "disciple whom Jesus loved." John was the loving man because he was the loved man. The secret of all love is the love of Christ.

At the age of seven, John Leech was sent to the Charterhouse School, but his mother hired a room in one of the houses that overlooked the ground. Here, unknown to him, she would sit behind a blind day by day, happy and content if only she could have glimpses of her loved boy. Thus ever does love watch over others and make its warmth felt in loving ministry.

2. *The water of a cleansing influence should be in the laver of our life.* Paul Dwight Moody, the son of the great evangelist, D. L. Moody, shared this story of his father's influence on him:

"An incident which impressed me deeply then and its impress has never faded, happened when I was about ten years old. My father had told me to go to bed. I honestly thought he meant when I had finished a quite legitimate and proper occupation, for I was hobnobbing with a little crony of my age who had come to the house with an older person.

"I remained talking with him. My father, later passing through the room and finding that I had not obeyed him, spoke with that directness of which he was capable, called brusqueness by some, and ordered me to bed at once. There was no delaying my going after this.

"I retreated, frightened and in tears, for such a tone of voice was a new experience in my life. I hurried to bed, but before I had time to fall asleep, my father was at my bedside, kneeling and asking my forgiveness for the harsh way in which he had spoken to me, the tears falling down over his rugged, bearded face.

"That was nearly half a century ago, but I would exchange any memory of life before I would surrender that. For all unknowing he was laying for me the consciousness of the Fatherhood of God, and the love of God. No sermon on the prodigal's father, and no words on the love of God have cast quite such a light as his huge figure kneeling in the twilight by my bed, asking the forgiveness of a child."

3. *The bread of a satisfying help should be on the table of our conduct.* The showbread had always to be on the table, and after it had been there a certain time, the priests were privileged to eat it. May we not believe the Lord is saying to us with regard to those around us, as He said to the disciples of old, "Give ye them to eat?" There are many who are hungering for the help of the sympathetic word, which shall light up the spirit with encouragement, even as Paul's "good cheer" did the people on the storm-tossed ship (Acts 27:22). Many are hungering for the considerate thoughtfulness which does little acts of kindness in a kind way, even as Joseph was mindful of his father's age and sent him provision and kindly words so that his downcast spirit revived (Genesis 45:27). Many are hungering for the attentive ear into which to pour their heart's sorrow, that they

may share their burden with another and so lighten the pressure upon themselves. As we thus act, we feed the spirits of many, to their encouragement and cheer. George Macdonald says, "If I can put one touch of a rosy sunset into the life of any man or woman, I feel I shall have worked with God." Or, to give another quotation as James Russell Lowell says in speaking of womanly grace in the commonplace things of life:

"She doeth little kindnesses
Which most leave undone or despise;
For nought that sets our heart at ease,
And giveth happiness or peace,
Is low esteemed in her eyes.

She hath no scorn of common things,
And though she seems of other birth,
Round us her heart entwines and clings,
And patiently she folds her wings
To tread the humble paths of earth.

Blessing she is, God made her so,
And deeds of week-day holiness
Fall from her, noiseless as the snow;
Nor hath she ever chanced to know
That aught were easier than to bless."

4. *The light of a kindly testimony should be heard from the tongue of our speech.* The sevenfold light which came from the golden lampstand was the only light in the holy place. It is typical of Christ as the Light of the world and of the believer. That which is true of Him is said of us, as He Himself declares, "Ye are the light of the world." There are two expressions which occur in connection with the lampstand which are significant. The lampstand was to be set "over against the table" (Exodus 26:35); and the light is said to be "over against the candlestick" (Numbers 8:2, 3). These two passages of Scripture, where we have the words "over against," plainly indicate the purpose of the lampstand. It was to light up the table of shewbread and also to reveal the beauty of the lampstand itself. The same thing is true of the believer's testimony. It should make evident the glory of the Lord Jesus. At the same time the life of the witness should reflect a character made luminous with the love of Christ. There is one thing we should especially cultivate, and that is the kindly tone in our testimony. There should certainly be the light of truth, but it may be dimmed by the wind of a harsh tone. One thing which will help to bring this about is to see the best in everything.

There is a legend about the Lord Jesus. On one occasion it is said He and His disciples saw a dead dog. While the disciples were filled with loathing at the sight, the Master exclaimed, "What beautiful teeth the creature has!" Dr. Miller well comments upon the lesson found in the legend. "We should see beauty even in loathsomeness. Miss Mulock tells of a gentleman and a lady passing through a lumber-yard, by a dirty, foul-smelling river. The lady said, 'How good the pine boards smell!' 'Pine boards!' exclaimed her companion, 'Just smell this foul river!' 'No, thank you,' the lady replied, 'I prefer to smell the pine boards.'

She was wiser than he. It is far better for us to find the sweetness that is in the air than the foulness. It is better to talk to others of the smell of pine boards than of the heavy odors of stagnant rivers."

> "If any little word of mine
> May make a life the brighter—
> If any little song of mine
> May make a heart the lighter—
> God help me speak the little word,
> And take my bit of singing,
> And drop it in some lonely vale,
> To set the echoes ringing."

5. *The incense of a prayerful spirit should be on the altar of our devotion.* The golden altar in the holy place is called "the altar of incense" (Exodus 31:8) because upon it was burned "the pure incense" (Exodus 37:29). It is a type of the Lord Jesus in the personal worth of His priestly character as He ever lives to make intercession for His people (Hebrews 5:25); it also typifies the consecrated devotion of the priestly intercessions of God's people (Revelation 5:8).

There are two words in the New Testament which are associated with the burning of incense. *Thumiama* is rendered "*odors*" (Revelation 5:8; 18:13) and "*incense*" (Luke 1:10, 11; Revelation 8:3, 4); and *Osmee* is translated "*odor*" and "*savor*" (John 12:3; Philippians 4:18; Ephesians 5:2; 2 Corinthians 2:14-16). Both of these words signify the fragrant burning of incense. The first is associated with the altar of incense and the second is connected with the altar of burnt offering.

I call special attention to the latter word, because of the settings in which it is found. Notice the first reference is to Christ Himself. "He gave himself an offering and a sacrifice to God for a sweet-smelling *savor*" (Ephesians 5:2). The burnt-offering which went up to God as a sweet-smelling savor (Leviticus 1:9) is a type of Christ in the Godward aspect of His life and death, in His whole-hearted consecration to God's will. The thought was expressed by Christ Himself when He said to the Father, "I have glorified thee on the earth." Paul uses the word in speaking of service, as he was led about by Christ as a trophy of His grace. Christ made known His power through Christ, thus made "manifest the *savor* of his knowledge"; and whether men believed in the Savior or not, the apostle and his fellow-laborers were a sweet savor in Christ. To the perishing, however, they were a "*savor* of death," and to the saved "a *savor* of life."

The two passages where *osmee* is rendered "*odor*" are found in connection with gifts given to Christ. The first calls attention to the costly box of ointment with which Mary anointed Him for His burial, when the house was "filled with the *odor*"; the second refers to the gift which the saints at Philippi sent to Paul to meet his personal need. This went up to the Lord "an *odor* of a sweet smell, a sacrifice acceptable, well-pleasing to God."

The practical thought in these last two verses is this: our priestly intercession for others will always cost us something, but the cost will not trouble us when it is done for the Lord's sake. We cannot pray for the heathen without helping them. We cannot plead that the need of some brother in want may be met, without helping to meet it. We cannot ask that others may be consecrated without consecrating ourselves. This kindly, thoughtful help is always an accompaniment to true prayer. A little girl at Mr. Spurgeon's funeral was crying most bitterly. When asked the reason of her grief, she replied, "He always put two lumps of sugar in my tea." That was characteristic of the man. Two things always impressed those who came into the inner circle of the great preacher's life: the fervor of his intercessions and the kindliness of his thoughtful help.

6. *The law of a Divine ideal should always be in the ark of our being.* In the ark of a covenant were placed the tables of stone upon which were written the ten commandments (Deuteronomy 10:1). The Holy Spirit now writes His law upon the fleshly tablets of our heart (2 Corinthians 3:3; Hebrews 8:10). This choice tribute was once given to a Christian woman: "Her natural life was so completely Christian, that her Christian life became completely natural." Spontaneity is the feature of the true Christian life. We do not seek to obey a code of laws, urged by the lash of compulsion; but we keep the law of love, because love is the law operating in our hearts, like the life in the plant which causes it to grow. This leads me to say that the Divine ideal is possible because of the Divine Idealizer within us. "I can do," says the apostle, because "Christ strengtheneth me." In this way the ideal becomes actual. Thus, while the law of the Divine ideal should always be within us, it can only be made a matter of experience through the indwelling Christ. "My religion won't give me up," was the answer of one to whom the possibility of giving up her religion was suggested. It was such a pervading power in all her life. Therefore it was no more possible to separate it from her than it is possible to have the sunlight without the medium of the atmosphere.

7. *The glory of a God-like demeanor should be in all our actions.* The Shekinah glory, the symbol of the Divine presence, was between the cherubim (Exodus 25:22). The glory of the Lord's presence is not now located in any one particular *place,* although it is confined to one set of *persons,* namely, believers in Christ. To them the word is, "Know ye not that ye are the temple of God, and that the Spirit of God dwelleth in you?" (1 Corinthians 3:16). Charles Simeon once wrote to one of the grandsons of John Venn: "I wish you had known your honored grandfather; the only end for which he lived was to make all men see the glory of God in the face of Jesus Christ." O that the glory of the Divine love may color all our love. O that the glory of the Divine holiness may shine from all our ways. O that the glory of the Divine power may be felt by all those with whom we come in contact. O that the glory of the Divine compassion may operate in all our hearts. O that the glory of the Divine grace may empower us at all times; and the glory of the divine presence be manifest in all our life.

When these things are in the tabernacle of our home-life, then we will worship God in spirit and in truth. When we show piety at home, it will reveal itself abroad and, above all, rise "good and acceptable before God."

Service

The fourth word rendered "*worship*" means to serve God in a religious manner. The service is not that of a slave but rather that of a priest occupied in the service and worship of the temple. The word *latreno*, in the Scriptural use of it, signifies Divine service. That the word has a priestly association may easily be gathered, for it is rendered "*serve*" in speaking of those who "*serve* the tabernacle" (Hebrews 13:10), and of the redeemed in glory who are said to "*serve*" the Lamb (Revelation 22:3), and also of the great multitude who have come out of the great tribulation, who are said to be "before the throne of God, and *serve* him day and night in his temple" (Revelation 7:15).

There are three main thoughts which are found within the circle of this aspect of worship as connected with the use of the word *latreno*. These are: *Whom* we are to worship; *Why* we are to worship; and *How* we are to worship. The latter thought is the principal one.

1. *Whom we are to worship*. "*Worship* God" is the unmistakable utterance of the Holy Spirit (Philippians 3:3). "Him only shalt thou *serve*" (Matthew 4:10; Luke 4:8) was Christ's rejoinder to the tempter's suggestion to worship him. The purpose which the Lord had in cleansing the conscience from dead works by the blood of Christ was that we might "*serve* the living God" (Hebrews 9:14). When he was before Felix, Paul gave this answer to the charge of heresy: "After the way which they call heresy, so *worship* I the God of my fathers" (Acts 24:14). In each of these scriptures there shines forth with unmistakable brilliance the *Object* of true worship, God Himself. We are not to worship superstition with its halo of painted glory, but God in the reality of His personality. We are not to worship some fetish with its reputed charm, but God in the might of His living power. We are not to worship the creature in the fallibility of his weakness, but God in the infallibility of His truth. We are not to worship the Bacchus of worldly gratification, but God in the attractiveness of His grace. We are not to worship the Venus of fleshly desire, but God in the purity of His love. We are not to worship the Dagon of covetousness, but God in the fatherhood of His humanity. We are not to worship the Goliath of self, but God in the personal lowliness and loveliness of Christ. God first, last, and always is the One whom we are to worship with Divine service.

2. *Why we are to worship*. Shakespeare, in his *Julius Caesar*, has Mark Antony say, in reference to Caesar's will:

> "Let but the commons read this testament—
> Which, pardon me, I do not mean to read,
> And they would go and kiss dead Caesar's wounds,
> And dip their napkins in his sacred blood;
> Yea, beg a hair of him for memory,
> And, dying, mention it within their wills,
> Bequeathing it, as a rich legacy,
> Unto their issue."

One thought in the above lines is, gratitude on the part of those who are named in Caesar's will because of what he has done for them. His gifts beget their gratitude. In the best sense, it should be the same with the child of God. The reason for our service is found in God's salvation. The gift of God's grace in blessing us is that we should give Him our heart's gratitude in thanksgiving. He has blessed us with His mercies, and we should bless Him with our praises.

God's intention in bringing Israel out of Egypt was, as Stephen expresses it, that they might "*serve*" (worship) Him "in this place" (Acts 7:7). He brought them out of the house of bondage that they might live in the house of blessing. His loving-kindness to them was to be the motive of their living to Him. The apostle Paul recognizes the same thing when he says, in speaking of his relationship to the Lord: "Whose I am, and whom I *serve*" (Acts 27:23). Because Paul had been claimed by Christ, he consecrated himself to Him. "*Whose I am*" tells out what Christ had done for him for before he could be the Lord's, the Lord must pay the ransom price for him, even His own most precious blood. "*Whom I worship*" proclaims Paul's consequent gratitude, for when he speaks of service, he is not referring to the outward sweat of compulsory labour, which a slave would give his owner, but to the sweetness of inward gratitude which rises to God acceptably, for this is the service which God wants, as M'Cheyne says, "God gets more glory from an adoring look of a believer on a sick bed than from the outward labor of a whole day without it."

Our topic, in this aspect of it, is further illustrated in the three "*Blesseds*" of Ephesians 1:3; 2 Corinthians 1:3 and 1 Peter 1:3. The first blessed takes in the riches of our possessions, hence, our song of praise is, "*Blessed* be the God and Father of our Lord Jesus Christ, who has blessed us with every spiritual blessing in the heavenly places" (RSV). The second blessed refers to the present supply which is ministered to the believer, hence, our thanksgiving is, "*Blessed* be the God and Father of our Lord Jesus Christ, the Father of mercies and God of all comfort, who comforts us in all our affliction" (RSV). The third blessed bids us go up the steps of faith and look out of the window which Love has opened for it bids us view what God has in store for us. Peter's doxology is, "*Blessed* be the God and Father of our Lord Jesus Christ! By his great mercy we have been born again to a living hope through the resurrection of Jesus Christ from the dead, and to an inheritance which is imperishable, undefiled, and unfading . . ." (RSV).

In each of these blesseds, the anthem of worship is for something done, some blessing bestowed, or some promise of future recompense, thus demonstrating the point upon which we have been meditating, namely, that it is as we apprehend the down-coming of God's blessing to our enrichment and betterment, there is to be the up-rising of our grateful praise in loyal service to Him.

3. *How we should worship*. Three of the most important *how's* of the New Testament are, "Take heed *how* ye hear," as to our treatment of the Word of God; "*How* ye ought to walk," is the stimulating word, as to the care which should be exercised in our life; and"*How* ye ought to answer" is the restraintive injunction in the exhortation of the Spirit when He urges us to see that our speech is seasoned with the salt of grace (Luke 8:18; 1 Thessalonians 4:1; Colossians 4:6). Of equal importance is it that we should exercise care in worshipful service. We are not left in the dark as to how we should act in this matter. There are at least seven Scriptures as to how we should worship, found in association with the word *latreno*, rendered "*serve*" and "*worship*."

First, *Scripturally*. In speaking of the priests under the Levitical economy, the Holy Spirit says, "Who *serve* unto the example and shadow of heavenly things, as Moses was admonished of God when he was about to make the tabernacle:

for, see, saith He, that thou make all things according to the pattern shewed to thee in the mount" (Hebrews 8:5). Before the priests could serve in God's worship in the tabernacle, there were certain things which had to be done for them and which they had to do, according to the instructions given to Moses. They had to be washed with water, clothed in priestly garments, anointed with the sanctifying oil, identified with the consecrated offering, sanctified by the blood of separation, their hands filled with the wave-offering, and their garments sprinkled with the blood of atonement (Leviticus 8:6, 7, 12, 18, 23, 24, 27, 30).

All these things have their typical import in the priestly service of the believer. The body of our spiritual nature must be cleansed in the renewing laver of God's truth, for this is the *forerunner of worship* (Hebrews 10:22; Ephesians 5:26; Titus 3:5); the garments of the new man, which are the graces of the Holy Spirit, must adorn the life, for these are *accompaniments of worship* (Galatians 3:27; Ephesians 4:24; Colossians 3:10-12); the anointing of the Spirit's unction in the consecrating influence of His presence must be upon us, for this is the *power of worship* (1 John 2:20, 27; 2 Corinthians 1:22; Acts 6:38); the identification with Christ in His death, as severing from sin's servitude, self's mastery, and the world's contamination, is the *pre-requisite of worship* (Romans 6:11; 2 Corinthians 5:15; Galatians 2:20; 1:4); the separation to God by the blood of Christ is the *qualification of worship* (1 Peter 4:1; Hebrews 10:19; 13:12); and the appreciation of Christ's worth and merit, as the wave-offering of His triumphal gladness, is our *plea in worship* (Hebrews 13:15); and our hearts being sprinkled from an evil conscience is the *condition of worship* (Hebrews 10:22). These things are plainly set forth in the pattern of God's Word, and the observance of God's plan is always the securer of His power. Nothing is left to the false light of man's reason, but all true worship is regulated by the light which shines from the sanctuary of God's truth.

Second, *Reverently*. "Let us have grace, whereby we may *serve* God acceptably, with reverence and godly fear: for our God is a consuming fire" (Hebrews 12:28, 29). The strange fire of irreverence must not be in the censer of our worship. It is not without meaning that it is said of the seraph and his wings, "With twain he covered his face, and with twain he covered his feet, and with twain he did fly" (Isaiah 6:2). Four wings are passive and two are active. The holiness of Jehovah makes the seraph conscious of his unlikeness to the pure Being in whose service he is employed. That is why he bows in adoring humility before Him. The same is true of those who are in the right spirit as they are about the Lord's service. They utter His name reverently, as Abraham did when he called the angel "My Lord" (Genesis 18:3); they handle the truth of God carefully as Josiah did when he read to his people from the discovered book of the law, which led to their restoration (2 Kings 23:2, 3). They serve Him faithfully as did Elijah when he told Ahab his faults (1 Kings 18:18). The wings of loyal justice, and the wings of loving mercy, should ever be coupled with the wings of lowly service, for the very essence of vital godliness is "To do justly, and to love mercy, and to walk humbly with thy God" (Micah 6:8).

Third, *Purely*. In speaking of his service to God, the apostle Paul says, "Whom I *serve* from my forefathers with pure conscience" (2 Timothy 1:3). The French proverb says: "There is no pillow so soft as a clean conscience." When there is no stain of sin on the conscience, then the gladness of joy sings to its heart's content; and when no dust of impurity clouds the lens of the conscience, then the vision is clear enough to see God through the telescope of faith. To worship the Lord with a pure conscience is to have the sun of God's love to warm us in trial, His truth to arm us in conflict, His joy to gladden us in sorrow, His peace to calm us in trouble, His power to strengthen us in weakness, His grace to beautify our life, and His presence to embolden us in testimony.

Fourth, *Holily*. "*Serve* him . . . in holiness" (Luke 1:74, 75). Holiness is conformity to God's nature, and His nature is love. Therefore holiness is not a sentimental theory but a correspondence of action with God. It has been said, "He only is great of heart who floods the world with a great affection. He only is great of mind who stirs the world with great thoughts. He only is great of will who does something to shape the world to a great career. And he is greatest who does the most of all these things, and does them best." And may we not add, he is greater than the greatest who does these things, not because of the halo of glory which they cast around the doer, but because they bring blessing to others. God blesses because He delights to do so, irrespective of anything it may bring to Him. We are like Him when we love for love's sake—do good for good's sake—do right because it is the right thing to do.

Fifth, *Righteously*. "*Serve* him without fear, in . . . righteousness" (Luke 1:74, 75). Righteousness is conformity to God's law. In other words, righteousness is the art of doing right—giving to God His right and the same to man. Righteousness never takes advantage of another's ignorance, never represents an article to be what it is not, never condones a wrong action under the plea that the end justifies the means, never sells an inferor garment for all wool, but ever acts according to the straight rule of the Word of God. Righteousness, in practical sense, means the reproduction of the truth of God by being true in all our ways.

Sixth, *Prayerfully*. Of aged Anna it is said she "*served* God with fastings and prayers night and day" (Luke 2:37). Who can estimate the worth of prayer? It gives *grace to life*, as Mary of Bethany found as she sat at Jesus' feet (Luke 10:39). Prayer gives *grit in trial*, as Nehemiah experienced when persecuted by his enemies (Nehemiah 4:9). Prayer gives *guidance in difficulty* as Eliezer discovered when he was led to Rebekah in answer to his pleading (Genesis 24:12-15). Prayer gives *go to work*, as Paul's experience illustrates, for it was after it was said, "Behold he prayeth," we read "Straightway he preached Christ" (Acts 9:11, 20). Prayer gives *grip to testimony* as the disciples discovered when, after waiting upon God in prayer, they testified in power (Acts 4:31). Prayer gives *growth in grace*, as the apostle implies when he prayed that the faith of the saints in Thessalonica might be perfect (1 Thessalonians 3:10). Prayer gives *glow in worship*, as may be gathered when Paul and Silas were imprisoned, for we read, they "prayed and sang praises unto God" (Acts 26:25). Prayer leads on to praise.

Seventh, *Spiritually*. "*Worship* God in the Spirit" (Philippians 3:3). The Holy Spirit has aptly been called the Executive of the Godhead, for the possible attainments of the Christian life are His accomplishments. He is the *Sap* of the believer's life for He is called "the Spirit of Life" (Romans 8:2); He is the *Seal* of the saint's assurance for He is God's mark upon us that we are Christ's (Ephesians 4:30); He is the *Strength* of the sufferer's endurance for He is the Spirit of Glory to cheer those who are suffering for the sake of Christ (1 Peter 4:14); He is the *Source* of the worker's power for apart from the Spirit of God we have no might (Acts 1:8); He is the *Spring* of the pilgrim's joy for it is through Him that we can sing psalms and hymns and spiritual songs (Ephesians 5:18, 19); He is the *Secret* of the disciple's knowledge for all we know of Divine things is through His instruction (2 Corinthians 2:10); and He is the *Soul* of the worshipper's adoration for it is only through Him that we can approach God in a manner which is acceptable (Ephesians 2:18). Since these things are so, how important that we should keep in touch with the Spirit. It is only as we are in the current of His will that we are in the place of His power.

From what has been said, it will be seen that worship is not confined to attendance at a so-called "place of worship," but that it involves the whole of the believer's life. Principal Moule has tersely summed up the subject: "We worship—ours is a hallowed, dedicated, and reverent life. It is spent in a sanctuary. Whatever we have to be, or to do, as to externals; whether to rule a province, a church, a school, a home; whether to keep accounts, or sweep a room; whether to evangelize the slums of a city, or the dark places of heathenism, or to teach language, or science, or music; whether to be active all day long, or to lie alone to suffer; whatever be our actual place and duty in the world, we worship. 'We have set Thee always before us.' We have 'sanctified the Christ as Lord in our hearts.' We belong to Him everywhere, and we recollect it. Let us reiterate the fact; ours is a hallowed life, for it belongs to a Divine Master; it is a reverent life, for that Master in His greatness is to us an abiding presence. The fact of Him, the thought of Him, has expelled from our lives the secular air, and the light and flippant spirit. We are nothing if not worshippers."

24

The Discipler's Weakness

There is one thing for which we are all crying to the Lord continually—and that is, more power. May I say, we do not need more power. Rather, we need to be in such a condition of soul that we may realize and utilize the power we have. The Lord had distinctly given the disciples power to cast out devils and yet we find that the disciples could not cast them out. This was because of their unbelief. They had the authority and the power to cast out demons but they were not in the right condition of soul for God to use them. So often this is the case with us as workers for Christ (compare Luke 9:1, 2; and 37-41).

Thus we need to be in the right condition of soul, that the power of Christ may rest upon us. The one condition necessary to realize the power of God is *weakness*. If we have any strength of our own, if we think we have any ability of our own, we will surely fail. Let us remember 2 Corinthians 12:9. Three times Paul prayed to the Lord that the thorn in his flesh might be taken away; but the Lord said, "My grace is sufficient for thee: for my strength [or as the Revised Standard Version puts it, 'for my power'] is made perfect in weakness. Most gladly therefore will I rather glory in my infirmities, that the power of Christ may rest upon me."

There are two words rendered *power* in the New Testament, one meaning *authority*, and the other meaning *ability*. The first is found in John 1:12, "As many as received him, to them gave he power [authority] to become the sons of God." In speaking of Himself, the Lord Jesus Christ says, "The Son of man hath authority on earth to forgive sins"; and "All power [authority] is given unto me in heaven and in earth." It is one thing for a policeman to have the *authority* to apprehend a person, but it is another thing for him to have the *strength* to do it. There may be forces coming in between him and the person so that he is hindered from doing what he is commissioned to do. We find the two words occurring together in Luke 4:36: "And they were all amazed"—when they saw Christ casting out the demons—"and spake among themselves, saying, What a word is this! for with *authority* and *power* he commandeth the unclean spirits, and they come out."

The Lord Jesus Christ had not only the *authority* but He had the *ability*. If we are in the right condition of soul, we not only have the authority to overcome sin, and go forth in work for the Master, but we have the ability. As Ralph Erskine says, "All God's biddings are His enablings." Or, as Augustine prayed, "Give what Thou dost command, and then command what Thou wilt." When He tells us to do a thing He gives us the power to do it. As workers we want power to go forth and testify for the Lord—power with men, power to be used of God. The only thing then for us is to be weak enough and low enough, for God Himself to take us up and use us. His power must rest upon us that He Himself may be glorified in us.

There are five things mentioned in 1 Corinthians 1:27, 28, which God uses as instruments in His service to accomplish His purpose. It is not insignificant there are *five*, for the number five as found in association with man is symbolical of weakness. But when it is found in connection with God the number five is typical of grace. These two thoughts are generally found together when this numeral is used. When God in His grace brought Israel out of Egypt, they came out "*five* in a rank" (Exodus 13:18, margin). God's promise to Israel was, "*Five* of you shall chase an hundred" (Leviticus 26:8), in speaking of their victories over their enemies. When David in his weakness went against Goliath in the power of God, he only took "*five* smooth stones" (1 Samuel 17:40). When Christ fed the five thousand, He did it with "*five* loaves" and "two small fishes" (John 6:9). There might be many other illustrations given, but the above will suffice to show that God uses the weak and insignificant things. If we get into the lowest place we are on the way to the highest. Many years ago an old Methodist at Brighton used to pray a prayer we could not for some time understand. It was, "Help us to deeper sink, that we may higher rise." We said then, "Whatever does he mean?" But we think we have learned that he meant the deeper he sank in his own estimation, and lost sight of himself, the higher he would rise. And the more God Himself would be able to use him. Let us look at the five classes of workers the Lord uses in His service.

God Uses Foolish Things

"God hath chosen the foolish things of the world to confound the wise." The word "foolish" means a simpleton. God can use a simpleton to confound the wise, or to put them to shame, as the sentence might be rendered. The same expression is found in Luke 13:17, where we read that Christ's adversaries were ashamed. I remember being some years ago in the little village of Bidford, near Stratford-on-Avon. A young fellow there, who is now a local preacher, was brought to the Lord during the meetings. Before his conversion he was very ignorant. His aunt said to him one day—

"Charlie, find out who 'whosoever' is."

He went to work, but puzzled his brain about it all day. When he got home his aunt said, "Have you found out who 'whosoever' is?"

"No," he replied.

"Why, of course it is you," she said.

A day or two after he was converted, he was working in a field: the devil came to him and began to tempt him. He fell upon his knees and prayed to the Lord. He did not know that some of his mates were watching him. When he got up from his knees they said, "Charlie, you are half a fool."

He was very much discouraged at this. The same night he walked over to a meeting we were holding four miles from that place. The subject happened to be "The Fool." I said there were two kinds of fools mentioned in God's Word: first, "those who allow the devil to cheat them out of all Christ is willing to give them; and second, those who are willing to be fools and despised for Christ's sake, that God Himself may be glorified."

The young man went back to the village, and the next day met his mates, and said to them, "You called me half a fool yesterday; by God's grace I intend to be a whole fool for Christ."

We want to be "whole fools" for Christ in that sense—fools enough to follow Him, to do as He tells us, to be completely sold out to Him.

The people of Jericho must have thought the children of Israel fools as they were marching around Jericho blowing the rams' horns. Can we not imagine them, saying, "Do they think they will pull down the walls of this strong city by blowing rams' horns"? They forgot that God was at His people's back, and, to their surprise, they found the walls did come down through the blowing of those rams' horns.

The late Dr. S.D. Gordon once related how a gentleman held a baby, while its mother was in the inquiry room. How foolish the man must have looked as he tried to quiet the child. But he was amply rewarded, for the mother was brought to Christ. Dr. Gordon says of it, "I think a special blessing rested upon that work, for not only was the mother saved, but that little girl came to Christ when she was twelve years old. And I haven't a more aggressive Christian than that baby has grown to be."

God Uses Weak Things

The meaning of the word "*weak*," is sickly, feeble, impotent, strengthless. It is used of the "*impotent* man at the beautiful gate" (Acts 4:9); of Paul's bodily infirmity when he says he "is *weak*" (2 Corinthians 12:10); of the "*sick*" Epaphroditus (Philippians 2:27); of the "*sickly*" Corinthians (1 Corinthians 11:30); and of the state of the sinner when he is described as being "*without strength*" (Romans 5:6). "God hath chosen the weak things of the world, to confound the things which are mighty." We not only need to be fools, but *weak*. When the Lord told Gideon to go against the Midianites, at first he had 32,000 men. "The Lord said unto Gideon, The people that are with thee are too many for me to give the Midianites into their hands, lest Israel vaunt themselves against me, saying, mine own hand hath saved me" (Judges 7:2). Then the Lord thinned the men out to 10,000, and so on until there were only 300. Then, He practically says, "Yes, that will do. Now, I have all the men who are whole-hearted, those who are willing to be used by Me, and give all the glory to Me." Away they went; the Lord used them, and got glory by doing so. We want to be like them—to lay ourselves down at the Master's feet that He may take us up and He Himself get glory by us.

God Uses Base Things

Yes, He not only uses weak things, but *base things*, that is, ignoble ones, those who have no social standing. Have you noticed the "base things" that God used

(Matthew 1) in connection with the genealogy of the Lord Jesus Christ? Of the four women mentioned, one played the harlot (Tamar), another was a Gentile (Ruth), another was an adulteress (wife of Urias), and the fourth a harlot (Rahab); yet God used these base things to accomplish His purpose. If He wishes, God can use Satan himself for His glory. In 2 Timothy 2:26 it is plainly stated, if we take the marginal reading of the Revised Version, for it says, "taken captive by the devil unto the will of God."

God Uses Despised Things

"Things which are despised hath God chosen." The word *"despised"* means contemptible. In speaking of Christ being mocked by Herod and his men of war it is rendered *"set at nought"* (Luke 23:11). Paul uses the same word when he refers to what the Corinthians might say of his speech as being *"contemptible"* (2 Corinthians 10:10). When David went against Goliath he was despised in his eyes, for when the giant saw him, "he disdained him" (1 Samuel 17:42); but David replied, "I am come against you in the name of the Lord, and the Lord will deliver you into my hands today." Though David was despised, God used him for His own glory. The Lord Jesus Himself was despised and rejected of men, but what wonders God has accomplished through Him! We are therefore in good company when we, too, are despised.

God Uses Things That Are Not

These also He has chosen for His service. "What is that in thine hand, Moses?" Only a rod; yet trace the history of that rod and see what God accomplished by it. O if we are just willing to be low at the Master's feet, the Lord Himself will use us. Let us ask, Is there anything between our souls and God—anything that hinders God from using us, anything that hinders the life of Christ from being manifested through us, any doubtful thing? How often we hear Christians say, "I do not think there is any harm in this or that!" Well, it may be there is no harm in it; but remember, "Whatsoever is not of faith is sin." That is the standard for us to go by. "He that doubteth is condemned." If we are satisfied with Christ, we will not want any of these second-hand things. Christ not only saves and sanctifies, but He satisfies the heart.

Does Christ satisfy? Of course, if we are going after worldly pleasures, it shows we are not satisfied with Christ. Only recently I heard of one Christian who said to another, "Why, you are going to meetings again; you are always going to meetings." The Christian who is in communion with Christ loves to meet with those who love Him. Are we satisfied with Him? Let us be very practical. If Christ Himself satisfies us, we will not want to compromise, and make bargains with the world. The Lord Jesus will fill every nook of our hearts. We will be ready to do anything He wishes, if His love fills our hearts. It will thrust us forth. With the apostle Paul we will say, "The love of Christ constraineth us, and we must tell others of it."

25

The Discipler's Growth

In the spring-time we have watched the new life of the tree manifesting itself in the buds and blossoms it has put forth. As we have done so, we have been reminded of the power within the tree. Sometimes we have noticed a few of the old leaves remaining, but the power of the fresh life soon throws them off. And we have also noticed those who have had evil habits—like old leaves—clinging to them, but who, by the power of the new life growing in them, have thrown off these evil habits. The leaves of a simple confession of Christ and the fruits of the Spirit have been seen instead.

There are five thoughts suggested by the subject of growth in the Divine life.

1. Growth implies life. 2. Growth implies progress. 3. The things in which we are to grow. 4. How to grow. 5. What we are to grow like.

Growth Implies Life

A friend was preaching in the open air in Scotland upon the subject of grace. He was accosted after he finished by a man who said that his minister had been preaching upon that subject and *that he was trying to grow into grace*. The evangelist pointed to a tree by the roadside and asked him if the tree grew *into* that place, or if it was planted there, and then grew where it was planted?

"Why, of course it was first planted in the place, and then grew where it was planted."

"And so," said the evangelist, "you must first be planted in grace before you can grow in grace. There is no such thing as working for grace and life, or growing *into* grace; but being saved by grace, we are to grow in grace." We who are believers in Christ rejoice in three blessed facts:

1. *We are saved by grace*. It was not anything we were, had done, could do, or promised to do; it was wholly and entirely of God's free unmerited favor that He saved us.

2. *We are now brought into a new standing*. We no longer stand upon our own dignity, or in the old Adam, but our standing is in Christ; it is no longer a question of what we are, but of what *He* is, and what He has done for us.

3. *We are born again.* That is, we have a new life, a new principle, a new nature. We find that now there is a principle at work within us which is opposed to the flesh, or the evil principle we have naturally. Up to the time we were born again, we followed that old nature.

We have an illustration of this in the case of Ishmael and Isaac. Until Isaac was born, Ishmael had it all his own way; but when Isaac was weaned, Ishmael was found mocking Isaac (Genesis 21:8, 9), and because of this Ishmael was cast out. The apostle takes up this as an illustration of the two natures: "Now we, brethren, as Isaac was, are the children of promise. But as then he that was born after the flesh persecuted him that was born after the Spirit, even so it is now" (Galatians 4:28, 29).

There are many Christians who say, "Why, I never had this conflict before I was born again. Now it is a continual conflict. Not only that, but I find that this evil nature or principle within me is stronger than the new nature or principle; in fact, my experience is described in the words of Paul, 'For the good which I would I do not: but the evil which I would not, that I practice'" (Romans 7:19 RSV) We know this is often the experience of Christians; but it is not proper Christian experience. The man in Romans 7 mentions himself forty-one times (see the pronouns "I," "me," and "my"), and the Lord Jesus only once: no wonder he got into bondage. Afterwards, in Romans 8, he sees the One who is to give him the power, namely, the Holy Spirit, who is to enable him to follow the desires of the new nature.

Many Christians, when they wake up to this fact—that by the power of the Holy Spirit they may have continual victory over the flesh—say they have received the second blessing. As to point of *experience*, it may be so; but as to actual *fact*, it was theirs as soon as they believed; and it was through ignorance and unbelief that they did not live in the power of the Holy Spirit. We remember hearing a quaint old man once saying, "Praise the Lord! when He saved me He made a clean job of it." And that is so. What we want to do is to live in the power of that cleansing by faith.

Recently, passing by a shop that was shut up, we noticed a placard stating, that in a few days it would be opened "under entirely new management." It is for us to remember that when we believed in Christ, we came under entirely new management—that is, under the management of the Holy Spirit. And remember this also, the evil principle within is not cast out (cast off as to its *power*, but not as to its *presence)*; for although Ishmael was cast out of the house, he was still in the land, and the seed of Ishmael was ever a source of annoyance to the seed of Isaac (Psalm 83:5, 6) even till the present day. What we have to do is to follow the new nature and not the old: "For they that are after the flesh do mind the things of the flesh but they that are after the spirit" (new nature), "the things of the spirit" (new nature). "For the mind of the flesh is death; but the mind of the spirit (new nature) "is life and peace . . . But ye are not in the flesh, but in the spirit" (new nature), "if . . . the Spirit of God dwelleth in you" (Romans 8:5-9, RV.)

Growth Implies Progress

In Genesis 2:9 we read that God made every tree to grow; and we know that God's purpose in saving us by His grace is that we should *grow in grace.*

We have four illustrations of growth or progress in the New Testament—1. The corn; 2. The plant; 3. The child; 4. The building.

1. *The corn.* "The kingdom of God is as if a man should cast seed into the ground; and should sleep, and rise night and day, and the seed should spring and grow up, he knoweth not how. For the earth bringeth forth fruit of herself; first the blade, then the ear, after that the full corn in the ear" (Mark 4:26-28). And in springtime we have repeatedly seen this. As in nature, so in grace; there is the *seed* of the new life implanted by the Word and Spirit, then the *blade* of confession of Christ and love to the brethren, then the *stalk* of upright conduct, then the ear of fruit-bearing, and the *full corn* in the ear of usefulness, communion, and joy.

2. *Plant growth.* There are four things necessary for a plant to grow. First, it must have a *good soil;* and we must be "rooted and grounded in love" if we are to grow in grace (Ephesians 3:17). Second, a plant must be in a good *atmosphere;* and if we are to grow, we must be separate from the world and be meditating in the Word of God. Then we shall be "like a tree planted by the rivers of water, that bringeth forth his fruit in his season" (Psalm 1:3). Third, a plant must have *sun,* or else it will be sickly; and we must be not only "rooted," but "built up" in Christ (Colossians 2:7) and "grow up into him in all things" (Ephesians 4:15). Fourth, a plant must have *water;* and we must have Him of whom water is an emblem, namely, the Holy Spirit, for it is only as we feed on the Word by the power of the Spirit that we grow in grace.

3. *Child growth.* There are four stages given us in the Word: *Babes:* those who are born into God's family; and as such, they need "the sincere milk of the Word, that they may grow thereby" (1 Peter 2:2). There are two things a mother wants for her baby, and these are sleep and food; and there are two things a babe in Christ wants—rest of conscience through faith in the perfect sacrifice of Christ, and to be feeding continually upon the sincere milk of the Word.

Children: those who not only know that they are born into the family, but who are rejoicing in the blessings Christ gives and whose sins are forgiven for His name's sake (1 John 2:12).

Young Men: those in whom the Word of God is abiding, and who have victory thereby, over the wicked one (1 John 2:13).

Fathers: those who have personal dealings with Christ, who not only rejoice in the blessings He gives, but who rejoice in the person of Christ and have fellowship with Him. Here we see progress.

4. *Building growth* (Ephesians 2:21). We have watched a house being built: we have seen the foundation laid, and then, brick by brick, or stone by stone, the building has gone on until it is finished. Peter seems to have this idea when speaking of adding to our faith, virtue or courage, knowledge, temperance or self-control, patience, godliness, brotherly kindness, and love (2 Peter 1:5-8). In fact, we might call this the progress of faith, for—

What is virtue or courage but faith undaunted?
What is knowledge but faith apprehending?

What is temperance but faith overcoming?
What is patience but faith untiring?
What is godliness but faith imitating?
What is brotherly kindness but faith in practice?
What is love but faith at work?

Thus, Peter says, "if these things be in us, and abound, they make us that we shall neither be barren nor unfruitful in the knowledge of our Lord Jesus Christ" (2 Peter 1:8).

The Things in Which We Are to Grow

1. *In grace*. It is not "grow in *graces*," although as we will see, we are to grow in them. It is growth in *grace*. We love to think that it is ever Christ Himself who is presented to us in the Word, not a set of doctrines only, or a mere system of theology, but a living Person. We are to be growing up in *Him*. There are three points we would notice: first, the *downward* growth in the Word; second, the *upward* growth in Christ; and third, the *outward* growth in blessing to others.

First, *the downward growth in the Word*. When we were in Galloway some years since, during a terrific storm in which thousands and thousands of fir-trees were blown down, we particularly noticed one plantation because not a single fir-tree was left standing. Here and there, however, we noticed a beech tree. What was the real cause of this? The fir-tree shoots its roots along the surface of the ground, while the beech-tree shoots its roots deeply downward.

In the parable of the sower, the Master tells us that those hearers who are compared to the stony ground have *no root* in themselves; they hear and receive the Word with joy, but in the time of temptation fall away. Again and again we have we seen this; many who received the Word with joy—and seemed to have been truly born again—have in the time of temptation fallen away. Like Simon Magus, they have made profession, but there has been no real evidence of the Spirit working in their lives (see Acts 8). The new life is not merely hearing the Word, and saying "Hallelujah!" What it is we see in the different accounts of the parable of the sower: in Matthew, it is *hearing* and *understanding* the Word; in Mark, *hearing* and *receiving* the Word; in Luke, *hearing*, *keeping*, and *doing* the Word. Notice these four steps.

Hearing and understanding the Word. Understanding what it says about ourselves, the utter worthlessness, badness, and helplessness of the flesh, so that we may abhor it, and put no confidence in it; understanding the all-sufficiency of the work of Christ to satisfy the claims of God and to give perfect rest to our conscience; understanding the all-satisfying glories of Christ, to fully satisfy our hearts; understanding the purpose of God in saving us that we should be "holy and without blame before Him in love"; understanding the almightiness, the all-sufficiency of Christ that we might fully trust Him.

Hearing and receiving the Word. Receiving it honestly that we may bring forth fruit; receiving it in simplicity that we may be blessed; receiving it as food that we may be strengthened; receiving it joyfully that we may be gladdened; receiving it wholly that we may judge our walk, thoughts, and actions; yes, our whole life by it.

Hearing and keeping the Word. Keeping it as a treasure, securely; as a light, carefully; as water, to cleanse; as food, to support; as a fire, to warm; as a sword, to kill every evil thing; as honey, to sweeten. Keeping the Word and yet being kept by it; in a word, hiding it in our heart that we sin not against our heavenly Father.

Hearing and doing the Word. Doing it cheerfully as obedient children; doing it lovingly as saved sinners; doing it wisely as skilled ambassadors; doing it constantly as true witnesses; doing it thoroughly as faithful servants; doing it carefully as good stewards; doing it always, at all times and under all circumstances; thus shall we be growing downward, rooted and grounded in Him, established in the faith.

Second. *The upward growth in Christ.* To illustrate the truth of growing up in Christ, we will take the two names, "*Christ Jesus,*" as we find them in the third and fourth chapters of Philippians. Remember, they never occur together in the Gospels, and are peculiar to Paul's epistles, thus reminding us that it is with an exalted, living, anointed Savior, we have to do.

Growing in our boasting in Him. "We are the circumcision, who worship by the Spirit of God, and *glory* in CHRIST JESUS, and have no confidence in the flesh" (Philippians 3:3, R.V.) The word "rejoice" in the A.V. is translated "glory" in the R.V. We dare not glory or boast in ourselves or our attainments, for we know that in our flesh dwells no good thing; even as Fletcher of Madeley once said in writing to a friend, "I compare myself to Lazarus, with this difference, Lazarus' sores were all outside, but mine are all *inside*."

If there is anything good or Christlike manifested in our life, it is not us, but the grace of God that is the cause of it. And how is it that we are thus enabled to boast or rejoice in the Lord? The whole secret is in the above verse. We find there that we are separated to the Lord—cut off from the world—and with Paul we say, "Far be it from me to glory, save in the cross of our Lord Jesus Christ, through which the world hath been crucified unto me, and I unto the world" (Galatians 6:14). We find, too, that we are enabled to worship God by the Spirit, not needing earthly or outside help. And also, as a consequence on the one hand we dare not trust or put any confidence in the flesh; and on the other hand, we are entitled only to glory, to boast in the Lord, not in one another, not in our own gifts, not in our attainments, nor in anything of man. Like the Psalmist, we make our boast in the Lord, and we grow in our boastings, *in*, *of*, and *for* Him.

Growing in our knowledge of Him. "I count all things but loss for the excellency of the *knowledge* of Christ Jesus my Lord" (Philippians 3:8). What marvels His grace has done for us! Think of His electing, seeking, finding, pardoning, justifying, keeping, preserving, helping, sustaining, bearing, and uniting grace. Think of what He has done, is doing, and will yet do. Think of the blessings He has given, is giving, and has yet promised to give; but let your eyes look higher still—look not only to the blessings but to the *Blesser*.

When Ruth lay at the feet of Boaz, she received six measures of corn: that certainly was more than she got when gleaning in the field, although then she had the "handfuls of purpose"; but when she was married to Boaz then all the corn in his granaries belonged to her because she belonged to him. But do you think she was thinking of her riches? No; her *one* object and thought was Boaz *himself*. And do not let us be taken up with the blessings that we have in Christ, but rather let us be taken up with Him who purchased them at such a cost—the shedding of His life's blood.

O to know Him; His sufferings for us; His love to us; His power to keep us! To know Him as our Strength to uphold us; as our Peace to rule us; as our Joy to fill us! To know Him in all the sufferings of His death; in all the power of His resurrection; in all the glory of His Person; in all the all-sufficiency of the offices and relationships He holds *to*, and *for* us; in all the abundance of His grace and the love of His heart.

Growing in our apprehension of Him. "That I may apprehend that for which also I was apprehended by Christ Jesus" (Philippians 3:12, R.V.) There are two thoughts here: first, a fact stated—"I was apprehended by Christ Jesus"; and second, Paul's desire to know the reason why. It is very helpful to notice that God's purpose in whatever truth we take up is that we should be holy. If we look at the death of Christ, we find that He died that we should live to Him. If we look at the resurrection of Christ, it is that we may know its power and walk in newness of life. If we look at the blood of Christ, we find that the same blood (which is the basis of everything) has also separated us to God from the world. If we look at the cross of Christ, we find we are also to take up our cross and follow Him. If we look at the sufferings of Christ, we are also to suffer for and with Him. If we look at the exaltation of Christ, it is that we should be taken up with, and look to Him. If we look at God's predestinating us, it is that we should be conformed to the image of His Son. If we look at God's electing grace, it is that we should be holy.

We rejoice that we have peace with God. Don't stop there, but go on to enjoy the peace of God. We shall enjoy it as we are careful for nothing, prayerful in everything, and thankful for anything. We rejoice that we are saved; then let us work out our own salvation with fear and trembling. We rejoice that we have been called with a high and holy calling; then let us walk worthy of it. We rejoice that we are kept by the power of God; then let us keep ourselves from idols and in the love of God. We rejoice that we have eternal life; then let us lay hold on eternal life. We rejoice that the Holy Spirit lives in us; then let us live in the Spirit. We rejoice because of our union in and with Christ; then let the life of Christ be seen in our life. We rejoice that we are made nigh by the blood; then let us continually draw near to God. We rejoice that we are accepted in the Beloved; then let us labor to be acceptable, or well-pleasing, to Him as servants. We rejoice that we shall not come into judgment; then let us continually judge ourselves by the Word of God. We rejoice that the blood of Jesus Christ, God's Son, cleanses us from all sin; then let us cleanse ourselves from all filthiness of the flesh and the spirit, perfecting holiness in the fear of the Lord. We rejoice that the Father loves us as much as He loves His Son; then let us love Him with all our heart.

O that we, indeed, knowing Christ has laid hold of us, may lay hold of Him; lay hold of His wisdom, power, and love; in a word—Himself!

Growing in Him and seeing His calling. "I press on toward the goal for the prize of the upward call of God in Christ Jesus" (Philippians 3:14 RSV).

In Ephesians we read of "the hope of His calling" (1:18), and "the hope of our calling" (4:4). The hope of His calling is the joy of Christ's own heart, in our sharing His own glory with Him. We are too apt to be taken up with our thoughts of Christ, instead of His thoughts to and of us. He will never be satisfied till we are with Him; and we shall never be satisfied till we awake in His likeness. This latter is the "hope of our calling." But the thought in Philippians 3:14 is this: Paul wanted not only to know Christ's delight in him, but he also wanted to delight in Christ that when He returned he might hear the Master's "Well done, good and faithful servant." He wanted to be well-pleasing to Him as a servant, which we must all acknowledge is the highest goal we can or want to reach.

Growing in Him and seeing His keeping power. "Have no anxiety about anything, but in everything by prayer and supplication with thanksgiving let your requests be made known to God. And the peace of God, which passes all understanding, will keep your hearts and your minds in Christ Jesus" (Philippians 4:6, 7 RSV).

"Consider the lilies how they grow; they toil not, neither do they spin." Many Christians make a great mistake in relation to growth in grace. Instead of trusting the Lord, they are worrying and looking to themselves, to see if they are growing. There will be no progress all the while they are doing that. A boy does not try to grow—he eats, sleeps, works, and exercises; all the while he is growing and ministering to his growth by so doing, although he himself is unconscious of it. If we would have a knowledge of Christ's keeping power, there must be on our part, a *perfect trust* in His *perfect keeping* power, and as a natural consequence, we shall enjoy *perfect peace*. As an old man once said, "I do the *trusting*, and He does the *keeping*."

A little servant girl was one day asked by a lady whether she knew Christ as her Savior, and she answered, "Yes." The lady then went on to tell her, it was her privilege to take all her troubles and trials to Christ, and she replied:

"I do so; and more than that, I *leave* them with Him, when I do take them."

Instead of doing this, we are too apt to be like the man who was walking along a country road carrying a heavy pack upon his back. When a horse and cart came along he asked the driver for a lift. But when the man got up into the cart, he did not take the pack off his back but continued to carry it. Presently the driver said:

"My friend, won't you put your pack down into the cart?"

"No, thank you," said the man, "you have been so kind as to give me a lift, I will not trouble you with my pack."

We smile at the foolish man, but are we not very often like him? We carry a pack of doubts and fears, a pack of trouble and care, when all the time the Lord is saying, "Roll your *burden* on Me; roll *yourself* on Me; roll your *way* on Me; roll your *works* on Me."

O that we may commit ourselves unreservedly into the hands of the Lord! like the Scotch lad, who, when he was asked if he had a soul, said, "No."

"What do you mean?" asked the minister; and he began to speak against heretical notions, thinking the lad was an unbeliever. Then the lad said:

"I did have a soul till the other day, but I gave it to the Lord Jesus, and now He has it."

Growing in Him and having all supplied. "My God will supply every need of yours according to his riches in glory in Christ Jesus" (Philippians 4:19 RSV). God does not promise to give us all we *want*, but He does promise to supply all our *need*. If a child wants a knife, the parent does not give it because the child would cut himself; and sometimes we ask the Lord for knives, and He does not give them to us because we should do ourselves harm. He will supply all our temporal need, and also all our spiritual need; and notice, the measure or standard of blessing is not according to our need, or asking, but "according to his riches in glory in Christ Jesus."

Growing in Him, and seeing our standing in Him, and our relationship one to another. "Greet every saint in Christ Jesus" (Philippians 4:21 RSV). God already sees us in heaven, in the person of His Son; but there is another side we are apt to forget, and that is this: all believers in Christ have the same standing, and we should recognize, not only our oneness in Him, but also our oneness with each other, and act accordingly. What bickering and jealousy, believers would be saved from, if they recognized that the success or failure of others was their own, for we are members one of another. Thus the success of one is the success of all and *vice versa.*

Third. *Outward growth in blessing to others.* If we look up the following Scriptures in connection with the word "*abounding,*" we will see how we may grow outwardly, in blessing to others:

Abounding in *fruit-bearing* (Philippians 4:17) that others may see the evidence of life in us.

Abounding in *love* (Philippians 1:9) that others may see the truth of the Master's words, "By this shall all men know that ye are my disciples if ye love one another."

Abounding in *contentment* (Philippians 4:12, 18) that others may see the spirit of the Master manifested by us.

Abounding in *thanksgiving* (Colossians 2:7) that others may glorify God on our behalf as they see His grace in us.

Abounding in *ministering to the need of others* (2 Corinthians 8:7, 8) that others may see that we love, not only in word but in deed.

Abounding in *suffering for* and *with* Christ (2 Corinthians 1:5) that others may see the patience and love of Christ manifested by us.

Abounding in *work for* and *with* Christ (1 Corinthians 15:58) that others may be blessed.

It is to the last we confine ourselves here. "Therefore, my beloved brethren, be ye steadfast, unmovable, always abounding in the work of the Lord, forasmuch as ye know that your labor is not in vain in the Lord"; in this verse we briefly notice seven things.

First. A *plea for steadfastness.* Do we not find the plea, the reason for steadfastness, as expressed in the word "therefore," for it brings before us the truths enumerated in 1 Corinthians 15, for in it we see the death of Christ, His resurrection, His glorious victory over death, His coming glory which we shall share with Him, the first fruits which He has become, and the certainty that we shall triumph over all our foes. As we see these things we will be steadfast in our *adherence* to Christ (Ruth 1:18); steadfast in our *hearts'* allegiance to Him (1

Corinthians 7:37); steadfast in holding fast our confidence in Him (Hebrews 3:14); steadfast in *looking for* Him (Acts 1:10); steadfast in *looking to* Him (Acts 7:55); steadfast in our *faith in* Him (Colossians 2:5); steadfast in our *resistance of* Satan with the Word (1 Peter 5:9); steadfast in *growing* in grace (2 Peter 3:17); and steadfast in our *work for* Christ (1 Corinthians 15:58).

Second. A *firm stand—"unmovable."* We stand on resurrection ground, keeping our position, because we are kept by the power of God through *faith*.

Third. A *persevering heart—"always abounding."* We are not to be working by fits and starts, but in prayerful, believing, loving, and persevering effort, and also abounding therein.

Fourth. *An important reminder—"in the work of the Lord."* We are to see that our work is *in* the Lord, *for* the Lord, and *with* the Lord; not for the glory of self, or to bring honor to any party.

Fifth. A *blessed assurance*—"forasmuch as *ye know* . . ." Whatever we do for Him does not escape His notice, and although it is only a cup of cold water, it will not lose its reward.

Sixth. *An encouragement—"labor."* It is not play, but hard work, and yet easy, because it is with Him who loved us and gave Himself for us.

Seventh. A *sure reward—"not in vain."* Working for Christ on such lines, in such a manner, and with such ends, it can never miss its reward. Thus seeking to be used by the Lord in blessing to others, we ourselves shall be growing in grace and become more Christlike, for it is said of Him that "He went about doing good."

2. *Grow in knowledge*. Mere head knowledge puffs up, but holding the truth in love builds up; and if we remember that the object of all true knowledge is that we become more Christlike, the more knowledge the better.

Growing in the knowledge of *God*, as we walk worthy of the Lord, we will be fruitful in every good work (Colossians 1:10).

Growing in the knowledge of *Christ*, we will become like Him in fellowship with Him (Matthew 11:29).

Growing in the knowledge of *His will*, by doing it (Colossians 1:9), we will be initiated into His secrets.

Growing in the knowledge of *His love*, in communion with Him (Ephesians 3:19), we will be satisfied in Him.

Growing in the knowledge of *His power*, by trusting Him (Philippians 3:10), we will be equipped for all that comes.

Growing in the knowledge of *His glory*, by looking to Him (2 Corinthians 4:6), we will live in the power of the world to come.

Growing in the knowledge of *His purpose*, as we are taught by the Spirit through the Word (John 16:13), we will know His mind and have fellowship with Him in consequence.

3. *Grow in love*. In 1 Corinthians 13 we have described what the character of true love is, and what it does. Let our love grow in *firmness*—"rooted and grounded in love"; let it grow in *extent*—"abounding in love"; let it grow in *intensity*—"constrained by the love of Christ"; let it grow *practically*—"love not in word, but in deed and in truth."

4. *Grow in humility.* Notice Paul's growth in humility: at first we find him saying, "I am the *least* of the apostles" (1 Corinthians 15:9); then, five years afterwards, I "am *less* than the *least* of all saints" (Ephesians 3:8); and just before he finished his course, "I am the *chief of sinners*" (1 Timothy 1:15). Yes, lower than this was he, for in writing to the Corinthians he said, "Though I be *nothing*" (2 Corinthians 12:11). Let us remember that while we seek to grow in humility, we must never be proud of it. Those who are most humble are most unconscious of it themselves.

5. *Grow in faith* (2 Thessalonians 1:3). Let our faith grow in *passiveness* by resting only in the Lord; let it grow in *firmness* by believing all the Word of God; let it grow in *dependence* by trusting everything to the Lord; let it grow in *constancy* by always looking to Him: let it grow in *simplicity* by receiving everything from Him; let it grow in *activity* that others may be blessed; let it grow in *extent*—never be satisfied, go on from faith to *faith*, from strength to *strength*, from grace to *grace*, from peace to *peace*, from joy to *joy*, from glory to *glory*, shining more and more unto the perfect day.

How to Grow

If a gardener wishes his standard rose trees to grow, there are two things he must do. First, he must keep down, or rather cut off, the suckers of the brier, and in the next place, he must cultivate the rose. And so with us. The answer to the question, "How am I to grow?" is, "Keep down the old nature; put off the old man with his deeds; and minister to, and cultivate the new nature"; or rather, as the Holy Spirit puts it, "Laying aside all malice, and all guile, and hypocrisies, and envies, and all evil speakings, as new born babes, desire the sincere milk of the Word, that ye may grow thereby" (1 Peter 2:1, 2).

There are three things essential to growth—*liberty*, *food*, and *exercise*—and these three things we have illustrated in the three persons whom Christ raised from the dead.

1 *Liberty.* When Lazarus came forth from the grave at the Lord's command, we read that he was "bound hand and foot," and a napkin was over his face; he had life, but not *liberty*. There are many Christians in the same condition spiritually; they have life but not liberty. Their hands are bound by laziness or fear for they seldom do any work for Christ; their feet are bound by worldliness and self-will; they are not running the way of the Lord's commandments; and there is the napkin of doubt and a conscience burdened by failure and backsliding, which obscures their vision of the Lord. This ought not to be; it is our privilege to stand and rejoice in the liberty wherewith the Lord has made us free, and not be entangled in the bondage of law, self, or the world.

2. *Food.* After Christ had raised the ruler's daughter from the dead, the first thing that He said was, "Give her something to eat." We who are brought from death unto life can praise God for the great love He has for us, that He has quickened us together with Christ; but do not let us forget that the Divine life within us needs to be ministered unto, and sustained, just as much as the natural life. Food for the believer in Christ is nothing *more*, and nothing *less*, than the

Word of God, which is milk to nourish, food to strengthen, and meat to build up.

3. *Exercise*. After Christ had raised the widow's son, He gave the boy back to his mother. Evidently this only son had been the support of his mother up to the time of his death. When he died, she lost her earthly supporter, and Christ's object in delivering him back to his mother was that he should still be her stay and help. Here we get the thought of exercise; and if we would grow in grace, there must be exercise. Exercising ourselves to have "a conscience void of offence toward God, and toward men" (Acts 24:16). Exercising ourselves in godliness (1 Timothy 4:7). Our senses exercised that we may discern between good and evil (Hebrews 5:14). Make no mistake; we do not mean by exercise a painful struggling to do work for Christ, but we mean being right in our own souls before God, down at the Master's feet, where He can take us up and use us; as one has said, "I used to work for Christ with *one* hand, and hold Him with the other: but now I let Christ hold me, and I work with *both* hands." We should be so filled with the love of Christ that we cannot keep it to ourselves; and so filled with the Spirit that out of us will flow rivers of living water.

What We Are to Grow Like

1. *Grow like the almond tree for wakefulness*. The almond blossoms are the earliest of any fruit trees. "From the circumstance of its blossoming the earliest of any of the fruit trees, and before it is in leaf, it has its name, from a verb, signifying to *make haste*, to *be in a hurry*, to watch or to *awake early*." If we would grow like the almond tree, we must be fully awake to our privilege and responsibility to live and shine for Christ. We must be on the lookout for Him and so be ready for Him when He comes.

2. *Grow like the corn for bountifulness*. If a corn of wheat remains unplanted, it abides alone; but if it is planted, it dies and brings forth much fruit. We have received much from the Lord; let us therefore be bountiful in our praise to Him in sharing Him with others, and in ministering to the wants of poorer saints as we have means and opportunity.

3. *Grow like the ivy for tenacity*. The ivy is a parasite. It lives on another. We have often seen it clinging around a tree, striking its roots into the bark and living upon it. We are parasites in a spiritual sense. We live not by ourselves, but by Christ; yes, it is Christ who lives in us. And as the ivy, by the power of the life that is in it, is enabled to cling to the tree; so we, by the power of the Holy Spirit, who lives in us, should *cleave* to the Lord with purpose of heart (Acts 11:23).

6. *Grow like the vine for fruitfulness*. Christ has ordained us that we should bring forth *fruit*, *more* fruit, *much* fruit, even that our fruit should *remain*. We once brought forth fruit unto death; but now we are to bring forth fruit unto holiness; to be filled with the fruits of righteousness; to be fruitful in every good work; and to bring forth the fruit of the Spirit, or rather let Him bring it forth in us.

5. *Grow like the oak for stability*. We are not to be like Reuben, "unstable as water." We shall not "excel" if we are. Firmly rooted in Christ, in love, and in

the Word, not carried about by every wind of doctrine, we will be established in grace and in the truth.

6. *Grow like the olive for richness*. Rich in faith, giving glory to God; and rich in good works, that others may see the power of His grace in and with us.

7. *Grow like the lily for purity*. "Keep *thyself* pure," is a most practical injunction. May we keep our *mind* pure; bring every thought into captivity to the obedience of Christ. The most practical definition of holiness that we know is found in the words of Paul: "Cleansing ourselves from all filthiness of the *flesh* and of the *spirit*; perfecting holiness in the fear of the Lord" (2 Corinthians 7:1). May we keep our *motive* in work for Christ pure, constrained by nought but the mighty propelling and compelling love of Christ! May we keep our *object* in work pure, the glory of God alone, not the honor and the applause of men! In a word, let us keep ourselves because we are kept by the power of God, our whole spirit, soul and body, blameless unto the coming of our Lord Jesus. Remember, our bodies are purchased by the blood of Christ, are members of Christ, and the temple of the Holy Spirit.

8. *Grow like the palm for uprightness*. We read that Noah was perfect, or as the margin says, "*upright*" (Genesis 6:9). Again, God said to Abraham, "Walk before me, and be thou perfect," or, as in the margin, "*upright*" (Genesis 17:1). Again, the word "perfect" in the New Testament in some cases means "*full-grown*" (Philippians 3:15).

And what will be the result, Godward, manward, and in our own experience, as we walk, work, and worship uprightly before the Lord? We have that given us in the book of Proverbs; we refer very briefly to a few passages. The Lord is a Buckler to us (2:7); we have a sure dwelling-place (2:21); are strengthened by walking in the way of the Lord (10:29); shall be guided (11:3); shall have deliverance (11:6); shall be a blessing to others (11:11); the Lord is pleased with us (11:20); we shall deliver others (12:6); we shall be kept (13:6); we shall have prosperity (14:11); the Lord will delight to answer our prayers (15:8); we shall have discernment to walk aright (15:21); our aim will be separation from all evil (16:17); we shall be on the winning side (21:18); we shall carefully consider (margin) our way (21:29); we shall be a contrast to the wicked (28:10); and hated by the world (29:27).

26

The Discipler's Motive

One of the four things which will be revealed at the judgment seat of Christ will be our motive in Christian work. When we stand in our glorified bodies before our Lord Jesus, as Lord, we shall have reviewed—1) Our whole life since we believed in Christ, according to 1 Corinthians 4:5; 2) Our conduct toward our fellow-believers as shown in Romans 14:1-10; 3) Our work, of what sort it is; and our reward will correspond to the amount that stands the fire as we read in 1 Corinthians 3:12-15; 4) Our motive in our life and service as implied in 2 Corinthians 5:9-16.

Before we refer to three signs as evidences that we are working for Christ's sake alone, let me ask a few practical questions which will revolve around this main question, "Why are we workers?"

Do we work because we hope to effect our salvation by it? This describes a class unhappily only too numerous among those known as Christian workers. A lady who was inviting a believer to a mission was asked by him if she knew her sins forgiven, and if she had peace with God. To his surprise the lady replied, "No," but that she hoped it would be all right, meaning that her zeal in Christian work would entitle her to salvation. This lady was ignorant of the knowledge that salvation is the gift of God, "Not of works, lest any man should boast" (Ephesians 2:9). God justifies without works the ungodly who believe in Jesus (Romans 3:20,24; 4:4, 5). Yes, man's works are dead ones (Hebrews 9:14). And, besides, those who are in the flesh cannot please God (Romans 8:6-8). And everyone is in the flesh, and of the flesh, until he is born again (John 3:5, 6). We do not, and cannot, work to be saved, but we are saved to work.

Do we work because others are engaged in it? If so, we are following others and not Christ, and, like Peter's companions, we go fishing because the suggestion, "I go a fishing," is given to us. One takes up a work and others follow because of the one who leads. They have not been to the Lord inquiring, "What will You have me to do ?" They are influenced only by what others do. They work with others, as Lot with Abraham, instead of working with the Lord, as Abraham walked with Him.

Do we work because we like it? Then Christian work with us may be but a pastime, a hobby, just as a man takes pleasure in keeping pigeons or having his yard in trim. An unconverted young lady once told me that she "would like to visit some elderly Christian women." It was simply a whim, to be relinquished for the next fancy. Our work should not be chosen merely because we like it. In this, as in all circumstances, the Lord should be Judge in such matters. If we love Him we will love to do as He bids us for His sake alone. To know that we are in the will of God gives lasting peace. It was this that enabled Madame Guyon to sing in her solitude in the Bastille. Had she chosen for herself she would probably have been surrounded by friends of kindred spirit. But knowing that the Lord willed her there, she could sing:

"A little bird I am,
Shut from the fields of air,
And in my cage I sit and sing
To Him who placed me there;
Well pleased a prisoner to be,
Because, my God, it pleaseth Thee.

"Naught have I else to do;
I sing the whole day long:
And He whom most I love to please
Doth listen to my song;
He caught and bound my wandering wing,
But still He bends to hear me sing.

"Thou hast an ear to hear;
A heart to love and bless;
And though my notes were e'er so rude,
Thou would'st not hear the less;
Because Thou knowest, as they fall,
That love, sweet love, inspires them all."

Do we work because people—religious people—think well of us? It may be pleasing to hear the complimentary "How earnest he is!" "How well he speaks!" "What devotion she manifests!" but is there not a bit of Simon Magusism when we are pleased simply because *we* are well spoken of? Simon Magus gave himself out to be some great one: he was inflated with pride and swelled like the frog in the fable with conceit (see Acts 8). Bunyan watched against this spirit and put the cap on the right person, when, in answer to a friend's remark, about how well he had preached, he said, "The devil told me that before you did."

Do we work because it may introduce us into good society? Then we are like those young ladies who were said to have changed their sphere of work (or engaged in Christian work for the first time), hoping by such means to throw themselves in the way of young men and "pick up a husband." Or are we like the shrewd worldling who associates himself with Christian work so as to enlarge his business?

Do we work because it is fashionable? There is a so-called "Christian" work that is fashionable—entertainments for the people, bazaars to raise funds to carry on God's (?) work; "sacred" concerts at which unconverted people sing to amuse, and in which Christians help. It is something akin to Jehoshaphat's policy when he allied himself to ungodly Ahab and brought on himself the censure of the prophet of the Lord: "Shouldest thou help the ungodly, and love them that hate the Lord? therefore is wrath upon thee from before the Lord" (2 Chronicles 19:2).

Let us guard against the *wrong* motive in Christian work. The apostle had to warn Titus of some who were working "for filthy lucre's sake" (Titus 1:11). Let us be careful lest we work for self's sake, pride's sake, praise's sake, friends' sake, people's sake, ministers' sake, or any others' sake. Perhaps we may have mixed motives, like the Jews who came "not for Jesus' sake only, but that they might see Lazarus" (John 12:9).

If we are living and working for the sake of Him to whom we owe everything, for whose sake we have been forgiven and blessed, even as David for Jonathan's sake honored Mephibosheth (2 Samuel 9:1, 7), there will be seen in us *denial* of self, *devotion* in service, and *delight* in suffering.

Denial of Self

The Lord says, "If any man would come after me, let him deny himself and take up his cross daily and follow me. For whosoever would save his life will lose it; and whoever loses his life for my sake, he will save it" (Luke 9:23, 24 RSV). And also in John 12:24-26, "Truly, truly, I say unto you, unless a grain of wheat fall into the earth and dies, it remains alone; but if it dies, it bears much fruit. He that loves his life loses it; and he who hates his life in this world will keep it for eternal life. If any one serves me, he must follow me; and where I am, there shall my servant be also; if any one serves me, the Father will honor him" (RSV.). What the Lord insists upon, if we would follow Him in service, is *not self-denial, but the denial of self*.

Note the difference. Self-denial is denying self something, as in the case of David, when he denied himself the draught taken at so great a risk from the well of Bethlehem (1 Chronicles 11:17, 18). But the denial of self is denying self itself, and using Peter's words to self, not to Christ, "I know not the man" (Matthew 26:74). Self-denial is often Pharisaical and prides itself upon its almsgiving and fasting; while the denial of self is letting Christ *have* all, and letting Him *hold* all. Self-denial is self at work, while the denial of self is seeing and reckoning self to be dead with Christ. Paul knew this when he said, "I am crucified with Christ; nevertheless I live; yet not I, but Christ liveth in me" (Galatians 2:20).

> "I once lived, but now I'm dead,
> And Christ—He lives in me instead."

O horrid self! In how many ways it seeks to show itself! There is *humble self* who is very proud of his humility; there is *hypocritical self* who gives utterance to what he knows nothing of in his experience; *covetous self* who cares not who sinks so long as he swims; *ambitious self* who seeks to be big, and will not be anything if he cannot be at the top of the tree; *conceited self* who fancies himself like King Saul, head and shoulders above everyone else; *earnest self* who is so carried away by enthusiasm as to lose sight of the glory of God. Then there is *religious self* who thinks himself holier than others: this Dagon is very tenacious of life and dies but slowly, as is illustrated in the following story:

"In the parish where Mr. Hervey preached, when he inclined to loose sentiments, there resided a ploughman whose seasonable advice made Mr. Hervey a debtor. Being advised by his physician for the benefit of his health to follow the plough in order to smell the fresh earth, Mr. Hervey frequently followed the ploughman in his rural employment. Understanding that the ploughman was a serious person, one morning he asked him, 'What do you think is the hardest thing in religion?'

"To which he replied, 'I am a poor, illiterate man, and you, sir, are a minister. I beg leave to return the question.'

"'Then,' said Hervey, 'I think the hardest thing is to deny sinful self'; and he applauded at some length his own example of self-denial.

"The ploughman replied: 'Mr. Hervey, you have forgotten the greatest act of self-denial which is to deny ourselves of a proud confidence in our own obedience.'

"Mr. Hervey looked at the man in amazement, thinking him a fool; but in after years, when relating the story, he would add, 'I have clearly seen who was the fool—not the wise old Christian, but the proud James Hervey.'"

A good way to lose sight of self is to do with it what we do when we do not want to see our shadow; that is, keep our face to the light and then our shadow will be behind. We cannot be proud of ourselves if we are walking in the light, for we will see that all advancement in Christian life and labor is not our working at all, but the result of the Lord working through us.

"Come after Me," says Christ, who leads while He invites us to follow. He gave His life on the cross for us, and He has found it in a sense in which He never would have found it had He not denied Himself. And now He bids us follow Him in losing the self-life and knowing the Christ-life. The following little incident may help to illustrate this.

A boy at a certain school was noted for his aptitude in a game of marbles. The other boys did not like this and they consequently shunned his company. Meeting his pastor one day, the boy unburdened his mind, and, after listening attentively, the pastor said, "Well, Ernest, you do win a good many marbles, don't you?"

"Why, yes, sir; of course I do."

"I wonder, now, if you ever ask the Lord Jesus about this marble playing?"

"Yes, sir; I do."

"And what do you ask Him?"

"I ask Him to let me hit."

"Ernest, do you ever ask Him to let another boy hit?"

"No, sir; of course I don't."

"Why not?"

"Why, I want to get all the marbles I can."

"It seems as if the other boys might like to win sometimes," said the pastor thoughtfully. "Ernest, are you trying to show God to the boys?"

"Yes, sir, I am."

"Do you ever talk to them about God?"

"Yes, sir, I do; I'd like to have the boys know Him."

"Well, do they seem to want to love Him much?"

"No. I think the boys don't care much about God."

"Well, Ernest, I don't know that I wonder much at it. The God they see is your God. He lets you have all that you want, but does not tell you to ask Him to give them anything. You are not showing them the God who laid down His life."

"What do you mean, sir?"

"Giving up the thing that we want is the very heart of religion. Christ laid down His life for us, and we are to lay down our lives for others. If we lose our life—that is, our will, our way, our pleasure, our advantage—for Christ's sake, we shall find the real life which He only can give. Try it, Ernest; lose your life among the boys, and see if they won't think better of your God."

Too many of us are very much like the boy. As long as we succeed, it is well; but let us fail, and it is bad. If we are living and laboring for Christ's sake, we must remember that the very first principle is the denial of self.

Devotion in Service

There is no one who so fully illustrates this as the apostle Paul. How frequently he uses the word "sake" in reference to the Lord Jesus and His gospel, as the reason why he and others should be devoted in service! In asking an interest in their prayers, Paul says, "I beseech you, brethren, for the Lord Jesus Christ's sake, and for the love of the Spirit, that ye strive together with me in your prayers to God for me" (Romans 15:30). In speaking of his persecutions, and how he was counted a man out of his mind, he says, "We are fools for Christ's sake" (1 Corinthians 4:10). In mentioning the subject matter of his preaching, he assures the Corinthian Christians: "We preach not ourselves, but Christ Jesus the Lord; and ourselves your servants for Jesus' sake" (2 Corinthians 4:5). In mentioning his willingness to identify himself with any persons, and to take up any position, that he might thereby gain the souls of men for Christ, he says, "This I do for the gospel's sake" (1 Corinthians 9:23). And when Paul, a prisoner in Rome, writes to Philemon about his runaway slave Onesimus, he entreats the master to receive the slave back "for love's sake" (Philemon 9).

Out of love to David his three mighty men risked their lives among the Philistines; Shammah kept the field of lentils against the Philistines; and Dodo fought against the same people till his hand stuck to his sword (2 Samuel 23:9-17). Let us remember that there can be no true service, except as it is the outcome of love to Christ and for the sake of Christ alone. Abundant gifts there may be, and ability to minister, but love there *must* be. The Holy Spirit would have us remember this. Look at 1 Corinthians 12, 13, and 14. First Corinthians 12 speaks of gift; 1 Corinthians 14 speaks of ministry; while 1 Corinthians 13 tells of the moving power of gift, and the motive power of ministry, which is LOVE, LOVE, LOVE. Without love the gift is mere sound without reality: and the ministry is dry, instead of refreshing and fruitful.

Delight in Suffering

Paul was no stranger to suffering. "I will show him how much he must suffer for the sake of my name" (Acts 9:16 RSV), were the words with which the Lord introduced His chosen vessel to the regard of Ananias. Paul's future life fully bore this out. He was "delivered unto death for Jesus' sake" (2 Corinthians 4:11). And in writing of his thorn in the flesh, and the power of Christ resting over him as a tabernacle, he tells us that he takes "pleasure in infirmities, in reproaches, in necessities, in persecutions, in distresses for Christ's sake" (2 Corinthians 12:10). He reminds the church at Colosse that Christ was suffering through him, as he, for the Church's sake, was enduring hardship: "Now I rejoice in my sufferings for your sake, and in my flesh I complete what is lacking in Christ's afflictions for the sake of his body, that is, the church" (Colossians 1:24 RSV). He reminds the Philippians that it is given unto them "in the behalf of Christ, not only to believe on him, but also to suffer for his sake" (Philippians 1:29).

We do not wonder that the early Christians took joyfully the spoiling of their goods; went calmly to the arena to be devoured by lions; sang praises to God while their backs were lacerated, and their feet were held fast in the stocks; rejoiced that they were counted worthy to suffer shame for the name of Christ, for Christ was all to them. The person of Christ was the one joy of their lives. Like Mephibosheth, it mattered little to them what they had of this world's goods, or what they lost. The world could take, and have all, so long as their Lord the King was theirs (2 Samuel 19:30).

And if we glory in the Person of Christ, and know His living power and presence, we will long to "know him, and the power of his resurrection, and the fellowship of his sufferings, being made conformable unto his death" (Philippians 3:10).

It seems to us that there are three classes of Christian workers.

Some are like *canal boats* and have to be dragged along by a power outside of them. These workers engage in Christian work because they have been influenced by some around them. Let the leader fail and the work ceases.

Then there are other workers who may be compared to *sailing vessels*, dependent on wind and tide. These workers labor well, so long as the wind of approval is favorable and the tide of public opinion is high. Let contrary winds assail them, and forthwith there is the tacking of self, and the running before what others say.

Lastly, there are workers who may be likened to *Atlantic liners*. These go on, no matter what the wind or tide may be. Why? Because they are not dependent upon their surroundings: for the power is within them.

Under which heading do we come? Let us be like the last. The love of Christ, in the power of the Holy Spirit, constraining us, our surroundings will not deter us but only bring us into the happy knowledge that He who is in us is the moving and motive Power of all.

To sum up, the lines the Christian worker should follow in his service for the Lord are:

The love of God should be our motive power in service (2 Corinthians 5:14; 1 John 3:16).

Likeness to God should be our moral strength in service (1 Peter 1:15; 1 John 2:6).

To please God should be the highest delight in service (2 Corinthians 5:9, R.V.; 1 Thessalonians 2:4).

The truth of God should be our mighty lever in service (Acts 4:29; 8:35; 1 Corinthians 2:13).

Consulting God should always be the prelude to all service (Acts 9:6; Philippians 4:6; Acts 13:2). The Spirit of God should be our power in service (Colossians 1:29; Acts 1:8; 4:29). The glory of God should be our aim in all service (1 Corinthians 1:31; 10:31; John 17:4).

27

The Discipler's Lord

To have Christ as our Lord means for us that there is *submission to Him as such*. Our *blessings* are connected with the exalted Man, Christ; our *responsibilities* are connected with Him as *Lord*. We see the two appearing in the Epistle to the Ephesians, viz., *in Christ*, and *in the Lord*; and the latter phrase, to which we now refer, occurs *seven* times.

Submission of Way in the Lord

"Faith *in the Lord* Jesus" (Ephesians 1:15). Saul of Tarsus was going on his own way when he was persecuting the saints, but the Lord stopped him; and when He did so, Saul immediately answered the question, "Saul, Saul, why persecutest thou me?" by saying, "Who art thou, *Lord?*" He recognized the despised Nazarene as Lord. This is but an illustration of what the Lord has done for everyone who now believes in Him. We were going on in our own way until He stopped us, and the light of the glorious gospel dispelled the darkness of sin and unbelief. When through faith in Jesus our way was changed, we submitted to Jesus as Lord.

Submission of Will in the Lord

"In whom the whole structure is joined together and grows into a holy temple *in the Lord*" (Ephesians 2:21 RSV). The thought in this verse seems to be, growing in holiness, or the new nature growing by the power of the indwelling Spirit—thus God's purpose carried out in us to the glory of Christ. For this, there must be submission of will—laying aside our own will; and like our Master, who ever pleased His Father, we should ever please our Lord.

The following incident illustrates this. There was a famous preacher living in the middle ages at Strasburg. His name was Tauler. Considered by far the most eminent preacher of his day, he was looked up to by his townsmen as their spiritual guide and director; yet he felt himself deeply in need of some Priscilla or Aquila who could instruct him in the way of God more perfectly. Penetrated by this conviction, he prayed earnestly and constantly for the space of two years that someone might be sent to instruct him. At the end of that time, he was directed (by what means we are not told) to go to a certain church porch at a given time, where he would meet with someone who would grant his request. Accordingly he went. When he got there, he found no one but an old beggar. Tauler concluded that his instructor was not come and waited long, but at last he spoke to the beggar, and said, "God give thee a good day, my friend."

"I thank God," said the beggar, "I never have a bad day."

Tauler was surprised, but, changing his salutation, said, "God give thee a happy life, friend."

"I thank God," said the beggar, "I am never unhappy."

"Never unhappy!" said Tauler; "what do you mean ?"

"Well," replied the beggar, "when it is fine, I thank God; when it rains, I thank God; when I have plenty, I thank God; and when I am hungry, I thank God; and *since God's will is my will, and whatsoever pleases Him pleases me, why should I say I am unhappy when I am not?"*

"But, *what if it were God's will to cast you hence into hell*—how then?"

At that point the beggar paused a moment. Lifting up his eyes towards Tauler, he replied, "And if He did I should have two arms to embrace Him—the arm of my faith, wherewith I lean upon His holy humanity, and the arm of my love, wherewith I am united to His ineffable Deity, and, being one with Him, He would descend thither with me; *and I would sooner be in hell with Him, than be in heaven without Him."*

Tauler was astonished at the beggar's reply and asked, "Who are you?"

"A king," replied the beggar.

"But where is your kingdom?" said Tauler.

"Within me; 'the kingdom of God is within you,'" replied the beggar.

"And when did you find this out?"

Mark well the reply of the beggar.

"When I left all the creatures and looked to God alone."

And in like manner, if we would glorify Christ, it must be by entirely submitting ourselves to Him; not seeking to please self or others, but ever having our mind set on Christ—yes, our whole spirit, soul, and body yielded up to Him.

Submission of Witness-bearing in the Lord

"Testify *in the Lord*" (Ephesians 4:17). Paul was conscious that he was speaking *from* the Lord, *for* the Lord, *of* the Lord, and *in* the Lord. As Christ came witnessing *of* the Father, *from* the Father, *for* the Father, and *in* His Father's name, so it should be with us. As the Father sent Jesus to witness of Him, so Jesus sends us to witness of Himself. *From Him:* this tells us of our *commission. For Him:* this tells of our *responsibility*. "Ye are my witnesses" (Luke 24:48); not "You may be," but *"Ye are."* We are responsible to witness for Him in life and testimony. *Of Him:* this tells us what we are to witness of—Himself alone, Himself always—and let it be manifestly seen that we are submitting to Him as Lord. *In Him:* this tells us of our *power*; if it is *in* the Lord, it will be in the power of the Spirit, in subjection to Him, and to the glory of the Father and Son.

Submission of Walk in the Lord

"Light *in the Lord*" (Ephesians 5:8). This tells us what we *were*—"darkness"; what we *are*—*"light in the Lord"*; and what we *should do*—"walk as children of light." "Walk" in Scripture refers to the whole tenor of our daily life. *Social walk:* we must not be mixed up, or yoked together with unbelievers, whether in *marriage*, *pleasure*, *company*, or *business*; we must always remember this—it must be *in the Lord*. *Private walk:* the thoughts brought into subjection to the obedience of Christ, the mind set on Christ, the heart only for Christ, the tongue only to speak for Him, the hands only to work for Him, the feet only to walk in His ways. And what will be the result? Our Lord will be glorified, we shall be blessed, and others will see and feel the power of the Lord resting upon us.

In one of the large American cities some years ago there was a small room with one occupant. The hand of poverty was there, but it was the abode of a child of God—a young seamstress. It was her closet for prayer, as well as the spot for plying her needle. When employment failed, she knelt in prayer and trusted in her Heavenly Father. One morning, she had been thus engaged, with unusual earnestness, when there was a knock at the door. In stepped a creature full of life and gaiety, with a large bundle.

"Can you sew for me?" asked this dashing young lady.

The question was met with a smile. "It is just what I have been praying for," she said. The bundle contained rich dresses and rich materials for more.

"I am an actress," said the young visitor. "I am under an engagement to play in Philadelphia, and those dresses must be altered, and these must be made up at once. I will pay you handsomely."

"I do not know about this work," said the seamstress. "It is true I have been praying for work, and am in much need of it, but I do not know about doing this," she said, hesitatingly.

"Why?"

"Because it seems to me that in doing this I should be serving the devil instead of the Lord Jesus," she answered meekly.

"But did you not pray for work?"

"Yes."

"And has not this come in answer?"

"It seems so, and yet I feel as if I ought not to do it."

"Well! What will you do about it?"

"I will ask my Heavenly Father. Will you kneel with me?"

She poured out her heart to God and prayed that she might not fall into sin, urging her petition with childlike simplicity, not thinking of any effect that her prayer was having upon her visitor. Then in agony of spirit, the latter threw her arms around the seamstress's neck and cried, "O do not pray any more about the dresses, but pray for me!"

The poor seamstress was taken by surprise. Now she prayed, that if her visitor was not in earnest, she might be made so, and there and then give herself to the Lord Jesus, to be His forever. She also prayed that the young actress would forsake the sinful manner of life she had been living. They rose from their knees and looked at each other in silence.

"I shall not let you do this work," said the actress; "no one shall do it."

"What will you do?"

"I will leave it as it is."

"You have an engagement in Philadelphia."

"I will write to the manager that I cannot play for him, and I will pray for him."

"How long have you been connected with the stage?"

"Five years; and I have followed it with an enthusiasm that swallowed up my life. But I shall quit the stage forever. I will not put my foot on it again."

"Then what will you do with these things?"

"I will keep them, in their present state. They shall remain as a memento of this hour and this room, and of God's mercy in arresting me here."

"How will you live now?"

"I do not know; but I will do all for Christ and ask counsel of Him."

Thus Christ was glorified by the consistent life of the seamstress and a precious soul was saved.

Submission to the Word in the Lord

"Children, obey your parents *in the Lord*" (Ephesians 6:1). In chapters 5 and 6 of Ephesians, we have *seven* relationships mentioned—1) *Husbands* who are to love their wives as *Christ* loved the Church; 2) *wives* who are to be subject to their husbands as unto the *Lord;* 3) *children* who are to honor their parents and obey them in the *Lord;* 4) *fathers* who are not to provoke their children to wrath, but to bring them up in the nurture and admonition of the *Lord;* 5) *mothers*—the name is not mentioned here, but they are responsible to pray for, and so to walk, so that their children shall be attracted to the *Lord;* 6) *servants* who are to obey their masters, and to do their service as unto the *Lord;* 7) *masters* who are to treat their servants in love, remembering that they have a *Master* in heaven. "You call me Teacher and *Lord:* and you are right, for so I am. If I then, your *Lord* and Teacher, have washed your feet, you also ought to wash one another's feet. For I have given you an example, that you also should do as I have done to you" (John 13:13-15 RSV). These are the words of our Master to us; and He also says, "If you know these things, blessed are you if you do them." (John 13:17 RSV). What we have to do is to be submissive to the Word of the Lord. We are to do as He tells us, and we will indeed be blessed as we obey Him.

Submission in Warfare in the Lord

"Be strong *in the Lord*" (Ephesians 6:10). The first principle in a soldier's life is obedience—to obey his captain's orders; so it must be with us. We do not have to fight to overcome our enemies; Jesus has already done that. We do not have to fight to gain a position; God has placed us on resurrection ground. Now what we have to do is to be strong in the Lord, that we may be able to *stand* where He has put us, having on the whole armor of God, and so *withstand* all the assaults of the enemy. If we are obedient to our Captain's orders, we will never be defeated, but in His power, we shall be more than conquerors.

Submission of Work in the Lord

"Tychicus, a beloved brother and faithful minister *in the Lord*" (Ephesians 6:21). "Son, go work today in My vineyard," is the command of our Father; "Occupy till I come," is the command of our Lord. We are to submit to Him, with regard to *what* the work shall be, and *how* it is to be done, the Word of the

Lord being our guide. What our Lord wants of us is to be what Tychicus was—faithful; faithful to Him and His Word.

We hear a good deal of talk about *success*, and also, that "the end justifies the means"; but that is not according to the Word of the Lord. God told Moses to *speak* to the rock, but Moses *smote* it *twice*. The end was the same —the water came out of the rock; but did the end justify the means? Hear what God Himself says: "Because ye believed me not, to sanctify me in the eyes of the children of Israel, therefore ye shall not bring this congregation into the land which I have given them" (Numbers 20:12).

Moses was kept out of the land because of his disobedience. Beware, fellow-believer, of this snare of the evil one—this lie that is forged in hell and propagated by the devil—that the end justifies the means. But be faithful to keep to the Word of the Lord, which shows how His work is to be done. When He comes, may He say, "Well done, good and faithful servant, enter thou into the joy of thy *Lord*."

In the Acts of the Apostles we have the name of the Lord Jesus as Lord, again and again, and the different things that are said of Him imply our surrender and submission to Him. As we sanctify Christ as Lord in our hearts, the *name* of the Lord will be our *delight* (Acts 2:21; 8:16; 9:29; 10:48; 15:25, 26; 19:13, 17; 21:13; 22:16); the *presence* of the Lord will be our *stay* (3:19); the *word* of the Lord will be our *authority* (8:25; 11:16; 13:12, 48, 49; 15:35, 36; 16:32; 19:10, 20); the *disciples* of the Lord will be our *companions* (10:28); the *Spirit* of the Lord will be our *power* (8:39); the *fear* of the Lord will be our *guard* (9:31); the *hand* of the Lord will be our *support* (11:21); the *grace* of the Lord will be our *supply* (15:11); the *way* of the Lord will be our *path* (18:25); the *things* of the Lord will be our *study* (18:25); and the *will* of the Lord will be our *will* (21:14).

28

The Discipler's Ambition

The discipler's ambition should be not to please men (Galatians 1:10), but to please God. We please Him when we are—

Obedient to Him, as Christ was, who could say, "I do always those things that please him" (John 8:29); confident in Him, as the Old Testament saints were, for "without faith it is impossible to please him" (Hebrews 11:6); separate to Him, as Paul said to Timothy, "No man that warreth entangleth himself with the affairs of this life; that he may please Him who hath chosen him to be a soldier" (2 Timothy 2:4); walking with Him, as Enoch did, of whom it is said, he "pleased God" (Hebrews 11:5 Genesis 5:22); helping others for Him, as the Spirit bids us, "To do good and to communicate forget not: for with such sacrifices God is well pleased" (Hebrews 13:16); increasing by Him, "Ye ought to walk and to please God, so ye would abound more and more" (1 Thessalonians 4:1); and sympathetic with Him, "Let every one . . . please his neighbor for his good to edification. For even Christ pleased not himself" (Romans 15:2, 3).

The discipler's ambition is that Christ may be glorified *in* him, and that thus God may be glorified *by* him. It is one thing to be saved and another to know why God has saved, or what purpose He had in view. We are plainly told in Ephesians 2:7 what His purpose was: "That in the ages to come he might show the exceeding riches of his grace in his kindness toward us through Christ Jesus," and thus He might be glorified in us. It is our privilege and responsibility to remember this, that our highest aim and one object in Christian life and work should be to glorify God.

Before we direct further attention to the subject which heads this chapter, let me trace the successive steps up to it. Man has come short of God's glory (Romans 3:23); man has been tried and found a failure at every point. Man was tried in innocence and failed; he was left to his own conscience and failed; he was tried under law and failed. God sent His Son and man murdered Him. Now men are rejecting the Lord and despising the Holy Spirit. Man having failed in every point, Christ came to glorify God on behalf of those who would believe in Him. Christ glorified God in the work He gave Him to do, as He Himself says, "I have glorified thee on the earth: I have finished the work which thou gavest me to do" (John 17:4). The Father has glorified Christ by raising Him from the dead (Philippians 2:9); the Spirit has been sent down to glorify Christ (John 7:39; 14:14) and we, by the power of the indwelling Spirit, glorify the father and the Son.

There are three passages where Christ is spoken of as "glorified in His saints." The *first* has reference to what Christ *has done for us*—"I am glorified in them" (John 17:10); the *second*, what God *does in us* by the power of the Spirit—"That the name of our Lord Jesus Christ *may* be glorified *in* you" (2 Thessalonians 1:12); the *third*, what He will *yet do for us*—"When he comes to be glorified in his saints, and to be admired in all them that believe in that day" (2 Thessalonians 1:10). We might sum it up thus:

1. Christ glorified in us by the work He *has* done *for* us.
2. Christ glorified in us by the work He *is* doing *in* us.
3. Christ glorified in us by the work He will *yet* do for us.

It is our purpose here to confine ourselves to the first—

Christ glorified in us by the work He has done for us. This, of course, implies that we are His saints, He having quickened us by the Spirit, and enabled us by simple faith to rest in Jesus as our Savior. We, thus becoming children of God, He calls us saints; hence—

1. *He is glorified in our salvation*.—"His glory is great in thy salvation" (Psalm 21:5).

When the sisters of Lazarus sent to Jesus to ask that He would come and heal their brother, He said, "This sickness is not unto death, but for the glory of God, that the Son of God might be glorified thereby" (John 11:4); and He did not go at once but tarried two days where He was. In the meantime, Lazarus died. When Jesus reached Bethany he was already buried. Christ might have prevented him dying, but that His power might be seen, and He Himself glorified thereby, He let him die.

A servant of Christ, addressing a children's meeting at Brighton, put the following question to the children:

"Would you rather Adam had never sinned?"

Immediately a little fellow got up and said, "I wish Adam had never sinned."

"I don't," said the friend; "for man was made a little *lower* than the angels, but by grace he is made an heir of God, and a joint-heir with Christ, and thus is made *higher* than the angels."

As we see in Revelation 5:6, 11, the redeemed in glory are round about the Lamb, but the angels are round about them, an outer circle. It appears, therefore, that God is infinitely more glorified by saving the believer from the punishment, power, and presence of sin, and making him one with Himself, than if he had remained in innocence.

2. *He is glorified by the standing into which He brings us*.—We are sinners in a threefold sense. 1) *Sinners by our connection with Adam*, for when he sinned, we fell in him, he being the federal head or representative of the whole race of mankind, as we have it in Romans 5:12: "As by one man sin entered into the world, and death by sin and so death passed upon all men, for that all have sinned," or, as the margin puts it, "in whom" (Adam) "all sinned." 2) *Sinners as*

to our sinful nature. When we were born into this world, Adam was formed in us, just as we read in Genesis 5:3: "Adam lived an hundred and thirty years, and begat a son in his own likeness, after his image." 3) *Sinners as to our practice*. A crabapple tree can only bring forth crabapples; a stinging nettle will sting—it is its nature to do so; so a sinner with a sinful nature can only bring forth sins.

We are saints in a threefold sense:

1. *Saints as to our standing in Christ*. We are no longer in the flesh (Adam), but in Christ all that He is, is ours, and all that He has done, is reckoned to our faith in Him. In Christ—*what are we in Him?* In Christ we are dead to sin; in Christ we are buried; in Christ we are risen; and in Christ we are seated at God's right hand.

What have we in Him? When I was preaching in the south of Scotland, a friend gave me the following on a slip of paper: "In Christ we are complete. In Him we have a *life* which can never be forfeited; in Him we have a *righteousness* which can never be tarnished; in Him we have a *pardon* which can never be reversed; in Him we have a *justification* which can never be cancelled; in Him we have an *acceptance* which can never be questioned; in Him we have a *peace* which can never be broken; in Him we have a *rest* which can never be disturbed; in Him we have a *hope* which can never be disappointed; in Him we have a *glory* which can never be clouded; in Him we have a *love* which can never be darkened; in Him we have a *happiness* which can never be interrupted; in Him we have a *strength* which can never be exhausted; in Him we have a *purity* which can never be defiled; in Him we have a *comeliness* which can never be marred; in Him we have a *wisdom* which can never be baffled; in Him we have an *inheritance* which can never be alienated; in Him our *resources* can never be exhausted; and in Him our *future* can never be uncertain."

2. *Saints as to our nature*.—In this respect also we are saints. We are born of God and made partakers of the Divine nature, for he that is "born of God doth not commit sin; for his seed remaineth in him: and he cannot sin, because he is born of God" (1 John 3:9).

3. *Saints as to practice*.—The new nature, by the power of the indwelling Spirit, will triumph over the old nature, and it will be seen by the fruit which we bear that we are saints.

But we wish more particularly to dwell upon the fact that Christ is "glorified" by the position into which He brings us. As an illustration, take the cherubim* in the tabernacle.

First. *The cherubim on the veil* (Exodus 26:31; Matthew 27:51). The veil of the temple was rent in twain; and what does this tell us but that we are dead—that in the person of our Representative we have borne the punishment due to our sin ?

Second. *The cherubim on the beautiful covering that was over the sanctuary*

---

* The cherubim actually are the administrators of God's righteous judgments (Genesis 3:24), or the upholders of God's throne (Ezekiel 10:20), or the executors of God's dealings in providence (Ezekiel 1), just as the seraphim are the administrators of God's mercy (Isaiah 6:2).

(Exodus 36:8; Ephesians 2:6). The high priest would look up and see them there. What does this tell us but this: as we look in the Word of God, and at the right hand of God, in the person of our Representative, we are risen with Him and seated together in heavenly places?

Third. *The cherubim on* (or *of*) *the mercy-seat*. The cherubim were made of the same piece of gold as the mercy-seat, as it says in the margin of Exodus 25:19: "And make one cherub on the one end, and the other cherub on the other end: even of the matter of the mercy-seat." The same thought is expressed in Hebrews 2:11: "He that sanctifieth and they who are sanctified are all of one." What does this tell us, but that we are united to, in, and one with our Lord Jesus Christ? That "as he is, so are we in this world"—called by the same name, having the same nature (1 John 4:17), and we will share the same glory (John 17:21, 22)? "What presumption!" says someone. It would be, if it was the imagination of man's mind, but it is the unalterable word of the living God; and how it exalts our blessed Lord and glorifies Him, when we remember it is all of His own free, unmerited favor, that He thus bestows such blessings upon us!

The Father loved us and gave us to Christ! Christ loved us and redeemed us with His own precious blood; the Spirit loved us and quickened us. He united us to our living, loving Lord. Glory be to His name!

> "Sovereign Lord and gracious Master,
> Thou didst freely choose Thine own;
> Thou hast called with mighty calling,
> Thou wilt save and keep from falling;
> Thine the glory, Thine alone!
> Yet Thy hand shall crown in heaven
> All the grace Thy love hath given;
> Just, though undeserved, reward
> From our glorious, gracious Lord."

We have already seen what Christ has done for us and the position into which He has brought us.

We now give a few hints as to how we may please God and glorify Christ.

We Glorify Christ as We Are Guided by Him

First. *Who* guides? The Lord by the Holy Spirit. "As many as are led by the Spirit of God, they are the sons of God" (Romans 8:14). Second. *Where* does He guide? 1. *Into the way of peace*. "To guide our feet into the way of peace" (Luke 1:79). 2. *In Christian life:* "I will instruct thee and teach thee in the way which thou shalt go: I will guide [or *counsel*] thee with mine eye" (Psalm 32:8). 3. *In conflict:* God saved Hezekiah out of the hand of the king of Assyria and guided him on every side (2 Chronicles 32:22). 4. *In service:* "Thou shalt guide me with thy counsel" (Psalm 73:24). 5. *In blessing:* "Even by the springs of water shall he guide them" (Isaiah 49:10). 6. *In every time:* "The Lord shall guide thee continually" (Isaiah 48:11). 7. *Into all truth:* "He will guide you into all truth" (John 16:13). It is in this that the Lord Jesus said of the Holy Spirit, "He shall glorify me; for he shall receive of mine, and shall shew it unto you." God never guides contrary to His Word, and if we would walk in the Spirit, we must walk in the truth—not ask the Lord to guide us and then go in our own way.

We remember a friend telling us the following incident:—He was in the north of Scotland, and when out walking one day, met an old woman at a place where two roads met. She had a stick or staff in her hand, and just as he got up to her, she flung it up about a dozen times. He asked her why she did so, and she laughed and said:

"When I come to two ways I always do that, to see which way I am to go."

"But why did you throw it up so many times?"

"Because," she said, *"the head of the staff would not go the right way*, so I threw it up until it did!"

Do we not sometimes ask the Lord to guide, and all the time our minds are made up as to what we are going to do? If we would glorify Christ, we must be guided by the Spirit in the truth.

We Glorify Christ as We Look to Him

It was the sight of Christ on the cross which made the centurion glorify God, for we read, "When he saw what was done, he glorified God" (Luke 23:47). Looking to Jesus crucified to see what He has done; looking to Him risen to see what He gives; looking to Him in His Word to see what He requires; looking to Him as our Example in prayer, work, humility, love to others, and doing the Father's will; looking to Him as our Leader, and as Gideon said to his followers, "Look on me, and do likewise" (Judges 7:17), so may we look to Him and follow wherever He leads. Looking to *Him*, not self, the world, Satan, temptations, strength, weakness, attainments, brethren, joys, gifts, work, afflictions, law, sins, love, righteousness, faith, repentance, feelings, or peace, but Jesus, Jesus only, we thus glorify Him.

Cyrus had taken captive a prince and his wife and children. When they were arrayed before him, he said to the prince, "What will you give me if I release you?"

"The half of my kingdom," said the prince.

"And if I release your children ?"

"The whole of my kingdom."

"And if I release your wife?"

"*Myself*."

Cyrus was so pleased with the devotion of the prince that he released them all gratuitously. After they had returned to their own country, the prince said to his wife—

"Wasn't Cyrus a handsome man ?"

The princess said:

"I did not notice; *I had eyes only for him who was willing to give himself for me*."

May we have eyes only for Jesus who was not only willing, but who *has* given Himself for us.

We Glorify Christ as We Are Obedient to Him

We read, the "King's daughter is all-glorious within" (Psalm 45:13). The *withinness* of glory was caused by the *withoutness* of obedience, for while it is perfectly true we must have the withinness of the Spirit's power for the *obtainment* of obedience, we can only have that glory by the *retainment* of obedience.

When Jesus washed His disciples' feet, He told them why He did it. He left them an example, how they were to serve each other, and said, "If ye *know* these things, *happy* are ye if ye *do* them" (John 13:17). Here we have three thoughts— 1. *Knowledge*. 2. *Doing*, or obedience. 3. *Happiness*, the result. These three always go together. Jesus has told us to abide in Him, therefore we know; now we are responsible to do it; and if we do so it will have a twofold effect—joy will be brought to our own hearts; and glory will he brought to God, for to abide in Him, and to be obedient to Him are the same thing: "All who keep his commandments abide in him" (1 John 3:24 RSV).

We Glorify Christ as We Are Ready for Him

The writer was preaching one Lord's Day afternoon in a village in Warwickshire upon the second coming of Christ. In the audience there was a local preacher and his wife. The truth was like a new revelation to them. A day or two afterwards the local preacher, who was a stone mason, was working in his shop at the quarry, and thinking about the Lord's coming. It became to him such a reality, that, with mallet in one hand and chisel in the other, he went and looked out at the shop door, to see if He were coming! Are we, who profess to be looking for Him, *really expecting and looking for Him*, and living as though we expected Him, and thus being ready for Him? If we are, we glorify Him in keeping in our hearts His own precious promise, "I will come and receive you unto myself," and rejoice in hope of the coming glory.

We Glorify Christ as We Identify Ourselves with Him in Rejection

We are exhorted to "glorify the Lord in the fires" (Isaiah 24:15). When we are in the fire of affliction, as Job was, we have the God-given opportunity to glorify Him by our patience (Job 2:3); when we are in the fire of persecution, as the three Hebrew young men were, we can be the instrumental cause of glorifying Christ by revealing Him to the ungodly (Daniel 3:25); when we are in the fire of temptation, as Joseph was, we glorify God by our resistance and enjoy His special presence (Genesis 39:7-21); when we are in the fire of trial, as Abraham was, we glorify God by our obedience to His will (Hebrews 11:17-19); when we are in the fire of misrepresentation, we glorify God in suffering as Christians (1 Peter 4:14-16); when we "glory in tribulation," in our "infirmities," that the grace of Christ may rest upon us, we glorify God (Romans 5:3; 2 Corinthians 12:9); and when we glory in the cross of Christ, that is, in having fellowship with Christ in suffering, we glorify God (Galatians 6:14, 17).

Rumor says that on one occasion the Queen, in speaking of the late Prince Consort, said: "He was such an one that I could have gladly walked barefooted around the world with him." Who would not do the same with Christ? To be with Him is the cry of the newborn soul, as is evidenced in the deliverance of the demoniac who prayed that he might be "with him" (Luke 8:38); it is the prelude to seeing Christ's glory, for Peter and the other two disciples were said to be "with him" before they saw His glory (Mark 9:2); it is the place of honor for the disciples were said to be "with him" before He instituted the Last Supper (Luke 22:14); it is the secret of witness-bearing, as the people owned for they took knowledge of the early disciples that they had been "with Jesus" (Acts

4:13); it is the power that separates from sin for we are said to be "dead with Christ" (Romans 6:8); it is the keeping-place of our life, for we are said to be hid "with Christ" (Colossians 3:3); it is the hope of the coming glory, for we shall forever be "with the Lord" (1 Thessalonians 4:17; 5:10; Colossians 3:4); and it is the joy of the sufferer for we know if we "suffer with him" we shall "be also glorified together" (Romans 8:17).

We Glorify Christ as We Are Fighting in Him

It is said that when the body of the Prince Imperial was picked up there was not a single wound in his back; the wounds were all in the front part of his body. That was an evidence that he kept his face to the foe; and if we would glorify Christ we must keep our faces to our spiritual enemies, standing upon resurrection ground, knowing our foes have been beaten by Christ. Having on the whole armor of God, fighting in His strength, we will be conquerors. After Jehovah had given deliverance to Israel at the Red Sea, He was acknowledged to be "glorious in power" and "glorious in holiness" (Exodus 15:6, 11); and as we trust Him, He will give us victory over our enemies too, and then, like Israel, we will glorify Him for what he has done.

We Glorify Christ as We Invite Others to Him

"They glorified God in me" (Galatians 1:24), says the apostle Paul as he refers to what "God had wrought among the Gentiles by his ministry" (Acts 21:19, 20). The brethren were bound to acknowledge the working of God through him. The seed of truth had been sown and a harvest of blessing results.

"Come, see a man who told me all things that ever I did: is not this the Christ?" said the woman of Samaria; and it must have rejoiced His heart to hear her speak thus of Him, for as He saw the crowd coming to Him, He said, "The fields are white unto the harvest"; thus He was glorified by the woman's simple testimony. So will He be by ours if done with a single eye to His glory.

To tell forth His love, to herald out His grace, to proclaim His truth, to preach His gospel, to enforce His claims, to witness to His faithfulness, and to invite others to Him is the privilege of those who are Christ's own.

We Glorify Christ as We Are Enduring in Him

Moses "endured, as seeing him who is invisible" (Hebrews 11:27). He met with opposition at home but he endured; he met with opposition from his brethren but he endured the pleasures of sin, the attractions of the world, and the riches of Egypt were put in his way, but he endured, as seeing Him who was more to him than earthly attractions. Looking at things from heaven's standpoint, he saw their hollowness, emptiness, and vain show. The secret of Moses' endurance is expressed in those two words, "*seeing him*"; and as we gaze upon Christ, He will fill our hearts with joy (John 20:20), so that the world will lose its attractions.

We Glorify Christ as We Are Delighting in Him

Some Christians do things because it is their *duty*, but that is bondage; but if we are living to and for Christ, and working for Him simply because we cannot help it, it is liberty and delight. There are many ways in which we can delight in the Lord. Delighting in *communion:* "I sat down under his shadow with great delight, and his fruit was sweet to my taste" (Song of Solomon 2:3). Delighting in *service* (Psalm 40:8). Delighting in *God's ways,* not our own (Isaiah 48:2). Delighting in the *Word of God* (Psalm 119:16, 24, 35, 47, 70, 77, 174). Delighting in God *Himself* (Job 27:10; Psalm 37:4). Delighting in doing *God's will:* "I delight to do thy will, O my God" (Psalm 40:8). Delighting to *worship* Him: the shepherds came and worshipped Christ and returned glorifying God (Luke 2:20); the palsied man who was healed returned to his house glorifying God (Luke 5:25); the woman who was made straight stood up glorifying God (Luke 13:13); it was the same with the leper (Luke 17:15) and blind Bartimaeus (Luke 18:43).

Gustave Doré, the great French artist, was once traveling in a foreign land. Through some accident he lost his passport. When he came to pass through the custom-house of another country, and his passport was demanded, he told the customs officer that he had lost it but assured him that he was Doré, the artist.

The customs officer did not believe him and said, mockingly, "O yes, we have a good many like you! You are Doré, are you?"

"Yes."

"Very well, then; take this pencil and paper"—and he handed these to him as he spoke—"and prove it."

"All right," said Doré, and with an amused smile playing on his face, he took the pencil and began to make a neat little sketch of a company of peasants on the wharf, with their piles of baggage and children playing about them.

The customs officer looked on with astonishment for a few moments as the life-like creation grew under the pencil, and then said: "That will do, sir. You are Doré, for no man but Doré could do that."

That is the way we are to prove our Christianity. We must carry our passport in our everyday conduct. A Christian spirit which shows itself in smiling face and kindly words, and right conduct, is the best introduction one can have. Sometimes it is a protection better than any armor. And the way for these ends to be achieved is to allow the Divine Artist, the Holy Spirit, to paint upon the canvas of our lives the lovely character of the Lord Jesus. Then, as others see this, He must be glorified.

29

The Discipler's Marks

Generally speaking, there are certain marks which a believer possesses that show he belongs to Christ:

1) *Heart-Marks*. The heart resting on Christ, cleansed, and possessed by Him (Romans 10:10; Matthew 5:8; Ephesians 3:17). 2) *Eye-Marks*. Looking to Christ for salvation, and gazing upon Him in sanctification (Isaiah 45:22; 2 Corinthians 3:18; Hebrews 12:2). 3) *Ear-Mark*. Listening to Christ, thus learning of Him (John 10:27; Luke 10:39). 4) *Face-Mark*. The glory of Christ reflected by us and shining from us because of communion with Him (Exodus 34:30; Acts 4:13; 6:15). 5) *Hand-Mark*. Laboring with Christ and ministering to Him in supplying the need of others (2 Corinthians 6:1; Matthew 25:40). 6) *Tongue-Marks*. Speaking as Christ, speaking for Him, and speaking to Him (2 Corinthians 13:3; Acts 1:8; Philippians 4:6; John 14:14). 7) *Forehead-Mark*. Every thought in submission to Christ (2 Corinthians 10:5). 8) *Feet-Marks*. Following Christ in service and suffering (Luke 9:23; John 10:27; 12:26).

While we call attention to these general marks, we especially call attention to what the apostle says in writing to the Church in Galatia. He says, "Henceforth let no man trouble me: for I bear on my body the marks of Jesus" (Galatians 6:17 RSV).

These are the words of a faithful and fearless man. Paul had been warning the Galatians of the insidious evils of Judaism. Though there were people who questioned his authority in speaking as he did, still he could point to those who had been blessed by his ministry—and also to what he had endured for the gospel's sake.

These are the words, too, of a determined man. He not only hoisted his colors—but nailed them up. Satan might urge his enemies to bring the weapons of their carnal opinions to bear upon him yet he fearlessly stood his ground against all comers, by the simple and soul-stirring truths of the gospel. And he was prepared to continue to do so for the Lord was beside him. By the Lord's grace he had passed through much suffering and persecution, as the marks on his body reminded him. When he looked at those marks he was encouraged to go on: for he was not alone—as he implies, in calling these marks, not those of *Paul*, but of *Jesus*.

Marks! The gnarled hand of the laborer tells us that he has been doing hard physical work. The knit brow of the merchant indicates his service as he sits in his office balancing his books. The thoughtful features of the student show his sacrifice in search of knowledge. The sailor's weather-beaten face tells of the rough life he lives. The soldier's scars and the medals which adorn his chest speak of battles fought and victories won. The wrinkled brow, the white hair, the failing memory, the feeble step, the shaking hand, and the dull ear are marks of old age. The worn features, the pale cheeks, the furrows on the brow, the sunken eyes and the thin hands are marks of suffering. So the scars which were upon the body of the beloved Paul told of his sufferings for Christ—and with Christ. And Paul glories in them, for they bear testimony to his loyalty to the Lord Jesus.

Five thoughts are suggested by the words of Paul:

Possession by the Lord

In speaking of the marks of Jesus, the apostle seems to say, "As the slave bears branded upon his body the marks of his slavery, proving him a slave, so I glory in the marks that are branded upon my body, for they evidence that I am the slave of Jesus Christ." There were four classes who were marked with brands: the runaway slave, as a mark of his rebellion; the slaves attached to some temple, or persons devoted to some heathen deity, thus speaking of their devotion; captives, in some instances, in token of their captivity; and soldiers who sometimes marked the name of their commander on some part of their body to denote their willingness to serve him. We may take it for granted that the apostle referred to his being the slave of Christ. It was a title in which he gloried—"the bondservant" of Jesus Christ (see Revised Version, margin, Romans 1:1; Philippians 1:1; Titus 1:1).

Suffering for the Lord

As the apostle saw the brands upon some runaway slave, stigmatizing the slave for life, so looking at the marks on his own person, he counted an honor what others might consider a disgrace. The scars on his back told of the rods of the Roman soldiers, twice inflicted. The long lines on his body spoke of the two hundred stripes imposed in the synagogue. "Once was I stoned," says the patient apostle, and traces of the cruel treatment were apparent. His wrists, too, bore the marks of the manacles. Endurance of such wrong proved the strong hold which the love of Christ had upon him. As has been hinted, he gloried in the knowledge of these marks, for they had been received in his service of the gospel. "Now I rejoice in my sufferings for your sake, and in my flesh I complete what is lacking in Christ's afflictions for the sake of his body, that is, the church" (Colossians 1:24 RSV). Paul seems to refer here to his life previous to his meeting with the risen Lord on the Damascus road and also to his experience in suffering on behalf of the Church. He seems to say, "I was causing Christ to suffer in His members, when stopped and reproved in the 'Saul, Saul, why persecutest thou Me?' So I see that my suffering now, is Christ suffering in, and through me"; hence, he gloried in the cross of Christ.

The blood of Christ, the death of Christ, and the cross of Christ are not synonymous terms. In connection with these expressions the Holy Spirit attaches a distinct significance to each.

The blood of Christ is the procuring cause of all the blessings which the believer enjoys. Thus we have *pardon* (Ephesians 1:7); *nearness* (Ephesians 2:13); *justification* (Romans 5:9); *peace* (Colossians 1:20); *access* (Hebrews 10:19); *sanctification* (Hebrews 13:12); *freedom* (Revelation 1:5 NIV); and *victory* (Revelation 12:11) —all through the blood.

The death of Christ is connected with this deep truth that in God's reckoning, Christ not only died for us, but *we died with Him*. This is seen if we look at the R.V. of Romans 6:8; 2 Corinthians 5:14; Colossians 2:20; 2 Timothy 2:11.

The cross of Christ indicates the treatment He underwent at the hands of sinful men in carrying out the will of God (John 19:7; Matthew 27:40; Galatians 5:11; Philippians 2:8; Hebrews 12:2).

When the apostle glories in the cross of Christ, he does not refer primarily to the blessings which were his through the atonement made by the blood of Christ nor to the benefits which flow from association with Christ, and His death. He alludes to the sufferings which it was his lot to endure through his faithfulness to Christ, "who for the joy that was set before him endured the cross, despising the shame" (Hebrews 12:2). In Paul's case, it was enough for the disciple that he was as his Lord.

Consecration to the Lord

Only the truly consecrated man could speak and act as Paul did. There were no half measures with him. He was thorough. As the oak sends its roots down into the ground and is thus firmly rooted and able to weather the storm, so the apostle was firmly rooted in the love of Christ. The very fiber of his spirit and the roots of his being were impregnated with the love of God. As the lighthouse at Eddystone (and many other places) is built on and into the rock, so the apostle was founded and grounded in the truth of God. He could thus defy the fiercest onslaughts of the prince of the power of the air and those through whom he worked. As the ocean liner is able to go ahead in spite of the wind and tide, because of the power within which impels it, so the apostle pressed onward, braving the waves of public opinion, rising above error and persecution in their subtlety and annoyance, because he was empowered by the Holy Spirit. Being right with God, Paul could be indifferent to what man did or said. He had looked into the face of God. Therefore, the face of man had no terrors for him. Have we these marks of Jesus in consecration to Him?

In speaking of the practical power of Christ's suffering endured on account of the believer, and its application to him, Bishop Hall said: "The crown of thorns pierces his head when his sinful conceits are mortified. His lips are drenched with vinegar and gall when sharp and severe restraints are given to his tongue. His hands and feet are nailed when he is, by the power of God's Spirit, disabled to the wonted courses of sin. His body is stripped, when all color and pretenses are taken away from him. His heart is pierced when the life-blood of his formerly reigning corruptions is let out."

Are we thus crucified with Christ? It is only as we are that we can be truly consecrated to Him. Are the marks of the purity and holiness of Jesus in our body? Are the marks of the patience, the humility, the cheerfulness, and the forgiveness of Jesus seen in our character? Are the marks of His love, compassion, and tenderness apparent in our life? Are the marks of the faith and faithfulness of Jesus evident to others?

Determination in the Lord

"Let no man trouble me," says Paul. He seems to say, "If you think that by your persecutions you will move me, or by your devices ensnare me, you are mistaken. I have had too much experience, and I trust in an unfamiliar Friend. He will help me." Paul had backbone. He was no weathervane to be turned by man's fickle mind. He calls himself contemptible in speech, weak in body, and not impressive in appearance; but he was rich in having holy stamina which was evidenced in the conflict he had with himself, when he said, "I keep under my body" (1 Corinthians 9:27). In his progress in the Divine life he was an ardent and determined athlete, saying, "I press toward the mark for the prize" (Philippians 3:14). In his sufferings and persecutions for Christ's sake he stood like a bold and solid rock in the sea around which the angry waves lash in vain. Only he could state, "None of these things move me" (Acts 20:24).

There is a determination which is born of self-will, a refusing to give in because self-interest is at stake. Not so in the case of Paul. His was a determination *in the Lord*. That is, he was moving along the lines of God's Word, and in His will; thus all that he had to endure came to him because of his faithfulness to his Lord; and knowing this, he was as fearless as a lion.

Honored by the Lord

Paul counted it an honor to have fellowship with the Lord in suffering, so he gloried in tribulations, knowing that they were to him what the grinding is to the diamond. They were working for him an experience like his Lord's, so that Divine grace should sparkle out in his life (Romans 5:3-5). He rejoiced in bodily weakness—the thorn in the flesh—because it was to him what the fire is to the sweet spices: it brought out the fragrance and gave Christ an opportunity for His power to rest upon him (2 Corinthians 12:9, 10).

When John Clark, of Meldon, France, was for Christ's sake whipped for three several days, and afterwards received a mark in his forehead as a sign of infamy, his mother, instead of being influenced by angry feelings, exclaimed exultingly, "Blessed be Christ, and welcome be these prints and marks of Christ," words which encouraged her son and showed how much that mother gloried in suffering for Christ.

The early Christians rejoiced that they were counted worthy to suffer shame for the name of Christ. Latimer said that "suffering for Christ is the greatest promotion that Christ gives in this world." Glover, the martyr, wept for joy at his imprisonment. Bradford said, "God forgive me for my unthankfulness for His exceeding great mercy, that among so many thousands He chooses me to be one in whom He will suffer." Eusebius, in speaking in the days of Severus, of the martyrs' release from prison, says, "They seemed to have come out of a perfuminghouse, rather than a prison-house. Merry they were, and much cheered that they were so much honored as to suffer for Christ."

These early Christians, knowing that suffering and glory were coupled together, rejoiced in suffering. An honored servant of Christ, in company with the writer, and sharing in the conversation about the sufferings of the apostle Paul, remarked, "Paul was what he was because his eyes were fixed on the glory." And so the Holy Spirit reminds us, through Paul, "If children, then heirs; heirs of God, and joint-heirs with Christ; if so be that we suffer with him, that we may be also glorified together. For I reckon that the sufferings of this present time are not worthy to be compared with the glory which shall be revealed in us" (Romans 8:17, 18).

30

The Discipler's Enemy

There are three enemies that oppose the Christian. These are *internal*, *external*, and *infernal:*

First. *The internal enemy*. The internal enemy is the evil principle that is called the "*flesh*" (John 3:6; Romans 7:18). This is opposed to the Holy Spirit and can only be overcome by Him (Galatians 5:16-26; comp. R.S.V.)

Second. *The external enemy*. The external enemy is the "*world*" (James 1:27; 4:4) and its trinity of evil (1 John 2:15-17). This can only be conquered by the Father in the Almightiness of His love (1 John 3 and 4).

Third. *Infernal enemies*. The infernal enemies are Satan and all his hosts as described in Ephesians 6:11, 12. These can only be defeated by the Lord who has already annulled the power of the wicked one (Hebrews 2:14; 1 John 3:8).

Thus while we have three enemies to meet, we have a *threefold power* to conquer them—*Father*, *Son*, and *Holy Spirit*.

In *Paradise Lost* Milton relates that, suspecting Satan to be in the garden of Eden, two angels instituted a search. They found a toad whispering evil in the ear of Eve, as she, together with her husband, reposed in one of its bowers. One of the angels (Ithuriel) touched the toad with his spear, and up rose, in all his fallen grandeur and malignity, the tempter, the devil. We are exposed to evil: when we would do good, evil is present with us. It is sometimes difficult to detect; but touch it with the sword of the Spirit, which is more powerful than Ithuriel's spear, and the evil will appear in its true colors.

As the imagined spear in the hand of the angel discovered Satan in his true character, so the Word of God is that which will reveal to us the *working*, as well as the *person* of the evil one. Satan's tactics lie in one of two extremes: he assumes one of two characters; knowing this, the child of God is forearmed for his "schemes" (2 Corinthians 2:11; Ephesians 6:11 NIV). There is nothing to fear when the believer is protected by the whole armor of God.

Satan comes as a roaring lion to persecute: or as an angel of light to patronize (1 Peter 5:8; 2 Corinthians 6:14)

Satan as an "angel of light" is more to be dreaded than Satan as a "roaring lion." A patronizing enemy is far worse than a persecuting one. In *Pilgrim's Progress* Bunyan brings this out strikingly. Christian had a hard fight with Apollyon in the Valley of Humiliation, and the enemy nearly overcame him; but the sword of the Spirit in the hand of Christian put even his strong enemy to flight.

Mark the contrast which Bunyan elsewhere presents. After Christian and Hopeful had been up the Delectable mountains and when they were proceeding on their journey, they came to two ways. There they stopped and conferred as to which they should take. Presently a black man in "a very light robe" asked the travelers why they were standing there. They told him of their perplexity and were led by him, as they supposed, in the right way. But instead of conducting them aright, the stranger led the travelers into a net. They woke up to know the wiles of the flatterer. It is a faithful picture of the deceitful workings of Satan.

In the early Church, Satan's policy was persecution. But persecution only caused the fire of truth to burn the more brightly. It made the Christians more zealous to spread the gospel. When Saul was persecuting the Church, the scattered flock "went everywhere preaching the Word" (Acts 8:1-4). Latimer may have thought of this at the stake when he turned to his companion, the saintly Ridley, with the cheering words, "We shall this day light such a candle, by God's grace, in England as I trust will never be put out." Now, as of old, where persecution exists, it acts like a bellows to increase the flame of truth and godliness. On the other hand, flattery, like water, puts out the fire.

But has not Satan changed his policy today? He does not so much attack the truth in the front as he seeks to undermine it through professed "supporters." He seeks to overthrow the kingdom of Christ—not so much by open persecution as by leading Christians to compromise by associating with the world and adopting its suggestions as to carrying on Christian work.

Satan comes as the adversary to accuse, or as the serpent to beguile

In the book of Job Satan is seen accusing that patriarch of serving God because it *paid* him to do so, because it was to his advantage (Job 1:9-11). He appears in the same character in the book of Zechariah. When God would act in grace toward His people, Satan stands up to resist the action (Zechariah 3:1, 2). Again, in the book of Revelation, he is said to be the *accuser of the brethren* (Revelation 12:10). These Scriptures lead us to believe that Satan has access into the presence of God. There he makes charges against the people of God. As Satan sought to thwart Christ in His mission by claiming homage (Matthew 4:9); as he opposed Him by seeking to divert Him from the path of suffering, using Peter as spokesman (Matthew 23); as he filled the heart of Judas to sell his Master for thirty pieces of silver (John 13:2); as he sought to sift Peter that the Divine life in him might be shaken so that he would deny his Master (Luke 22:31); as he hindered Paul from going to Thessalonica (1 Thessalonians 2:18)—so he seeks by every means still to oppose the child and servant of God.

Not only does Satan oppose and accuse, but he seeks to corrupt our minds from "the simplicity that is in Christ" (2 Corinthians 11:3). He overcame Eve by casting a doubt on the word of God. Thus he led her to suspect the goodness of God. In the same way our adversary accuses us to God. As the father of lies he misrepresents God to us.

One has said, "Satan would make us think hard things of Divine providence, and wicked things about Divine grace. Let us not believe his slanders of our Heavenly Father, for our Father does not heed what he says of us."

Satan seeks to make men represent him as an awful personage, or as a nobody

The late Bishop Villiers was once heard to remark on "the dangerous tendency of those old pictures, so familiar to us all, and so often exhibited to children, in which Satan was represented as some grim, dark, ugly monster, the very sight of whom it was terrible to behold."

A broad-shouldered Scotchman, looking at Schaefer's painting of "The Temptation of Our Lord," said, as he pointed to the figure of Satan, "If that chiel cam' to me in sic an ugly shape, I think he wud hae a teuch job wi' me too."

"I could not help smiling," adds John de Liefde, narrator of the incident; "but I felt there was much truth in the remark."

Satan realized that he had overstepped the mark in presenting himself as an ugly monster. Such representation was more likely, perhaps, to suit his purpose in the dark ages than today. Now he seeks to persuade men that he is not a person, and that all the devil there is, is to be found in men's hearts. This theory is described in the following quaint lines:

"Men don't believe in a devil now,
  As their fathers used to do;
They've forced the door of the broadest creed
  To let his form pass through.
There isn't a print of his cloven foot.
  Or a fiery dart from his bow.
To be found in earth or air today,
  For the world has voted so.
But who is it mixing the fatal draught
  That palsies heart and brain,
And loads the bier of each passing year
  With ten hundred thousand slain?
Who blights the bloom of the land today
  With the fiery breath of hell?
If the devil isn't, and never was,
  Won't somebody rise and tell?
Who dogs the steps of the striving saint,
  And digs the pit for his feet?
Who sows the tares in the field of time
  Whenever God sows His wheat?
The devil is voted not to be,
  And, of course, the thing is true;

But who is doing the kind of work
The devil alone should do?
We are told he does not go around
Like a roaring lion now;
But whom shall we hold responsible
For the everlasting row
To be heard in home, in Church and State,
To the earth's remotest bound,
If the devil by a unanimous vote
Is nowhere to be found?
Won't somebody step to the front just now,
And make his bow and show
How the frauds and the crimes of a single day
Spring up? We want to know.
The devil was fairly voted out,
And, of course, the devil's gone;
But simple people would like to know
Who carries his business on."

If there is no devil, where does the devilishness come from? If there is no devil, then the Word of God is not true; the temptation in the Garden of Eden is a myth; and the recorded utterances of Satan are simple fables.

Let's suppose a gang of bandits wishes to capture a party of travelers, who decline to pass a certain mountain because of reported danger. They wait for the arrival of a powerful escort. The bandits could not adopt a better policy than to send one of their number in disguise to the travelers with the assurance that their fear of danger is groundless. There are no robbers on the mountain! If the travelers believe the story of the disguised bandit, one can easily see how fatal the issue is likely to be.

Beware of this lie of the devil's, that there is no devil to lie. Mind this policy of the evil one which asserts that there is no enemy to frame a policy.

Satan seeks to induce men to attach little importance to doctrine and to exalt life at its expense, or else to make much of doctrine and little of the life

A very popular statement just now is, "It doesn't matter what you believe, so long as you are sincere." Can a building be constructed without a plan? Can a business be carried on without method ? No. Neither can character be formed apart from the truth.

The writer says, "Build yourselves up on your most holy faith" (Jude 20 RSV). Is the "most holy faith" here the act of believing—or the thing believed? We believe it is the same as that spoken of in verse 3 of the same epistle—the "faith which was once for all delivered to the saints." What is this but the truth of God? What is the truth but the doctrine or teaching of the Holy Spirit?

In his Epistles to Timothy and Titus, the apostle Paul speaks a great deal about doctrine. He speaks of things that are "contrary to sound *doctrine*"; of being "nourished up in the words . . . of good *doctrine*"; counsels Timothy to "give attendance to *doctrine*"; to "take heed unto the *doctrine*"; to "count worthy of double honor" those elders who "rule well," "especially they who labor in the

Word and *doctrine*." Servants are to "count their own masters worthy of all honor, that the name of God and His *doctrine* be not blasphemed." The apostle teaches that anyone who propounds other than "the *doctrine* which is according to godliness," is "proud, knowing nothing"; he tells Timothy he has fully known his *doctrine*; and he declares that the inspired Word is profitable for *doctrine*. He bids this "son in the faith" "reprove with . . . *doctrine*"; he also warns him of the time when men "will not endure sound *doctrine*" (1 Timothy 1:10; 4:6, 13, 16; 5:17; 6:1, 3; 2 Timothy 3:10, 16; 4:2, 3).

In writing to Titus he says that a bishop must be one who is "able, by sound *doctrine* . . . to exhort"; he charges him to "speak the things which become sound *doctrine*"; "in *doctrine*" to show "uncorruptness," and to admonish servants to "adorn the *doctrine* of God our Savior in all things" (Titus 1:9; 2:1, 7, 10).

Thus we see the importance which the Holy Spirit attaches to the teaching that is inspired by Himself. Dyer says that "Christ is not only the Root upon which we grow, but the Rule by which we square." The straight rule of God's truth is the only means whereby we can have a straight life. Therefore let us take heed to ourselves, by taking heed to the Word—the doctrine of Christ.

But while Satan works, on the one hand, in the line of depreciating doctrine he goes also to the other extreme with some and says, "It is most important that you should take heed to the doctrine—that you should be orthodox; correct definitions of truth are essential as also are clear ideas. But the life—well—that will be all right."

The man who acts upon this principle is like one who, while knowing that the ruler is straight, pays no heed to making a straight line with it; or like a builder who has laid the foundation of the house and yet does not build on it. He is like a traveler who, while knowing the way to his desired haven, fails to walk in it. He is like a diseased person who knows a remedy but refuses to take it.

Satan tries to introduce jealousy among believers or else to make them indifferent to each other

We have a painful record of the wrangling spirit possessing the disciples of the Lord Jesus at a time when He stood in need of their sympathy. When they should have been grieved at knowing the treatment to which their Lord must be subjected at the hands of unrighteous men, they were occupied with *inquiring which of them should be greatest* (see Luke 9:46). The disciples seem never to have rejoiced the heart of Jesus by seeking to know how they might the more resemble *Him*, their perfect Example. On the contrary, we find them thus wrangling for position.

In discoursing on the damaging effect which dissension produces, an old writer well says, "O consider what a dishonor it is to the gospel that those who profess themselves sons of the same God, members of the same Christ, temples of the same Spirit, heirs of the same glory, should be jarring one with another; it is strange and unnatural that they who are saints in profession should be devils in practice; that God's diamonds should cut one another! For wolves to devour the lambs is no wonder, but for lambs to devour one another is a wonder, and monstrous."

Now mark another scheme of the adversary. If he cannot cause open hostility and friction he will seek to induce indifference; if he cannot stir up opposition he will try what assumption will do. Among the many things which wrung the heart of the apostle Paul were contentions, strifes, debates, variances.[1] Of such divisions he had to complain particularly in writing to the Church at Corinth.

There were quarrelings and wranglings among the believers there, which speedily caused "divisions" or parties in the Church, one saying, "I am of Paul," another, "I of Cephas," and another, "I of Christ." Thus a rent[2] was caused, and instead of the Corinthian Church being spiritual, it was carnal. To defeat this spirit Paul enforces the truth that believers are members one of another, that all are in the mystical body of Christ—and that to set up divisions is to deny the Lordship of Christ, to fail in discerning the Lord's body by not apprehending the oneness of believers with Christ and consequent oneness with each other.

The secret of success and blessing in the Church of the first days undoubtedly lay in the recognition of each member as partaker of the one Spirit. In the Acts of the Apostles we have a sevenfold unity:

1. In *prayer* (Acts 1:14).
2. In *obedience* (Acts 2:1).
3. Of *presence* (Acts 2:1).
4. Of *purpose* (Acts 2:46).
5. In *praise* (Acts 4:24).
6. In *service* (Acts 5:12).
7. In *recognizing God's servants* (Acts 15:25).

Mark the words, "*one accord*" in these verses from Acts. Christians should be like a well-tuned harp upon which the Master of Assemblies can produce the melodies of righteousness of life, holiness of character, love to each other, and glory to God in the highest. But if we allow Satan to introduce jealousy, or lull us to indifference, our state will be like that of a harp out of tune whose discord will offend.

Satan seeks to inflate with pride, or else to cast down by discouragement

Pride is like Joseph's coat—of many colors. It presents itself in a variety of ways. There is *pride of gift*. Some Christian workers give one the impression that they are the only ones to do certain things, and that no one can match them in their chosen domain. They seem to think they are, like King Saul, head and shoulders above everybody else.

There is *pride of attainment*. Bunyan brings this out in his picture of Christian outrunning Faithful: "Then did Christian vaingloriously smile, because he had gotten the start of his brother; but not taking good heed to his feet, he suddenly stumbled and fell, and could not rise again until Faithful came up to help him."

---

1. The same Greek word is translated *strife* in Romans 13:13; 1 Corinthians 3:3; Philippians 1:15; 1 Timothy 6:4; *variance* in Galatians 5:20; *debates* in 2 Corinthians 12:20; *contentions* in 1 Corinthians 1:11; Titus 3:9.

2. The word rendered *division* in 1 Corinthians 1:10 is translated *rent* in Matthew 9:16.

Let us beware of boasting of our attainments. Let us leave the things that are behind and seek to apprehend that for which we are apprehended of Christ Jesus.

There is *pride of dress*. There is not much to be proud of in dress; as Matthew Henry says, "Clothes came in with sin; we had had no occasion for them, either for defense or decency, if sin had not made us naked to our shame. Little reason, therefore, have we to be proud of our clothes, which are but the badges of our poverty and shame."

There are many other phases of pride. Pride, like the chameleon, has many hues, but those to which we have called attention indicate some of its workings. As a rule its presence is prominent, for it climbs a tree—not to see Jesus, as Zaccheus did, but to be seen itself.

Now if Satan fails in his attempt to puff us up with pride and trick us into thinking we are *somebody*, he will go to the opposite extreme. He will try to persuade us that we are *nobody*. I remember reading somewhere of a conference in hell at which the subject was discussed. What was the most effectual way to overthrow the work of Christ in the heart of a faithful servant? One demon suggested putting before this saint the pleasures of the world in the most fascinating array. Another sought to bring dismay into the heart of the saint by picturing to him the sorrow and privations to which unflinching truthfulness would probably lead, and thus to get him to relax his service and devotion. But these propositions were considered to be inadequate, based on the fact that the pleasures at God's right hand were more powerful than those of sin and that the glory hereafter would enable the saint to bear present suffering. At last one said confidently that he had a plan which was sure to succeed: he would *discourage* the servant of God in his work. An exulting shout rose from each demon, all agreeing that this temptation would result in fiendish triumph.

How well the enemy succeeded with Elijah we know from the scene in 2 Kings 19. There the discouraged prophet requests that he may die. To be discouraged is a sin—it is disobedience to the injunction, "Be strong and of a good courage." Discouragement is a cancer which eats faith and strength away. It tends to produce such conduct as that of the children of Israel when they gave heed to the false report of the unbelieving spies (Deuteronomy 1:28).

Satan's policy is often to cause one to lean on self, or only partially to trust in Christ

Jesus said to Peter, "Satan demanded to have you, that he might sift you like wheat" (Luke 22:31 RSV), He was speaking of coming temptation. This should have put Peter on the alert and caused him to ask for the Lord's intervention. Instead of that, in his self-confidence he declared, "I am ready to go with thee, both into prison and to death" (verse 33). But Christ who knew Peter better than Peter knew himself told him that before the cock should crow he should deny Him three times. We know how successful Satan was in overthrowing Peter and what a miserable spectacle he made as he stood among the ungodly, denying his Lord with oaths and curses.

Self-confidence is *disobedience*, for the Lord has told us to deny *self itself* and to follow Him who pleased not Himself, but was always the dependent Man. He ever trusted His Father and acted in the Spirit's might. Self-confidence is *damaging*, for it precedes a fall—and the fall means loss of power and joy. Self-confidence is *presumption*. Christ has said that apart from Him we can do nothing, even as the branch of the vine cannot bring forth fruit of itself. Faith acts on the word of the Lord as the children of Israel at the Red Sea did when they obeyed the command, "Go forward"; but self-confidence goes, as did the Egyptians, without any command, and defeat and death are the consequences. Beware of this Satanic device for it makes men like Satan himself: he fell because of his self-confidence, and all who walk in his steps will meet with the same fate.

On the other hand, Satan frequently pursues a different policy; if he cannot influence us to trust in self *only*, he will suggest that we trust partly in Christ and partly in self. He turns preacher and says, "It is quite right to trust in Christ; but do not go too far. Be cautious; be reasonable. Put Saul's armor on; that will protect you should you get a nasty knock; and with it, you can go in the name of the Lord as well." We can see at once that this will not do when we remember our relation to our Lord. Is the Lord simply our guest? Or is He indeed the Lord and we His slaves? The latter most assuredly. We are what the apostle Paul gloried in being, the "bond-slaves of Jesus Christ." Since we are the property of the Lord Jesus Christ, it is for us to remember that all our responsibility is to do what He wills and says. And He has most distinctly told us to be strong in Himself and to trust in His arm alone.

The whole secret of our being able to detect the "schemes" (thoughts) and "wiles" (traps) of the devil (2 Corinthians 2:11 RSV; Ephesians 6:11) is to be found in the following—

Three Things of God

1. *The Spirit of God is our power.*—"Be strong in the Lord, and in the power of His might" (Ephesians 6:10). A similar expression occurs in Ephesians 1:19, and refers to the mightiness of the Almighty God, which He put forth when He raised Christ from the dead—the power of the Holy Spirit, as we know from Romans 8:11. Can we think of defeat when we know the power that is behind us; nay, within us, if we are living in Christ our Lord, and under the control of His Spirit?

2. *The armor of God is our covering.*—"Put on the whole armor of God" (Ephesians 6:11). We can obey this injunction only as we respond to the previous one. The Holy Spirit is the power to enable us to clothe ourselves in the armor of God. The Lord Jesus Himself is the One who answers to every piece of the armor of God. Hence we are told to "put on the Lord Jesus Christ" (Romans 13:14). We need a whole Christ to protect us, and if we apprehend Him as our Protector and Protection, we will be safe.

3. *The Word of God is our sword.* We are not only to stand on the defensive, but we are to be on the offensive in using the Word of God, which is able to give our enemy a thrust, setting him off to his confusion and defeat. Remember that Christ met Satan's trickery by wielding the sword of the Spirit.

Let us be *valid*, true, and upright, doing the will of God from the heart and taking care that there is no communication with the fleshly enemy within nor the infernal enemy without.

Let us be *vigilant* as Satan is ever on the alert; and if he can only catch us napping, he is sure to place us in some Doubting Castle or otherwise to hinder our usefulness.

Let us be *valiant*, not counting on defeat but remembering that we have to do with a conquered foe, one whom Christ has already defeated. Therefore let us not be afraid, since Jehovah says, "Fear thou not" (Isaiah 41:10).

31

The Discipler's All

The Lord Jesus is not only the One in whom all blessing rests, but He also answers to every blessing we need. He is the Embodiment of blessing. This is seen in the following alphabetical Bible reading. Christ is the—

Acceptance to justify	(Ephesians 1:6)
Blessing to enrich	(Deuteronomy 23:23)
Comfort to cheer	(2 Corinthians 1:4)
Deliverance to defend	(Psalm 67:20, R.V.)
Enjoyment to satisfy	(Jeremiah 31:13, 14)
Favor to charm	(Luke 2:52; Jeremiah 31:9, mar.)
Grace to strengthen	(2 Corinthians 12:9)
Health to invigorate	(Psalm 42:11; 43:5)
Instruction to enlighten	(Psalm 32:8)
Joy to gladden	(Nehemiah 8:10; Psalm 16:11)
Kindness to crown	(Psalm 103:4)
Light to reveal	(John 8:12)
Mercies to surround	(Lamentations 3:22-25)
Nurture to cherish	(Ephesians 5:29, 30, 32)
Owner to claim	(Isaiah 43:1)
Power to keep	(1 Peter 1:5)
Quietness to calm	(Isaiah 30:15; 32:17, 18)
Redemption to liberate	(Isaiah 61:1 Luke 4:18)
Sunshine to warm	(Psalm 84:11)
Truth to arm	(Psalm 91:4)
Union to secure	(Psalm 91:1, 14)
Virtue to purify	(Matthew 5:8; Ephesians 5:26)
Wisdom to guide	(1 Corinthians 1:30)
'Xperience to assure	(Galatians 2:20)
Youth to renew	(Isaiah 40:31)
Zeal to inspire	(John 2:17)

Let us not look at *something* but let us look to the SOMEONE—namely, to CHRIST HIMSELF; then we shall have the best of blessing in having *Him*.

One reason why the Holy Spirit takes up His abode in the believer is to make objective truth an inward reality, to cause our standing in Christ to be a matter of experience. The Holy Spirit directs the attention of the Church at Colosse to this very thing. For instance, the resurrection of Christ is a historical fact. It is also a truth that is put to the credit of the believer—who, in God's reckoning, rose when Christ rose. But the apostle carries the mind to the practical belief of this truth, and urges: "If ye then be risen with Christ, seek those things which are above" (Colossians 3:1). The effect of this association with Christ in resurrection is to lift the believer above sin and the world, to godliness of life and Christlike action.

The Holy Spirit also reminds us that in Christ's death we died (Colossians 3:3 RSV); that our life is "hid with Christ in God" as to our present security and comfort and we are to rejoice in the prospect that "when Christ, who is our Life, shall appear" *(be manifested)*, we also "shall appear" *(be manifested)* "with him in glory." Meanwhile, we are to be diligent to put to death the deeds of the body; to put off the old man and his deeds as we should discard a useless and unfit garment; and to put on the new man which is after Christ, and is of God's ordering and making—as were Aaron's garments of glory and beauty.

"Christ is all and in all"; that is, all who believe in Christ have one common standing. There are no distinctions in Christ. He does not give His gifts and graces to a select few, but Christ is in all who believe, whether they be bond or free, Jew or Gentile. It is not our intention to dwell upon the connection in which this expression, "Christ is all," occurs, but rather to take it as indicating what the worker's all is, namely, THE PERSON OF CHRIST.

Dyer says, "The Lord Jesus is fairer than the fairest, sweeter than the sweetest, nearer than the nearest, dearer than the dearest, richer than the richest, and better than the best. . . . He is a believer's *all*. Now that which is his all must needs be precious. Christ is his all; He is all that he has, He is all that he enjoys. Christ is all that he is worth, He is all that he is, he is no such thing without Him. Whatever he is worth, it is He that makes him worth it. It is not worth a man's while to live unless he live in Christ. Christ is the Gain of the believer, living and dying; so that whatever is good for a believer, he must say, For this I am beholden to Christ."

The Christian says of Christ what Phocion said of her husband when she was asked where her jewels were: "My husband and his triumphs are my jewels." Christ is our Gain and Glory.

There are four ways in which the worker specially delights to say "Christ is all."[1]

1. Christ is all in *Scripture*. 2. Christ is all in *Salvation*. Christ is all in *Sanctification*. 4. Christ is all in *Service*.

---

1. The Jews called the Shekinah by a word which means "all." With the Cabalists it is one of the names of God. This thought is expressed in Colossians 1:15-18.

Christ Is All in Scripture

To take Christ from the Scripture would be like taking the sun from our planet. All would be darkness and death. The Person around Whom all Scripture revolves and to Whom it all relates is Christ.

The Father points to Him. The voice from the throne of God comes to us like sweet music, borne upon the summer breeze, "Behold my Servant whom I uphold; mine elect, in whom my soul delighteth" (Isaiah 42:1). The Father seems to say to us, "See His condescension and grace in coming to the earth. Ponder His prayerful and loving manner. Meditate upon His willing and joyful obedience. Behold His pure and holy life. Mark His persevering and painstaking service. Look at His patient and providing love. Note His calmness and courage in trial. Consider His wondrous and loving compassion. Keep in mind His determination to do My will: His fidelity to My word and work: His life-purpose to please and glorify Me. Mark well His glorious work upon the cross, and the all-sufficient atonement He made there."

The Holy Spirit speaks of Christ. By type and title, by symbol and statement, the Holy Spirit sings the praises of Christ.

In Genesis, He is the promised Seed, and the Princely Shiloh.

In Exodus, the Redeeming Lamb, the Resident Leader, the Riven Rock, the Resuscitating Manna, and the Mighty Warrior.

In Leviticus, He is beheld as the Burnt Offering, for it typifies Him as the One who perfectly pleased and glorified God. In the Meat Offering, His perfect life and powerful ministry are portrayed; in the Peace Offering we behold Him who has made peace by the blood of His cross, bringing the believer into fellowship with God; in the Sin Offering we gaze upon Him—made sin for us—suffering outside the camp. In the Trespass Offering we note Him who bore our sins in His own body on the tree; and in the Drink Offering we see Him who poured out His soul unto death for us. In the cities of Refuge we are reminded of Him who is our Eternal Refuge.

In Numbers we see Him prefigured in the uplifted Serpent; while His coming is foretold by Balaam as the Star out of Jacob.

The characters recounted in the historical books represent on a small scale, the trials and triumphs of Him who is David's Son and Lord. And the glory of Solomon is obscured before the glory of Him, who is "greater than Solomon."

In the Psalms we have the inner life and experience of Christ, in the bitterness of the Suffering One of the twenty-second Psalm as well as in the blessedness of THE MAN of the first Psalm. His death on the cross is alluded to in the "sinking in deep mire" of Psalm 69; and His glory and gladness are hinted at in Psalms 16 and 24.

The prophetical books are full of the coming One and His glory.

Isaiah records His devotion in suffering to the death; His determination in doing the will of God, as well as the gladsome day for earth when He reigns as King.

Daniel, too, speaks of His coming as King and of Him who was "cut off" in death.

Micah predicts Him, in His twofold nature, as the One born in Bethlehem yet Whose goings forth were from eternity.

Zechariah points to Christ as the Shepherd smitten and as the kingly Priest reigning over His people in peace and blessing.

As the golden threads were interwoven into the vestments of Aaron, so the Golden One of heaven is inwrought in Scripture, from Genesis to Revelation. Think of HIM! Mark the characters He bears and remember how the Word of His Truth speaks of Him and reveals Him as bearing these. He is the Atonement to cover, the Advocate to look after our interests, the Brother to sympathize, the Bread of Life to feed, the Companion to cheer, the Captain to command, the Deliverer to liberate, the Day Star to guide, the Example to influence, the Emmanuel to dwell, the Friend to keep, the Foundation to uphold, the Guard to protect, the Guide to direct, the High Priest to represent, the Husband to cherish, the Intercessor to plead, the I AM to supply, Jesus to save, Jehovah to keep, the Life to ennoble, the Lovely One to attract, the Minister to serve, the Mediator to interpose, the Near kinsman to identify, the Nourishment to sustain, the Offering to atone, the Overseer to superintend, the Purifier to sanctify, the Passover to shelter, the Rock to hide, the Refuge to shield, the Strength to empower, the Shepherd to defend, the Teacher to instruct, the Truth to arm, the Understanding to enlighten, the Unction to empower, the Vine to enrich, the Virtue to bless, the Way into the holiest, the Wonderful to charm, yesterday, today, and forever the same; the Zeal to inspire us, and the Zone to encircle us.

Christ Is All in Salvation

Christ died to save us from the penalty and the guilt of sin; He lives to deliver from the power and government of sin; and He is coming again to emancipate from the presence of sin. Thus, salvation is threefold. It is past and complete to the one who rests in Christ and His finished work:—"By grace you have been saved through faith" (Ephesians 2:8 RSV), that is, from the consequence of sin, Christ having borne on the cross the wrath due to sin. Salvation is present and continuous. As we trust in the living Christ He is able to save *to* as well as *from* the uttermost, those who come unto God by Him (Hebrews 7:25). As we abide in Him, He saves us from the power and love of sin. He keeps us from consciously sinning. Salvation is also future and full. When Christ comes again we will be saved from the body that has been humiliated by sin (Philippians 3:20, 21), and we will be fashioned like Himself.

These three aspects of salvation are illustrated in the action of the high priest on the Day of Atonement. They are demonstrated in the three appearings in Hebrews 8:24-28.

On the Day of Atonement Aaron killed the bullock at the altar of burnt offering, which was afterwards burned outside the camp as the sin offering to make atonement for Israel. In the same way "Christ" once in the end of the world "appeared to put away sin by the sacrifice of himself."

Another action of the high priest's was to take the blood of the bullock and of the goat into the Holiest of all. There he sprinkled the blood seven times before the mercy-seat and once upon it. He sprinkled the blood for himself and for his house, and also for the whole nation of Israel. What is the comment of the Holy Spirit upon this? "By His own blood" Christ "entered in once into the holy place, having obtained eternal redemption for us . . . Christ is not entered into the holy places made with hands, which are the figures of the true; but into heaven itself, now to appear in the presence of God for us" (Hebrews 9:12, 24). By virtue of Christ's atonement He has gone into the presence of God for us, bearing in His body the marks of His suffering. Now He lives to bless, to keep, to cheer, to uphold, to plead, to represent, to sympathize, and to empower His own.

After the high priest came out of the Holiest of all he put off the holy linen garments and put on the garments of glory and beauty (Leviticus 16:23, 24). All the while the high priest was in the Holiest of all he was not seen nor heard by the people. But when he came out, clothed in his beautiful garments, they knew his work inside was finished. Even so, Christ shall "appear the second time without sin unto salvation," and when He is manifested, it shall be in power and great glory.

Thus Christ is all in salvation. Salvation! What a word! It is all that Christ is, has done, is doing, and will yet do. As Dyer says, "All that Christ did and suffered, it is for me; all that Christ has is mine. O soul, Christ's love is yours to pity you; Christ's mercy is yours to save you; Christ's graces are yours to beautify you; and His glory is yours to crown you. Christ's power is yours to protect you; Christ's wisdom is yours to counsel you; His angels are yours to guard you; His Spirit is yours to comfort you; and His Word is yours to teach you."

Christ Is All in Sanctification

Sanctification has two aspects. There is what might be called *positional* sanctification, or meetness for God's presence, and there is *practical* sanctification, or the manifestation of Christ in the life. The first is complete, and depends on Christ. The second is continuous and depends upon our willingness to allow Christ, by the Holy Spirit through the truth, to possess us. Let us briefly call to mind what our Lord says upon these aspects of holiness, which may be classed under two words, namely, *meetness* and *manifestation*.

First. *Meetness in Christ*. "Sanctified in Christ Jesus" (1 Corinthians 1:2). "By one offering He hath perfected for ever them that are sanctified" (Hebrews 10:14). "Giving thanks unto the Father, who hath made us meet [qualified us R.V.] to be partakers of the inheritance of the saints in light" (Colossians 1:12). The same word as is here translated "meet" is rendered "sufficient" in 2 Corinthians 3:5). "Accepted in the Beloved" (Ephesians 1:6). To sum up the above Scriptures, we find that the *Cause* of our sanctification is the Father; the *Agent* of it is the Holy Spirit; the *Ground* of it is the atonement of Christ; and the *Measure* of it is the Person and position of Christ. As the words "Holiness to the Lord," were graven upon the mitre of the high priest, that the children of Israel might always be accepted before the Lord (Exodus 28:36), so Christ the Holy One, with whom every believer is identified, is ever before God for us, and in Him we are always accepted.

Second. *Manifestation of Christ*. "I live; yet not I, but Christ liveth in me" (Galatians 2:20). "For to me to live is Christ" (Philippians 1:21). "Abide in me, and I in you" (John 15:4). The purpose of God in uniting us to Christ was that we should be possessed by Christ, that we should be able to imitate Christ, for we cannot copy Christ of ourselves. This is seen in John 1:29, 36. In those verses we have two "Beholds:"—the "Behold" of *salvation* —"Behold the Lamb of God, which taketh away the sin of the world"; and the "Behold" of *imitation*, as John directs his disciples the second time, to behold the Lamb of God while He walks, not saying anything about sin on that occasion. It was as if he said, "You saw the Lamb of God as your Sin-Bearer yesterday, and today you behold Him as your Example: follow Him, don't look to me." But in between these two "Beholds" we find John bearing testimony to the fact that Christ should baptize with the Holy Spirit. Is not the order in which the truth is presented Divine? First, Jesus the Sin-Bearer; second, Christ the Empowerer; and third, the Lamb as the Example.

And note this: we can only imitate the Christ *without* as revealed in the Word by the power of the indwelling Christ *within*. An illustration of this may be found in the following:—"Only the Spirit of the Lord within us can reproduce the image of the Lord that is set before us. Let us suppose that you have the original picture of Raphael's 'Transfiguration.' You desire to reproduce it; just as many people talk about copying or imitating Jesus Christ. You bring out your brushes, your paints, your pencils, and your easel, and set to work. When you have worked at it for a day, you will probably find what miserable work you are making of it. You try again and again, but by and by you become the laughing-stock of your neighbors, and they see very plainly that you are not an artist. Then you begin to be in despair and are ready to give it up. But let us suppose, if it were possible, that the spirit of Raphael should enter into you. Well, I do not say that he would produce the picture at once. It would take that spirit some time to get the mastery of your fingers, to train your eye to the delicate perceptions of proportion and perspective. But if Raphael's spirit were in you, he would more and more train your faculties to his use, till by and by he would perfectly reproduce Raphael's picture. So exactly does the Lord deign to set the portrait of Himself before us, and tells us to reproduce it, since He puts His Spirit within us. *It is only Christ who can produce Christ. It is only the Christ within that can reproduce the Christ without.*"

Remember how the "Acts of the Apostles" begins. No: they are not the "Acts of the Apostles," but the acts of Christ by the Holy Spirit, through the Apostles. How does the book begin? "The former treatise have I made, O Theophilus, of all that *Jesus began both to do and teach.*" As much as to say, "This which I now write is a continuation of His work." We see the devotion and determination, the consecration and courage, the service and suffering, the work and witnessing of the early Christians, and we know that all this was not natural to them, but that it was the supernatural presence of Christ working through them.

Christ Is All in Service

As the engine has no power to move itself and is only of use when the steam is up, so the worker has no might in himself. He can work only as God Himself works in him.

As Secker says, "Gracious hearts are like stars in the heavens, which shine not by their own splendor. He who takes the brick must give straw to make it. There is no water unless He smite the rock, nor fire except He strike the flint. . .

'Lord, Thy pound hath gained ten pounds.' It is not my pains, but Thy pound, that hath done it." Apart from Christ, we are nothing, and can do nothing (John 15:5); but with Him we can say with beloved Paul, "I can do all things through Christ which strengtheneth me" (Philippians 4:13).

Christ Is Our All-glorious Theme. "I determined not to know anything among you, save Jesus Christ, and Him crucified" (1 Corinthians 2:2). Some would seem to know everything but Jesus Christ. A certain abbé once preached before Louis XVI a sermon which contained a good deal of politics, finance, and government. As the king was leaving the building, he was heard to remark, "If the abbé had only touched a little on religion, he would have told us of everything." This will not be said of him to whom Christ is all, for all his theme is Christ, *Christ*, CHRIST. And nought else must be our theme. Christ beginning, middle, and end; Christ in the glory of His person as the Son of God; Christ in the graciousness of His love in dying for sinners; Christ in the perfection of His offices; and Christ in the glory of His kingdom.

Christ Is Our All-perfect Example. He is our Copy to imitate; in delighting in the Father's will, in keeping to the Father's word, in doing the Father's work, and in bringing glory to the Father's name. In sympathy for the lost, in zeal in service, in constancy in prayer, and in doing good to others, He is our Pattern. In His love for the Scriptures, in the purity of His life, in the gentleness of His manner, in the holiness of His walk, in His patience under provocation, in His faith in God, in His dependence upon the Holy Spirit, in His care of His disciples, in His teaching of the ignorant, in His use of the Word of God in temptation, in His humble living, and in the "pleasing not" of Himself, He is our Example.

Christ Is Our All-inspiring Motive. "The love of Christ constraineth us," says the apostle Paul in speaking of the power which impelled him and compelled him to serve and to suffer. As the electric current runs along the wire, and causes the carbon to ignite, so the love of Christ is the secret influence which causes the believer to shine in holy living. As the river bears on its bosom the loaded barge, so does the love of Christ bear the disciples on their errand of mercy to others. As the love that Jonathan had for David prompted him to give him his clothes and his crown, so the love of Christ constrains the worker to do service for his Lord and Savior. Dyer well says, "Christ has made every believer a king. It is Christ's beauty that makes us beautiful: it is His riches that make us rich: it is His righteousness that makes us righteous"; and we may add, it is the love of Christ which makes us love like Christ.

Christ Is All Our Glory. One has well said, "Christ is the glory of glories, the crown of crowns, the heaven of heavens; He is light in darkness, joy in sadness, riches in poverty, life in death; it is He who can resolve all your doubts, secure you in danger, save your souls, and bring you to glory, where all joys are enjoyed. Oh, therefore, let all the glory of your glory be, to give all glory and yourselves to Him." Is Christ all to us? The above is the ideal. Is it actual? Let us ask a few questions to bring this question to a practical issue.

Is Christ all in our home? "Christ is Master of this house." Such words were hung in the hall of a devoted Christian. But there is no need to advertise this on our walls; if Christ is Master, the truth will be seen and felt.

Is Christ all in our business? "In business for the Lord," one had placarded in his shop. But this is superfluous: if the Lord is in the business, the fact will reveal itself. As clothes that have been lying in lavender emit fragrance, so the believer who lives with Christ will reveal the secret by the righteous way in which the business is transacted.

Is Christ all in our work? "Whatsoever ye do in word or deed, do all in the name of the Lord Jesus" (Colossians 3:17). This is the Divine injunction. Christian work is not confined to teaching a class in the Sunday school, giving away tracts, preaching the gospel, ministering to the needy. Whatsoever is done in the name of the Lord is work which is accepted by Him, whether it be serving behind the counter or scrubbing the floor. This the little servant girl realized as she scrubbed the floor the more thoroughly because she knew it would please her Savior.

Is Christ all in our possessions? Do we realize that we are stewards, left in trust by our Lord, to whom we have to render an account? The faithfulness of Abraham's Eliezer was seen in the interested way in which that devoted servant carried out his master's wishes. Thus the Lord has put us in trust, not only with the gospel, but also with all we have. Not only are we not our own, but all we have is not ours, but His. "Holiness unto the Lord" (Zechariah 14:20) should be stamped on all our possessions.

Is Christ all in our plans? It is ours to follow the Lord's plan, and not our own. But we should have no plans. Some content themselves with drawing up plans and seeking the Lord's blessing and approval on them; but surely a better way is to let the Lord plan and seek to have grace to follow His leading. Too often it is with us, "Lord, bless and prosper me in this or that line of action," while we *ought* to say, "Lord, what will *You* have me to do?"

Is Christ all in our pleasures? "Is there any harm in this?" "Can I go there?" These are the questions frequently put. If we can answer "*Yes*" to each of the following five questions, the difficulties in regard to any matter of this kind will go away:

Can we seek the blessing of Christ upon it?
Can we take the presence of Christ with us?
Will Christ take us to it?
Can we witness of Christ at it?
Can we glorify Christ in it?

"May I go to a dance?" was the question of a young lady to the writer. She knew there would be ungodly people at the dance, so her question was answered by putting it to herself, "Can you go to the dance?" and the young Christian replied, "No." There are pleasures that are healthful and profitable, while others are hurtful and damaging.

Is Christ all in our heart? The writer remembers hearing an honored and beloved minister of Christ relate how a lady came and unburdened her mind by asking these questions:

"I have lost all my property, and have been obliged to take a situation: I don't like it: is this pride, or proper self-respect?"—"I have a number of girls under me, and sometimes I speak sharply to them: is this temper, or a proper business spirit?"—"I have a very dear friend whom I love very much: is this an idol?"

The servant of Christ answered all her questions thus: "I don't know but I can tell you this: your heart down here is all wrong with the Lord up there."

If Christ is dwelling in the heart by faith, He will keep things in order. If Christ has the center of our being, the presence and the power of Christ will be felt to its circumference. When an old Christian was spoken of once as being eccentric, he replied simply, "Whether this is so or not, I do not know; this I know, that I am centered in Christ." If this is so with us, it will be seen in us, just as the impression of the seal is left on the wax. May Christ in very deed be All to us, and with the martyr we shall say, "None but Christ! none but Christ!" or with Augustine, "O Lord, take away all: only give me Thyself!" or with another—

"Christ for sickness, Christ for health,
Christ for poverty, Christ for wealth,
Christ for joy, Christ for sorrow,
Christ today, and Christ tomorrow,
Christ my Life, and Christ my Light,
Christ for morning, noon, and night,
Christ when all around gives way.
Christ my Everlasting Stay,
Christ my Rest, and Christ my Food,
Christ above my highest good,
Christ my Well-beloved, my Friend,
Christ my Pleasure without end,
Christ my Savior, Christ my Lord,
Christ my Portion, Christ my God,
Christ my Shepherd, I His sheep,
Christ Himself my soul doth keep,
Christ my Leader, Christ my Peace,
Christ hath brought my soul's release,
Christ my Righteousness Divine,
Christ for me, for He is mine,
Christ my Wisdom, Christ my Meat,
Christ restores my wandering feet,
Christ my Advocate and Priest,
Christ who ne'er forgets the least,
Christ my Teacher, Christ my Guide,
Christ my Rock, in Christ I hide,
Christ the Ever-living Bread,
Christ His precious blood hath shed,
Christ hath brought me nigh to God,
Christ the Everlasting Word,
Christ my Master, Christ my Head,
Christ who for my sins hath bled,
Christ my Glory, Christ my Crown,
Christ the Plant of great renown,
Christ my Comforter on high,
Christ my Hope draws ever nigh."

32

The Discipler's Model

Christ is *the* Worker's Model, and His servants are models as Christ lives and works in them. There are seven places in the First Epistle of John where the words "*as he*" occur, which remind us how we are to live and labor. *Fellowship.* "If we walk in the light, *as he* is in the light, we have fellowship" (1:7). *Abiding.* "He that saith he abideth in him, ought himself also so to walk, even *as he* walked" (2:6). *Likeness.* "When he shall appear, we shall be like him for we shall see him *as he* is" (3:2). *Purity.* "Every man that hath this hope . . . purifieth himself, even *as he* is pure" (3:3). *Righteousness.* "He that doeth righteousness is righteous, even *as he* is righteous" (3:7). *Love.* "Love one another, *as he* gave us commandment" (3:23). *Representation.* "*As he* is, so are we in this world" (4:17).

The model for Christian workers is Christ Himself, but there are many Christian workers who may be taken as models, if Christ is living and acting in and through them. Thus, Paul is a model of devotion, Barnabas of consecration, Stephen of faithfulness, and Peter of earnestness. But next to the Lord Jesus Himself we think that Philip stands before us as the model in evangelistic work. In him we see the qualifications that are necessary to make a good evangelist.

In the brief mentions of Philip's name as deacon, or as the kind host, or in his life-work of evangelist, we have the complete character of the man given us by the Holy Spirit in the Acts of the Apostles.

Chapter 6 shows us the Lord's choice of Philip as deacon. We believe he had all the qualifications as a man of "honest report, full of the Holy Ghost and wisdom." Chapter 21:8 gives us a glimpse of his home life as he hospitably entertains the servants of the Lord. And as evangelist, we find him in Samaria, in the midst of a great revival, where a preached Christ brought joy to many hearts; or, at the Spirit's bidding, removed to the quiet of the desert, awaiting the arrival of the chariot to whose eager occupant he successfully preached Jesus (Acts 8:5-40).

As deacon, Philip serves the church; in his courtesy in entertaining the servants of the Lord, he shines at home; and in his fervor and faithfulness and accompanying success in preaching the gospel, he is a pattern to all evangelists. Let us study Philip under the following aspects:—

1. The Man. 2. His Mission. 3. His Message. 4. His Manner. 5. His Might.

The Man

The natural question we ask in speaking of a person is, What kind of a man is he? We can easily answer this in reference to Philip, for we find that when the apostles told the church to select seven men for the office of deacon, they were to be men of special characteristics—"Men of honest report, full of the Holy Ghost" (Acts 6:3). "Men of honest report"—men against whom there was no charge of inconsistency in the life. But they were also to be men "full of the Holy Ghost." All workers for Christ should be this, but especially an evangelist. What should characterize those who are filled with the Holy Spirit. All that the Holy Spirit is will be manifested. To be specific, there are four characteristics which adorn one who is under the control of the Holy Spirit and in communion with Him.

1. *The man who is filled with the Holy Spirit will seek to act before God in everything*. If we are acting before men and seeking to be men-pleasers, there will be bondage of soul and bitterness of spirit. Acting before God means to be like Christ. We read of Him that He was to grow up before the Lord (Isaiah 53:2). Acting before God means to be right in the life—"Walk before me, and be thou perfect" (Genesis 17:1). Acting before God means holiness before God and righteousness before men. This Zacharias indicated in speaking of the purpose of Christ's work—"That he would grant unto us that we being delivered out of the hands of our enemies might serve him without fear, in holiness and righteousness before him, all the days of our life" (Luke 1:74, 75). Acting before God means that we are delivered from the fear of man. Thus we are enabled to act and to speak with courage, like Elijah when he confronted the wicked king Ahab with—"As the Lord God of Israel liveth, before whom I stand" (1 Kings 17:1). Acting before God is to be conscious of His presence, as exemplified in the offering up of the sacrifices in connection with the cleansing of the leper. The priests offered before the Lord. No less than nine times does the expression "before the Lord" occur in Leviticus 14. Acting before God means obedience to His word. Aaron was directed to set in order the shewbread and to light the lamps before the Lord as He commanded Moses (Exodus 40:23, 25). Acting before God favors the development of our own spiritual life. "Samuel grew before the Lord" (1 Samuel 2:21). Acting before God means pleading for souls and persistency in prayer, like Abraham when supplicating, on behalf of Sodom—"Abraham stood yet before the Lord" (Genesis 18:22). Acting before God means His approval as to our life—"Thee have I seen righteous before me," was the Lord's estimate of Noah. Acting before God means to tell out the Word of God faithfully—"I charge thee before God . . . preach the Word," said Paul to Timothy. Acting before God means to rebuke faithfully those who are in fault, as the same apostle said, "Charging them before the Lord that they strive not about words to no profit" (2 Timothy 2:14). Acting before God means to be kind to those who are in need and to keep ourselves unspotted from the world—"Pure religion and undefiled before God and the Father is this, To visit the fatherless and widows in their affliction, and to keep himself unspotted from the world" (James 1:27).

Let us acquire the habit of acting before the Lord in the commonplace things of daily life. It is His standard; surely He means us to attain to it. "Whatsoever ye do in word or deed, do all in the name of the Lord Jesus" and to the glory of God (Colossians 3:17; 1 Corinthians 10:31); such is the command of the Holy Spirit. O if we more frequently realized the presence of the Lord, there would be no seeking to please men, but there would be a holy ambition to please God, and to be acceptable to Him. "Thus saith the Lord" would be our watchword, the glory of God would be our aim, and the will of God would be our delight.

2. *A man who is filled with the Holy Spirit is full of love.* Love to God for what He is and for what He has done; love to all who love the Lord Jesus because of our oneness with Him; and love to the perishing millions of the unsaved because of their need, and of the command of the Lord to go and preach the gospel to them. Christ is our Pattern in everything. In His love to the Father we see the example of our love to God. In Christ's love to His disciples we have the manner and measure of our love to the brethren. In Christ weeping over Jerusalem, in His patience and tenderness, His mercy and compassion, His sympathy and meekness, we have the pattern that should ever be before us for dealing with the unsaved. "The love of Christ constraineth us," said Paul, in speaking of the propelling power that made him labor so devotedly. The love of Christ! Ah, that is the power which should activate us! The love which wept over sinners and watched for souls; the love which prompted Christ to suffer for the unsaved, and to sympathize with them, while hating their sins. O for His heart of love to feel for sinners, His tears to weep over them, His tenderness to speak the truth, and his eyes of compassion to gaze upon the worth and way of the sinner!

This was said of an evangelist who was mightily used of God in Ireland, in 1859: "The secret of his power, after all, is his simple, unaffected manner; his intense earnestness; his solemnizing sense of responsibility; *the warmth of heart which sends all his thoughts glowing into the hearts of others and kindling them into sympathetic fervor.*" This is what we want, "warmth of heart." How are our hearts to be warmed? The Word of God supplies the answer: "Keep yourselves in the love of God." Some evangelists are as clear as crystal in their explanation of the plan of salvation, but they are also as cold. We may be as majestic in the presentation of our addresses as an iceberg, and as freezing. We may be as symmetrical as a building in our utterances and as lifeless. What we want is—*go, glow, grip, godliness, grace, gumption* and *grit*; the *go* of a sanctified enthusiasm, the *glow* of Christ's love, the *grip* of God's truth, *godliness* of life, the *grace* of God sustaining us, the *gumption* of sanctified common sense, and the *grit* of patient endurance in well-doing.

3. *A man who is full of the Holy Spirit is full of faith.* Faith in the *Lord* is the most practical thing under the sun. Men of faith are *men of power*—like Caleb, they follow the Lord fully. Men of faith are *men of prayer* although circumstances are against them. Elijah was a man of prayer all through his checkered and eventful life. Men of faith are *men of progress* as Joshua was. And men of faith are *men of perseverance* as was Noah. It is not only necessary to have faith in the Lord for ourselves, but as evangelists there must be faith in Him to bless others. In the Gospels again and again we find that the Lord honored the faith of those who brought the cases of others to Him. Just as we read in another case, Christ

could not do many mighty works because of their unbelief. The man who was sick of the palsy was healed because Christ saw the faith of the four men who brought the palsied one. The daughter of the Syrophoenician woman (Matthew 15:28), the son of the nobleman (John 4:50), and the servant of the centurion (Matthew 8:10-13), were all healed because of the faith of those who brought them to Christ. The man who does not believe in Christ and in His Word with all his heart, and who does not believe with all his soul that the Word of God cannot be preached without the blessing of God upon it had better leave the work at once for he is a hindrance rather than a help.

4. *A man who is filled with the Holy Spirit is constant in prayer*. May we with reverence say that if we importune God with prayer, He will baptize us with power? Steadfastness in prayer is essential to our own spiritual growth. All that is called prayer is not prayer. "Praying in the Holy Ghost" is the Divine method. What does "praying in the Holy Ghost" mean? It means praying in the name of Jesus (John 14:13); with nothing in the heart to condemn us (1 John 3:21, 22); in simple faith (John 14:14); and according to the will of God (1 John 5:14). Prayer is the *oil* that keeps the soul running smoothly along the rails of truth. Prayer is the *pipe* through which the supply of the Spirit comes so that we are refreshed and out of us flow rivers of living water. Prayer is the *air* that keeps the lungs of our spiritual being pure and clean. Prayer is the *hand* that brings the need of the soul to God and faith takes away the blessing. Pray *in* faith but *have* faith—not in prayer—IN GOD.

The Mission of the Evangelist

As an evangelist, Philip's duty was obviously to evangelize. What does that mean? To proclaim the glad tidings of the grace of God. We read of the apostles that they "ceased not to teach and preach Jesus Christ" (Acts 5:42). *Teaching* Jesus Christ is the work of the teacher while *preaching* Jesus Christ is the work of the evangelist. There are three special gifts which the Lord has given His church for its edification, namely, "evangelist, pastor, and teacher."

Perhaps we cannot do better than refer to the Levites as illustrating these three distinct offices and gifts. The tribe of Levi (chosen in place of the firstborn because of their fidelity to God at Mount Sinai) was divided into three sections in terms of their service in the Tabernacle. When the Tabernacle was being moved, each company had its particular part of it to move, to look after, and to pitch. The Merarites had charge of the silver sockets, which were the foundation of the boards and of the pillars of the Holiest of all; and also of the boards, the bars, the pins, the cords, and the sockets of brass, which were the foundations of the pillars of the court. The Gershonites had the custody of all the coverings, and also the beautiful curtains which were called "The Tabernacle." The Kohathites had charge of the ark, the table, the candlestick, the altars, and all the vessels of the sanctuary.

We may look at these three as illustrating the threefold ministry already referred to. As it was the office of the Merarites to lay the foundation, to erect the boards and pillars on the foundations, and to secure them by the bars and the cords and the pins, so the evangelist goes forth to the unsaved, telling out the fact that Christ is the only Foundation—all others being unstable and insecure—to rest upon. It is his task to get them to rely upon Him who has met the claims of God and who meets their needs as they do so. Then he has to tell this: trusting in Him in His twofold work, Godward and manward, as the board in the twofold socket of silver, they are one in Christ with all believers, as the boards were united; and they are held together by the power of the Holy Spirit (Ephesians 2:21, 22) just as the unseen bar that ran through all the boards held them together (Exodus 36:33). He proclaims also a living Christ, able and willing to keep them, just as the bars and rings kept the boards steady on the foundation. This is especially the work of the *evangelist*.

The work of the Gershonites may illustrate the work of the *pastor*, who seeks to comfort the distressed, to care for souls, and to correct the unruly.

The work of the Kohathites may illustrate the work of the *teacher*, whose office it is to explain the meaning of faith to believers, and to elucidate and expound the meaning of words and phrases. In a word, it is the teacher's task to give the sense of Scripture so that there may be a clearer apprehension of the mind of the Spirit, and to unfold in detail the doctrine of the Person and work of Christ.

But it is especially the work of the *evangelist* to proclaim to the sinner his need of salvation; the sufficiency of the salvation in Christ because of His accomplished, substitutionary work on earth; and to offer to all, in the name of Christ, a free and a full salvation. The evangelist is the herald who proclaims that there is in Christ, for those who believe in Him, acceptance for the unworthy, blessing for the needy, cleansing for the polluted, deliverance for the distressed, entrance into God's presence for the sinner, fullness of pardon and peace for the empty, grace for the prodigal, heaven for the hell-deserving, incorruptible inheritance for the beggar, joy for the miserable, a kiss of greeting for the wanderer, life for the dead, might for the feeble, nearness for those who are afar off, an open door to the glory for the undeserving, peace for the enemy, quietness for the troubled, righteousness for the unjust, salvation for the lost, triumph for the slave, union for the severed, virtue for the depraved, and a welcome for all. These blessings are for the sinner, upon his receiving Christ, and are given to him for Christ's sake and for His sake *alone*.

The Message of the Evangelist

Philip preached three things. He preached Christ (Acts 8:5); he preached Jesus (Acts 8:35); and he preached the kingdom of God (Acts 8:12). *Philip preached Christ*. He did not argue about the truth nor preach a set of dry doctrines; neither did he preach about preaching Christ, but he preached *facts about a person, and that Person was the Living Christ*. This was the burden of the evangelist's message to the city of Samaria.

When Philip approached the Ethiopian eunuch, while he was reading in the Scriptures, of Christ in His death and humiliation, Philip brought light to the perplexed spirit by pointing him to Jesus. Thus from Philip's preaching we know the theme of the evangelist's message. A glorious theme indeed!—Christ in the glory of His person; Jesus in the completeness of His work; and the claims of God upon those who believe.

We should preach Christ, not dogma. We must not argue about the truth, but present Christ, the Personal, Living, Ever-present, and All-sufficient One.

Preach Christ in all the glory of His Person. Preach Him as the Atonement to cover the sinner; as the Bread of life to feed the hungry; as the Captain of salvation who has defeated the powers of hell; as the Deliverer to emancipate the slave of sin; as the Emmanuel who has undertaken the sinner's cause; as the only firm Foundation on which the soul can rest; as the Gracious One who waits to bless; as the Hiding-place from the storm of God's wrath; as the Immutable One in whom we may safely trust; as Jesus the Savior who alone can save; as the Kinsman who has the right and power to redeem; as the Life Eternal, who secures eternal life for us; as the Mediator who acts between God and the sinner; as the Nourisher who alone can sustain as the Offering for sin, who alone could atone as the Passover which safely shields; as the Rock who makes immovable; as the Teacher who instructs in Divine mysteries: as the Unction of power which is in the believer by the Holy Spirit; as the Vine to enrich and to manifest His own fruitfulness; as the Way to the Father and the only way for blessing. Preach Christ! This we cannot help doing, if we are walking in fellowship with Him and having sweet converse with Him.

Preach Christ in the completeness of His work. Preach the necessity of His atonement. Man has sinned and sin must be atoned for; man has broken the law and its penalty must be borne. We cannot better illustrate the necessity and the nature of the work of Christ than by giving an extract from an address by Christmas Evans. Speaking at a conference of ministers on this subject he said:

"If, my brethren, I were to present to you in a figure the condition of man as a sinner, and his recovery by the cross of Christ, I should do it somewhat in this way. Suppose a large graveyard, surrounded by a high wall, and with only one entrance by a large iron gate, fast bolted and barred. Within these walls are thousands and tens of thousands of human beings, of all ages and of all classes, blighted by a terrible disease, bending towards the grave which yearns to swallow them up. This is the condition of man, and while he was in this deplorable state, Mercy, the darling attribute of the Deity, came down and stood at the gate, looked at the scene, and bending over it, exclaimed, 'O that I might enter in and bind up their wounds, I would heal their sorrows, I would save their souls!'

"While Mercy stood weeping an embassy of angels, commissioned from the high court of heaven to some other world, paused at the sight, and, seeing Mercy standing there, they asked, 'Mercy, Mercy, can you not enter? Can you look on the scene and not pity? Can you pity and not relieve? Why can you not enter?'

"Mercy replied, 'I can see,' and in tears added, 'I can pity, but cannot relieve. Justice has barred the gate against me, and I cannot enter.'

"At this moment Justice himself appeared, as if to watch the gate. The angels inquired of him why he did not let Mercy enter? Justice replied, 'My law is broken and must be honored; die they must, or Justice must.'

"Suddenly there appeared among the angels the form of One like unto the Son of God, who, addressing Himself to Justice, said, 'What are your demands?'

"Justice replied, 'My terms are stern and rigid. I must have ignominy for their honor; I must have death for their life; I must have sickness for their health. Without shedding of blood there is no remission.'

"'Justice,' said the Son of God, 'I accept your terms. On Me be this wrong. Let Mercy enter.'

"'When,' said Justice, 'will You perform this promise?'

"'Four thousand years hence, upon the hill Calvary, without the gates of Jerusalem, I will perform it in My own Person.'

"The deed was prepared and signed in the presence of the angels of God. Justice was satisfied, and Mercy entered, preaching salvation in the name of Jesus. The deed was committed to the Patriarchs and Prophets. Then, at the appointed time, Justice appeared on the hill of Calvary, and Mercy presented to him the important deed.

"'Where,' said Justice, 'is the Son of God?'

"'Behold Him,' said Mercy, 'at the bottom of the hill, bearing His own cross.'

"Mercy then departed and stood aloof. At the hour of trial Jesus ascended the hill. Justice immediately presented to Him the deed, saying, 'This is the day when the bond is to be executed.' When He received it, did He tear it to pieces? O no! He nailed it to His cross, exclaiming, 'It is finished!'

"Justice called down holy fire from heaven to consume the sacrifice. The fire descended; it swallowed up His humanity, but when it touched His Divinity it expired. And there was darkness over the whole heaven, but 'Glory to God in the highest, peace on earth, good-will towards men.'"

Let us remember that Jesus is not only the expression of God's love. In His death we see God's hatred of sin. Aaron on the "day of atonement" first went into the Holiest of all and sprinkled the blood on and before the mercy-seat; then he came out and blessed the people. In like manner, Jesus first met the righteous claims of God, before he could be the Savior of the sinner. Remember, God is Majesty as well as Mercy, Consuming Fire as well as Compassion, and Light as well as Love. Grace reigns because the justice of God has been met; and we say it with reverence, God could not possibly have dispensed His mercy at the expense of His justice.

Do not fail to preach Jesus in *the completeness of His work*, both Godward and manward—Godward because Christ has borne the wrath due to sin; manward because He, by His death and resurrection, meets the sinner's case. Thus, for Christ's sake, God can righteously forgive the sinner who believes in Him and can righteously accept him as His child.

Preach Christ as revealed in the Word of God. As there is no knowledge of God but in Christ, so there is no knowledge of Christ but in the Word of God. This comes only as we prayerfully seek the teaching of the Holy Spirit. The reason why there is such a small result from so-called Christian effort is that there is such an absence of the Word of God in preaching. We may safely say that the Holy Spirit has to bless His own Word. We have this illustrated in the case of Peter in the house of Cornelius. While Peter spoke the Word, the Holy Spirit fell upon all those who heard it (Acts 10:44).

Dr. Howard Crosby of New York has well said, "It is as preachers depart from the Word, that their preaching becomes barren and fruitless. The Divine Spirit will only accompany the Divine Word. His mighty power will act only in His own way, and by His own means. The Word is supernatural, and woe be to the preacher who leaves the supernatural for the natural . . . who sets aside the sword of the Spirit to use in its stead a blade of his own tempering!"

As to the evangelist's message, we cannot do better than preach the following seven S's:—

Sin and its blighting influence upon all (Romans 3).
Sovereign grace of God in providing a Ransom (John 3:16-18).
Sacrifice of Christ in becoming sin for us (2 Corinthians 5:21).
Salvation through faith in the Son of God (Acts 8:37).
Sanctification by the indwelling of the Holy Spirit (Galatians 5:22-25).
Service with Christ as a consequence of faith (2 Corinthians 6).
Second death for all who neglect the great salvation (Hebrews 2:3).

Preaching Jesus will produce conviction of sin, for where can we learn what sin is, and know what it deserves, as well as at the cross of Christ? Preaching Jesus will bring life as when the uplifted serpent in the wilderness brought life and healing to the people. Preach Christ as the Object of faith. Do not stress the faith, but point to Him as the Object. Speak not of the kinds of faith, but of the Object, and that Object Christ. Speak of the ground of faith which is the unalterable and unerring Word of the living God. Preach Christ the Living One at God's right hand who lives to intercede; who lives to bless; who lives to sustain; who lives to keep; who lives to direct; who lives to instruct; who lives to supply; and who lives to watch over us. Preach Christ the Coming One—the Hope of the Church; for this will urge us on in Christian life and will produce holiness of walk.

The Manner of the Evangelist

We have already touched upon this in speaking of the *"man,"* but there are yet one or two points suggested by the account of Philip's action.

1. Philip was *earnest*. The whole account in the eighth chapter of the Acts impresses one with this fact: he was intensely in earnest. This is brought out emphatically in connection with Philip running to meet the eunuch (verse 30). He felt and realized the importance and worth of the souls to whom he ministered. He spoke as one who knew in his own experience the truths he preached. There was no parrot-talk with him, but there was the glow of one who was in touch with His Master. If a man speaks in a light and listless way we do not wonder that people are not interested and aroused. The wonder would be if they were. One has well said, "If there is a pulpit on fire, people will go to see it burn"—meaning, of course, that if the preacher is deeply in earnest, people will be drawn to the truth.

2. Philip was *pointed*. He did not beat about the bush. He put the plain and pointed question to the eunuch, "Do you understand what you are reading?" (verse 30). "Some preachers round off their words so that they roll off the consciences of the people," said Rowland Hill. Remember what is said of "the preacher" in the book of Ecclesiastes: "The preacher sought to find out acceptable words: and that which was written was upright, even words of truth. The words of the wise are as goads, and as nails fastened by the masters of assemblies, which are given from one shepherd" (Ecclesiastes 12:10, 11). I well remember hearing a preacher in Scotland speaking of himself as if he were an unsaved sinner one

minute and a saved one the next. That kind of preaching only does harm. Another preacher kept apologizing for what he was saying. There was nothing of this in Philip. He was *direct*.

3. Philip was *illustrative*. He found the eunuch reading about Christ being led as a lamb to the slaughter. He began at once to explain the passage and to enforce the illustration used by the Holy Spirit. We must not give illustrations for the sake of giving them—to fill up the time, or to amuse the people, but to throw light upon the truth. Let us guard against the mistake of that evangelist who took twenty minutes to tell an anecdote which, after it was given, had no point. We want what a doctor told a young preacher was not in his sermon when the latter asked him how he liked his discourse. The doctor replied, "Not at all, for there were no 'likes' in it"— referring to the customary expression of the Lord Jesus: "The kingdom of heaven is *like*," etc. Our manner should be, and the evangelistic address should contain, all that is expressed in the following lines:

"It should be brief; if lengthy it will steep
Our hearts in apathy, our eyes in sleep;
The dull will yawn, the chapel-lounger doze,
Attention flag, and memory's portals close.

"It should be warm—a living altar coal,
To melt the icy heart and charm the soul:
A sapless, dull harangue, however read,
Will never rouse the soul, or raise the dead

"It should be simple, practical, and clear,
No fine-spun theory to please the ear;
No curious lay to tickle lettered pride,
And leave the poor and plain unedified.

"It should be tender and affectionate
As His warm theme who wept lost Salem's fate;
The fiery laws, the words of love allayed,
Will sweetly warn and awfully persuade.

"It should be manly, just, and rational,
Wisely conceived, and well expressed withal;
Not stuffed with silly notions apt to stain
A sacred desk, and show a muddy brain.

"It should be mixed with many an ardent prayer
To reach the heart, and fix and fasten there;
When God and man are mutually addressed,
God grants a blessing, man is truly blest.

"It should be closely, well applied at last,
To make the moral nail securely fast:
Thou art the man! and thou alone wilt make
A Felix tremble, and a David quake."

The Might of the Evangelist

The Holy Spirit was the might of Philip (Acts 8:29, 39). All our efforts, earnestness, arrangements, machinery, clearness, illustrations and preaching are useless without the Holy Spirit. He is the One who gives glow to effort; reality to earnestness; power to the machinery; effect to the illustration; and efficacy to the preaching.

"Honor the Holy Spirit next time you preach," said an experienced Christian to a young preacher. We honor the Father by preaching Christ for He is the "Brightness of His glory, and the express image of his person" (Hebrews 1:3). We honor Christ by speaking of the Father for we read forty-three times in John's gospel of Christ being sent by the Father. We honor the Holy Spirit by preaching the Word which was given by His inspiration, for in it are revealed the Father and the Son.

There is one thing that we must never forget: while the Holy Spirit is *in* us, as the seal of God that we are His, there must be the Holy Spirit *upon* us for life and service. The Holy Spirit within is perpetual and abiding; but there must be the seeking of the Holy Spirit—the *anointing*, as it is called—*upon* us by prayer for every fresh act of service. This is *typified* in the Old Testament; *exemplified* in the Lord Jesus; and *illustrated* in the experience of the apostles.

It is typified in the Old Testament. In Leviticus 2, in connection with the meat-offering, the fine flour was mixed with oil, and that oil was also poured upon it. Now we know that the meat-offering is *exemplified* in the Lord Jesus, as the perfect Man. The mixing of the oil with the flour, brings before us the fact that Christ was born of the Holy Spirit; and the oil that was poured upon the meat-offering, the fact that He was anointed for service so that we hear Him say the first time He stood up to preach, "The Spirit of the Lord is upon me, because he hath anointed me to preach the gospel to the poor" (Luke 4:18).

This anointing is illustrated in the experience of the apostles. On the day of Pentecost the Spirit of God came upon them and they were filled with the Holy Ghost. But we read of a subsequent filling, in Acts 4, while they were waiting upon God in prayer, and as a result the apostles went forth and boldly preached the Word. With great power they witnessed of the Lord Jesus.

What is the condition on our part for receiving this anointing? We must be abiding in Christ and have His Word abiding in us. What is the condition for the Lord's blessing upon us? Our conscience must be void of offence toward God and man. And what attitude must we have to have power for service? Waiting upon God in prayer, and in the study of His Word, so that we may be able to present the Person and Work of Christ as revealed therein. Doing this, there will be one of two results—either people will be pricked to the heart to their salvation, as in the case of the multitude on the day of Pentecost, under the preaching of Peter; or they will be cut to the heart to their condemnation and hardening, as in the case of the council which listened to Stephen! But whichever way, having been *faithful* to the Lord in preaching the gospel—whether the truth is a savor of life unto life, or of death unto death—we are in Christ, a sweet-smelling savor unto God.

33

The Discipler's Judgment

"We must all appear before the judgment seat of Christ" (2 Corinthians 5:10).

It has been said: "A careless reader of the Scriptures never makes a close walker with God." For instance, let us take the names and titles which are given to believers. If these are not distinguished we will neither see our privileges nor recognize our responsibilities. By way of illustration let us briefly note the following: The title "*sons*," or "children," reminds us of our filial relationship to God (John 1:12); as stones in God's building we see our oneness with Christ in His life and preciousness (1 Peter 2:4-7); as *sheep* in the flock of the good Shepherd we show we are such by hearing His voice and following Him (John 10:27); as *strangers* we show we are not at home in and with the world, our pilgrim character separating us from evil (1 Peter 2:11); as *stewards* we recognize our responsibility to the Lord in faithfully discharging the trust committed to us (1 Corinthians 4:2); as *soldiers* we have a defensive warfare in resisting evil and an offensive conflict in putting it down (2 Timothy 4:7; 2 Corinthians 10:4); and as *servants* of Christ we are told we are not our own and that we are responsible to follow the directions of Him whom we call "Master and Lord" (John 13:13).

The judgment of the believer at the judgment seat of Christ must not be confused with the judgment of the nations mentioned in Matthew 25:31 to 46. They who are judged there are judged according to their treatment of the Jews—the "brethren" mentioned—whose testimony concerning the coming Messiah they have received or rejected. This judgment takes place before the reign of Christ, on or over the earth for a thousand years. Before Christ can reign, He must send forth His angels to gather out everything that offends, according to Matthew 13:39-42. But someone says this takes place at the end of the world. No; I believe the word "world" is rightly rendered in the margin of the R.V. "age"; it means at the end of this dispensation. This throws light on the passage in Matthew 24:40, 41: "One taken and the other left." One taken away by judgment, and the other left on the earth for blessing. As it was in the days of Noah and Lot. The antediluvians were taken away by judgment, and Noah and his family were left for blessing. The Sodomites were taken away by the judgment of fire, and Lot was left.

We must not confuse the judgment seat of Christ with the judgment of the great white throne (Revelation 20:11) either. There, only "the dead" are judged, that is, those who died in their sins. This judgment takes place at the end of the thousand years of millennial glory on the earth.

To come to the subject before us. It will be well to put it in the form of question and answer.

Who will stand before the judgment seat of Christ?

"We." To whom is the apostle writing? To the Church at Corinth. To saints, not sinners (2 Corinthians 1:1). From this we must infer that only believers will be there. When, therefore, the plural pronoun "we" is used in the Epistles, believers, and believers only, are meant, as Dr. Denny says: "It is Christians who only are in view here." This is further seen if we note the connection of the "we" in 2 Corinthians 5. Let us look at seven places where it occurs:

Knowledge	"We know" (verse 1).
Possession	"We have" (verse 1).
Groaning	"We groan" (verses 2, 4).
Walk	"We walk" (verse 7).
Confidence	"We are confident" (verse 8).
Labor	"We labor" (verse 9).
Acceptance	"We may be accepted" (verse 9).

The knowledge of a glorified body which is in reserve for us, the earnest longing to possess it, the walk which corresponds to it, and the confidence, the labor, and the aim in relation to it, can only apply to those who are saved by Christ (2 Corinthians 1:10), sanctified in Him (1 Corinthians 1:2), and sealed from Him (2 Corinthians 1:22). Yet even these are to be revealed at the judgment seat.

A simple illustration may further clarify the meaning. A son who is in his father's business has a special department under his control. He has to give an account to his father and his father's partners at the end of the year as to the discharge of the trust committed to him. The reckoning is not to determine whether he is the *son* of his father, but to see how he has acted as a *servant* to the firm. Thus we stand before the judgment seat of Christ. It is not to determine whether we are sons or not, but to reckon with us as servants, as we gather from Matthew 25:19, where the Lord comes to reckon with His servants as to their work.

Where shall we stand?

Before the judgment seat of Christ. The "*Bema*" or judgment seat was the raised place where the judge sat and witnessed the Grecian games. He determined who were the successful competitors and from it he gave the prizes won. It was also the place of judicial authority, for the word is used to describe the seat where the judge sat when he had to hear cases upon which he had to adjudicate. Its use in the following Scriptures will determine its meaning:—Matthew 27:19;

John 19:13; Acts 12:21; 18:12, 16, 17; 25:6, 10, 17. The word is only used twice in connection with believers (Romans 14:10; 2 Corinthians 5:10); but from its use it will be seen that it is a place of judicial authority and discrimination. From it Christ tests the service of His servants and rewards them according to their faithfulness.

When will believers be manifest at the judgment seat of Christ?

After Christ comes *for* His people (1 Thessalonians 4:13-18), and before He comes *with* them (Jude 14). We infer this from Christ's own words for He says that the time for recompense is at the resurrection of the just (Luke 14:14). Now the recompense of the just must be before the *return* of the just with Christ for when He and they are manifest to the world they are seen coming forth as an army (Revelation 19:11-14); and this speaks of diversity of rank. The question arises, "Where did the saints get their appointments?" It must have been at the judgment seat for that is the time when rewards are given.

How will the saints be manifested at the judgment seat of Christ?

In glorified bodies. The first sight of Christ will transform us for when we see Him we shall be like Him (1 John 3:2; Philippians 3:21). Note this: believers will not have merely resurrection bodies but *glorified* bodies. The ungodly will be raised but their resurrection is spoken of as the "resurrection *of* the dead" (Hebrews 6:2), whereas believers are said to be raised "*from* the dead" (Acts 4:2; Romans 6:5); and not only so, but "changed," as we read in Philippians 3:21. The word "*changed*" is translated in 1 Corinthians 4:6, "*transferred*," and in 2 Corinthians 11:14, 15, "*transformed*." The use of the word suggests a change of place and a change of body. That change shall make us forever like Christ Himself in outward form and fashion.

Who will be the judge?

The Lord Jesus, as Lord. There are several different characters in which Christ is seen as the Coming One.

- As the Man of war He comes to dash in pieces His enemies (Isaiah 63:1-6; Revelation 19:11-21).
- As the King of kings and Lord of lords, He comes to judge the nations (Psalm 2; Matthew 25:31-46; Zechariah 14).
- As the Savior, King and Priest He comes to Israel (Zechariah 12:10; Psalm 110).
- As the King He comes to reign on and over the earth (Isaiah 32; Psalm 8; Hebrews 2:6-9).
- As the Bridegroom He comes for His bride (Ephesians 5:25-32; Revelation 19:7).
- As the Son of Man He comes to judge the wicked (John 5:27).
- As the Redeemer He comes to complete our salvation (Hebrews 9:28; Romans 8:23; Philippians 3:20, 21).
- And as Lord He comes to reward His servants (Luke 19:11-24; 1 Corinthians 4:5).

The Lordship of Christ is a much-forgotten truth now. That is the reason for the questionable methods adopted in so-called Christian work and the setting up of man's opinion in the place of God's truth; but Christ's Lordship will be recognized then, for His eyes will be as flames of fire to search into the motives of things. Everything that applies to our service will stand out in clear distinction then as seen by Him now.

What will be judged at the judgment seat of Christ?

Before we seek to answer this question, let us note what will *not* be judged. Our past life before our conversion will not be brought up, for the Lord has not only *forgiven* our sins, He has *forgotten* them. This is very strikingly illustrated in Hebrews 11. There we have an account of what faith in God did for the Old Testament saints, but not a word have we as to their failures. Why is this? Because in the previous chapter God had said, "Their sins and iniquities will I remember no more" (10:17). Now if He had recorded them in the eleventh chapter, it would have shown He had not forgotten them; therefore, since our sins are forgiven and forgotten, they cannot be brought up at the judgment seat of Christ.

Our sins confessed as children of God will not be brought up against us. Sins confessed are sins forgiven. If we do not confess our sins, the Lord deals in chastisement with us. Still we need to remember that sin in a penal sense will never be opened, for that was settled for us at the cross.

First. *The believer is to be made manifest at the judgment seat of Christ as he was known by the Lord in this present life.* "I judge not mine own self . . . He that judgeth me is the Lord. Therefore judge nothing before the time, until the Lord come, who both will bring to light the hidden things of darkness, and will make manifest the counsels of the heart: and then shall every man have praise of God" (1 Corinthians 4:3-5). As the electric light illuminates the darkness, so the light of the Lord's presence will illuminate our life and reveal every secret of our heart; for the counsels of the heart will be revealed, and the hidden things will be seen in the light. What a revelation it will be! Ambitions that are not of the Lord will be revealed. Black bitternesses against others will be detected. Covetousness of the heart will be unmasked. Deviations from the truth will be discovered. Envyings of others will become apparent. Fault-finding with our brethren will be discerned. Grumblings and murmurings will be disclosed. Heart backslidings and secret faults will be made known. Indulgings of the flesh and selfishness will be unearthed. Wrongful judging of others will be unfolded. Love of money, ease, and the world will be obvious. Mixed motives in work for Christ will be ferreted out. Opportunities lost for doing good and confessing Christ will be shown up. Perverseness of heart and pleasures not of God will be evident. Quarrellings, backbiting, anger and malice will be seen. Rebelliousness under God's chastening hand will be distinguished. Selfishness, slanderings, and self-will will be observed. Tremblings before the world will be palpable. Uncleanness of heart will be recognized. Willfulness and wanderings will be visible. We shall be heartily glad for the fire to burn up all this heap of rubbish and shall adoringly praise the Lord for His grace and love toward us.

Second. *The believer is to give an account of himself to the Lord as to his conduct towards fellow-believers*. "Why do you pass judgment on your brother? Or why do you despise your brother? For we shall all stand before the judgment seat of God" (Romans 14:10). In the fourteenth chapter of Romans, the Holy Spirit speaks of meats, drinks, and days. There was one of two errors into which the Christians at Rome were likely to fall. For instance, there was one brother who could eat and drink anything, and the weak brother was apt to judge him and say he was not the Lord's. On the other hand, the strong brother was only too ready to go to the opposite extreme and despise and look down on the weak brother because he could not eat and drink as he did. Here both are rebuked. To the weak brother the word is, "Why do you judge your brother?" To the strong brother the word is, "Why do you despise your brother?" It is to our Master we stand or fall and are responsible. If we look after our own estate, we shall have enough to do without throwing stones over the wall at our neighbor. Besides, very often when the mote is seen in the brother's eye, it is but the reflection of the beam that is in the eye of the beholder. We need to be as the Israelites under Nehemiah who were each concerned in repairing the wall "over against his house" (Nehemiah 3:10, 23, 28, 29, 30). If we repair our *own* conduct, we shall do well and be continually occupied. We are too ready to judge each other by what seems to be instead of getting to know the facts.

Fourteen times in the New Testament we are told to love one another (John 13:34, 35; 15:12, 17; Romans 13:8; 1 Thessalonians 4:9; 1 Peter 1:22; 1 John 3:11, 23; 4:7, 11, 12; 2 John 5). Love is the one essential that shall deliver us from unjust judgment and keep us from unkind reproofs. Peter the Great once said, "It is easy to splash mud, but I would rather help a man to keep his coat clean." That's what love does. I cannot always understand the reason of a brother's action; but I can always give the brother credit for a good motive till I find out to the contrary.

As to the judgment of our conduct towards fellow-believers, and as to the judgment generally, Principal Moule says on Romans 14:10, "We have here, as in 2 Corinthians 5:10, and again, under other imagery, in 1 Corinthians 3:11-15, a glimpse of that heart-searching prospect for the Christian, his summons hereafter, *as a Christian*, to the tribunal of his Lord. In all the three passages, and now particularly in this, the language is limited by context as to its direct purport, to the Master's *scrutiny of His own servants as such*. The question to be tried and decided (speaking after the manner of men) at His 'tribunal,' in this reference, is not that of glory or perdition; the persons of the examined are accepted; the enquiry is in the *domestic* court of the Palace, so to speak; it regards the reward of the King as to the issues and value of His accepted servants' labor and conduct, as His representatives, in their mortal life. 'The Lord *of those servants* cometh and reckoneth *with them*' (Matthew 25:19). They have been justified by faith. They have been united to their glorious Head. They 'shall be saved' (1 Corinthians 3:15), whatever be the fate of their 'work.' But what will the Lord say of their work? What have they done for Him in labor, in witness, and, above all, *in character*? He will tell them what He thinks. He will be infinitely kind; but He will not flatter. And somehow, surely, 'it doth not yet appear' how, but somehow, eternity, even the eternity of salvation, will bear the impress of that award, the impress of the *past of service*, estimated by the King, 'What shall the harvest be?'"

If we do the Lord's bidding and love each other as He has loved us, there will not be much to test at His judgment seat on this score.

Third. *Believers will have the quality of their work judged.* "For other foundation can no man lay than that is laid, which is Jesus Christ, Now if any man build upon this foundation, gold, silver, precious stones, wood, hay, stubble; every man's work shall be made manifest: for the day shall declare it, because it shall be revealed by fire; and the fire shall try every man's work of what sort it is. If any man's work abide which he hath built thereupon, he shall receive a reward. If any man's work shall be burned, he shall suffer loss: but he himself shall be saved; yet so as by fire" (1 Corinthians 3:11-15). Some have thought the material built on the Foundation refers to character, hence one has said, "Some build with the gold of faith, with the silver of hope, with the imperishable costly stones of love—others, again, with the dead wood of unfruitfulness in good works, with the empty straw of a spiritless, ostentatious knowledge, and with the bending reed of a continually doubting spirit." Undoubtedly this is true, but another seems to be nearer to the truth in the text when he says, "Believers have to take heed what superstructural doctrine they build upon Christ in themselves, and in those whom they influence." The context plainly tells us that the material built on the foundation has reference to doctrine, or what believers, as workers for Christ, add to Him as the Foundation.

Let us look at the different kinds of material mentioned and note their symbolical meaning.

1. *"Gold."* Gold is typical of the Divine nature of Christ as the Son of God. When the Holy Spirit speaks of Christ as to His eternal Sonship, He speaks of Him as the "Ancient of Days," and says in describing Him, "His hair is as white as snow and wool" (Revelation 1:14; Daniel 7:9); but in the Song of Songs the bride says, "His head is as the most fine gold" (Song of Songs 5:11), plainly denoting the same thing with the added thought of preciousness. All that pertained to the Lord and His worship is associated with gold. The vessels of the Tabernacle were all of gold, and these are typical of Christ (Exodus 25-28).

The whole building of Solomon's Temple was more or less covered with gold (1 Kings 6, 7), and with regard to the new Jerusalem its streets are said to be of "pure gold" (Revelation 21:18, 21). Gold is frequently used to express Divine glory. We may therefore say that the gold which believers are to build on the foundation of Christ's atoning work is *the gold of His Divine glory as the Son of God.* If the gold of Christ's Deity is taken away, we have only the leaden hue of mere humanity. There is no hand strong enough to pluck us from the waves of sin and despair into which we are sinking but the hand of God, as Browning says:

> "I say the acknowledgment of God in Christ
> Accepted by thy reason, solves for thee
> All questions in the earth and out of it."

And as he further says, in praying for one who disbelieved in the Christ Deity:

"May Christ do for him what no mere man shall,
And stand confessed as the God of salvation."

2. *"Silver."* Silver is typical of Christ's atonement. When the children of Israel were numbered they had to bring the half-shekel of atonement money to ransom themselves (Exodus 30:11-15). To this the apostle refers when he speaks of not being redeemed with silver and gold (1 Peter 1:18). On one occasion, Tennyson, when sojourning in an out-of-the-way country place, asked an old Methodist woman "after news," in seeking to ascertain if there was anything fresh. She replied, "Why, Mr. Tennyson, there's only one piece of news that I know, and that is, Christ died for all men." He responded, "That is old news, and good news, and new news." "Christ died for our sins," is the Gospel, the good, new news of God's gracious provision for guilty man.

3. *"Costly Stones."* In Exodus 28:15-21, we read of the precious stones that were in the breast-plate of the High Priest, which are typical of the moral perfection and variegated glory of our Divine High Priest, yet perfect Man as He appears in the presence of God for us. The different stones may be taken to represent Christ in His personal worth and work. There is the *red sardis* of His all-sufficient and God-glorifying death; the *golden topaz* of His beautiful and holy life; the *yellow fiery carbuncle* of His patient and lowly suffering; the *pure green emerald* of His righteous and perfect character; the *sky blue sapphire* of His heavenly and gracious humanity; the *brilliant diamond* of His unflinching and becoming immutability; the *variegated agate* of His true and manifold graces; the *purple amethyst* of His kindly and kingly glory; the *sea green beryl* of His unchanging love and sympathy; the *pinky white onyx* of His adaptedness and ability to keep; the *bright sparkling jacinth* of His devoutness and devotedness; and the *crystal jasper* of His purity and preciousness.

Tennyson, in speaking of the work of a true artist, says:—

"As when a painter, poring on a face,
Divinely, thro' all hindrance, finds the man
Behind it, and so paints him that his face
The shape and color of a mind and life,
Lives for his children ever at its best."

Thus the Holy Spirit has given to us in Holy Writ the beautiful and unsurpassing lineaments of the character of Christ, as we are fellow-workers with Him and as we in His power unfold the truth and attractiveness of Christ's personal worth.

4. *"Wood."* Wood is the product of earth and is typical of man in his self-conceit and fancied greatness, as Jeremiah indicates when the Lord says to him that he is to be an instrument of judgment in His hands. Why? Because the people and the prophets have inclined to their own thoughts instead of hearkening to His warnings. The Word is, "And the prophets shall become wind, and the word is not in them: thus shall it be done unto them. Wherefore thus saith the Lord God of hosts, because ye speak this word, behold, I will make My words in thy mouth fire, and this people wood, and it shall devour them" (Jeremiah 5:13, 14).

To build wood on the foundation signifies a Christian worker adding to the truth of God the deductions of his own reason. A case in point is found when Peter would not associate with Gentile believers because they would not put themselves under the bondage of a law which was done away with in Christ. When Paul got to know this he blamed Peter. He said if he were to act in a like manner, he would have to build again the things which he had destroyed (Galatians 2:11-19). When, therefore, a Christian worker builds on Christ the Foundation the legalism of the law, instead of the liberty of the Gospel, he is putting wood into the building which will be consumed at the judgment seat of Christ.

5. *"Hay."* The Greek word, *Kortos*, rendered *"hay,"* is elsewhere given *"grass"* and *"blade,"* and is used in James 1:10, 11, and 1 Peter 1:24 to denote the frailty of man and the mutability of his greatness. It is not without significance that in the latter passage the uncertainty of man is contrasted with the certainty and stability of God's Word. Therefore, it may be said we put hay into the building when we incorporate the earth-thoughts of frail man with God's eternal truth. When the man of God out of Judah listened to and acted upon the self-conceived thought of the old prophet of Bethel, he built into the Divine message which came to him the hay of man's opinion and suffered loss in consequence (1 Kings 13).

6. *"Stubble,"* or *"straw"* (RSV). The stubble mentioned is the stalk of grain after the ears are removed. Stubble, when used in a symbolical sense in the Scriptures, signifies that which is useless and unworthy of notice (Job 21:18; 41:28, 29; Isaiah 33:11; Jeremiah 13:24); hence Job says, "Wilt thou pursue the dry stubble?" (Job 13:25). What does it mean to build stubble on the Foundation? May we not take it to signify a Christian worker who is occupied with the mere stalk of religious ordinances and who has left out the grain of truth with which they are associated? For instance, take the subject of baptism. Bishop Lightfoot, in speaking of baptism, says: "Baptism is the grave of the old man and the birth of the new. As he sinks beneath the baptismal waters, the believer buries there all his corrupt affections and past sins; as he emerges thence, he rises regenerate, quickened to new hopes and a new life. This it is because it is not only the crowning act of his own faith but also the seal of God's adoption and the earnest of God's Spirit. Thus baptism is an image of his participation, both in the death and resurrection of Christ."

Looking broadly at the above quotation, without going into the question of the mode of baptism, we see that Dr. Lightfoot draws attention to its spiritual meaning hence, to the grain of truth. But let any worker call attention to the water alone, saying there is efficacy in it to regenerate, and omit its spiritual significance, then he is building on the Foundation the stubble or straw of error which will be consumed in the day of the fiery trial.

All this goes to show how careful we should be to build upon Christ the Foundation the doctrines of Grace, for if we build with the stubble of self-assertion, the hay of self-opinion, and the wood of self-deduction, these will all be destroyed, although we ourselves are saved as through fire.

34

The Discipler's Reward

There are two main tracks of truth which, while they run alongside of each other, must never be allowed in our thoughts to run into each other. These are eternal life and reward. The former is *given* to those who have faith in Christ (John 3:36; 1 John 5:11; Romans 6:23); but the latter is *obtained* by those who are faithful to Christ (Matthew 25:21, 23; Luke 19:17, 19). Our being in the realm of God's grace is the outcome of His infinite act of love (John 3:16); but our place in Christ's kingdom will be determined by our faithful devotion to Him since we believed in Him (Revelation 3:12; 1 Corinthians 3:13, 14). The failure to distinguish the difference between these two things has caused a good deal of confusion of thought and bondage of soul in those who have mixed up what God does for His people, and what He is willing to do in and through them. He has "perfected for ever them that are sanctified" (Hebrews 10:14). Let us not confuse the "perfected for ever," which is based upon the perfect offering of Christ and reminds us of what God does for His sake, with the perfection which the apostle says, "I follow after" (Philippians 3:12). The former speaks of the believer's salvation, standing, and sanctification, but the latter has reference to "the prize of the high calling of God in Christ Jesus" (Philippians 3:14). Paul was "apprehended of Christ Jesus" as to his salvation, but he had not apprehended the prize; hence, he was pressing forward to get it (Philippians 3:14). He had obtained mercy (1 Timothy 1:13), but he had not obtained the crown (1 Corinthians 9:24-27). Let us, therefore, direct our minds to the rewards which Christ will give to His own when they are manifested in their glorified bodies at His judgment seat.

There are some rewards which come to God's children in this present life. In keeping God's Word "there is great reward" (Psalm 19:11), for it gives light in darkness, joy in sorrow, guidance in difficulty, assurance in doubt, calmness in trouble, protection in conflict, and power in testimony.

There is reward in being faithful to the Lord by keeping from the world and in refusing to accept what it offers, for then the Lord comes and manifests Himself in some new and satisfying relation. Abram found it to be so, for it was after he had refused to accept any favors from the king of Sodom that the Lord appeared to him and said. "I am thy shield, and thy exceeding great reward" (Genesis 15:1).

A reward is found by God's people when they unite together in God's work, for more is accomplished when two saints work together than when they work separately. As the wise man said, "Two are better than one; because they have a good reward for their labor" (Ecclesiastes 4:9).

Reward is bestowed upon the one who is righteous in his actions for he who is right in his dealings with others ever has the reward of a good conscience. As the Word of God says, "One who sows righteousness gets a sure reward" (Proverbs 11:18 RSV).

The Christian worker who serves Christ without fee has a special reward in that he is independent of wages and is not open to the accusation that he works for money's sake. But with or without charge, the worker who willingly works for Christ because he has been called to do so, has the reward of the Lord's approval in being in the line of His will (1 Corinthians 9:17, 18).

The secret prayer has the reward of the outward blessing. Those who know how to feed the inner life in secret will have the open blessing of unmistakable and benign influence (Matthew 6:6, 18).

We should not, and we dare not, do anything for reward's sake, for that would bring against us the rebuke of the Lord's displeasure (Micah 3:11). We should be like the Lord's servant, of whom it is said, "He shall let go my captives, not for price nor reward, saith the Lord of Hosts" (Isaiah 45:13). On the other hand, while we work for the Lord's sake, He has promised to give us reward, as we may see if we ponder the promise of His Word (Jeremiah 31:16), the injunction of His truth (2 John 8), the encouragement of His love (2 Chronicles 15:7), and the announcement of Christ's return (Revelation 22:11).

Having said so much, let us dwell upon the passages of Scripture where reward is specially mentioned and mark the characters of those to whom recompense is promised.

The reward to the one who adds to his faith

Twice the Greek word occurs in 2 Peter 1. In the first instance, we are told what to "*add* to our faith" (verse 5), and in the second instance we are told what God will "minister" (add) to those who do so, namely, an abundant entrance into the kingdom of the Lord Jesus (verse 11). The word "add" is a striking metaphor. Literally, it means a chorus. As there are many parts which make the harmony of a perfect chorus; so there are many graces which make the Christian character a harmony of perfect melody to the Lord. The strong voice of courage, the true voice of knowledge, the trained voice of temperance, the skilful voice of patience, the rich voice of godliness, the tender voice of brotherly kindness, the mellow voice of love, and the leading voice of faith, as they sing in unison in the life of the believer, peal forth a Hallelujah Chorus which no Mendelssohn of earth could ever compose or sing. What is the reward as we thus chorus to God? He says He will add (chorus to us) an abundant entrance into the everlasting kingdom of the Lord Jesus.

There is all the difference between an Atlantic liner which has weathered the storm through the ability of the captain, the alacrity of all under him, and the perfect make and working of her machinery, coming triumphantly into port; and the liner which has lost her cargo, which has her deck broken and torn, and her machinery out of order, because of her unseaworthiness and the unskillful action of the captain, and which has to be towed into port by an insignificant tug. They both get in, but what a difference! Similarly, there is all the difference between an out-and-out believer, who has chorused to God's praise in an all around consecrated behavior, and who has the abundant entrance like Paul the apostle; and one who has only the end of his life, like the dying thief, or the half- heartedness of a Christian life, to give to the Lord. There may be *entrance* for such, but *abundant* entrance for the latter there can never be.

The reward to the self-denier

"He that loves his life loses it, and he who hates his life in this world will keep it for eternal life. If any one serves me, he must follow me; and where I am, there shall my servant be also; if any one serves me, the Father will honor him" (John 12:25, 26 RSV). The Lord Jesus, as in everything, is the great Example as to the denial of self. He lost His life to benefit us, and His reward has been, and will be, the "much fruit of redemptive spoil" in the many whom He will bring to glory. A like spirit will characterize us if we are following in His steps, and the reward will be this: special honor placed upon us by the Father.

"Just after the close of the civil war in America, the army that had marched in triumph through Georgia under General Sherman was to be reviewed in one of the great cities and march in triumphant parade. The night before the parade, General Sherman called General Howard to him and said: 'You know, General, you were at the head of one of the divisions that marched with me through Georgia, and you ought rightfully to ride at the head of your division in the parade tomorrow. But I find that through political influence a plan is being pressed to have the general who preceded you in the command represent the division, and as political pulls are sometimes stronger than personal rights, I hardly know how to meet the case.' Very naturally General Howard replied, 'I think I am entitled to represent my division, as it was I who led them to victory.' 'Yes,' said General Sherman, 'you are, but I believe you are a Christian, are you not? And I was wondering if Christian considerations might not lead you to make an exception, and even to yield your rights for the sake of peace.' 'Oh,' said good General Howard, 'If it is a matter of Christian consideration, of course I yield, and he can have the place.' 'All right,' said General Sherman, 'I will so arrange, and will you please report to me tomorrow morning at nine o'clock and you shall ride with me at the head of the army.'"

General Howard denied himself in giving up the place which was rightfully his, but he did not lose by so doing. Instead he was the gainer. So shall it be with those disciples of Christ who out of love to Him will allow others to elbow them out of their rightful place, for He will see they are not losers. Rather, they shall have greater reward because of their self-effacement.

The reward of the patient sufferer

Tribulation is what the Lord has told us to expect from the world (John 16:33), but even in the suffering there may be unspeakable joy. Pastor Homel, of the French Protestant Church, had all his bones so broken on the wheel that he only survived forty hours. But in his dying agony he said, "Though my bones are broken to shivers, my soul is filled with inexpressible joy." From the rough rock of persecution comes the gold of joy. The flail of tribulation knocks away the husk of impatience and makes the grain of God's enduring visible.

The world may rub the plate of our character, thinking to mar it, but they only make it shine the brighter when God's grace rests upon us. Persecution places us in good company, even in the fellowship of the Lord Jesus. To be hated with Him turns the hatred into a halo of glory (John 17:14, 22). Not to be known, because of our association with Him, makes the scorn of the world a mere figment: while to be known by heaven (1 John 3:2), lights up the darkest dungeon (Acts 16:25), makes every lion's den a gateway to heaven (Daniel 6: 22), and every fiery furnace a means of grace (Daniel 3:25). The persecutions of earth are but the piercings in the crown of glory which are requisite for the placing of the gems of reward (Matthew 5:12; Luke 6:22, 23).

Twice the words "*counted worthy*" occur in the New Testament in association with suffering. The early Christians rejoiced "that they were *counted worthy* to suffer shame for His name" (Acts 5:41), and the apostle cheers the suffering saints at Thessalonica by telling them that the persecutions and tribulations they had endured so manfully were but making them to be "*counted worthy* of the kingdom of God" for which they had suffered (2 Thessalonians 1:5). May we not say the reward for patient suffering for Christ now means a place in His kingdom, even as David's mighty men who shared with him when he was rejected (1 Samuel 22:4) afterwards were found with him in his exaltation (1 Chronicles 11:16). Of one thing we may be sure, and that is, suffering and glory are always found together (Luke 24:46; Romans 8:17; 2 Timothy 2:12; 1 Peter 2:20; 4:16). Therefore, the logical conclusion is that if we do not have the suffering we shall not have the glory; and further, the proportion of suffering here will determine the proportion of glory in Christ's kingdom.

The reward for the trial-endurer

"The trial" (R.V., "proof") of your faith, being much more precious than of gold that perisheth, though it be tried" (R.V., "proved") "with fire, might be found unto praise and honor and glory at the appearing of Jesus Christ" (1 Peter 1:7). The reference in these words is to the testing of faith and the reward bestowed upon the one who endures. Every anchor which leaves the British Isles is required to pass the test of the Board of Trade before it is stamped as fit for use. A severe hydraulic strain is put upon it, up to a given point, and if the anchor stands this, it is then passed as fit for service. In the trial of the believer's faith, there is that which corresponds to this. The "manifold temptations" which come to us are overruled for our blessing in that God makes them opportunities to trust Him, and as we endure, He lays up for us that which we shall have at the appearing of Jesus Christ. The reward is said to be "praise and honor and glory." The "praise" refers to the commendation of the Lord, the "honor" to the bestowment of the reward, and the "glory" that which accrues to the receiver as a consequence of the "praise" and "honor" already given: just as when the brave soldier receives the Victoria Cross. The V. C. is the "honor" conferred upon him, the King's word of commendation as he pins it upon his coat is the "praise," and the loud hurrah as he joins his comrades with proud step is the "glory."

The reward for the alert watcher

The Lord's charge to His servants during the time of His absence is "watch"; and we are to watch with girded loins and with lamps burning (Luke 12:35, 36). The girded loins indicate readiness for action (1 Kings 18:46), preparedness for service (John 13:4), and alertness of mind (1 Peter 1:13). The burning lamps suggest consistency of life (Matthew 5:16), faithfulness in testimony (John 5:35), and reflection of Christ's character (Philippians 2:15; Ephesians 5:8). Of the servants whom the Lord shall so find when He returns, He says, "Blessed are those servants, whom the Lord when he cometh shall find watching: verily I say unto you, that he shall gird himself, and make them sit down to meat, and will come forth and serve them" (Luke 12:37). The servants are waiting to serve their Lord and have prepared a feast for Him, but when He finds the attitude they are in, He girds Himself and makes them take His place. He then honors them in serving them, as a reward for their fidelity. Such an action reminds us of what Ahasuerus did for Mordecai when he caused him to be arrayed in the royal apparel, to ride upon the royal horse, and to have on the crown royal (Esther 6:8). Mordecai was treated as the king was accustomed to be honored, as a reward for the service he had rendered to him (Esther 6:3, 11). So shall the ever alert watcher be honored when the Lord Jesus comes back. He shall honor the servant as he wished to honor Him. What an honor that will be for the servant to be served by His Lord!

The reward to the talent-user

The talents represent the use of opportunities possessed by us. These are not possessed to the same extent by all. One servant had five talents, another had two, and the third had only one. They were given according to each one's "several ability." The Lord did not expect so much from the one who had only one talent, as He did from the servant who possessed five. But He did expect every man to use what he had. The man who did not use his talent received no reward, while the other two were rewarded according to the use they had made of their talents. This parable reminds us of our individual responsibility to use what powers we have in the Lord's service.

Scripture will serve us to illustrate what talents are, if we note the natural traits in the lives of some of its characters. Daniel used his skilful mind in the apt manner in which he filled the office of legislator in the kingdom of Babylon. David, the sweet singer of Israel, used his voice and pen in singing and setting forth the grace and glory of God to His praise. The keeper of the Egyptian prison recognized the natural ability which Joseph had in giving him the oversight of all the prisons under his care. That talent was further manifested in the rule which Joseph exercised under Pharaoh. Elijah evidently recognized by the way in which Elisha handled the plough, he would make a fit successor to himself; for he who could make such straight furrows, would be sure to go about the Lord's business with equal integrity.

There will be many who will say, I do not have the talents of Daniel, the abilities of Joseph, the qualifications of Abraham, the astuteness of Solomon, the poetry of David, or the eloquence of Paul. That may be. The Lord does not expect from us what we have do not have, but He does expect us to use what we have. If we do so, we can have no greater commendation and wish no greater reward than the woman received from the Lord Jesus, "She hath done what she could"; for after all, "The highest life consists not in doing magnificent things, but rather in doing common things in a magnificent way."

The reward to the pound-employer

The parables of the talents and pounds are sometimes thought to be one and the same, but one general observation is sufficient to prove they are not. In the parable of the talents there is a diversity of abilities. One man has five talents and the other only one; but in the parable of the pounds, each man receives alike; we read that the nobleman called his ten servants and "gave them ten pounds, and said to them, 'Trade with these till I come'" (Luke 19:13 RSV) That each servant got a pound is evidenced, for in the reckoning day each servant says to his Lord, "Your pound." The question naturally arises, "What is represented by the pound?" I think it is the gospel. Every child of God is a servant, and to each of us is committed the word of reconciliation (2 Corinthians 5:18), with which we are to trade till our Lord returns. Then the question will be asked, "What use have you made of the gospel I gave you?" The use of the pound does not mean preaching the gospel, although that is included, but each of us in our several spheres are to testify to its power.

The mother can do this with the children, the father with the son, the employer with his employee, and the employee with his employer, the merchant with the customer, and the customer with the merchant, the friend with friend, and so on. By kindly word, by consistent action, by sympathetic look, by timely help, by generous self-denial, by loving letter, by unflinching faith, by buoyant hope, by intense zeal, by ardent love, and by patient endurance we can trade with the gospel. In so doing we increase what we have by passing the seedlings on to others. These shall grow up into trees of blessing.

The reward for faithfully trading with the gospel will be in proportion to the use we make of the pound. What the rule over the ten cities may mean, we cannot say, but something real, tangible, and enduring is evidently represented. Some position of rule and authority is unmistakably meant, for nothing else but this would answer to the "authority over ten cities" and "five cities" (Luke 19:17, 19).

The reward to the faithful steward

The office of a steward is repeatedly referred to in the New Testament. The Lord's servants are stewards "of the mysteries of God" (1 Corinthians 4:1), and of "the manifold grace of God" (1 Peter 4:10). As such we are to be "blameless" in life (Titus 1:7), and "faithful" in service (1 Corinthians 4:2). Faithfulness is the one thing which is "required" in stewards, and where it is found it will meet with the Master's "Well done."

One of the most touching incidents of faithfulness is found in this story of how a faithful dog lost its life in serving its master: "One night in the Scottish highlands, when the snow was deep upon the mountainside, a shepherd found that two of his flock were still out in the storm. Calling his faithful collie, or shepherd's dog, he roused her from her warm kennel where she was lying with her young. Pointing through the open door, he held up two fingers and said, 'Go.' Well she understood his meaning, and gave one pitiful look at her little pups, and then one appealing glance at him, but there was no relenting in his look. Quietly and promptly she went out through the open door into the dark and wintry night. It was late in the night when the shepherd was roused by a scratching on the door. As he opened it, there was one of the lost sheep, and the tired dog dragged herself through the door to lie down once more in her kennel with her young. He carefully nursed the tired sheep, and then again he called the faithful dog, and pointing his finger through the open door, he called, 'One is still lost, Go.'

"Tenderly she gazed once more at her young. Longingly she clung to her little brood, pleadingly she gazed into the shepherd's eyes and seemed to say, 'Must I go again?' But still there was no reprieve in that glance. There was but one message and that was, 'Go.' And slowly she dragged herself again to the door and went forth into the darkness. The dawn had come before the shepherd was again awakened to find the lost sheep there, and the poor dog scarcely able to drag herself to her corner, lay down to die. As she pressed her little ones to her breast and gasped out her last breath, he gently patted her head and tried his best to say, 'Good and gentle servant, you did your best.' She was but a dog. For her there was no heaven, no crown of bright reward, no higher motive than obedience. Beloved, with so much more for us in the future shall we be less faithful than a shepherd's dog?"

The reward for the true worker

"If any man's work abide which he hath built thereupon, he shall receive a reward" (1 Corinthians 3:14). "Whatsoever ye do, do it heartily, as to the Lord, and not unto men; Knowing that of the Lord ye shall receive the reward" (Colossians 3:23, 24). The first passage is found in connection with the quality of material which the builder puts upon the foundation; and the second Scripture has reference to work generally. As we have already seen in the chapter on *The Discipler's Judgment,* the material specified denotes the doctrines of grace, or otherwise. The "whatsoever" of Colossians 3:23 reminds us that all our actions may be service for the Lord.

A little boy was lying in the hospital. His hand had been amputated. In response to his request, the nurse brought the amputated hand to him. As he felt it with his other hand, it was cold and lifeless. The little lad felt he could not part with the member which had been so useful to him without a parting greeting. As he handed it back to the nurse, he said, "Good-bye, I'll get you back at the resurrection." Ah! there are a good many things which we shall get back at the resurrection, and among the many will be the works—the deeds done in the body (2 Corinthians 5:10)—for these will determine the kind of reward we shall receive.

The reward for the considerate helper

The Word of God abounds with promises of reward to those who minister to the need of others, especially those who help those who are not able to make any return (Matthew 6:4; Matthew 25:35-40; Mark 9:41; Luke 14:12-14). There is no greater joy than to give joy to others. He who feeds others feeds himself. He who helps others helps himself. Those who help others for the sake of Christ never think of the pains it gives them but of the pleasures it gives those who are helped for His sake. The highest good, next to being good, is to do good, for this goes up to God as a sweet-smelling aroma (Hebrews 13:16).

It is said that Ivan of Russia used sometimes to disguise himself and go out among his people to find out their true character. One night he went, dressed as a beggar, into the suburbs of Moscow, and asked for a night's lodging. He was refused admittance at every house until at last his heart sank with discouragement to think of the selfishness of his people. At length, however, he knocked at a door where he was gladly admitted. The poor man invited him in, offered him a crust of bread, a cup of water, and a bed of straw. Then he said, "I am sorry I cannot do more for you, but my wife is ill, a babe has just been given her, and my attention is needed for them." The Emperor lay down and slept the sleep of a contented mind. He had found a true heart. In the morning he took his leave with many thanks.

The poor man forgot all about it until a few days later. Then the royal chariot drove up to the door and, attended by his retinue, the Emperor stopped at the peasant's humble abode.

The poor man was alarmed. Throwing himself at the Emperor's feet, he asked, "What have I done?"

Ivan lifted him up. Taking him by both his hands said, "Done! You've done nothing but entertain your Emperor. It was I who lay upon that bed of straw, it was I who received your humble but hearty hospitality, and now I have come to reward you. You received me in disguise, but now I come in my true character to recompense your love. Bring hither your new-born babe." And as he brought him, he said, "You shall call him after me, and when he is old enough, I will educate him and give him a place in my court and service." Giving him a bag of gold, he said, "Use this for your wife, and if ever you have need of anything, don't forget to call upon the poor tramp who slept the other night in that corner."

Something similar will happen when our Lord returns. For every cup of water given in His name, for every kindly word spoken for His sake, for every meal given out of love to Him, for every encouragement given to others, for every self-denying act to our brethren, there will be recognition and recompense from our Lord Jesus Christ.

The reward for the resolute endurer

The child of God is called to endure many things. We are called to endure hardness as good soldiers of Jesus Christ (2 Timothy 2:3); chastening as God's children (Hebrews 12:7); afflictions as workers for Christ (2 Timothy 4:5); grief, as Christians (1 Peter 2:19); contradictions as partners with Christ in His sufferings (Hebrews 12:3); temptation as tried believers (James 1:12); we are even called to endure "all things" for the elect's sake (2 Timothy 2:10).

The reward for those who endure is the victor's crown. There are some seven references to the victor's crown, all of which are associated with endurance.

Endurance under temptation meets with the reward of the "crown of life" (James 1:12). Endurance in the heavenly race of progress in the Divine life meets with the reward of the incorruptible crown (1 Corinthians 9:25). Endurance in faithful service meets with the reward of "the crown of righteousness" (2 Timothy 4:8). Endurance in shepherding the flock meets with the reward of "the crown of glory" (1 Peter 5:4). Endurance under persecution meets with the reward of "the crown of life" (Revelation 2:10). Endurance in keeping God's Word preserves us from losing the victor's crown (Revelation 3:11); and the endurance of those who have received the truth through others means that they have a "crown of rejoicing" in the day of awards at the judgment seat of Christ (Philippians 4:1; 1 Thessalonians 2:19).

The reward to the willing loser

There are two ways in which we may lose things in this life. We may lose what we actually have, as the Hebrew Christians did who "took joyfully the spoiling of their goods" (Hebrews 10:34); and there is a losing of riches which would surely come if a given course of action was followed, but the course is abandoned in faithfulness to Christ. Why did Moses give up the "riches of Egypt"? Because "he had respect unto the recompense of the reward" (Hebrews 11:26). What made the saints take the spoiling of their goods with such good heart? Because they had "in heaven a better and an enduring substance" (Hebrews 10:34). The glamors of earth were eclipsed by the glories of heaven. The sun of God's love made the lights of earth to be of little moment. For everything lost in this life for the Lord's sake, there shall be a corresponding and compensating blessing in the life to come. As Christina G. Rossetti has said, "For the books we now forbear to read, we shall one day be endued with wisdom and knowledge. For the music we will not listen to, we shall join in the song of the redeemed. For the pictures from which we turn, we shall gaze unabashed on the beatific vision. For the companionship we shun, we shall be welcomed into angelic society, and the companionship of triumphant saints. For the pleasure we miss, we shall abide, and evermore abide, in the rapture of heaven. It cannot be much of a hardship to dress modestly, and at a small cost, rather than richly and fashionably, if, with a vivid conviction, we are awaiting the 'white robes of the redeemed.'"

Further, we have the promises of the Lord Jesus that there is compensation for loss. On one occasion, Peter reminded Christ that he and his fellow disciples had left all to follow Him. In answer to the question Jesus said, "Every one that hath forsaken houses, or brethren, or sisters, or father, or mother, or wife, or children, or lands, for my name's sake, shall receive an hundredfold, and shall inherit eternal life" (Matthew 19:29). Whatever the reward may be, the Lord assures us that we are to receive *ten thousand per cent*, for the hundredfold does not refer to a hundred per cent, that is, one for every one given, but a hundred for every one.

Some true-hearted believer will say, as a lady once said to me in Maine, "I don't want to serve Christ for what I can get!"

"Certainly not," I replied, "we give up, we serve Him and others *for* His name's sake, and *not* for the reward's sake; but none the less, He assures us we shall be compensated."

The reward to the offering-giver

Some of the most precious of God's pronouncements and promises flow out of the giving of the Lord's people and the exhortations to the "grace" (2 Corinthians 8:9).

To give but three examples. I call your attention to the *great Example of giving* right in the midst of a series of exhortations upon ministering to the need of God's saints, in the words, "Ye know the grace of our Lord Jesus Christ, that, though he was rich, yet for your sakes he became poor, that ye through His poverty might be rich" (2 Corinthians 8:9).

The spiritual blessing of giving is sandwiched between the words, "God loveth a cheerful giver," and, "It is written, he hath disperseth abroad: he hath given to the poor; his righteousness remaineth for ever." The words between are, "Every man according as he purposeth in his heart, so let him give; not grudgingly, or of necessity: for God loveth a cheerful giver. And God is able to make all grace abound toward you; that ye, always having all sufficiency in all things, may abound to every good work. [As it is written, He hath dispersed abroad; he hath given to the poor: his righteousness remaineth for ever]" (2 Corinthians 9:7-9). In this verse of spiritual blessing the verse of the five alls, if we make the word "every" read "all"—we have

All Grace
For
All Times
For
All Emergencies
For
All Things
For
All Work

The third example reminds us of the *counterpart of giving*. Giving to the Lord always brings its own reward (Luke 6:38). This is brought out in what the apostle said after he received the gift from the saints at Philippi. He said in so many words, "You have supplied my need, and now 'my God will supply every need of yours according to his riches in glory in Christ Jesus'" (Philippians 4:19 RSV).

There are seven ways of giving, somebody has said. The first is the *careless way*, giving something to everything that comes along, giving to get rid of the nuisance of the appeal. The second way is the *impulsive way* of giving, giving when you feel like it, when your emotions are stirred. Then there is the *lazy way* of giving. Get somebody to get up a fair, or festival, or an ice cream social. That is the lazy way of giving, and it is the most expensive in the end. Then there is the *selfish way* of giving, giving for your organ, for your Sunday school, for your preacher, for something that you are to receive from it. Then there is the *systematic way*, setting aside a certain per cent of your means, and I am glad to say that this is growing among intelligent Christians. Then there is what we might call the *fair way* of giving, giving as much for the Lord as we use upon ourselves. And finally, there is the *heroic way*, the self-sacrificing way, giving more than you can, giving until it hurts, and then giving until it does not hurt.

The difference between giving in a heroic and in a careless way, was aptly put by a friend at a Convention held at Asbury Park, New York. Or as he put it, it was the difference between "a collection" and "an offering." A little boy, who evidently had had the difference explained to him while sitting at the dinner table, was about to give the dog Fido the leg of a chicken which had been placed upon his plate.

"My boy," said the father, "you must not do that. Eat the meat, and then give Fido the bone." The boy did as he was told, and then handed Fido the bone. But as he was doing so, he said, "Fido, I intended to give you an offering, but you have only got a collection."

The reason why God's people *give* so little is that they *get* so little. When the grace of God lives in the heart, it will loosen the hand. There would be more open hands to give to others if there were more open hearts to receive God's grace. If we stint and starve our hearts of God's grace, no wonder there is stinginess in our giving. There are too many like the man who rented a farm on the condition of giving one-third of what he raised to the owner. The harvest passed and the owner did not receive anything. He called upon the tenant and reminded him of the arrangement into which they had entered. He said, "How is this? You were to give one-third of what you raised to me, and keep two-thirds yourself!"

"Yes," replied the tenant, "that is so, but there were only two-thirds. When I came to gather up the harvest, I 'lowed there would be three loads, and there were only two!"

We call the man a trickster, but are there not some like him? Those who give to the Lord the mere pittance out of their plenty are to be pitied, for they have no joy in it, and certainly they will have no reward in the hereafter.

What is the reward? Christ indicates it in His application of the parable of the unjust steward. He says, "Make to yourselves friends by means of the unrighteous mammon; that when it fails they may receive you into eternal habitations" (Luke 16:9 RSV). Christ does not mean for us to make friends of the mammon of unrighteousness, that is, to love money; but He does desire we should "make friends *by means*" of it, as the Revised Standard Version indicates. Then we shall have a welcome from those we have helped. They shall accord us such an ovation in the next life as shall more than compensate for what we did for them here.

The reward to the victory-gainer

Eight times in the book of the Revelation is the promise of Christ given to the overcomer. In many instances what is to be overcome is indicated by the promised reward.

The reward promised to the overcomer of the Church in Ephesus is to "eat of the tree of life" (Revelation 2:7). To eat of the tree of life suggests the thoughts of abiding fellowship and enduring vitality. The cherubim and the flaming sword were placed in the garden of Eden to prevent man from eating of the tree of life after he had fallen. If he had eaten in his sinful state, he would have been fixed in that state forever. So the redeemed overcomer eating of the tree of life is in a state of holy bliss from which it is impossible to fall. The Church at Ephesus had left their first love, hence they had lost vitality and were out of fellowship. So they were exhorted to get back into the position from whence they had fallen, that the means of vitality might be restored; and the incentive to this is the reward promised to the overcomer.

The reward to the overcomer of the Church in Smyrna is this, that he is assured he will not be hurt of the second death. No believer can ever come under the power of the second death, for Christ assures those who believe in Him that they shall not come under condemnation, but are passed from death unto life (John 5:24). Further, all believers evidence their faith in Christ in some degree by overcoming the world (1 John 5:5). But all believers may not be overcomers while passing through the fiery ordeal of persecution with death staring them in the face. Those who are faithful unto death are assured by Christ that they will not be hurt of the second death, thus all fear of their souls' salvation is removed. This is grandly illustrated in the words which fell from the lips of Polycarp, the bishop of this Church, when he was called upon by his judges to recant. He said, "Fourscore and six years have I served the Lord, and He never wronged me; how then can I blaspheme my King and Savior?" The timid believer who denies his Lord has good ground to fear, but he who is faithful is fearless.

The reward to the overcomer of the Church in Pergamos is the hidden manna and the white stone. The thought here is secrecy, for the "manna" is said to be "hidden," and the new name inscribed on the white stone is only known to the receiver (Revelation 2:17). The hidden manna and the white stone take our thoughts back to the Aaronic priesthood. Some of the manna which fell in the wilderness was placed in a pot, which was put in the ark of the covenant (Exodus 16:33; Hebrews 9:4); and the white stone may have reference to the Urim and Thummim which were in the breastplate of the high priest, by means of which the Lord gave secret directions to him (Exodus 28:30; Numbers 27:21). Commentator Fausset says, upon the promise of Christ to the Church in Pergamos: 'The new name is Christ's' (Revelation 3:12). Some new revelation of Himself hereafter to be imparted to His people, which they alone are capable of receiving. The connection with the 'hidden manna' is thus clear, as the high priest alone had access to the manna hidden in the sanctuary. What believers had to contend against at Pergamos were idol meats and fornication, put in their way by Balaamites. As Phinehas was rewarded with an 'everlasting priesthood' for his zeal against these sins, so the heavenly high priesthood is the reward promised to those who are zealous against the New Testament Balaamites."

The reward to the overcomer of the Church in Thyatira is authority over the nations and the morning star. The morning star gives the thought of kingly glory (Numbers 24:17; Matthew 2:2; Revelation 22:16), and the "authority" of kingly power. These rewards were to be bestowed for faithful rule in God's assembly by repudiating the evil of Jezebel's false doctrine, and the necessary false practice which accompanied it; and the holding fast to Christ's word and works "unto the end."

The reward to the overcomer of the Church in Sardis is to be clothed in white raiment, an assurance that his name will not be blotted out of the book of life, and confession of him before the Father and the angels (Revelation 3:5).

The not defiling the garments, *i.e.*, being clean in life and right in action (Revelation 19:8) meets the reward of being "clothed in white raiment." Not having the name blotted out of the book of life,[1] shows they had spiritual life and not merely a name that they lived (Revelation 3:1). The confession by Christ is in recognition of their watching and holding fast.

The reward to the overcomer of the Church in Philadelphia is to be a pillar in the temple of God and the new name inscribed upon him (Revelation 3:12). The Church in Philadelphia had proved themselves stable in their faith, sterling in their love, and faithful in their testimony. Now the Lord promised them a permanent place in His glory. They had not "denied His name," and in appreciation He promises to write upon them His new name. When Admiral Dewey returned from the Spanish-American war, a monumental arch and a number of pillars were erected in the city of New York. Upon these are words of American appreciation and emblems of the victories gained. These monuments are already showing signs of decay for they were comparatively flimsy erections, made of wood and plaster. Those which Christ shall make, however, will be enduring in nature and eternal in character.

The reward to the overcomer of the Church in Laodicea is to sit with Christ on His throne (Revelation 3:21). The one who overcomes amid the worst condition of things has the highest reward.

"So you intend to be a reformer of men's morals, young man," said an aged peer to Wilberforce. "That," and he pointed to a picture of the crucifixion, "that is the end of reformers."

"Is it?" replied Wilberforce, "I have read in an old Book this: 'I am He that liveth, and was dead; and behold I am alive for evermore, Amen, and have the keys of hell and of death.' That is the end—not death, but dominion. And if we are faithful, doing our duty, the end shall not be exhaustion, but 'sit with Me on My throne.'"

The promises to the overcomers reach their apex when the Lord promises those who overcome that they shall "inherit all things" (Revelation 21:7). What the sweep of this promise includes no pen can write, no tongue can tell, but something real, tangible, and enduring is evidently meant. The Phillips paraphrase reads, "*these* things" instead of "all things." "These things" refer to the absence of everything that frets, such as pain, sorrow, and death. These shall be "no more"; and on the positive side "these things" denote the glory of the new Jerusalem, the companionship of the Lord, and the peculiar relationships which He will hold with regard to His people that shall satisfy His heart and theirs (Revelation 21:1-6).

There is one fact we would briefly note in concluding these promises to the overcomer, and that is, the counterpart of the promise is found in the Book of the Revelation. The promise of the "tree of life" to the Ephesian overcomer is

---

1. "A register of citizens was kept in ancient states; the names of the dead were erased. So those who have a name that they live and are dead, are blotted out of God's roll of the heavenly citizens; not that in God's electing decree they ever were there . . . Many are enrolled among the *called* to salvation, who shall not be among *the chosen* at last."—*Canon Fausset*

referred to in Revelation 22:2, where the properties of the "tree of life" are stated. The promise to the Smyrnan overcomer as to not being "hurt of the second death" is explained in Revelation 20:14, where we are told the second death is "the lake of fire." The promise to the Pergamos overcomer of the "new name" finds a counterpart in Revelation 14:1, where the 144,000 have the "name of the Father" written on their foreheads. The promise to the Thyatiran overcomer of "power over the nations" finds its correspondence in Revelation 20:4, where a company are described who "live and reign with Christ for a thousand years." The promise to the Sardian overcomer of the "white raiment" meets its counterpart in Revelation 4:4, where the four and twenty elders are seen "clothed in white raiment"; and the "name in the book of life" has its likeness in Revelation 13:8 where we read that those who worship the beast have not their names in the Lamb's book of life. The promise to the Philadelphian overcomer is the permanent place in God's temple. It has its answering feature in the New Jerusalem and its citizenship as described in Revelation 21:10-27; and the promise to the Laodicean overcomer of sitting on Christ's throne finds its counterpart in the throne-sitters who are mentioned in Revelation 4:4 and 20:4.

Let us remember that not a single action done out of love to Christ shall miss His commendation and reward in the day of His reckoning. Everything done for "His name's sake" is recorded for our reward. He records the ardent faith of a clinging soul (Matthew 15:28); the generous heart which gives its all although it be but two mites (Luke 21:3); the grateful thanks of a cleansed man are noticed by Him (Luke 17:18, 19); the true confession of Himself is music in His ears and calls forth His approbation (Matthew 16:17); He appreciates the breaking of the costly box of ointment over His person and makes a lasting memorial of it (Matthew 26:13); He commends the earnest desire of David to build Him a temple and puts the building down to His account, although he never placed a stone in it (2 Samuel 7:2-7; 1 Chronicles 28:2); He is careful to give as much reward to the prophet's host as He gives to the prophet himself (Matthew 10:41); and the cup of water given to one of His own is accepted as done to Himself (Mark 9:41).

"Our labor and our pleasure,
Be this, to do His will,
To use our little measure,
In loving service still.
The cup of water given
For Him, will find reward
Both now, and soon in heaven,
Remembered by the Lord.

Lord, may Thy love constrain us,
Through all the 'little while;'
Nor fear of man restrain us,
Nor love of praise beguile;
Thus till Thy glorious coming
Enough, O Lord, if we
Then hear Thy voice approving
Aught we have done for Thee."

Author Index

Subject Index

Scripture Index

Acts

Romans

1 Corinthians